HISTORY
OF THE
RISE OF THE MAHOMEDAN POWER
IN
INDIA,
TILL THE YEAR A.D. 1612.

HISTORY
OF THE
RISE OF THE MAHOMEDAN POWER
IN
INDIA,
TILL THE YEAR A.D. 1612.

TRANSLATED FROM THE
ORIGINAL PERSIAN OF MAHOMED KASIM FERISHTA,

BY

JOHN BRIGGS, M.R.A.S.
LIEUTENANT-COLONEL IN THE MADRAS ARMY.

TO WHICH IS ADDED,
AN ACCOUNT OF THE CONQUEST,
BY THE KINGS OF HYDRABAD,
OF THOSE PARTS OF THE MADRAS PROVINCES
DENOMINATED
THE CEDED DISTRICTS AND NORTHERN CIRCARS.

WITH COPIOUS NOTES
IN FOUR VOLUMES.

VOL. IV.

GYAN

Published by

Gyan Publishing House
5, Ansari Road
Daryaganj, New Delhi-110002
Phone: 011-47034999, 9811692060
E-mail: books@gyanbooks.com

Distribution Network
gyanbooks.com
India, USA, Canada, UK, Australia, France

ISBN : 978-81-212-2289-1 (Set)
ISBN : 978-81-212-2285-3 (PB)
First Published, 1910

2nd Impression 2021

Printed at: Gyan Press, Delhi.

History
of the
Rise of the Mahomedan Power in India,
Till The Year A.D. 1612.Vol. IV
Translated by: John Briggs

HISTORY

OF THE

RISE OF THE MAHOMEDAN POWER

IN

INDIA,

TILL THE YEAR A.D. 1612.

TRANSLATED FROM THE

ORIGINAL PERSIAN OF MAHOMED KASIM FERISHTA,

BY

JOHN BRIGGS, M.R.A.S.

LIEUTENANT-COLONEL IN THE MADRAS ARMY.

TO WHICH IS ADDED,

AN ACCOUNT OF THE CONQUEST,

BY THE KINGS OF HYDRABAD,

OF THOSE PARTS OF THE MADRAS PROVINCES DENOMINATED

THE CEDED DISTRICTS AND NORTHERN CIRCARS.

WITH COPIOUS NOTES.

In Four Volumes.

VOL. IV.

CALCUTTA:

PUBLISHED BY—R. CAMBRAY & CO.,

LAW BOOKSELLERS & PUBLISHERS,

6, HASTINGS STREET,

1910.

CONTENTS

OF

THE FOURTH VOLUME.

CHAPTER IV.

HISTORY OF THE KINGS OF GUZERAT.

MOOZUFFUR SHAH I.

AHMUD SHAH I.

MAHOMED SHAH.

KOOTB SHAH.

DAWOOD SHAH:

MAHMOOD SHAH I.

ENTITLED BEGURRA.

MOOZUFFUR SHAH II.

SIKUNDUR SHAH.

MAHMOOD SHAH II.

BAHADUR SHAH.

SOOLTAN HOOSHUNG GHOORY.

GHIZNY KHAN.

SURNAMED SOOLTAN MAHOMED GHOORY.

SOOLTAN MAHMOOD KHILJY.

SOOLTAN GHEIAS-OOD-DEEN.

SOOLTAN NASIR-OOD-DEEN.

SOOLTAN MAHMOOD II.

CONCLUSION OF THE HISTORY OF MALWA.

CHAPTER VI.

HISTORY OF THE KINGS OF KANDEISH.

MULLIK RAJA FAROOKY.

MULLIK NUSEER.

ENTITLED NUSEER KHAN FAROOKY.

MEERAN ADIL KHAN FAROOKY.

MEERAN MOOBARIK KHAN FAROOKY.

MEERAN GHUNY.

COMMONLY CALLED ADIL KHAN FAROOKY I.

DAWOOD KHAN FAROOKY.

ADIL KHAN FAROOKY II.

ENTITLED AZIM HOOMAYOON.

MEERAN MAHOMED KHAN FAROOKY.

ENTITLED MEERAN MAHOMED SHAH.

MEERAN MOOBARIK KHAN FAROOKY.

CHAPTER VII.

SECTION I.

HISTORY OF THE KINGS OF BENGAL AND BEHAR, COMMONLY CALLED POORBY.

FUKHR-OOD-DEEN POORBY.

ALLA-OOD-DEEN POORBY.

HAJY ELIAS.

ENTITLED SHUMS-OOD-DEEN POORBY.

SIKUNDUR POORBY.

GHEIAS-OOD-DEEN POORBY.

SOOLTAN-OOS-SULLATEEN POORBY.

SHUMS-OOD-DEEN POORBY II.

RAJA KANS POORBY.

JEETMUL.

ENTITLED JULAL-OOD-DEEN.

AHMUD POORBY.

NASIR-OOD DEEN GHOLAM POORBY.

NASSIR POORBY.

BARBIK POORBY.

YOOSOOF POORBY.

SIKUNDUR POORBY.

FUTTEH POORBY.

THE EUNUCH SHAHZADA.

FEROZE POORBY.

MAHMOOD POORBY.

CHAPTER VII. (CONTINUED.)

SECTION II.

HISTORY OF THE KINGS OF JOONPOOR, DENOMINATD SHURKY.

CHAPTER VIII.

THE HISTORY OF THE KINGS OF MOOLTAN.

SHEIKH YOOSOOF.

KOOTB-OOD-DEEN LUNGA.

HOOSSEIN LUNGA.

MAHMOOD LUNGA.

HOOSSEIN LUNGA II.

CHAPTER IX.

THE HISTORY OF SIND AND TUTTA.

MAHOMED KASIM.

NASIR-OOD-DEEN KUBBACHA.

ACCOUNT OF THE DYNASTY OF SOOMUNA,

ENTITLED JAM.

SHAH BEG ARGHOON:

SHAH HOOSSEIN ARGHOON.

MIRZA EESY TURKHAN.

MIRZA MAHOMED BAKY TURKHAN.

MIRZA JANY BEG TURKHAN.

CHAPTER X.

THE HISTORY OF KASHMEER.

SHUMS-OOD-DEEN.

JUMSHEED.

ALLA-OOD-DEEN.

SHAHAB-OOD-DEEN.

KOOTB-OOD-DEEN.

SIKUNDUR BOOTSHIKUN,

OR,

ALEXANDER THE ICONOCLAST.

ALLY SHAH.

ZEIN-OOL-ABID-DEEN.

HEIDUR.

HUSSUN.

MAHOMED.

IBRAHIM.

NAZOOK.

YOOSOOF SHAH CHUK.

CHAPTER XI.

APPENDIX.

To face page 1. Vol. IV.

GENEALOGY OF THE KINGS OF GUZERAT.

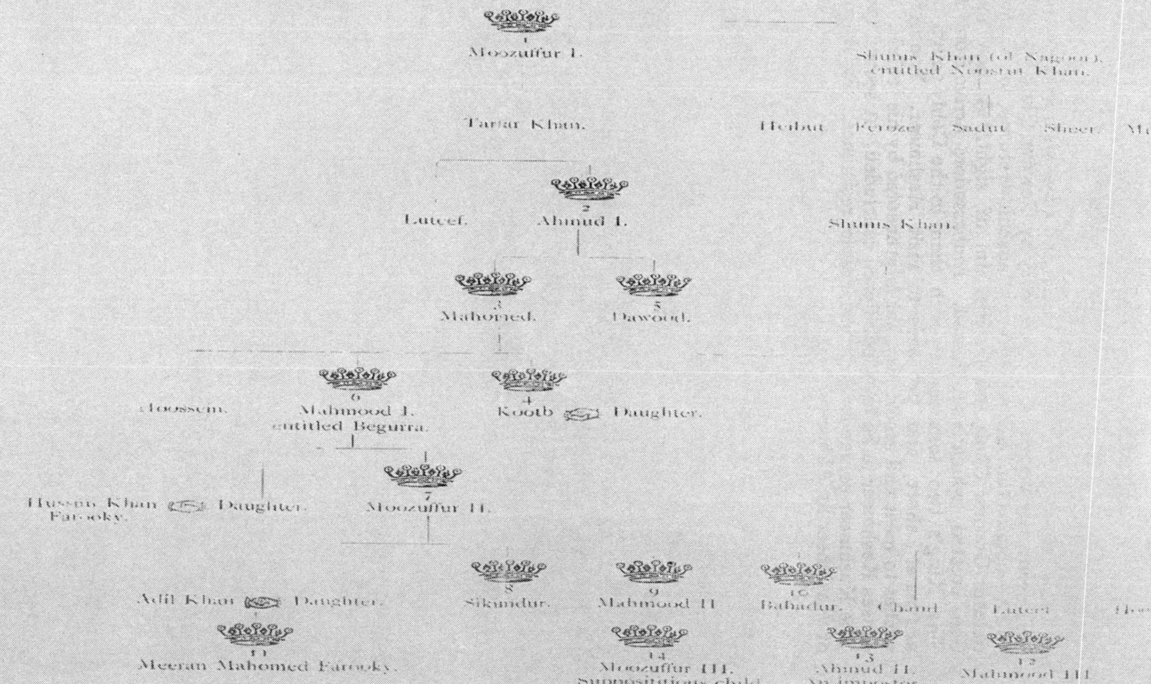

HISTORY

OF THE

MAHOMEDAN POWER IN INDIA.

CHAPTER IV.

HISTORY OF THE KINGS OF GUZERAT.

MOOZUFFUR SHAH I.

Cause of his nomination to the office of viceroy of Guzerat —the insignia of royalty are conferred on him at court—is opposed by the governor of the province at Sidpoor.—The governor is killed.—Moozuffur marches against Idur, and compels the Ray to pay tribute—forms a treaty with Adil Khan Farooky, ruler of Kandeish—levies tribute from the rajas of western Guzerat and Mundulgur—assumes the title of King—proceeds to Idur a second time, and levies tribute. —The King of Dehly expelled from his throne by Teimoor (Tamerlane)—seeks shelter in Guzerat, but is compelled to quit it.—Moozuffur Shah proceeds to Idur a third time—finds it evacuated, and occupies it with a force—marches to Somnat, which is evacuated—continues his route to Diù—the town opens its gates, but the inhabitants are put to the sword, and the Hindoo raja trod to death by an elephant. —Death of Tartar Khan at Suntpoor—contradictory accounts of the cause of that event.—Sudden death of

Dilawur Khan, ruler of Malwa.—War between Moozuffur Shah and his son and successor Hooshung.—Hooshung taken prisoner.—Moozuffur Shah leaves his brother, Noosrut Khan, in charge of the government of Malwa.—Noosrut Khan expelled from Malwa.—Hooshung reinstated, and the title of Sooltan and regalia conferred on him by Moozuffur Shah.—Death of Moozuffur Shah.

In the reign of Feroze Toghluk of Dehly, Furhut-ool-Moolk was nominated to the government of Guzerat, in which office he was confirmed by that monarch's successor, Gheias-ood-Deen Mahomed Toghluk II. Removed at a great distance from the capital, Furhut-ool-Moolk became desirous of establishing his independence; and in order to gain popularity for the furtherance of that object, he encouraged the Hindoo religion, and thus rather promoted than suppressed the worship of idols.

A. H. 793.
A. D. 1391.

In the year 793, the learned and orthodox Mahomedans of Guzerat, fearing lest this conduct should be the means of eventually superseding the true faith in those parts, addressed petitions to the throne, pointing out the probable political views of Furhut-ool-Moolk, as well as the danger to the true faith, if he were permitted to retain his government. On receipt of these addresses Mahomed Toghluk II. convened a meeting of the holy men at Dehly, and in conjunction with them appointed Zuffur,* the son of Wujee-ool-Moolk, one of the most respectable noblemen of the court, to the office of viceroy of

* Proselytes are usually the most zealous of all sectarians. Zuffur Khan was born a Hindoo prince, but became a convert.

Rubbee-oos-Sany 1. A. H. 793. March 6. A. D. 1391. Guzerat; and on the 1st day of Rubbee-oos-Sany of the same year he received the title of Moozuffur Khan, and was honoured with a dress of instalment. To add to his dignity, also, he was presented with a white canopy, and scarlet pavilion, such as are exclusively used by kings.

Moozuffur Khan was born at Dehly on the 25th of the month of Mohurrum, in the year 743 (30th of June, A.D. 1342). His family had been elevated from menial stations in the household of the kings of Dehly*; but the subject of the present history ranked among the most accomplished noblemen of the empire. It was on this account he received the honour of being appointed viceroy of Guzerat; and after making the necessary preparations for his journey, he left Dehly in the beginning of the year 794; about which period, the wife of A. H. 794. A. D. 1391. his son, Tartar Khan, was delivered of a son named Ahmud, of whom particular mention will be made hereafter.

On the arrival of Moozuffur Khan at Nagoor, many complaints against Furhut-ool-Moolk reached him from the inhabitants of Cambay, and other places, representing his oppression in the shape of accumulated taxes and imposts. Upon this he

* The author of the Mirut-Iskundry says, that Zuffur Khan was the wine-distiller at the court of Feroze Toghluk; that he was subsequently ennobled, as well as his brother, who received the title of Shums Khan; but that Tartar Khan, the son of Zuffur Khan, was detained at court about the King's person when his father was appointed viceroy of Guzerat.

wrote to that officer, informing him of his approach as governor, and recommending him to repair to court, with the balances of revenue so long withheld from the crown. Furhut-ool-Moolk returned an answer sufficiently indicative of his determination not to yield his authority quietly; and instantly collecting a force, composed chiefly of Hindoos, marched to oppose Moozuffur Khan. The new governor advanced to Yessavul, and having ascertained that his rival's army consisted of from ten to twelve thousand men, which he had collected with the intention of disputing his advance, he deputed an officer to him at Nehrwala (since called Puttun), warning him against opposing the legal authority, as in that case he must be considered, and would be treated, as a rebel.

Furhut-ool-Moolk not only insulted this officer, but returned an insolent answer to Moozuffur Khan, who at length being compelled to raise an army, in order to support his commission, he enlisted a body of four thousand cavalry, with which he made rapid marches to Nehrwala. Furhut-ool-Moolk with ten thousand of his troops, to whom he made liberal donations, marched as far as Sidpoor,* situated within twenty-four miles of Puttun, where the armies met. An engagement ensued, in which the rebels were routed, and Furhut-ool-Moolk lost his life; after which Moozuffur Khan continued his march to Nehrwala.

* The author of the Mirut-Iskundry states, he built a town on the spot where the battle took place, which he called Jeetpoor, "the Town of Victory;" probably the Chitpoor of our maps.

A. H. 796. A. D. 1393. In the year 796, the Ray of Idur having refused to pay the customary tribute, Moozuffur Khan marched to enforce it. Several skirmishes ensued, in which the new governor was generally victorious, until he arrived before the town of Idur, which he closely invested. The siege being protracted, the garrison became so distressed for provisions, that it is said they consumed cats and dogs, not before these animals had begun to feed on each other. The Ray at length sent out his son to prostrate himself before Moozuffur Khan, and to beg the lives of the inhabitants; a boon which was granted on condition of the payment of a quantity of jewels, and a large sum in specie.

Moozuffur Khan intended to have marched thence immediately to the city of Somnat, situated near the island of Diù; but he received information that Mullik Raja, entitled Adil Khan, not content with occupying that portion of the territory of Kandeish which lies contiguous to Talnere and Kuronde, had now extended his rapacity towards certain districts belonging to Guzerat, such as Sooltanpoor and Nundoorbar.

Moozuffur Khan accordingly deemed it proper, in the first instance, to turn his arms towards Kandeish; but Adil Khan retreated to Talnere, and sent a person to negotiate with Moozuffur Khan, and so completely succeeded in appeasing him, that a treaty of alliance was formed in consequence. On the return of Moozuffur Khan to Guzerat, he learnt that in the western Puttun district the Ray of Jehrend, an idolater, refused allegiance to the

Mahomedan authority. To this place Moozuffur Khan accordingly marched, and exacted tribute. He then proceeded to Somnat, where having destroyed all the Hindoo temples which he found standing, he built mosques in their stead; and leaving learned men for the propagation of the faith, and his own officers to govern

A. H. 798. A. D. 1395. the country, returned to Puttun in the year 798.

During the government of Furhut-ool-Moolk, the Rajpoots of Mundulgur acquired such strength as to expel the Mahomedans from their territories, refusing, also, to pay the usual tribute to the state. Moozuffur Khan accordingly moved in that direction. He besieged Mundulgur with battering rams and catapultas, and caused subterraneous passages to be dug, in order to enter the fort by that means; but all his endeavours would have proved futile had it not been for a pestilence which broke out in the town, and which induced the besieged ray, whose name was Doorga,* to send out deputies to treat for a surrender. These persons came with shrouds on their shoulders and swords suspended from their necks; at the same time, several women and children exposed themselves almost naked on the works, begging for mercy. The Khan agreed, at length, to raise the siege, on the payment of a large sum in gold and jewels. From Mundulgur Moozuffur Khan marched to Ajmeer, to pay his devotions at the shrine of Khwaja Moyin-ood-

* Mundulgur was a dependency of the Rana of Chittoor. Ferishta, like the Portuguese and other historians, sometimes (as in this distance) mistakes a lieutenant for a principal.

Deen Hussun Sunjury, from the whence he went towards Guzerat. On reaching Julwara, he destroyed the temples; and after exacting heavy contributions, and establishing his authority, he returned to Puttun. It is related in the Tareekh-i-Alfy, that after his return from Julwara, in the year 799, Moozuffur Khan caused him-

A. H. 799. A. D. 1396.

self to be proclaimed King, under the title of Moozuffur Shah, and directed coin to be struck in his name.

In the Dehly histories we are informed, that Tartar Khan, the son of Moozuffur Shah, became prime minister to Gheias-ood-Deen Mahomed Toghluk II. of Dehly, and that he afterwards raised a force and rebelled. Mulloo Yekbal Khan, an officer of that government, was sent to oppose him, and proceeded to Paniput, where Tartar Khan was encamped. The latter, by a forced march, avoided a battle and reached Dehly; but being unsuccessful in his attempt on that city he was obliged to relinquish his plans, and to fly precipitately to his father in Guzerat. Moozuffur Shah was induced, in consequence, in the year 800, to take the field in person, in sup-

A. H. 800. A. D. 1397.

port of his son; but hearing that Mirza Peer Mahomed Jehangeer, the grandson of Ameer Teimoor, had already advanced into Hindoostan, and occupied Mooltan, he suspended his intentions for the present; and we find him, in the year 801, engaged in another

A. H. 801. A. D. 1398.

attack on Ray Runmul, Raja of Idur. The Ray was obliged, as on the former occasion, to purchase forbearance by the payment of tribute ; and as the court of Dehly was now in a state of the utmost confusion, and many rivals were contending for the crown, Moozuffur Khan and Tartar Khan declined at present making any attempt in that quarter, but returned quietly to Puttun. In the year 803, Mahomed Toghluk, who had now been driven from his throne, fled to Guzerat; but Moozuffur Shah, conceiving it impolitic to allow him to remain in his dominions, obliged him to quit them, and he took refuge in Malwa.

A. H. 803.
A. D. 1401.

Moozuffur Shah, in the same year, again marched to levy the tribute of Idur ; but the Raja fled, on his approach, to Beesulnuggur, leaving the King to occupy Idur with his own troops. In the following year, 804, he marched to Somnat, and after a bloody action, in which the Mahomedans were victorious, the Ray fled to Diù. Moozuffur Shah having arrived before Diù laid siege to it, but it opened its gates without offering resistance. The garrison was, however, nearly all cut to pieces, while the Ray, with the rest of the members of his court, were trod to death by elephants. One large temple in the town was rased to the ground, and a mosque built on its site ; after which, leaving his own troops in the place, Moozuffur Shah returned to Puttun.

A. H. 804.
A. D. 1402.

One author relates that in the year 807 Moozuffur Shah projected the reduction of Dehly, and the placing of his son Tartar Khan on the throne; that he actually conferred on him the titles of Gheias-ood-Dowla-

A.H. 807.
A.D. 1404.

ood-Deen Mahomed Shah ; and that to this end he marched his army as far as the town of Suntpoor, where Tartar Khan, being taken dangerously ill, died.* Other historians state, with more probability, that Tartar Khan, taking advantage of the age and infirmities of his father, seized and imprisoned him in the town of Yessavul, since called Ahmudabad ; that he dignified his uncle Shums Khan with the title of Noosrut Khan, and causing himself to be proclaimed King, coined money under the name of Mahomed Shah Guzeratty, and then collecting an army, marched towards Dehly, for the purpose of assuming the title of King of Hindoostan ; he, however, only reached the town of Suntpoor, when Moozuffur Shah procured a letter to be written to his own brother Shums Khan, entitled Noosrut Khan, pointing out the wickedness of Tartar Khan, in having deposed him, and the futility of his enterprise on the throne of Dehly. He concluded his letter by instigating his brother to put Tartar Khan, the usurper, to death, and to return to Yessavul. In consequence of this, Noosrut Khan is said to have poisoned his nephew that very night at supper, and on the following day marched back and replaced his brother on the throne.

A.H. 810. A.D. 1407. About this period Dilawur Khan, the ruler of Malwa, died, and it was generally believed that his son Hooshung, who succeeded him, had poisoned him. A close

* The author of the Moontukhib-oot-Towareekh states, that Moozuffur Shah abdicated his throne in favour of his son Tartar Khan, but afterwards repented of having done so, and caused him to be poisoned.

alliance having subsisted between Moozuffur Shah and Dilawur Khan, the former marched with a force to D'har to avenge his untimely death, where he was opposed by Hooshung, who, after a severe action, was taken prisoner. Moozuffur Shah left his brother Shums Khan, entitled Noosrut Khan, in the government of Malwa. On the return of the army to Guzerat, Hooshung was delivered over to the Prince Ahmud, grandson of Moozuffur, and son of Tartar Khan, to be retained by him in a hill-fort. Hooshung had the address to gain the esteem of the young prince, his keeper, and some-time afterwards, when Noosrut Khan was obliged to fly from Malwa, the Prince Ahmud was prevailed on to write petitions in favour of Hooshung, which were graciously received at court, and he was permitted to accompany Hooshung, and reinstate him in his authority. At the same time he was directed to confer on him, in the name of Moozuffur Shah, the title of Sooltan, and the white canopy and scarlet pavilion.

On the return of the Prince Ahmud to Guzerat, Moozuffur Shah was taken dangerously ill, and seeing his own end fast approaching, nominated his grandson to succeed him on the throne of Guzerat.* He shortly afterwards died, on the 6th day of Rubbee-oos-Sany, in the year 814, in the seventy-first year of his age, after a reign of nearly twenty years.

Rubbee-oos-Sany 6. A.H. 814. July 27. A.D. 1411.

* The author of the Moontukhib-oot-Towareekh states, that the King placed his grandson, Ahmud, on the throne during his lifetime, and that he survived that measure five months and sixteen days.

AHMUD SHAH I.

Ahmud, the son of Tartar Khan, ascends the throne, agreeably to the will of his grandfather.—His uncles collect a force at Cambay to dispute his claim.—The confederates proclaim Feroze King—they solicit aid from Sooltan Hooshung of Malwa—they disagree, and dissolve their union.—Feroze retires into Baroach—he submits, and is pardoned.—Ahmud Shah builds the city of Ahmudabad.—The Prince Feroze again urges his pretensions to the throne, and unites with Ray Runmul, the exiled Raja of Idur.—Feroze is joined by his brother, Futteh Khan, and occupies Rungpoor.—Rungpoor taken.—Feroze and Ray Runmul of Idur make their escape.—The King proceeds against the Raja of Jhalode.—The latter is supported by Sooltan Hooshung, King of Malwa.—An insurrection created by Ahmud Sheer Kutchy.—The King marches against the King of Malwa, and deputes his brother, the Prince Luteef, against the insurgents under Ahmud Sheer Kutchy.—Ahmud Sheer is defeated, and flies to the Raja of Girnal (Joonagur).—The King proceeds to that fort.—The Raja becomes tributary.—Military operations carried on against the Hindoo chiefs of Guzerat.—The King proceeds to Kandeish and Buglana, where he hears of a formidable confederacy of the Hindoo rajas, in which Sooltan Hooshung of Malwa is connected.—The King returns to Guzerat.—Battle of Kaliada—the Malwa troops are defeated.—Peace concluded.—Ahmud Shah levies tribute from the Ray of Champanere—besieges Mando—raises the siege, and proceeds to Sarungpoor.—Battle of Sarungpoor.—Pestilence in the Guzerat army.—Ahmud Shah retreats—proceeds to attack Idur, which had been recovered by the Hindoos.—The King constructs a fort near it to watch the garrison, to which he gives the name of Ahmudnuggur.—The Ray agrees to pay tribute.—The King marches to Julwara.—Kanha Ray of Julwara flies to Kandeish—is supported by Nuseer Khan, and by

Ahmud Shah Bahmuny, King of Bidur.—The Deccanies are defeated.—A second campaign.—Battle of Manukpoonj.—Bombay and Tanna taken by the Deccanies—recovered by the Guzerat troops.—Ahmud Shah marches to Champanere.—The Deccan army invades Buglana.—The King countermarches and opposes the Deccanies at Tumbole.—Peace concluded.—Ahmud Shah marches into Malwa to support the claims of Musaood Ghoory.—Plague in Malwa.—The King retreats to Guzerat.—His death.

AHMUD SHAH was born at Dehly, A.H. 793 (A.D. 1390), and ascended the throne at the early age of twenty-one. During the year 815, Feroze* Khan, the eldest of the sons of the late Moozuffur Shah, hearing of the accession of his nephew Ahmud Shah, collected together some of the discontented nobles, such as Hissam-ool-Moolk, Mullik Sheer, Mullik Kureem, Mullik Khoosrow, Jeevundas, and Vinaikdas Kuhtry,† and through their means raised a force and marched to Cambay, where they formed a junction with Ameer Mahmood Toork and the Prince Heibut Khan, who had also formed an army at that spot. Upon this intelligence being made known to the other brothers, the Princes Sadut Khan and Sheer Khan also joined; and

A.H. 815.
A.D. 1412.

* The authors of the Moontukhib-oot-Towareekh and Mirut-Iskundry distinctly state, that Feroze was the *nephew* of Moozuffur Shah, and son of his brother Shums Khan Dundany, and that he afterwards fell in action against the Rana of Chittoor.

† The mention of these Hindoo names at this period proves that this class of people had now been associated in the offices of the government; a measure to which the Moslems were long averse.

a council being held, it was resolved to march, in the first instance, with their army (consisting of between seven thousand and eight thousand men) to Baroach, where they encamped on the Nerbudda. Feroze Khan was proclaimed king, and assumed the white canopy and scarlet pavilion. He invited Sooltan Hooshung of Malwa to march to his assistance; but the latter required a promise from him that in case of success the confederates should pay him one hundred thousand tunkas* for every march that his army made.

Ahmud Shah, however, took timely precautions for the security of his crown. In the first place, he sent deputaions to his uncles, and at the same time caused a small force to advance and keep the confederates in check; but this detachment was attacked and defeated by Raja Vinaikdas. Dissenions, however, shortly after arising among the pretenders, an affray ensued, in which Vinaikdas lost his life, and many of the troops went over to the King's army, so that Feroze Khan was obliged to break up his camp on the Nerbudda, and to take post in the fort of Baroach.

Ahmud Shah, respecting the ties of blood which

* The tunka of this part of India differs from one-half to two-thirds of a rupee; so that the sum would be in the one case 50,000, in the other 66,666 rupees. This practice of paying a certain sum for each march seems to be of ancient date, and it prevailed till a very late period. On the occasion of the defeat of Shooja-ood-Dowla, Nabob of Luknow, by the British troops at the battle of Buxar, in 1764, he called on Mulhar Row, the grandfather of the present Holkar, to aid him, and agreed to pay his army at the rate of a lack of rupees for each march, and half a lack for every halting-day during the campaign.

subsisted between him and the pretender, sent people into Baroach, urging Feroze Khan and his brothers to desist from further hostility, and they, finding themselves daily deserted by their troops, and that their finances were much reduced, submitted to the King's clemency. Ahmud Shah received them kindly, and restored them to the respective estates which they had held under the late king. Sooltan Hooshung of Malwa, however, who had not yet effected a junction with the army of the insurgents, was employed in devastating the eastern provinces of Guzerat; and Ahmud Shah sent Imad-ool-Moolk to expel him, an object which was not effected without difficulty.

The King, who had always professed himself extremely partial to the air and situation of the town of Yessavul, situated on the banks of the Saburmutty, in the latter end of this year (being 815) laid the foundation of a new city, which he caused to be called Ahmudabad; and the town of Yessavul formed one of the mohullas or parishes in the suburbs of that city, which afterwards became the capital of the kings of Guzerat. The houses of Ahmudabad are in general built of brick and mortar, and the roofs tiled. There are three hundred and sixty different mohullas, each mohulla having a wall surrounding it. The principal streets are sufficiently wide to admit of ten carriages abreast. It is hardly necessary to add that this is, on the whole, the handsomest city in Hindoostan, and perhaps in the world. Feroze Khan, in the latter end of this year, having again set up his pretensions to the crown, was joined by

Rookn Khan, the governor of Mahrasa,* with a considerable force, and he even promised to reinstate Raja Runmul in his possessions at Idur, on condition of his joining his standard with five or six thousand horse, and a number of foot. In the mean time, Ahmud Shah having collected a large force, marched to Mahrasa, where the rebels had taken post. Futteh Khan, the younger brother of the pretender, was sent in advance against him, but he treacherously deserted with his whole party to Feroze Khan, who having left Mullik Budr and Rookn Khan to defend Mahrasa, marched with Ray Runmul to Rungpoor, a town situated at the distance of ten miles. Meanwhile Ahmud Shah employed persons to induce Rookn Khan and Mullik Budr to abandon the cause of the pretender; but finding his remonstrances of no avail, the King quitted Mahrasa, and invested Rungpoor. On the following day, Rookn Khan, Mullik Budr, Zungy Khan, and Seif Khan, made a sally on the King's troops, but were repulsed.

Ahmud Shah continued during the siege to send messengers to the fort, dissuading his uncle, in vain, from further resistance; till at length Mullik Budr and Zungy Khan, having stated that they were empowered to enter into negotiations with certain officers of the royal army whom they named, and who were sent for that purpose; on approaching the fort-gate near the ditch, a party

* Ferishta always spells this word مهراسه and I have felt myself bound to follow his orthography: Mowrasa, I believe, is more correct.

sallied and succeeded in taking some of the King's deputies prisoners. Notwithstanding this act of treachery, Rungpoor was carried by storm two days afterwards, and both Rookn Khan and Mullik Budr fell in the assault, while Feroze Khan and Ray Runmul fled for refuge to the hills.

These circumstances are otherwise related by different historians; but I have selected the authorities which I consider best entitled to credit. It is said that soon after Ray Runmul and Feroze Khan had some disagreement, and the former seized the horses, elephants, and other effects of the latter; and in order to gain favour with the King he sent them to him. Feroze Khan fled to Nagoor, where he was put to death by the governor.

A.H. 816. A.D. 1413. In the following year, Ahmud Shah proceeded to attack the Raja of Julwara. The latter solicited the assistance of Sooltan Hooshung of Malwa, who accordingly marched and plundered some of the eastern provinces of Guzerat; in which direction Ahmud Shah no sooner moved, than his attention was distracted by commotions in another quarter. Ahmud Sheer Kutchy,* and Sheer Mullik, the son of Sheikh Mullik Adum of Bhukkur, officers of the late court, taking advantage of the King's absence, committed depredations on Guzerat; and though Ahmud Shah had actually marched towards Malwa, he was compelled, on arriving in the district of Champanere, to make two detachments from his

* An inhabitant of Kutch or Cutch.

army: the one under the command of Mullik Imad-ool-Moolk Samarkandy, to attack Sooltan Hooshung, and the other under the command of his younger brother, the Prince Luteef Khan, whom he appointed, under Nizam-ool-Moolk, to attack Ahmud Sheer Kutchy and Sheer Mullik.

Sooltan Hooshung, too well acquainted with the troops of Guzerat in the time of Moozuffur Shah, fled on the approach of the detachment, without halting till he arrived at the fort of D'har; while the other detachment under the Prince Luteef Khan defeated and pursued the rebels so closely as to take all their baggage. The author from whom I write states, that Sheer Mullik having escaped, found refuge with the Raja of Girnal.*

Ahmud Shah having a great curiosity to see the hill-fort of Girnal pursued the rebel in that direction; and as none of the former rajas had yet bent their necks to the Mahomedan yoke, he took advantage of the circumstance of the Raja having afforded an asylum to Sheer Mullik to make it a plea for invading his country. On his arrival at the hills in its vicinity, the King was opposed by the Hindoo prince, who, unaccustomed to the brunt of Mahomedan warfare, was defeated, and pursued to the fortress of Girnal, now called Joonagur. After a short time, the Raja, having consented to pay an annual tribute, made a large offering on the spot. Ahmud Shah left officers to collect the stipulated amount, and returned to Ahmudabad; on the road to which place he destroyed the temple of Soma-

* Properly Girnar.

poor, wherein were found many valuable jewels, and other property.

A.H. 817.
A.D. 1414.

In the year 817, Mullik Tohfa, one of the officers of the King's government, was ennobled by the title of Taj-ool-Moolk, and received a special commission to destroy all idolatrous temples, and establish the Mahomedan authority throughout Guzerat; a duty which he executed with such diligence, that the names of Mawass and Girass* were hereafter unheard of in the whole kingdom.

A.H. 819.
A.D. 1416.

In the year 819, Ahmud Shah marched against Nagoor; on the road to which place he plundered the country, and destroyed the temples. After his arrival there, he attacked the fort, and carried it by storm; but hearing that Khizr Khan, who had at this time assumed the government of Dehly, was on his march towards it, he retreated, and passing along the confines of Malwa, returned towards Ahmudabad.

A.H. 821.
A.D. 1418.

In the year 821, the King learned that Mullik Nuseer of Aseer and Sooltan Hooshung of Malwa had united and committed depredations on the districts of Sooltanpoor and Nundoorbar. He in consequence marched in that direction; whence he proceeded

* The Mawassy and Girassy chiefs appear to have been much like the zemindars of Hindoostan, and the poligars of the south. They only acknowledged Mahomedan supremacy when it was enforced by the presence of troops; and they have, till within the latest period, felt themselves bound in honour to withhold tribute till a body of soldiers appeared against them, even under the British government.

to the fort of Tumbole,* and compelled the Raja to pay a considerable sum of money.

The rains having set in, Ahmud Shah was desirous of retiring to his capital, but he obtained information which induced him to prepare for war in another quarter. During his absence in Buglana, the rajas of Idur, Champanere, Mundulgur, and Nadoot, had written petitions to Sooltan Hooshung, inviting him to the invasion of Guzerat. This intelligence was confirmed by a letter which the King received about the same time from his cousin Feroze Khan, the son of his uncle Shums Khan, which was brought in nine days from Nagoor to Nundoorbar; in which he stated positively, that Sooltan Hooshung, taking advantage of the King's absence, contemplated the conquest of Guzerat; that he had made overtures to him for that purpose, setting forth, that he had been invited by frequent applications from the zemindars to invade the kingdom, and that he had now absolutely commenced his march. Feroze Khan † also adds, "The King of Malwa, calcu-

* Tumbole, a small hill-fort in the district of Buglana. This district, from its local position, naturally belongs to Kandeish; but it had, from a very early period, rajas independent of that province.

† In the early part of this reign, Feroze Khan, who is denominated the son of Moozuffur Shah, sets up pretensions to the throne. He is defeated, but escapes, and no other mention is made of him. Here we have a Feroze Khan, the son of Shums Khan, the King's uncle, who holds the government of Nagoor. It appears to me probable they are one and the same person, especially from the remarkable concluding sentence of his letter to Ahmud Shah. Feroze, therefore, instead of being

"lating on my not being on good terms with your "Majesty, proposes to add the district of Nehr-"wala to my estates." The movements of Sooltan Hooshung confirmed this information ; so that the King, notwithstanding the rains, crossed the Nerbudda, and encamped his army on the banks of the Mehndry ; from whence, having selected a small force, he made rapid marches towards Ahmudabad, and thence to Mhowrasso. The Raja of Sorut * having heard of the projected invasion by Sooltan Hooshung, refused to pay the usual tribute. Mullik Nuseer, also, taking advantage of the moment, attacked his brother Mullik Iftikhar in the fort of Talnere, with whom he had previously consented to divide the province of Kandeish, and to whose aid Sooltan Hooshung had detached his son Ghizny Khan. These confederates now invaded the district of Sooltanpoor.

Such was the state of affairs when Ahmud Shah returned to Guzerat. He therefore deputed Mahmood Toork to levy the tribute from the Raja of Sorut, and Mahomed Toork and Mokhlis-ool-Moolk to disperse the forces of Mullik Nuseer and Ghizny Khan. These officers succeeded in effecting the object on which they were employed ; but the King reserved the punishment of Sooltan Hooshung of Malwa till the following year, when he marched

---

the son of Moozuffur Shah, appears to me to be the son of Shums Khan, entitled Noozrut Khan, the brother of Moozuffur Shah, of whom mention has already been made in his reign.

* The western peninsula of Guzerat is called Sorut or Sowrashtra ; but this province must not be confounded with the city and district of Surat, on the sea-coast.

in person against that prince, leaving Nizam-ool-Moolk in charge of the affairs of his government, with orders to attack the Raja of Mundulgur.

Having thus provided for his absence, Ahmud Shah marched by the route of Mahrasa into Malwa, and found Sooltan Hooshung with a large army posted in a strong position, with his rear thrown back on the village of Kaliada, having a number of low prickly hedges partly protecting his front. Ahmud Shah, after reconnoitring his position, made immediate dispositions to attack the enemy. Mahomed Toork commanded the right wing, and Mullik Fureed, the son of Imad-ool-Moolk, the left. The action commenced by the Guzeratties skirmishing, in order to draw the enemy from his strong position, a manœuvre which only partially succeeded, till one of the Guzerat elephants becoming furious, charged the enemy's line, broke through it, and opened a passage to the cavalry. On this occasion, Ghizny Khan, Prince of Malwa, received an arrow-wound which obliged him to fall back with his elephants; and this circumstance having caused some confusion, was taken advantage of by Mullik Fureed, who galloping round the village fell upon the rear of the Malwites, and completed the defeat. Sooltan Hooshung fled to Mando, and the Guzerat troops pursued the flying enemy till within a few miles of that place. The rainy season having set in, Ahmud Shah returned to Guzerat, and rewarded in the most liberal manner all those officers who had distinguished themselves in the late action.

After the rains, the King having caused the fortress of Soangur to be repaired, proceeded in person to Idur, from whence he detached a force into Malwa to lay waste that country. On the following year an envoy arrived from Sooltan Hooshung, and a peace was concluded between the Malwa and Guzerat sovereigns; but the latter resolved to punish the Ray of Champanere, one of the confederates, who had originally invited Sooltan Hooshung to the invasion of Guzerat. He therefore marched and invested that place, and the Ray consented to pay an annual tribute.

A. H. 822.
A. D. 1419.

Notwithstanding the recent treaty which had been formed, such was the restless character of Sooltan Hooshung, that in the course of two years Ahmud Shah was again compelled to take the field against him. He marched a force directly to Mando, without meeting opposition; and having encamped opposite the Sarungpoor gate of the fort, he commenced the siege by regular approaches.

Sooltan Hooshung, confident in the strength of the fortress, left Mando, and taking six thousand horse with him, went to Jajnuggur,* where he intended to obtain some elephants, in order to make a stand in the field against Ahmud Shah. For this reason he left the place in charge of a confidential officer, and returned at the expiration of six months, during which time the siege continued; but it is most extraordinary, that he marched out and came back without the besiegers

* A city situated on the Mahanuda river, which empties itself into the sea in the province of Orissa. The forests of which have always been famous for wild elephants.

being aware he had left the garrison. The first intimation which Ahmud Shah received of the circumstance was on the return of Sooltan Hooshung, which was announced by flags being hoisted on the bastions, accompanied with the sound of drums and trumpets.

Ahmud Shah, ashamed and vexed, raised the siege, and vented his rage in plundering the country. In this warfare he was frequently opposed by the Malwites, but the Guzeratties were, in general, victorious. The following is an extract from the Tareekh Alfy of Moolla Ahmud, which appears to give a clear and more probable account of the whole campaign, and the cause of its commencement:—

A. H. 825.
A. D. 1422.

"In the year 825," says Moolla Ahmud, "Sooltan Hooshung having "assumed the dress of a horse-mer-"chant, went to Jajnuggur in order to procure "elephants. Ahmud Shah of Guzerat having "heard that he had left his kingdom, and that "his officers had divided it among themselves, "took advantage of this state of affairs to invade "Malwa. In the first place, he reduced the fort "of Meheswur, and thence marched to Man-"do, detaching, at the same time, small bodies of "cavalry to plunder the country. He continued "the siege of Mando but a short period, when the "rains setting in, he proceeded to Oojein, leaving "detachments in the several districts of Malwa, to "assist in collecting the revenues of the khurreef "or autumnal crop. Meanwhile, he ordered bat-

"tering rams and engines to be brought from Gu-"zerat, for the purpose of besieging Mando; which "having arrived under Mullik Mokurrib from "Ahmudabad, he renewed the siege, detaching "Mullik Mokurrib to secure the approach by the "Tarapoor gate.*

"At this period intelligence was received that "Sooltan Hooshung was on his return to Malwa; "Ahmud Shah therefore raised the siege of Mando, "and calling in his different detachments, marched "with the whole army towards Sarungpoor. Sool-"tan Hooshung, having timely intimation of Ah-"mud Shah's movement, made rapid marches, and "reached Sarungpoor before him. Whence he de-"puted messengers to Ahmud Shah, to endeavour "to detain him by negotiation, till he should have "time to repair the ditch and the boundary "hedge† of Sarungpoor.

"Ahmud Shah, however, marched on; but he "had no sooner reached the place than Sooltan "Hooshung made a night-attack on his camp, "though his ambassador was still with him. The "Guzeratties being surprised, were many of them "cut to pieces, and Ahmud Shah made his escape "with difficulty, attended by only one domestic. "When he had got clear of the camp he halted, and "ordered his attendant to go and bring him in-

* The southern entrance.

† It is usual to form strong hedges either of the cactus or aloe around fortified towns, at the distance of two or three hundred yards, to prevent the enemy bringing their approaches closer to the works; which answer all the purposes of an abatis.

"formation how the Malwites were engaged. "The messenger returned, and reported that they "were chiefly employed in plunder. On which, "collecting his scattered army during the night, "he was enabled to muster one thousand horse. "With this small body, he anxiously waited on "the confines of the camp till daybreak, when he "attacked it. The Malwa troops, fatigued with "the former night's work, had, for the most part, "given themselves up to sleep, while some few "were still engaged in plundering; they conse-"quently made but feeble resistance, and the "slaughter among them was severe. Ahmud "Shah not only recovered on this occasion all the "elephants he had formerly lost, but he acquired "seven other large ones, which had been brought "from Jajnuggur.

"Sooltan Hooshung fled to the fort of Sarung-"poor, to which Ahmud Shah laid siege; but he "was obliged, in consequence of an epidemic that "raged in the camp, to abandon his purpose, and "commence his retreat; in which he was closely "pursued by Sooltan Hooshung, who hung "upon his flanks, and harassed him on the line of "march. At length Ahmud Shah halting, brought "on a general action, in which Sooltan Hooshung "was defeated with the loss of four thousand nine "hundred men; which enabled Ahmud Shah, "though not without much difficulty, to bring off "his army; and, in consideration of what his troops "had suffered during this campaign, he abstained "from any foreign attacks for some years."

A. H. 829. A. D. 1426. In the year 829, he marched to retake Idur. On the banks of the river Hatmutty,* in the vicinity of Idur, he constructed a fort, which he called Ahmudnuggur, and then returned to his capital. On this occasion the Raja Poonja Ray made some defence; but being defeated, fled to the hills of Beesulnuggur.

A. H. 830. A. D. 1427. In the year 830, the King was induced to return to the country of Idur, having heard that Poonja Ray had collected a force in that neighbourhood. The two armies meeting, a severe conflict ensued, in which the Ray's army was defeated, and himself killed; when Ahmud Shah ordered a detachment to lay waste the country of Beesulnuggur. Meanwhile the son of Poonja Ray promised to pay into the treasury of Guzerat an annual tribute of three lacks of tunkas of silver. From Idur the King marched into the district of Gilwara.

Suffur 6. A. H. 832. Nov. 14. A. D. 1428. In the year 832 he marched again to Idur; and on the sixth of Suffur carried by storm one of the principal forts in that province, wherein he built a magnificent mosque. In the following year, Kanha Ray, the Raja of Jhalode, perceiving the system which Ahmud Shah pursued towards the Hindoos, fled with his family and property to Aseer, and presented Nuseer Khan, the Prince of Kandeish, with two elephants, which he had succeeded in bringing

* Ferishta writes Hatmutty; it should evidently be Saburmutty, the same river that flows through Ahmudabad.

away with him when he escaped from a detachment sent in pursuit by Ahmud Shah.

The Ray having thus secured the interest of Nuseer Khan (who was connected with Sooltan Ahmud Shah Bahmuny), that chief prevailed on the King of the Deccan to furnish a small body of troops to accompany the Ray, in order to recover his country. Instead of marching towards Jhalode, however, the Raja plundered the districts of Sooltanpoor and Nundoorbar, on which Ahmud Shah sent a force under Mullik Mokurrib, with his son the Prince Mahomed Khan, to punish the invaders. The armies met near Sooltanpoor: the Deccany troops were defeated, and the few who escaped fled to Dowlutabad.

This intelligence reaching the ears of Ahmud Shah Bahmuny, he appointed his son Alla-ood-Deen, accompanied by a force commanded by Khan Jehan and Kuddur Khan, to retrieve the character of the Deccany arms. This force assembled under the walls of Dowlutabad, where it was joined by the Raja of Jhalode and by Nuseer Khan Farooky of Aseer, whose daughter was married to the Prince Alla-ood-Deen. It moved several marches in the direction of the Guzerat troops, and encountered them on the top of the Manukpoonj pass, where an action ensued, in which the two commanders-in-chief, Mullik Mokurrib of Guzerat and Kuddur Khan of Deccan, were personally opposed to each other. The latter being unhorsed was killed in the fall; but the Deccanies, who were retreating, rallied, and forming into a solid body, made a desperate charge on the Guzeratties. They were, however, so steadily opposed that they fell back, and became subsequently completely routed. The Prince of the Deccan fled to Dowlutabad, and the Raja of Jhalode and Nuseer Khan took refuge in the hills of Kandeish; after which the Prince Mahomed Khan returned to Ahmudabad.

In the same year, Kootb Khan, the governor of Mahim,* dying. Sooltan Ahmud Shah Bahmuny thought this a favourable opportunity to obtain possession of that island, which he effected without loss. Ahmud Shah instantly deputed his youngest son, Zuffur Khan, with a force commanded by Mullik Iftikhar Khan, to retake it. For this purpose, orders were sent to Diù, Gogo, and Cambay, to collect shipping; and a fleet was formed, consisting of seventeen sail, on which part of the army embarked, while the remainder marched to Tanna by land, which had now also fallen into the hands of the Deccanies.

In the first place, Tanna was invested by Mullik Iftikhar, and the fleet anchoring off the port, all communication was cut off both by sea and land. The officer commanding the garrison made two or

* Bombay. This island seems, at this time, to have consisted of two parts; the one denominated Mahim, from the village of that name in the N. E. corner, and the other Mumby from an idol to which a temple is still dedicated, and is known by the appellation of Mumbydevy, or the Goddess Mumby, which by Europeans has been corrupted into *Bombay*. The separation of the two islands would be again complete, if the dam called Breach Kandy were removed, which keeps out the sea on the west face of the island. Colonel Tod is of opinion, that Mumbydevy is also a corruption from Mama Devy, "Mater Dea," the Divine Mother, or Alma Mater.

three vigorous sallies; but being always repulsed with loss, and finding himself incapable of making any effectual defence, and despairing of succour, he fell back on Mahim. The fort of Tanna capitulated next day, and Mullik Iftikhar marched on to the attack of Mahim. On his arrival, he found that Mullik-oot-Toojar, the Deccany general, had formed a very strong wattled breast-work on that face of the island by which the Guzeratties must necessarily approach; and though this barrier proved a very serious obstacle, it was by no means insuperable. The Guzerat troops stormed and carried the stockade with great gallantry, but not without considerable loss. They now found themselves opposed to the whole of the Deccan line. A severe action ensued, which was undecided at night-fall; on which occasion, the heroes on both sides lay down on the variegated carpet, deeply tinged with each other's blood. During the night, Mullik-oot-Toojar retreated to the contiguous island;* which being closely blockaded by the fleet and by the troops which were also landed, he escaped to the continent, where he effected a junction with a body of Deccanies, consisting of ten thousand horse and sixty elephants, under the command of Khwaja Jehan, accompanied by the Bahmuny Prince Mahomed Khan. This force had been sent in consequence of Mullik-oot-Toojar's requisition for reinforcements, even before the attack on Mahim.

With this army the Deccany prince marched to

*That part of the present island then separate, and called Mumbydevy.

retake Tanna ; but the Guzerat prince having intimation of his movement, proceeded in person with a strong detachment to intercept the Deccanies. Both armies arrived before Tanna on the same day; and another action ensued, which lasted from break of day till sunset, when the Deccanies were ultimately defeated, and dispersed. Mullik-oot-Toojar took refuge in Chakun, while the Prince and Khwaja Jehan did not halt till they reached Dowlutabad. Among the articles taken on the island of Mahim were some beautiful gold and silver embroidered muslins, with which vessels were laden and sent to Ahmudabad.

A. H. 835. A. D. 1431. In the year 835 Ahmud Shah, leaving his eldest son at the capital, marched in person to Champanere; and Ahmud Shah Bahmuny, in order to have his revenge, also marched at the head of an army to Buglana, a district contiguous to Surat, which he completely devastated. The King receiving information of this attack countermarched from Champanere to Nundoorbar, destroying Nadout on his march.

Ahmud Shah Bahmuny, who was at this period engaged in the siege of Tumbole, retreated to his capital, and Ahmud Shah of Guzerat returned towards Ahmudabad; but he had scarcely reached the river Tapty, when he received intimation that Ahmud Shah Bahmuny had returned to the attack of Tumbole, a measure occasioned, it seems, by the King of the Deccan mistaking for pusillanimity the offers made by Ahmud Shah to negotiate a peace. Ahmud Shah of Guzerat now returned towards the enemy, and arrived within a few miles of the town of Tumbole, when Ahmud Shah Bahmuny resolved to make an attempt to carry the place by escalade that night. A few Naigs were in consequence selected for this service; some of whom succeeded in gaining a footing on the ramparts before they were discovered; but the alarm being once given, the commandant of the garrison, Mullik Sadut Sooltany, having collected a small party, attacked the assailants, and nearly destroyed the whole. A few threw themselves over the works. At the same time the garrison made a sally on the enemy's camp, by which the besiegers suffered severely before they could oppose the attacking party, which escaped back to the fort under cover of the night, without loss.

On the next morning the Guzerat army arrived; and Ahmud Shah Bahmuny, stung with vexation at the repeated defeats his arms had suffered during the late campaign, seemed determined to retrieve the character of the Deccanies in a general action. When the two lines were drawn out opposite to each other. Ajdur Khan, a young Deccany nobleman, galloped forth and challenged any of the nobles of Guzerat to meet him singly. The offer was accepted by Azd-ool-Moolk of Guzerat, and they both fought as the opposing armies advanced. Ajdur Khan was severely wounded, and taken prisoner, soon after which the action became general. It was severe on both sides, and continued till sunset, when the retreat was mutually sounded; and this would have been considered a drawn battle, but the King of the Deccan having experienced a very heavy loss in killed and wounded, commenced his retreat during the night.

Ahmud Shah on the next day went into the fort of Tumbole, and with his own hands conferred donations and titles on Mullik Sadut and his brave garrison, which he reinforced, and then marched to Talnere; whence he proceeded to Nadout; and having left Ein-ool-Moolk in charge of that district, returned to Ahmudabad.

In the Siraj-oot-Tareekh Bahmuny, the account of the siege of Tumbole is somewhat differently related; but I think the Deccan historian is not so clear in his account as the Guzerat author, to whose text I have adhered, though God only knows which authority is most to be relied on.

In the year 836, Ahmud Shah hav-
A. H. 836. ing contracted his son Futteh Khan in
A. D. 1432. marriage with the daughter of the Ray of Mahim, marched towards Nagoor and Mewat. On his arrival at Dongurpoor, he received large presents, and exacted tribute from the Raja; thence entering the country of the Kolies and Bheels, subject to Rana Mokul of Chittoor, he laid it waste; and proceeding into the district of Meywar, he levied contributions from the rays of Kota, Boondy, and Nowlaye. During this campaign he was joined by Feroze Khan of Nagoor, who made an offering of several lacks of tunkas, which, however, were not accepted by Ahmud Shah. He now returned to Ahmudabad.

A. H. 839. In the year 839, Mahmood Khan
A. D. 1435. Khiljy, one of the officers of the Malwa

government, having rebelled, drove Musaood (the grandson of Sooltan Hooshung Ghoory) from the throne, who sought protection at the court of Guzerat. In the following year, Ahmud Shah felt himself bound to march an army in order to reinstate him. On his arrival at Basowda he detached part of the force in advance towards Mando to intercept Khan Jehan,* the father of the usurper, then on his march from Chundery; but when the latter heard of the movement of Ahmud Shah, he made forced marches to the capital and reinforced his son, now styling himself Sooltan Mahmood Khiljy.

A. H. 840.
A. D. 1436.

Ahmud Shah at length arrived before Mando, and the Malwites made several trifling sallies; but in a night-attack, of which Ahmud Shah obtained previous information, they were so completely repulsed that they almost all fell victims to their temerity. On the following morning Ahmud Shah detached his son Mahomed Khan, with a body of five thousand horse, to plunder the country of Sarungpoor, with orders to join Oomr Khan, a son of the late King of Malwa, who, having raised a force, was also on his march from Chundery to the capital. Sooltan Mahmood Khiljy, in spite of these disadvantages, was enabled to hold out in the fort; for he had laid in store a large quantity of ammunition and provisions, while the besiegers found it difficult to subsist. In this state of affairs he made a sally from the Tarapoor gate, leaving his

* His real name is Mullik Mogheis Khiljy, and he is much distinguished in the history of Malwa under that name.

father in charge of the fort, and marched to Sarungpoor. On the road, having encountered Mullik Hajy Ally of Guzerat, who was posted to guard a ford on the Chumbul, he attacked and completely defeated him, compelling him to seek refuge in Ahmud Shah's camp. Sooltan Mahmood, following up his success, attacked the Prince Oomr Khan, whom he also defeated and slew, and eventually established himself on the throne of Malwa. At this time the plague (a disease very unusual in India*) broke out in the army of Ahmud Shah, so that many of the dead remained unburied. The King of Guzerat was, therefore, induced to quit Malwa, and to retreat to Ahmudabad, where he eventually died, on the 4th of Rubbee-ool-Awul, in the year 847, after a reign of nearly thirty-three years.

Rubbee-ool-Awul 4. A. H. 847. July 4. A. D. 1443.

* As this is the only instance, I believe, on record, of the disease known to Europeans by the name of the plague having made its appearance in India, notwithstanding the constant intercourse between its coasts and Egypt, I think the author from whom Ferishta quotes must be mistaken. The word is written طاعون

MAHOMED SHAH.

Espouses the daughter of the Raja of Idur—exacts tribute from the Raja of Dongurpoor—attacks the Raja of Champanere, who obtains aid from the King of Malwa.—Mahomed Shah retreats.—Invasion of Guzerat by the Malwa troops.—The pusillanimity of Mahomed Shah—flies to Diù—is poisoned by his queen at the instance of his officers.

THE Prince Mahomed, the eldest son of the late king, succeeded his father, under the appellation of Mahomed Shah, and immediately after, having marched to Idur, espoused the daughter of the Ray, to whom he restored his ancient rights in that district. Thence proceeding to Dongurpur, he exacted tribute from the Raja, and returned to Ahmudabad.

A.H. 853. A.D. 1449. In the year 853 he marched towards the fort of Champanere, where being opposed by the Raja Gungadas, he defeated and compelled him to seek refuge in his capital. Gungadas, thus situated, wrote to Sooltan Mahmood Khiljy of Malwa, stipulating for the payment of a lack of tunkas of silver to his army for every march. Sooltan Mahmood, in consideration of the pecuniary subsidy, and smarting with resentment under the treatment he had experienced in the beginning of his reign from the late king of Guzerat, assented, and in the end of the same year marched towards Champanere.

Mahomed Shah, having lost many of the carriage-cattle of his army during the campaign, no sooner heard of the advance of Sooltan Mahmood than he set fire to the greater part of his heavy baggage, and commenced his retreat to Ahmudabad, in spite of the earnest remonstrances of his officers. Some time afterwards (in the
A.H. 855. year 855), when Sooltan Mahmood of
A.D. 1451. Malwa, perceiving the timidity of the present sovereign of Guzerat, advanced with a force of one hundred thousand men, with the resolution to conquer and annex it to the kingdom of Malwa, Mahomed Shah, so far from opposing him, endeavoured to retreat to the island of Diù; but the Guzerat officers, feeling for their character, resolved to cut him off, and instigated his own wife to administer poison to him.*

Mahomed Shah reigned eight years, nine months, and four days, having obtained, during that period, the name of Kurreem, or the Merciful, an appellation to which, from his mild nature, he seems to have been entitled.

* This event, according to the Moontukhib-oot-Towareekh, occurred on the 10th of Mohurrum, A.H. 855, which answers to the 12th of February, 1451.

KOOTB SHAH.

In induced to oppose the King of Malwa.—Battle of Surkech.—The King of Malwa retires.—Peace concluded.—Shums Khan, the son of Feroze Khan of Nagoor, solicits the King's aid against the Rana Kombha of Chittoor.—Reinforcements sent to Nagoor.—The King's troops defeated.—Treaty of offensive alliance against the Rana concluded between the kings of Malwa and Guzerat at Champanere.—Aboo taken by the King of Guzerat—he compels the Rana to pay one thousand one hundred and seventy-six pounds weight of gold.—Death of Kootb Shah.

On the death of Mahomed Shah he was succeeded by his son Kootb Khan, under the title of Kootb Shah. This prince was born at Nundoorbar, on the night of Monday the 8th of Jumad-oos-Sany, in the year 855, (8th of August, A. D. 1451,) and ascended the throne in the forty-ninth year of his age. The King of Malwa, Sooltan Mahmood Khiljy, in prosecution of the war, obtained possession of the town of Sooltanpoor, by gaining over the governor Mullik Alla-ood-Deen Sohrab Toork. He appointed that officer commander of his troops, and made rapid marches to the capital of Guzerat. Kootb Shah was advised by some of his courtiers to retreat to Sorut,* and allow the King of Malwa to occupy for the present the eastern provinces;

* Western Guzerat, called also Kattywar.

when it was proposed, that, after his return to Mando, Kootb Shah should attack the Malwa troops, and recover his losses. This advice was so entirely in unison with the King's feelings, that he actually suggested it to the officers of the army; who, with one voice, protested against a measure so fraught with disgrace and inevitable ruin.* They reminded the King of the deeds of his warlike grandsire and ancestors, and used every means in their power to induce him to lead his army to oppose the invader; a measure to which he reluctantly assented, and made one march towards the enemy.

Mullik Alla-ood-Deen, the Guzerat officer who had betrayed the fort of Sooltanpoor to the enemy, and who now held the high post of commander-in-chief of the Malwa army, on finding that Kootb Shah was actually on his march to resist the invasion, returned to his allegiance, and went over to his king, who received him with such marks of favour, that during one levee he bestowed upon him seven different khiluts, and conferred on him the title of Alla-ool-Moolk.

When the two armies were within six miles of each other, the Guzeratties at the village of Sur-

* The spirited conduct of the nobles on this occasion must not be mistaken for patriotism. They had each considerable landed estates for the maintenance of troops, which they must have lost in the event of the King of Malwa succeeding in subduing Guzerat. Their motives for fighting, therefore, appear quite natural; so that, although this mode of paying the army seems, in some respects, exceptionable, yet it tended greatly to promote union in cases of invasion by a foreign enemy

kech, and the Malwites at Butwa, Sooltan Mahmood addressed some verses, conceived in taunting language, to Kootb Shah, who returned for answer that the present generation had not forgotten the conquest of Malwa by Moozuffur Shah, the capture of Sooltan Hooshung, and the restoration of his kingdom at the hands of his grandfather, Ahmud Shah.

Suffur 1. A. H. 856. Feb. 10. A. D. 1453.

On the night of the 1st of Suffur, A.H. 856, Sooltan Mahmood mounted at dusk, with the intention of surprising the Guzerat army, but lost his way in the night among some ruined walls near his own camp. Kootb Shah, hearing of his failure, ordered out his line, and at day-break attacked the Malwa forces, who were also by this time under arms. In this action, the left wing of the Guzerat army was repulsed, and fled to Ahmudabad, but the right wing succeeded in defeating the body of the enemy to which it was opposed. Notwithstanding this circumstance, Sooltan Mahmood of Malwa, although deserted by all his army excepting thirteen troopers, charged with this small party as far as the royal tents of Guzerat. From which he brought away the crown, the King's girdle, and many other valuable jewels, to his own camp. On his arrival, he caused a report to be circulated, that he intended to attack the Guzerat army again on the same night; which becoming known to the enemy, as he intended, induced the Guzeratties to remain on the alert. This enabled Sooltan Mahmood, whose troops had been severely handled to retreat without molestation, if we except the opposition he experienced from the Kolies and Bheels. Kootb Shah, congratulating himself sincerely on having got rid of the Malwa forces with such facility, returned to the city of Ahmudabad with his spoils, consisting, among other articles, of sixty elephants. A considerable detachment was now sent to retake Sooltanpur; which being effected, a peace was concluded between the two sovereigns, by which it was agreed each should retain whatever places his troops now occupied; and one article enjoined the parties to wage perpetual war against Hindoos, whose destruction was solemnly agreed on.

A. H. 860.
A. D. 1455.

In the year 860, Feroze Khan, the occupant of Nagoor, died, and his brother Mujahid Khan, having expelled Shums Khan, the son of Feroze Khan, kept possession of the estate. Shums Khan immediately applied to Rana Koombho of Chittoor for aid; and as the Rana's family had long wished for an opportunity to humble the chief of Nagoor, he marched against him. The garrison, without offering resistance, agreed to receive Shums Khan; and he was formally re-instated with the understanding that he was to dilapidate part of the battlements,* in token of submission to the Rana, after which he returned. So far from doing this, however, Shums Khan improved the fortifications, and set the Rana at defiance; who, enraged at this con-

* It was usual to require refractory chiefs to allow part of the battlements of their castles to be broken, in token of submission. The act of repairing them, without permission, was the signal of rebellion.

duct, returned to Chittoor, only to collect a large force, and then marched against Nagoor. Shums Khan, unable to cope with him, left the place, under charge of one of his best officers, and proceeded to Ahmudabad to obtain reinforcements.

Kootb Shah became so well pleased with Shums Khan, that he not only required him to reside at his court, but he even married his daughter, and ordered an army, under the command of Ray Ramchundur and Mullik Gudday, to reinforce the garrison of Nagoor. These troops no sooner arrived than an action ensued with the Rana, who completely defeated the Guzeratties, and killed many brave officers and men. Kootb Shah, hearing of this disaster, marched in person; but despairing of reducing Chittoor, he proceeded in the direction of Sirohy, the Raja of which was closely connected with the Rana of Chittoor. He was opposed by the Rajpoots of Sirohy, whom he defeated, and afterwards entering the hills, he reached Koombulmere. Here the Rana attacked the Moslems, but was defeated in several engagements, and sued for peace, consenting to pay a large sum in specie, and a quantity of jewels; after which Kootb Shah returned to Ahmudabad.

On his road to Guzerat he was met by Taj Khan, an ambassador from the court of Malwa, who had been sent to propose an offensive alliance against Rana Koombho of Chittoor, whose country it was agreed should be divided between the allies. All the towns to the southward, and lying contiguous to Guzerat, were to be attached to the kingdom of Kootb Shah, while the districts of

Mewar* and Aheerwara should be reduced and retained by the Malwa forces. This treaty was solemnly signed by the respective envoys at the

A. H. 860.
A. D. 1456.

town of Champanere, in the latter end of the year 860.

A. H. 861.
A. D. 1457.

On the following year, pursuant to the treaty of Champanere, Kootb Shah marched towards Chittoor, and on the road stormed and carried the fortress of Aboo, where having left a garrison, he pursued his march. At the same time Sooltan Mahmood Khiljy also commenced his attack on the side of Malwa. The Rana was desirous of opposing the Malwa army first; but Kootb Shah's approaches were so rapid, that he reached Sirohy, and entered the hills, compelling the Rana to come to a general action, in which the Rajpoot army was entirely defeated. Kootb Shah followed up his success, and shortly after brought the Rana again to action: he was defeated a second time, and fled to the hills, whence he deputed an ambassador, and purchased the retreat of the King of Guzerat by the payment of fourteen maunds† weight of solid gold, and two elephants which conveyed the treasure. A seasonable donation was at the same time made to Sooltan Mahmood Khiljy, who was also induced to retreat to Malwa.

* The entire dominions of the Rana constitute according to Colonel Tod, Méwar, or properly Med-war, the midland or central region of India.

† A maund of Chittoor is equal to eighty-four pounds: the whole amount would weigh one thousand one hundred and seventy-six pounds.

A. H. 862. A. D. 1458. On the following year, 862, the Rana broke the treaty, and marched to attack Nagoor with fifty thousand horse and foot; intimation of which the governor immediately despatched by a messenger to the King at Ahmudabad. Kootb Shah was at the time engaged in a course of debauchery, from which he could not be recalled; notwithstanding which, the prime minister, Imad-ool-Moolk, collecting part of the army, made one march from the capital, but was obliged to halt for a whole month, before the equipments could be prepared. The Rana, hearing that the troops had actually moved, retired to Chittoor; and the King returning to Ahmudabad, continued to spend his time in licentious excess.

In the latter end of the same year he marched to Sirohy; the Raja of which place being related to Rana Koombho, and apprehensive of the Mahomedan arms, fled to the hills of Koombulmere, while the Guzeratties laid waste his country; a simultaneous movement was also made by the Malwa forces against Chittoor. Kootb Shah having pursued the Rana to the fort of Koombulmere, found that he was unable to take it, and contented himself, therefore, after plundering the country, with retreating to Ahmudabad. Shortly after his return to which city, he was taken dangerously ill, and died on the 23d of Rujub, 863. He was buried in the vault of Mahomed Shah. It was generally believed at the time of his death that the King had been poisoned by Shums Khan of Nagoor, whose daughter he had married; and

Rujub 23. A. H. 863. May. 25. A. D. 1459.

that chief suffered death in consequence, but it was afterwards proved he was perfectly innocent.* Kootb Shah is entitled Ghazy (the Champion of the Faith), and reigned seven years and seven months, during which period many scenes of the most wanton cruelty took place. He was of a violent and capricious temper, and of a sanguinary disposition, often putting to death, without the slightest cause, some of his most confidential servants and favourites, who usually suffered during the time of his disgraceful debauches.

* The author of the Moontukhib-oot-Towareekh says, that Kootb Shah's mother, suspecting the Queen, her son's wife, made her over to the vengeance of her eunuchs, who literally tore her in pieces.

DAWOOD SHAH:

He succeeds to the throne of his nephew—ennobles persons of low birth—is deposed by his courtiers.

AFTER the death of Kootb Shah, his uncle Dawood, at the instance of Imad-ool-Moolk and the rest of the nobility, was elevated to the throne ; but shortly after his accession, he ennobled one of the common sweepers of the household, and conferred on him the title of Imad-ool-Moolk. This and other acts of imbecility induced the same nobles who raised him to power to depose him on the seventh day, and to place his nephew Mahmood, a youth of only fourteen years of age, on the throne of his elder brother.

MAHMOOD SHAH I.

ENTITLED BEGURRA.

A conspiracy threatens to subvert the throne, but is suppressed by the great vigour displayed by the King—he makes two campaigns to the Deccan to assist Nizam Shah Bahmuny against the King of Malwa—marches into the province of Sorut—reduces Girnal—makes an inroad through Kutch as far as the Indus—builds Moostufabad in Sorut—reduces Champanere—builds the town of Mahomedabad—constructs the city wall of Ahmudabad—proceeds to Dowlutabad in the Deccan.—Arrival of the Turkish fleet from the Red Sea at Diù—it is joined by the Guzerat fleet, and they proceed to attack the Portuguese.—Battle of Choul, in which both parties suffer severely, and each claims the victory.—Death of Mahmood Shah Begurra.

SHORTLY after the accession of Mahmood Shah, the affairs of the state, which had been so much neglected during the reign of Kootb Shah, began to assume a form of regularity. Five or six months after, however, four nobles, who held small governments at a distance from the capital, jealous of the increasing influence of the minister, Imad-ool-Moolk, formed a conspiracy against him, and insisted on his removal; the even went so for as to threaten, if he were not instantly disgraced, to dethrone the present king, and to place his younger brother Hoossein on the musnud. The names of these officers were,—

Boorhan-ool-Moolk,
Azd-ool-Moolk,
Hissam-ool-Moolk,
Suffy-ool-Moolk.

In the history of Nizam-ood-Deen Ahmud it is related that these officers represented to Mahmood Shah that Imad-ool-Moolk projected to dethrone him, and intended to place the crown on the head of his own son, Shahab-ood-Deen. Notwithstanding the nature of this accusation, so likely to poison the mind of this young prince, he had sufficient discretion to see the matter in its true light, and at the same time too much prudence openly to avow his sentiments. He, therefore, dissembled his feelings, and determined to avail himself of the first favourable opportunity to expose the accusers. In the first place, he caused Imad-ool-Molk to be confined in chains, thanked the informers for their loyalty and attachment, and assured them, that he would punish the traitor by putting him to death with his own hands.

This conduct, while it elated the four conspirators with hopes of placing the Prince Hoossein on the throne, lulled them into security from any apprehension of a discovery of their plot.

On the following day the King having taken his measures, ordered the accused minister to be conveyed into the palace-yard, opposite the hall of audience. Upon his arrival, he desired him to be brought into his presence, in order that he might put some questions to him before his death, when he suddenly caused his fetters to be removed.

Some of the conspirators observing this, and concluding they were discovered, threw themselves from the palace, on the pavement below, while others falling on their faces prostrated themselves at the King's feet, and begged his mercy. In order that the triumph of the minister over his enemies might be complete, the King allowed him to stand on the right hand of the throne, where he received the congratulations of the court.

Hajy Mahomed Kandahary relates, that when the four conspirators heard of the enlargement of Imad-ool-Moolk they proceeded with a body of thirty thousand men towards the palace, where the King remained with three hundred attendants only. On this occasion, some resolved to shut the palace-gates, and defend themselves behind the walls; while others proposed to collect the crown jewels, and make their escape. Mahmood Shah, however, in spite of the inequality of numbers, and though merely a boy, slung his quiver at his back, and with a bow in his hand sallied forth, attended only by three hundred horsemen, and accompanied by all the royal elephants, which did not amount to two hundred. On quitting the palace, he caused the approaches leading to it to be occupied by elephants, proceeding himself through the main street in slow procession, with the royal music playing before him. By this coolness and intrepidity, several of his nobles were enabled to join him: and in a short time they formed a very considerable force, though infinitely inferior to that of the insurgents.

The rebel troops having no room to oppose a

large front dispersed among the streets, and plundered the inhabitants; while the conspirators themselves, being in a very short time deserted, fled, and were pursued. Boorhan-ool-Moolk, being of an unwieldy bulk, threw himself for temporary safety into a ditch which runs into the Saburmutty, in the village of Surkech, where he was taken, and, by the King's orders, trod to death by elephants. Azd-ool-Moolk fled among the Girasias, who, recognising him to be the same person that had on a former occasion plundered them, put him to death. Hissam-ool-Moolk took refuge with his brother Rookn-ood-Deen, the chief magistrate of Puttun, from whence both fled to Malwa; and Suffy-ool-Moolk was taken prisoner; but, as he was not considered so guilty as his confederates, the King spared his life, causing him to be confined in the fort of Diù, where he died. Order being restored, Imad-ool-Moolk requested permission to resign the seals of office, and spend the rest of his days in retirement and devotion; and the King (to convince the world of his attachment to his old minister) appointed his son, Shahab-ood-Deen, to his situation, with the title of Mullik Ashruf.

A. H. 866.
A. D. 1462.
In the year 866, Ahmud Nizam Shah Bahmuny of the Deccan, attacked on all sides by his enemies, particularly by Sooltan Mahmood of Malwa, who had marched towards his capital, solicited the aid of Mahmood Shah. The King no sooner received this communication than he determined immediately to march to his assistance; but his officers and nobles recommended that he should send an army, and

himself remain at home, in order to provide against any contingences which might occur during his absence. With an ardent disposition, and ambitious of glory, he could not be averted from his resolution ; and he assumed command of the army in person, consisting of a large body of cavalry and infantry, besides five hundred elephants. With this force he marched to Nundoorbar, where he was joined by Khwaja Jehan of Gavulgur, and proceeded to make a diversion by attacking the territory of the King of Malwa. This circumstance compelled Sooltan Mahmood Khiljy to retreat from Ahmudabad Bidur, to which place he had penetrated, in order to return and protect his own country ; but the passes on his direct route being occupied, he was reduced to the alternative of marching by Elichpoor, from whence, penetrating through the Gondwana woods, he arrived in Malwa.* Such was the end of this campaign.

In the following year, Sooltan Mahmood Khiljy renewed his attack on the Deccan ; and the King of Guzerat, at the entreaties of Ahmud Nizam Shah Bahmuny, marched to his relief, but did not arrive in sufficient time to prevent Sooltan Mahmood laying waste all the fertile country in the vicinity of Dowlutabad, and carrying off many prisoners. The King of the Deccan on this occasion paid a large sum for the assistance of the Guzerat troops to Mahmood Shah, who, on returning to Ahmudabad, addressed a letter of remonstrance to Sooltan Mah-

* The Moontukhib-oot-Towareekh states, that Sooltan Mahmood of Malwa lost one thousand men, who perished by thirst in this retreat.

mood Khiljy to this effect :—" It is surely far from " the principles of the faith for you to wage war " with true believers. On the other hand, it is as " discreditable to refuse to meet your enemy in the " field. Desist, therefore, from these invasions, or "you may rely on it that the moment you commence " your march again towards the Deccan, we will " make a predatory incursion into Malwa." This letter was answered by a promise of refraining in future from any other invasion of the Deccan.

A. H. 869. A. D. 1465.

Two years afterwards (869), Mahmood Shah marched with a large army towards Bavur, an extraordinary hill-fort, considered impregnable by the inhabitants. From thence he proceeded to Doora* and Purnalla, places situated between Concan † and Guzerat, and defeated the infidels in several actions; and the Raja was obliged to give up his forts, and to throw himself on the mercy of the Mahomedan conqueror, who, after having obtained from him a large sum of money, restored his country into his hands.

As an instance of the impartial justice of Mahmood Shah it is related, that in the year 870,

A. H. 870. A. D. 1466.

while on a hunting party near Ahmudnuggur, Baha-ool-Moolk, the son of Aluf Khan, one of his principal nobles, in a fit of passion put to death a trooper,

* Probably Durampoor.

† The country lying below the western range of mountains of the peninsula of India north of Goa is denominated Concan, and is divided into northern and southern Concan by the Panwell river, which disembogues into the harbour of Bombay.

and for fear of being taken fled to Idur. The King immediately sent Mullik Hajy and Imad-ool-Moolk, two of the secretaries of the government, to seize him; but they, in order to screen the real murderer, on account of his rank, gave a sum of money to two of Baha-ool-Moolk's servants, to acknowledge that they perpetrated the deed; and the secretaries promised to save their lives, by using their influence with the King. These unfortunate men, allured by the largeness of the bribe, and relying on the fair promises of the two officers, avowed the commission of the crime, and being delivered over to the court of justice, were tried, condemned, and executed. Sometime after, when the King discovered the real state of the case, he caused the heads of the secretaries to be struck off, notwithstanding they were men of noble family, and in high favour at the time. After their execution their skins were stuffed with straw, and hung over the gates of the town, as public examples, to the rest of the nobles of the court.

A. H. 872. A.D. 1468.

The author of the history of Mahmood Shah relates, that in the year 872 the King saw the holy Prophet (Mahomed) in a dream, who presented before him a magnificent banquet of the most delicate viands. This dream was interpreted by the wise men as a sign that he would soon accomplish a conquest by which he would obtain great treasures; which prediction was soon after verified in the capture of Girnal.

A. H. 873. A. D. 1469.

In the year 873, Mahmood Shah marched towards the country of Girnal, the capital of which bears the same name. This place is situated on a mountain, on which is constructed the strongest fortress in that part of India. Its reduction had been frequently in the contemplation of the kings both of Dehly and Guzerat, but they had not yet been able to effect it, and many of the ancient rajas of India had in vain attempted to seize that formidable fortification. The accomplishment of this object was reserved for Mahmood Shah Begurra. The mountain on which the fortress stands is surrounded by lower hills situated at some distance, and ravines and broken ground surround its approaches on all sides, which lead through narrow defiles. One of these, the Dumodry G'hat has a strong outwork at the entrance, called at the present day Joonagur. There are, besides, two other works, called Mohabilla. Nearly nineteen hundred years had elapsed since this fortress first came into possession of the family of Mandulik* Raja, who

* This is the first time that Ferishta speaks of a Mandulik raja. The title implies Petty Chieftain, and it is generally supposed they were originally Hindoo military chiefs, frequently near relatives of the superior king, entitled Sarwabhoom, "Lords of the whole Country." As the power of the Sarwabhooms declined, or passed into other hands, the Mandulik rajas became independent. They have the same description of authority as dessayes, natgowrs, reddywars, zemindars, and poligars, so called in different parts of India; under which appellations they have, at various times, become known to the British government. Viewed abstractedly, they are the officers of some greater state; but circumstances frequently render them entitled to be treated as independent princes. The Moontukhib-oot-Towareekh gives this petty prince the name of Humbur Ray.

held it when Mahmood Shah marched to attack it; and excepting Mahomed Toghluk and Ahmud Shah of Guzerat, no foreign prince had penetrated into that country.

Mahmood Shah, relying on the interpretation of his dream, marched towards Girnal with perfect confidence of reducing it to his subjection. On his arrival within eighty miles, he detached a force of one thousand seven hundred men, under his uncle Toghluk Khan, in advance; and presenting every man of the party with a dirk in a scabbard mounted with gold, ordered that the works called Mohabilla should be occupied at all hazards before his arrival. As the approach of this force was unexpected, the Rajpoots, who bear the name of Row, and who were intrusted with the charge of the post, were attacked by surprise, and cut off.

Mahmood Shah with the main body following soon after, passed the defile without opposition. The Ray of Girnal, hearing of the occupation of the Mohabilla post, descended from the hill-fort, and attacked Toghluk Khan, and might have repulsed him, but for the arrival of the King with the main body, when the Ray sustained a total defeat, being himself severely wounded. The victorious army, without attacking the fort of Girnal, destroyed all the temples in the vicinity; and the King sending out foraging parties procured abundance of provisions for the camp. The Ray, rather than sustain a siege, purchased a cessation of hostilities by present submission, and by the payment of a large amount in jewels and in specie; after which, the army returned to Ahmudabad.

A. H. 874.
A. D. 1470

In the year 874, the King, who only wanted some excuse to invade Girnal a second time, urged, as a cause of complaint against the Raja, his habit of assuming the ensigns of royalty. He, therefore, ordered an army of forty thousand horse to march to Girnal, and to exact a fine from him on this account. The Ray, who was neither able nor willing to oppose the Mahomedan arms, paid the sum required; and Nizam-ood-Deen Ahmud states in his history, that Mahmood Shah distributed the money produced by this expedition, in one night, amongst a set of female dancers.

About this period a curious incident occurred, and the anecdote will serve to illustrate the character of Mahmood. He was engaged on a hunting excursion, when a *must* elephant, running towards him, attacked that on which the King was seated. All the rest of the party instantly took to flight, and the King was left alone. The circumstance by no means disconcerted him; but with a presence of mind which never deserted him, he received the animal with undaunted bravery, and with a spear assisted his own elephant and driver in such a manner, that the infuriated beast became so severely wounded as to give up the contest and fly.

In the latter end of the year 874, the King again marched by way of Sorut to Girnal. The Ray declared his willingness to pay any sum of money he could produce, to protect his subjects from the oppression and horrors of war. Mahmood insisted on his abdicating the throne and government in his favour. The Ray made no answer, but shut himself up in the fort of Joonagur, to which the King laid siege. Shortly after, having evacuated Joonagur, in the beginning of the year 875, the Raja again retired to Girnal; but seeing no end to his misfortunes, he at length consented to become a proselyte to the Mahomedan faith, when he was dignified with the title of Khan Jehan; and his descendants have ever since occupied one of the most respectable stations at the Guzerat court. The author of the Mirut-Iskundry relates the circumstance of the conversion of the Ray of Girnal in the following words:—

"The Mandulik Raja," says that author, "being taken prisoner, was sent to Ahmudabad. "One day, perceiving a grand procession going "towards the residence of the holy Shah Alum at "Russoolabad, the Ray enquired who Shah Alum "was, and in whose service. He was told that "this holy person acknowledged no master, but "the Supreme Being. Struck with admiration at "the reply, he resolved to visit him, and was "afterwards persuaded by him to become a "proselyte to the faith."

The King, being desirous that the tenets of Islam should be propagated throughout the country of Girnal, caused a city to be built, which he called Moostufabad, for the purpose of establishing an honourable residence for the venerable personages of the Mahomedan religion deputed to disseminate its principles; Mahmood Shah also took up his residence in that city. Having by this measure withdrawn his court into a corner of the Kingdom, the greater part of his dominions was left to the bad management of his officers, who during his absence neglected their duty, the evil effects of which soon became apparent. The public roads were so infested by robbers, that it was dangerous for single travellers, or small parties, to pass to and fro in Guzerat, sothat the King found it necessary to establish a more active police. Accordingly Jumal Khan, the son of Sheikh Mullik, ennobled with the title of Mohafiz Khan, was appointed to this duty, with orders to reside at Ahmudabad, and he was authorised to increase the police establishment. In a short time, five hundred thieves were publicly executed ; and some idea may be formed of the number of the police retainers when it is known, that Mohafiz Khan had, at one time, in attendance one thousand seven hundred bargeer-i-khass, or persons equipped by him, and riding his own stable horses. His power was, in fact, so little within control, that his son Mullik Khizr, in the absence of the King, marched without orders, and obliged the rays of Idur, Wagur, and Serohy, to pay him tribute.

The King, who was still at Moostufabad superintending the building of the new city, now heard that the inhabitants of Kutch, far removed from Dehly, had long thrown off all allegiance from that government. This people having but little to subsist on, were in the habit of plundering their neighbours, and had lately invaded Guzerat. Mahmood Shah, who only wanted an object to excite him to action, readily seized this opportunity of gratifying his ambition, enriching himself, and of propagating the faith. Accordingly,

A. H. 877. A. D. 1472. in the year 877, he proceeded towards Kutch, and by forced marches came suddenly upon the enemy's encampment at Sheevur with only three hundred cavalry, the rest of his troops having been left behind during a march of sixty coss* without a halt. The Kutchies consisted of four thousand archers, who drew up in good order. Mahmood Shah dismounted to put on his armour, and with his small party charged the enemy, which, notwithstanding the disparity of numbers, was (by the assistance of God) defeated, and numbers of them slain; after which, the remainder came forward with their weapons slung round their necks, to implore mercy. Mahmood Shah, wishing to ascertain if they had any knowledge of the principles of the true faith, questioned them as to their religion. They replied, they were men of the desert, without teachers: they knew there was a sky, earth, and water, and fire; that they had no wants but the necessary articles of food; but begged his Majesty to send teachers among them, in order that they might become true Mahomedans.† The Kutchies are a large, tall, robust race, extremely active, and notoriously good archers. Many of the chiefs of the tribe accompanied the King on his return to Moostufabad, where they imbibed the true principles of the faith; after which, a constant intercourse was kept up between that

* According to ordinary computation, not much less than ninety miles.

† It would appear from the original that the Kutchies were, at this time, Mahomedans. They are no longer so.

city and these people. From them the King learned, that beyond the country of Sheevur, in the province called Sind, were four thousand inhabitants of the Jutt and Buloch tribes, who also excelled in the use of the bow to that degree, that it was said of them that they could split a hair with an arrow. These Bulochies, as well as their neighbours the Bulochies of Persia, are of the Sheea persuasion, and live by depredations, sometimes penetrating as far as the Guzerat provinces.

In the end of the same year, Mahmood Shah marched towards Sind. On arriving at Sheevur, he selected a detachment of one thousand cavalry, each trooper leading a second horse with a week's provender; and by making forced marches accross the desert, he reached the frontier of that country. On the evening of his arrival he halted, in order that his men and horses might be effective on the following day, when he attacked the enemy's camp. This delay, however, enabled some persons who were tending their camels to give intimation of this sudden inroad, so that many of the Bulochies made their escape in consequence, and the King found the tents deserted, except by a few persons who had concealed themselves. These were dragged out on being discovered by the soldiery, and put to death; and their camp was delivered up to plunder; after which the King retreated to Moostufabad, having penetrated on this occasion as far as the Indus.

Mahmood Shah's next effort was against the port of Jugut, with a view of making converts of the infidels, an object from which he had been hitherto deterred by the reports he received of the approaches to it. The cause of making the attempt at this time arose from the capture of Mowlana Mahmood Samarkandy by the people of Jugut. This holy man was one of the most learned philosophers of his age. He had spent the greater part of his life in the service of the Bahmuny kings, and being in the decline of life was returning to his native country. Having embarked in a vessel bound to Ormuz, it was driven into the port of Jugut, where the inhabitants, at the instigation of the bramins, boarded the ship, and having taken the Mowlana and family prisoners, plundered him of all he possessed, permitting him with his two children to go, but detaining his wife.* The holy man brought his complaint to Mahmood Shah at Moostufabad; stating that his wife had been seized and detained by Raja Bheem of Jugut; and he persuaded the King that he was bound in duty to attack these infidels, who had thus dared to lay hands on the faithful. Mahmood Shah, having harangued his army, stated the necessity of making another campaign against the infidels of Jugut, to which, although the troops had been sadly harassed during the last three or four years, by severe marches, they cheerfully consented.

The King, after an arduous march, at length arrived before the fort of Jugut, a place filled

* The pirates of Jugut and Béte have been notorious for many ages, and they are little less infamous, I fear, in the present day than they were several centuries ago. Local circumstances account for their propensity and for their success.

with infidels, misled by the infernal-minded bramins. They were terrified at the appearance of the Mahomedans, and fled in confusion to the island of Béte. The spot on which the King encamped was full of wild beasts, such as lions, leopards, and wolves. Snakes, also, were so numerous, that within the enclosure occupied by the royal tents no fewer than seventy* were killed in one day. The army was employed in destroying the temple at Jugut, and in building a mosque in its stead; while measures, which occupied three or four months in completing, were in progress for equipping a fleet to attack the island of Béte. During this time the enemy attacked the King's flotilla on twenty-two different occasions. At length the Mahomedans reached the island, and landed, and having got into the town, put to death a vast number of Rajpoots Raja Bheem effected his escape in a small boat during the attack, though he was overtaken and made prisoner by some vessels sent in chase; and being put in fetters was carried in the train of the King to Moostufabad, where he was delivered over to the holy man on whose account the war had

* This number of venomous reptiles being killed within an area of two or three acres may appear to the European reader incredible; but it will not surprise those persons who have had occasion to move about much in Asia, and may be thus accounted for: When the royal tents, occupying an area of two or three acres of land, are pitched, and the spot enclosed by screens, the whole superficies is levelled, and rendered smooth to walk on: in doing this, snakes' nests are frequently turned up, and vast numbers of those venomous reptiles are disturbed.

been undertaken, to whom also his wife and property were restored. The Raja was, subsequently, at the instigation of Mowlana Mahmood, dragged around the city of Ahmudabad, and put to death, in order to deter others from similar conduct.

Mahmood Shah, conceiving his dominions too extensive for his own immediate management, divided Guzerat into separate provinces, appointing governors to each, himself residing at Moostufabad.

Béte and Jugut,—Furhut-ool-Moolk,
Songier,—Imad-ool-Moolk,
Godra,—Kowam ool-Moolk,
Tanna,—Nizam-ool-Moolk,
Ahmudabad,—Khoodabunda Khan.

The latter individual was the preceptor of the Prince Moozuffur Khan.

A short time after this arrangement took place, Khoodabunda Khan, in conjunction with Ray Rayan, and some other officers, concerted a plan to dethrone Mahmood, and to place his son, the Prince Moozuffur, on his throne, and proposed taking advantage of the Rumzan fast to carry their project into effect. Among others to whom they communicated their plan was Imad-ool-Moolk, governor of Songier, whom they swore to secresy. The force which he commanded being at that time at the seat of his government, he had not the power, even had he wished it, to oppose the conspirators; he therefore pretended to enter into their project, and in the mean time sent messengers to order his troops to Ahmudabad.

On the last day of the Rumzan,* Imad-ool-Moolk went to the Prince's court, accompanied by his troops, and attended him, as usual, to read prayers at the Eedgah, and he returned without making any attempt to place him on the throne, as was expected. The conspirators, though disappointed, were overawed by the force of Imad-ool-Moolk, and looked on the plot as having failed. In the mean time, Keisur Khan, an officer of the household, mentioned the affair privately to the King, who proceeded forthwith to Gogo, and embarking in a vessel sailed to Cambay. On his arrival there, he was met by most of the confederates, who came to welcome him. On the first court-day, in order to discover how they were disposed towards him, he addressed his courtiers, saying, that as his son Moozuffur had now arrived at years of discretion, and as he understood that some of the nobles looked up to the Prince in preference to him, he had come to the resolution of abdicating the throne in the Prince's favour, and proceeding to Mecca to pay his devotions at the holy shrine. Imad-ool-Moolk of Songier entreated the King, in the first place, to proceed to Ahmudabad. This observation from Imad-ool-Moolk at once convinced him

*The month of Rumzan is kept as a fast throughout all Mahomedan countries. On the last day of which, the whole of the people proceed to a building erected for the purpose, and say their prayers. This spot is called the Eedgah, "the Place of Rejoicing," after the month's mourning and fasting. The edifice consists of a stone platform, on one side of which is built a single wall several feet high, facing Mecca.

that he had nothing to apprehend from that quarter, he therefore marched to Ahmudabad, declaring, that, after his arrival, he would not eat till the nobles consented to his visiting Mecca. The chiefs, having by this time discovered that the King only wanted to try their fidelity, forbore to urge him; and Nizam-ool-Moolk recommended him to proceed and subdue the fort of Champanere, from the plunder of which the expenses of the pilgrimage might be defrayed. The King replied, "God willing, let it be even so." For some days after he avoided conversing with Imad-ool-Moolk, whom he knew to be loyal; but although acquainted with the whole plot, he had yet communicated nothing to the King. An explanation, however, at length took place, when the King disgraced the minister Khoodabunda Khan, and caused the person employed in the meanest office of his household to be called by his name, in order to show that the minister was worthy of no higher station. Mahmood Shah, after remaining for some time at Ahmudabad, proceeded to Puttun, from whence he deputed Imad-ool-Moolk and Keisur Khan to levy tribute on the rajas of Julwara and Aboogur. During the first march, while encamped at the shrine of Sheikh Hajy, Mujahid Khan, the son of the late degraded minister, took the opportunity of revenging himself on Keisur Khan, who had given the first information of his father's defection, and entering his tent at night, put that nobleman to death. The King's suspicions of the murder fell first on Ajdur Khan, who was known to be hostile to Keisur Khan, and he was placed in fetters; but the real murderer and his accomplices having fled from camp the next night, the King caused Khoodabunda Khan to be imprisoned, and Ajdur Khan to be released. The King now returned to Ahmudabad, and then proceeded to Moostufabad, where he remained for some years. In the year 887, he prepared an army to move towards Champanere; but about that period, hearing that the Bulsar pirates had gained such an ascendency at sea as to threaten the invasion of his dominions, and had already intercepted the trade, he collected a fleet, on board of which he embarked a force consisting of gunners, musketeers,* and archers, with which he sailed from Cambay. After some days the fleet fell in with the enemy and gave chase; a running fight was sustained for some hours, during which several of the piratical vessels were captured. The fleet returned to Cambay, and the King repaired to Ahmudabad.

A. H. 887.
A. D. 1482.

During this year, in consequence of an unusual drought, famine prevailed in Guzerat, of which many thousands of the inhabitants perished. On the 1st of Zeekad, the King commenced his preparations for marching against Champanere. This fortress,†

Zeekad 1.
A. H. 887.
Dec. 3.
A. D. 1482.

*This is the first mention of artillery and musketry in the Guzerat history. They were probably introduced by the Arabs and Turks from the Red Sea and Gulf of Persia.

† It is now called Pawrungur, or the Stormy Rock, owing, it is said, to the violent winds which prevail on its summit. The appellation may be modern, but it seems to have superseded that of the Mahomedan historian.

situate on a high hill, was surrounded by strong works of solid masonry, and was in possession of Beny Ray, a chief of the Rajpoot tribe. It is so ancient that no tradition even exists of the time of its foundation. The princes of Champanere had possessed the government from time immemorial; and sixty thousand Rajpoots formed the army of the Raja, who were devoted to his person with an enthusiastic attachment. It is by no means, therefore, to be wondered at, that this fort had not yet been subdued, or that its rulers had never bent their necks to the Mahomedan yoke.*

When the Ray heard of the determination of Mahmood Shah, he began to lay waste the country contiguous to Rusoolabad, and put to death many of the faithful. On the King's arrival at Baroda, repenting of his conduct, the Ray sent ambassadors to solicit forgiveness; but Mahmood Shah, enraged at the devastation committed on Rusoolabad, refused to listen to any accommodation.

A. H. 888.
A. D. 1483.

It was in the beginning of the year 888 before all the preparations were ready, that Taj Khan, Beiram Khan, Etibar Khan, and Azd-ool-Moolk, were sent in advance, and arrived at the foot of the hill on the 7th of Suffur, A. H. 888. After this the enemy repeatedly attacked these troops without much effect, till at length the King having reached the fort, he

Suffur 7. A. H. 888. March 17. A. D. 1483.

* The Raja of Champanere was a Chowhan by descent, of the tribe of Keechy, and nearly allied to the head of the family who then occupied Gagrone as his capital; but on being dispossessed by the race of Hara, he built the fort of Ragoghur-Tod.

encamped at Girnary on the Malwa road. Beny Ray deputed ambassadors, offering to pay two elephant loads of gold if Mahmood Shah would desist from his purpose; but finding neither his entreaties nor offers of any avail, he collected his troops, consisting of sixty thousand men, beside the auxiliaries furnished by the neighbouring rajas. With these troops the Rajpoots made frequent attacks on the besiegers; till at length they compelled them to raise the siege; and the Raja drew up his army to engage the King, who now appeared at the head of his forces. The action which ensued was sanguinary, and obstinately contested on both sides; and the Hindoos, though repulsed, retreated in good order, with a compact body of twelve thousand men. The King having followed the enemy to the foot of the hill-fort, renewed his disposition for the prosecution of the siege, and returned in person to Girnary. Shortly after, a convoy of provisions and stores, under Syud Mudun Lung, was attacked by the Rajpoots, and the whole convoy seized. In consequence of this, the King repaired to the camp, and superintended in person the operations of the siege, both in constructing the trenches and carrying on mines. The flower of the Rajpoot army had been destroyed in the late action; and the Raja, beginning to despair of saving his capital, or of appeasing Mahmood's rage, sent his minister Shew Ray to Mando, promising Sooltan Gheias-ood-Deen Khiljy of Malwa to pay him a lack of tunkas of silver for every march he should make in coming to his assistance. Gheias-ood-Deen assembled his army for this purpose at the town of Nalcha; when Mahmood Shah, leaving orders for the continuation of the siege, marched to attack him. On arriving at D'har, Mahmood Shah heard that Sooltan Gheias-ood-Deen, on being reproached by his nobles and officers for entertaining an intention of marching to the assistance of an infidel, had disbanded his army and returned to Mando. Mahmood Shah, in consequence, countermarched to Champanere, and caused a mosque to be built in the lines, in order to convince his troops that it was his resolution not to desist from the siege of the fort till it was reduced. The mines were now carried on with increased exertion, and the approaches brought within a short distance, so much so that the besiegers discovered that the Rajpoots left the place through a sally-port every morning in order to perform their ablutions. The King, taking advantage of this circumstance, ordered a party on the morning of the 2d of Zeekad, A.H. 889, to be close to the walls at daylight; and as the besieged quitted them, many of the Mahomedans rushed into the place, and penetrated as far as the second gate, while Mullik Eiaz Sooltany,* with a small party, escaladed the western wall, where a breach had been made a few days before by one of the batteries, and got possession of the main gate. The Rajpoots seeing no chance of escape, and finding that the King rejected all overtures for surrender, made a funeral pile within the walls, and having brought their property, their wives, and their children, set fire to it, and con-

Zeekad 2. A. H. 889. Nov. 17. A. D. 1484.

* This is the celebrated admiral who engaged the Portuguese fleet off Choul, and who commanded for many years at Diù.

sumed them to ashes; after which, they resolutely awaited the storm. Meanwhile they made every effort to expel Mullik Eiaz Sooltany from the position he had gained; but a shell* falling on the palace of the Raja, it was deemed unlucky. Mahmood Shah, who was ready in the lines, sent more troops to support Mullik Eiaz, who opened the gates, and admitted the Mahomedans. With this reinforcement the King arrived in person; and having planted the colours on the works, obtained entire possession of the ramparts. The Hindoos, thus situated, collected in a body, and running to some water near the spot, bathed, with their naked swords and spears in their hands, and then rushed on the Mahomedans. The Rajpoots were for the most part killed in this assault, though the victors also suffered severely, both in killed and wounded. The Raja Beny Ray, and his prime minister Dongursy, were both wounded, and fell into the hands of the King's troops.

After this victory, Mahmood Shah caused public prayers to be read, and directed the wounds of the prisoners to be attended to. Having sent for Beny Ray, he asked him what could induce him to hold out so long, before so large a force. The Ray replied, with undaunted firmness, "I "hold this territory by hereditary right, and being "descended from a line of noble ancestors, have "been taught to respect that name which they "handed down to me. I determined, therefore,

* The word is *hooka*. The use of shells at this early period is remarkable, although it is mentioned that the Moslems employed *grenadoes* in their ships at the time the Portuguese reached India.

"not to act in a way so as to disgrace my family." Mahmood, admiring this spirited and manly conduct, ordered every attention to be paid to the Raja's wants and comforts.

During the time the King was detained by his sick and wounded at Champanere, he laid the foundation of the city of Mahmoodabad, and also of a beautiful mosque, in which was a pulpit with this sentence inscribed upon it commemorating the date of its completion :—

خطبه و منبر

"Prayers and the pulpit."

Beny Ray having recovered from his wounds, the King used every effort to persuade both him and his minister to embrace the Mahomedan faith. They, however, persisted in refusing, swearing that they preferred death to abjuring their religion. Mahmood Shah was in hopes of shaking their constancy by confining them separately, and treating them harshly. This conduct only tended to support their resolution, till at length the King, at the instigation of some holy men about his person, ordered them to be put to death.

At this period, he caused the city of Ahmudabad to be surrounded by a wall and bastions; and on its completion had the following sentence, commemorative of the date of that event, inscribed on one face of the fortification :—

مَن دَخلهٗ كَانَ اٰمِنًا

"Whosoever is within is safe."

A. H. 892. A. D. 1486. In the year 892, some merchants travelling from Dehly with horses for Guzerat were plundered in passing the territories of a Hindoo chief.* The King immediately sent a person to demand restitution of the property; and such was the awe Mahmood Shah had inspired, that the merchants were not only well reimbursed, but the messenger was handsomely entertained, and magnificent presents sent back with him to the King.

A. H. 900. A. D. 1494. In the year 900, one Bahadur Geelany, an officer of the Deccan government, having revolted from his master, collected a force consisting of from ten to twelve thousand men, and also a fleet, with which he not only seized on the ports of Goa and Dabul, but went so far as to lay hands on some Guzerat vessels trading along the coast. He afterwards landed, and took possession of the island of Mahim,† giving up the town to plunder. On information of this event, the admiral, Sufdur-ool-Moolk, was sent to Mahim by sea, and Kowam-ool-Moolk marched with a force by land. The fleet experienced a heavy gale off the port, in which most of the vessels were stranded; on which occasion the enemy came down to the beach, and massacred the crews as they were washed ashore. The admiral himself was taken prisoner, and all the fleet fell into the enemy's hands. Kowam-ool-Moolk hearing of this disaster, on his arrival near Mahim, sent a messenger to the King, and halted

* The name and country of this chief is omitted in the original.

† Bombay.

till further orders. Mahmood Shah now deputed an envoy to the King of the Deccan, complaining of the outrage committed by Bahadur Geelany; and that monarch marching against the rebel (notwithstanding a disaffection of the nobles of his court), seized* his person, and caused him to be executed; and Sufdur-ool-Moolk, the Guzerat admiral, was released from prison, and the fleet of the late Bahadur Geelany, which fell into the hands of the King of the Deccan, was delivered over to the admiral's charge. After the necessary equipments, Sufdur-ool-Moolk sailed from Mahim to the northward, taking with him some valuable presents from the King of the Deccan, and also a letter, requesting the interference of Mahmood Shah with the officers of his army, and the nobles of his court, who were in a state of actual revolt. Mahmood Shah, perceiving that matters had gone too far to be enabled to render him any aid, declined engaging in the affairs of his court.

A. H. 901. A. D. 1495. In the year 901, Mahmood Shah marched towards the countries of Wagur and Idur, from the rajas of which places he exacted large offerings, and returned laden with treasure to Mahomedabad Champanere.

A. H. 904. A. D. 1498. Three years afterwards (A. H. 904), having heard that Aluf Khan had raised the standard of revolt, the King ordered Sheikh Burra Deccany, the Kazy-ool-Koozat † of

* Bahadur Geelany was killed in action, fighting against a detachment of the Deccan army in the vicinity of Kolapoor. Vide vol. ii. p. 543.

† Chief judge.

Ahmudabad, to march against him ; upon which the rebel fled to Malwa, where he shortly afterwards died by poison. On the following year (A. H. 905) Adil Khan Farooky,
A. H. 905. A. D. 1499. ruler of Kandeish, following the example of Aluf Khan and the officers of the Deccan, raised the standard of revolt, and refused to pay the usual tribute. Sheikh Burra was also sent against him ; but Adil Khan coming in person to Mahomedabad Champanere, threw himself on the King's mercy, bringing with him the arrears of tribute, as a peace offering. Some historians state that Mahmood Shah marched in person against Adil Khan, and having arrived on the river Tapty, received his submission there.*

About this period Mullik Ashruf,† the governor of Dowlutabad, wrote to Mahmood Shah, stating that he had possession of that strong fortress, and was besieged by the Deccan army under Ahmud Nizam Shah Bheiry ; offering, at the same time, if the Guzerat monarch would march to his assistance, to give him possession, and hold it as his tributary. Mahmood Shah, in consequence, marched to the south, and Ahmud Nizam Shah raised the siege, and retreated to Ambur. The King of Guzerat did not halt till he reached Dowlutabad ; where having received handsome presents

* It is difficult to fancy a more wanton exertion of power than that of the Mahomedan King of Guzerat demanding tribute from the independent Mahomedan principality of Kandeish, whose rulers derived their titles and authority from the very same sovereign as did the kings of Guzerat.

† The history of Mullik Ashruf is fully detailed in that of the Nizam Shahy kings of Ahmudnuggur. Vide vol. iii p. 204.

from Mullik Ashruf, he returned to Mahomedabad Champanere.

A. H. 906.
A. D. 1500.

In the year 906, the King having discovered a conspiracy among some of the nobles of Ahmudabad, for the purpose of dethroning him, went thither, and by strong measures dictated by policy as well as by necessity, removed some from their offices, and caused others to be executed.

A. H. 913.
A. D. 1507.

In the year 913, the infidel Europeans,* who had of late years usurped the dominion of the ocean, endeavoured to occupy for themselves some port on the Guzerat coast, on which they wished to settle; and the Grand Seignior of Constantinople, desirous of opposing this measure, deputed Ameer Hoossein† with a fleet from the Red Sea to engage them in this quarter. Ameer Hoossein arrived off the Guzerat coast in this year; and Mahmood Shah, also, anxious to aid in the expulsion of these strangers, sailed with a fleet first to Daman, and then to Mahim. On his arrival at the former port, he ordered Mullik Eiaz Sooltany, the Ameer-ool-Omra, with a large fleet, to sail from Diù to attack the enemy in concert with the Turkish fleet, whose ships were of a larger description than those of Guzerat.‡

* This is the first mention made of the Protuguese in the Guzerat history.

† This is the same person the Portuguese call Meer Hashim.

‡ The Portuguese historian states, that the Turks in Arabia, having no means of constructing ships there, procured timber to be sent form the mountains of Dalmatia to Alexandria, whence it was conveyed to Cairo, and over the desert of Suez

The combined fleets fell in with the Portuguese off the port of Choul, where an engagement took place, in which the flag-ship of the enemy (valued at a crore of rupees*) was sunk, and every man on board perished. Mullik Eiaz, having thus defeated the Portuguese fleet, returned victoriously; for "although four hundred Turks were honoured with "the crown of martyrdom, no fewer than three "thousand or four thousand Portuguese infidels "were, at the same time, sent to the infernal re- "gions." After this event, the King having placed the Guzerat ports in security from the enemy's attacks, returned to Mahomedabad Champanere. Shortly after, news arrived that Dawood Khan Farooky, ruler of Kandeish, was dead, and that a revolution had taken place in that country. Adil Khan Farooky (the grandson of Mahmood Shah) deputed a person to the King, asserting his right to the government, and claiming assistance from him on the score of relationship. In the year 913, therefore, Mahmood Shah
A. H. 913. marched with a small force towards
A. D. 1507. Aseer. On the road thither he halted

---

on camels. The fleet consisted of twelve sail, and carried one thousand five hundred men, under the command of Ameer Hoossein, who, with Mullik Eiaz, the admiral of Guzerat, united and attacked the Portuguese in Choul harbour; on which occasion the latter took two of the Turkish vessels, and lost one of their own, which was blown up. Faria-e-Souza, tome i. part ii. chap. ii.

* A million pounds sterling. This affords some notion of the estimation in which they held the European vessels.

† Faria-e-Souza states the Portuguese to have lost eighty-one men, and estimates the enemy's loss at six hundred.

to celebrate the Rumzan at the town of Chikly, on the banks of the Nerbudda; where he learned that Alum Khan Farooky, being invited by one Hissam-ood-Deen of Kandeish, and supported by Ahmud Nizam Shah Bheiry, and Imad-ool-Moolk ruler of Berar, had assumed the reins of government in Aseer. On Mahmood Shah reaching Talnere, he was met by Adil Khan, and thence he sent a Guzerat detachment in advance to Boorhanpoor. In consequence of which, the united forces of Berar and Ahmudnuggur retreated, and Adil Khan was placed at the head of the government. Larun Khan Khiljy, one of the pretenders to Kandeish, was gratified by receiving the title of Khan Jehan; and he obtained the district of Ahwas in jageer. Mahmood Shah, on this occasion, conferred titles also on many other of the Aseer officers attached to Adil Khan, and left a body of Guzerat troops to support his authority. In order to deter Hissam-ood-Deen from making any future attempt on the government, he conferred on him the town of Dhoor, in the district of Sooltanpoor. Notwithstanding these arrangements, internal commotions occurred at Aseer during the following year, which were amicably adjusted through the agency of Mahmood Shah, who sent his own son to carry into effect his orders, and to confirm the authority of Adil Khan.

It is worthy of remark, that an embassy, accompanied by valuable presents, was sent on the following year from Sikundur Lody of

A. H. 915. Dehly to Mahmood Shah of Guzerat,
A. D. 1509. thereby acknowledging, for the first

time, the independence of that kingdom.* In the latter end of the same year, Mahmood Shah made a tour of his kingdom; proceeding, first, to Nehrwala Puttun, where he solicited the prayers of the holy men dwelling in that place; and subsequently to Ahmudabad, when he paid his devotion at the shrine of Sheikh Ahmud Geesoo-Duraz, and returned thence to Mahomedabad Champanere; where falling dangerously ill, he sent for his son the Prince Moozuffur, the heir apparent, from Baroda. Shortly afterwards, recovering sufficiently to transact business, he permitted him to return to his government; but in a few weeks after, having a relapse of his complaint, he again sent for the Prince. At this period, Yadgar Beg Kuzilbash† arrived as ambassador from Shah Ismael, King of Persia; but

Rumzan 2. A. H. 917. Nov. 23. A. D. 1511.

before he could obtain an audience, Mahmood Shah died, on the 2d of Rumzan, A. H. 917, in the seventieth year of his age, and the fifty-fifth of his reign.‡

He was surnamed Bègra, or Bè Gurra. Historians differ with regard to the origin of this appellation: some assert it was given to him because bègra signifies curled, as the horns of a cow, allud ing to the shape which his mustachios assumed.

* The Guzerat historian, who prides himself much on this event, seems to forget that the empire of Dehly had also changed its master, and that the power of the Toghluks had passed into the hands of the Afghans since the establishment of the kings of Guzerat.

† Kuzilbash, or Red-head, is an appellation given to the Toorks settled in Persia, owing to their wearing red caps. Vide p. 80.

‡ He is buried at Surkech, near Ahmudabad, in the shrine of Sheikh Ahmud Kutloo.

Shah Jumal-ood-Deen Hoossein, however, in his history, gives his opinion in these words:—"The word bè, in the Guzeratty language, signi-"fies two, and gurra a hill-fort, from whence the "name Bè Gurra, derived from Mahmood Shah "having reduced two hill-forts on the opposite "sides of his dominions, before deemed impreg-"nable; viz. Girnal on the west, and Champanere "on the east." This derivation appears to me sufficiently rational and probable.

MOOZUFFUR SHAH II.

He ascends the throne without opposition—engages to assist the King of Malwa, who is expelled from his throne by the Hindoos—besieges Mando, and takes it by storm, on which occasion fifteen thousand Rajpoots lose their lives—replaces the King of Malwa on his throne.—The King of Malwa defeated by Rana Sanka of Chittoor—receives aid from Moozuffur Shah, whose army besieges Chittoor.—Peace concluded with the Rana.—Bahadur, the King's second son, quits his father's court in disgust, and proceeds to Dehly.—Death of Moozuffur Shah II.

MAHMOOD SHAH was succeeded by his son Moozuffur, who was born on Thursday, the 20th of Shuval, A. H. 875, (10th April, 1470,) and ascended the throne in the forty-first year of his age; immediately after which he nominated Mullik Khoosh Kuddum, entitled Imad-ool-Moolk, and Mullik Rusheed, entitled Khodawund Khan, his two ministers. On the following month, Yadgar Beg, the Persian ambassador, reached the capital, and all the principal officers and heads of departments were deputed to meet him at some distance from the city, in order to welcome him in the King's name, and to escort him to a handsome palace fitted up for his reception. At his first audience, the ambassador delivered his credentials and some of the rarities of Persia, when he and the rest of his suite were honoured with robes.

Sometime afterwards the King went to Baroda, the name of which town he caused to be changed to Dowlutabad.* Upon his arrival there, he found Sahib Khan † (a prince of the blood-royal of Malwa), who had fled from the persecution of his brother. Moozuffur Shah received him with attention, and treated him with the consideration due to his rank. The King then proceeding to Mahomedabad Champanere, directed Keisur Khan to go to Dohud, in order to ascertain the state of affairs in Malwa. This measure was adopted previously to sending any troops in aid of the fugitive prince, Shaib Khan, whose impatience he restrained by telling him that at present the rains had set in, and it would be imprudent to commence a campaign ; but that when the season was more favourable he would, God willing, restore to him his just rights.

During his residence at court, Sahib Khan unfortunately contracted a close intimacy with the Persian ambassador, who, together with his suite, had become extremely obnoxious to all classes, and were called by the inhabitants Soorkh Koolla, in allusion to the name of their tribe, Kuzilbash signifying in the Toorky language Red-head. The result of this intimacy, on the part of Sahib Khan, at length ended in a scuffle between the Kuzilbashes and his people in the ambassador's palace. Swords were drawn on both sides ; and the Indians being routed, the Kuzilbashes pursued them into the street

* It is no longer known by the latter appellation.

† The adventures of Sahib Khan will be found in the Malwa history.

armed with bows and arrows, and wounded several persons wholly unconnected with the affray. A rumour immediately spread through the town that the Toorkmans (that is to say, the Kuzilbashes,) had seized the person of Sahib Khan, and it was some time before peace was restored. The Malwa prince, who felt himself to blame, was so ashamed of his conduct, that he quitted the court without taking leave, went to Aseer and Boorhanpoor, and ultimately to Berar, where he solicited the assistance of Imad-ool-Moolk. A more full account of Sahib Khan's adventures will be found in the Malwa history.

The departure of Sahib Khan was followed by intelligence that the Poorby Rajpoots had completely defeated Sooltan Mahmood Khiljy of Malwa, an event which induced the King to go to Godra in order to make arrangements for a campaign in Malwa. Ein-ool-Moolk, governor of Puttun, was directed to bring his division to Ahmudabad, when Bheem Ray of Idur, taking advantage of his absence, plundered and laid waste the surrounding country as far as the Saburmutty. In consequence of this proceeding, Ein-ool-Moolk was ordered to proceed to Mahrasa, where he was attacked and defeated by the Idur Raja; and Abdool Mullik, an officer of distinction, with two hundred men, were left dead on the field.

The King, hearing of this disaster, instantly marched towards Idur. On reaching Mahrasa he caused the whole of the Idur district to be laid waste. Bheem Ray took refuge in the Beesulnuggur mountains; but the garrison of Idur, consisting of only ten Rajpoots, defended it against the whole of the King's army with obstinacy; they were, however, eventually put to death on the capture of the place; and the temples, palaces, and garden houses, were levelled with the dust. Meanwhile the Ray deputed one Mudun Gopal, a bramin, as envoy to the King; stating that Ein-ool-Moolk had wantonly devastated his country, and that the action which had been fought occurred in consequence of his outrages. Bheem Ray expressed his regret at the circumstance, and sent one hundred horses and two hundred thousand tunkas, as an offering, which, in consideration of the projected campaign in Malwa, the King accepted, and overlooking the conduct of Ray Bheem, gave the money to Ein-ool-Moolk to raise troops, with orders to join the army. On the King's return to Godra, having left his son Sikundur Khan in charge of Mahomedabad Champanere, he marched to Dohud, from whence he directed Keisur Khan to occupy the town of Dydla; but having heard there was good hunting ground in the vicinity of D'har, he left the army under Kowam-ool-Moolk, and proceeded, with an escort of two thousand cavalry and one hundred and fifty elephants, to that place, where he was for some time engaged in the amusement of the chase. At this period, Nizam-ool-Moolk, who had been sent with a foraging party to Nalcha, was attacked by a body of Poorby Rajpoots of Malwa, but succeeded in repulsing them without loss. Intelligence was now received, which compelled the King to return to Guzerat; and this partial skirmish led to no other event. The information alluded to was that of the death of Bheem Ray of Idur, who had been succeeded by his son Bharmul; but the latter was shortly afterwards deposed by Rana Sanka* of Chittoor, who placed his son-in-law Raymul, the son of Soorijmul, at the head of the government. In the year 921, Bharmul deputed persons to wait on Moozuffur Shah, soliciting his aid; and the King ordered Nizam-ool-Moolk, with a detachment, to restore to him the country of Idur. Having succeeded in this object, Nizam-ool-Moolk took upon himself to pursue Raymul the usurper into the Beesulnuggur territory, where an action ensued, in which the Mahomedan general was defeated, and many of his best officers and soldiers slain. The King, who had by this time returned to Ahmudabad, reproved Nizam-ool-Moolk severely for acting beyond his instructions, and recalled him; but on his arrival in the King's camp he was appointed governor of Ahmudnuggur.

A. H. 921.
A. D. 1515.

In the year 923, Raymul again appeared in the Idur district, and Zeheer ool-Moolk marched against him, but was killed at the head of the cavalry; on which occasion two hundred and seven men fell, and the Guzeratties were defeated. Mullik Noosrut-ool-Moolk was now directed to march to Beesulnuggur, and to plunder and lay waste

A. H. 923.
A. D. 1517.

*Sanga, and not Sanka, is the true pronunciation; but as the same person is mentioned (vol. ii.) in the histories of Babur and Hoomayoon, and the name is there spelled Sanka, it has not been altered in this place.

the whole of that country, which the King, in his orders, calls " the receptacle of renegadoes, " and the asylum of rebels."

In the same year, Sheikh Humeed of Bhilsa, and Hubeeb Khan the Kazy of Choly Meheswur,* fled from the persecution of the Rajpoots, and arrived at the Guzerat court. They had also succeeded in expelling the King of Malwa from his capital, and had obliged him to seek safety in Dohud,† where he was received by the governor, who made a representation to court, reporting the circumstance. Moozuffur Shah immediately sent to the King of Malwa the white canopy and scarlet pavilion, and a respectable body of troops, with which he marched against the Rajpoots. Moozuffur Shah soon followed with his own army, and defeated the Hindoos in several actions, but not without considerable bloodshed on both sides. The Rajpoot chief, Bhew Ray, was at length compelled to take refuge in the fort of Mando, wherein he was closely besieged.

At this period Medny Ray, the late minister of the King of Malwa, wrote a letter to his son Bhew Ray, desiring him to hold out in the fort for one month only, by which time Rana Sanka of Chittoor would be able to collect the Marwar Rajpoots, and march to his assistance. Upon this Bhew Ray made overtures to the King; and stipulated, that if he would raise the siege for one month (during which period all the Rajpoot women

* Properly Maha-Iswur.

† This town is considered the boundary between Malwa and Guzerat.

and children would be enabled to quit the fort), the place should be evacuated, when he would submit himself to the King's mercy. Although Moozuffur Shah placed little reliance on the promises of this perfidious infidel, he withdrew his army six miles from the place, where he remained twenty days; a measure he adopted out of consideration for the royal family of Malwa, who were still in the fort, hoping to save them, by obtaining the place by capitulation. On observing, however, that elephants were frequently passing towards the fort, the King became suspicious of treachery, more particularly as he heard that Rana Sanka of Chittoor had arrived, with a large force, within a few miles of Oojein. In this state of affairs, Moozuffur Shah directed Adil Khan, the ruler of Kandeish (who had lately joined the army), accompanied by Kowam-ool-Moolk and a Guzerat force, to march against the Rana of Chittoor, while the King himself again proceeded to invest Mando. From that day the Mahomedans made false attacks four nights successively, as if they intended to escalade; a manœuvre which succeeded in wearing out the garrison with fatigue, and on the fifth night, ladders being applied, Mando fell, but not without much slaughter; for the Rajpoots, finding that their enemies had succeeded in gaining a footing on the ramparts, according to custom, set fire to their property, their women, and children, and collecting in bodies, charged the assailants with fury. On this occasion, no fewer than nineteen thousand Rajpoots lost their lives.

After the fall of Mando, Sooltan Mahmood asked what was to be his fate; on which the King of Guzerat, with a magnanimity and generousity which along belongs to the brave, said, "It is true "I have fought hard, but I have fought for you; "and I am happy to be now enabled not only "to confirm to you the white canopy and scarlet "pavilion, but to restore you to the capital of your "kingdom, which I trust God will long preserve "to you."

On the following day, Moozuffur Shah marched against Rana Sanka, who received the information of the fall of Mando from one of the Rajpoot officers who had been wounded in the assault, and had made his escape. This man was so agitated in describing the scene he had witnessed, that his wounds burst during the relation, and he bled to death in open durbar. On hearing of the approach of Moozuffur Shah, Rana Sanka retreated to Chittoor; and Adil Khan Farooky, with a small body of light cavalry, went in pursuit. He succeeded in daily cutting off some of the Rajpoot stragglers, but did not overtake the Rana before he received orders of recall from Moozuffur Shah.

At this time, Sooltan Mahmood of Malwa invited the King to a grand entertainment at Mando, whither he repaired, attended by the Princes Bahadur Khan and Luteef Khan, as also by Adil Khan Farooky. When the King of Guzerat arrived, his host treated him in every respect as his superior, seating him upon the throne of Malwa, and standing himself at the foot of it. So far was this humility carried, that the King of Malwa waited on Moozuffur Shah at the entertainment, in the capacity of a menial servant. Magnificent presents were then offered to him and to his sons; after which, Moozuffur Shah, having left Mando, was accompanied by Sooltan Mahmood Khiljy as far as D'har, when the King wished Sooltan Mahmood to return, and ordered Asuf Khan, with two thousand cavalry, to remain with him in Malwa as an auxiliary force. Sooltan Mahmood however, persisted in accompanying Moozuffur Shah as far as Dydla, whence he repaired to Mando, and Moozuffur Shah proceeded to Champanere.

Scarcely had the King of Guzerat reached his capital, when he received intelligence that Raymul, having sallied from the Beesulnuggur hills, had devastated the country of Puttun, and sacked the town of Gilwara. but that he had been compelled to fall back again by Mullik Noosrut-ool-Moolk, who commanded at Idur. This information determined the King to make arrangements for seizing the person of Raymul after the rains; and in the year 925 he marched towards Beesulnuggur, and laid waste the country, but returned to Mahomedabad Champanere without having gained any other object.

A. H. 925.
A. D. 1519.

Shortly after his arrival, news were brought that Sooltan Mahmood Khiljy, accompanied by the Guzerat auxiliaries under Asuf Khan, having attacked the combined forces of Medny Ray and Rana Sanka, had sustained a defeat, and that many valuable officers of the Malwa forces had been killed. Among the Guzeratties, the son of Asuf Khan lost his life, Sooltan Mahmood himself was severely wounded, and fell into the enemy's hands, and Rana Sanka proceeded to Mando. Moozuffur Shah lost no time in sending reinforcements to the remainder of the Malwa army. At this time, Noosrut-ool-Moolk was removed from the government of Idur, and Moobariz-ool-Moolk nominated to that office. Shortly after his arrival at Idur, some person ventured to extol the bravery of Rana Sanka,* on which the governor was much incensed, and an altercation ensued. Moobariz-ool-Moolk, to show the contempt he had for the Rana, caused a common cur † to be tied up at the fort-gate, directing it to be called Rana Sanka. The Rana, hearing of this insult, was so incensed, that he immediately marched towards Idur, and pillaged the country as far as Serohy.

The King, having left Kowam-ool-Moolk at Ahmudabad to act against the Girasia chiefs in that vicinity, marched to Champanere on his way to Malwa. Rana Sanka arrived at Bagry, where he was joined by the raja of that province, who

* It will be recollected he had just defeated the King of Malwa and the Guzerat auxiliary troops, a subject on which the Guzerat officers would naturally be very sore.

† This mode of evincing contempt is not confined to the Mahomedans. Many persons must recollect the time when it was the custom to call black dogs in England by the name of Tippoo. The practice in the East, however, is particularly offensive. An officer in a high diplomatic situation with Lord Lake's army in the field, in 1805, discovered, by accident, that he had given great offence to his Mahomedan friends by calling a young lioness Fatima, the name of the daughter of their prophet, which he instantly changed; a compliment that, no doubt, smoothed his future diplomatic communications.

owed allegiance to the crown of Guzerat. Both the Hindoo princes proceeded to Dongurpoor, when Moobariz-ool-Moolk thought it necessary to write to court for reinforcements. Some individuals about the King inimical to Moobariz-ool-Moolk represented that he had wantonly drawn upon himself the vengeance of Rana Sanka, and that he was now so alarmed as to apply for aid even before he was attacked. The King in consequence suspended the march of any troops to assist him till after the rains; and Moobariz-ool-Moolk, having called a council of war, evacuated Idur, and retreated to Ahmudnuggur. On the next day Rana Sanka arrived, and was joined by several Girasia chiefs who had fled from Kowam-ool-Moolk. These assured him that Moobariz-ool-Moolk was not a person likely to fly without opposition; but that his own opinion had been overruled by his officers, who recommended him to fall back on Ahmudnuggur, where he expected to obtain reinforcements; on which the Rana marched towards that place. Moobariz-ool-Moolk, hearing that he was in pursuit, and had sworn he would not take rest till his horse drank out of the ditch of Ahmudnuggur, resolved to make a desperate stand, and, undaunted by the superiority of the enemy's numbers, drew his small party out in front of the walls of the town, on the opposite bank of the river. The Rana's army, which exceeded that of the Mahomedans as ten to one, not only received the Guzeratties with great steadiness, but charged in the most gallant manner. Assud Khan and many other officers of distinction were killed; and Sufdur Khan and Moobariz-ool-Moolk being severely wounded, the King's army was compelled to retreat to Ahmudabad, leaving Rana Sanka to plunder the surrounding country. At Burnuggur, the Rana finding the inhabitants to be chiefly bramins, exempted them from pecuniary exactions. The Rana then proceeded to Beesulnuggur, where he was gallantly opposed by the governor, Mullik Hatim, who lost his life in its defence. Having thus successfully plundered the country, the Rana returned, unopposed, to Chittoor. The King, during this time, was on the Malwa frontier; but Kowam-ool-Moolk, the viceroy of Guzerat, placed a respectable force at the disposal of Moobariz-ool-Moolk, and enabled him to return to Ahmudnuggur. On the march thither, he was opposed by a body of Kolies and Girasias from the Idur district, who were defeated, and sixty-one Girasias killed; but on his arrival at Ahmudnuggur, finding the country destitute of provisions and inhabitants, owing to the late ravages, he was compelled to fall back on Puranty. The King, hearing of these circumstances, directed Imad-ool-Moolk and Keisur Khan to proceed to Ahmudnuggur; but the famine which prevailed obliged them also to retreat. Determined, however, not to allow Ahmudnuggur to be abandoned, the King remanded them back at all hazards during the rains, resolving after that season to march in person against Rana Sanka.

Mullik Eiaz Sooltany, originally a slave born in the King's family, offered to march with the

Surat division, consisting of twenty thousand horse and a quantity of artillery and rockets, to reduce Rana Sanka; representing that it was beneath the King's dignity to proceed in person against a common marauder. The King gave no answer; but in the month of Mohurrum, in the year 927, marched to Ahmudnuggur, where he directed his army to assemble. Mullik Eiaz now repeating his request, the Guzerat army, composed of one hundred thousand cavalry and one hundred elephants, were placed under his orders, of which the reserve, consisting of twenty thousand men, followed, under the command of Kowam-ool-Moolk. On the arrival of the army at Mahrasa, Taj Khan and Nizam-ool-Moolk also joined with their divisions. Mullik Eiaz representing that so large a force was quite unnecessary, left behind him nearly the whole of the elephants, and the greater part of the cavalry, which had lately joined. Sufdur Khan, in command of the advance, plundered the district of Mahrasa on his route, putting many Rajpoots to death, and also taking many prisoners; and Mullik Eiaz, proceeding by Dongurpoor and Banswala, reduced those towns to ashes, and thence marched on to Chittoor. One day Mullik Shooja-ool-Moolk and Sufdur Khan, the officers in advance, obtained intimation that Oody Sing the Ray of Poloh, and Oogur Sein Poorby, were lying in wait at the back of some hills, near which they were encamped, intending to make a night-attack upon them. The Guzerat officers anticipated the measure, and leaving their tents

Mohurrum, A. H. 927. Dec. A. D. 1520.

standing, fell upon the Rajpoots with only two hundred men; on which occasion the Rajpoots were defeated with the loss of eighty men killed, and Oogur Sein Poorby was severely wounded. Mullik Eiaz, hearing of the attack, ordered the line under arms, and galloped towards the scene of action; but he was too late to witness even the defeat. The success of the Mahomedans had been complete; and Mullik Eiaz publicly applauded the gallantry of this daring little party. On the following day Kowam-ool-Moolk was ordered to pursue the fugitives; and although he did not come up with them, he so laid waste the country of Banswala that he did not leave even a blade of grass. Mullik Eiaz now marched on to the attack of Mundsoor, while Rana Sanka also moved in the same direction, and encamped within twelve coss.* Here Rana Sanka proposed sending an envoy to the King, consenting, as a preliminary, to acknowledge fealty to the crown of Guzerat; connected with this overture, however, there were certain conditions so extravagant that Mullik Eiaz determined to prosecute the sieze of Mundsoor. The attack was in much forwardness, and the mines in progress, when an officer arrived in camp, stating that Sooltan Mahmood, King of Malwa, was in full march to co-operate with the Guzerat army; shortly after which he arrived. In a very few days Kowam ool-Moolk had brought the approaches so close as to be capable of effecting a breach; but Mullik Eiaz, jealous lest the former should gain all the credit of the

* Twenty-four miles.

siege, ordered him back to the lines, a circumstance which gave general offence in the army. On the following morning, Moobariz-ool-Moolk, with a party of Guzerat horse, marched without orders to attack Rana Sanka; but Mullik Eiaz, leaving the camp, intercepted and brought him back to the lines. The object of Mullik Eiaz was to wait till the springing of one of the mines, and then to head the assault, and ensure to himself the honour of the capture. The mine was at length exploded, and a practicable breach effected; but the Rajpoots, having discovered the point to which it was directed, had already cut off the breach, and the attack failed in consequence. On this event Rana Sanka made further overtures to Mullik Eiaz; the preliminary of which was an acknowledgment of allegiance to Guzerat; promising, besides, to return all the elephants taken in the battle of Ahmudnuggur. Mullik Eiaz availed himself of this second opportunity of putting an end to the war, foreseeing that no co-operation could take place between him and the other Guzerat officers. A suspension of hostilities was accordingly agreed on, until communications could be receive from the King. In spite of this agreement, some of the junior officers formed a plan, in concert with Sooltan Mahmood of Malwa, to attack the Rana's camp on the ensuing Wednesday. Mullik Eiaz, having obtained information of their intention, deputed a confidential officer to wait upon the King of Malwa, informing him that the King of Guzerat had been pleased to appoint him commander-in-chief of the forces in the province of Chittoor, with discretionary powers to conclude the war ; but having heard that part of the Guzerat army had resolved to march in concert with a body of his troops against Rana Sanka, he thought it his duty to protest against the measure, saying, that there was every reason to dread that so disgraceful a breach of faith would end in defeat. No reply being received to this message, Mullik Eiaz ordered the Guzerat line under arms on the day appointed for the attack; and instead of marching against Rana Sanka he moved to Khiljipoor, where he conferred honorary dresses on the Rana's agents, and gave their dismissal. On this Sooltan Mahmood Khiljy returned to Mando, and Mullik Eiaz to Champanere, where he was honoured with a title, and was created governor of Diù. Moozuffur Shah, at the same time, made up his mind to march in person against Rana Sanka on the following year. Mullik Eiaz, having learned the King's intentions, despatched a confidential person secretly to the Rana, saying, "As we have contracted a friendship during the "late negotiations, it is but fair that we should "assist each other by advice. I think it my duty, "therefore, to inform you that the King is highly "displeased that the army returned without "having effected any object of importance, and "he, in consequence, intends in a few months "more to march in person to plunder your country. "I therefore advise you to send, as soon as possible, "your eldest son as ambassador to this court with "a number of valuable presents, regretting the "differences which exist, and begging to be "considered as a vassal of this crown. This "appears to me to be the only mode by which "you can secure your own safety, or avert "the evil of a war."

A. H. 928.
A. D. 1521.

In the year 928, the King proceeded from Champanere to Ahmudabad; but while collecting his army at Kakreea, in order to attack Chittoor, he heard that Rana Sanka had deputed his son with large presents to intercede for him, and that the young rana had already reached Mahrasa on his way to Ahmudabad. Moozuffur Shah accordingly halted, and received the embassy, ordering an honorary dress to be given to the Rana's son, with assurances of reconciliation. The King then broke up the army and came to Ahmudabad; when he heard of the death of Mullik Eiaz, on whose son he conferred his father's government and honorary titles.

A. H. 929.
A. D. 1522.

In the year 929, the King marched in person to Champanere, to quell an insurrection in that quarter, and he subsequently caused the town of Mahrasa to be repaired. It was about this time that the Prince Julal Khan, the son of Sikundur Lody of Dehly, who had, in a fit of rage, put to death one of the principal nobles of his brother's government, reached the court of Guzerat. Julal Khan had previously applied repeatedly for the aid of Guzerat troops to assist in dethroning his brother Ibrahim; and on the present occasion Moozuffur Shah ordered a force to accompany him to Dehly for the purpose; but a full account of the transactions connected with this event has already been given in the history of Dehly.*

A. H. 931.
A. D. 1524.

In the year 931, the King marched towards Idur; on which occasion the Prince Bahadur Khan complained that his allowances were insufficient to maintain the establishment due to his rank, and requested that they might be made equal to those of his elder brother, Sikundur Khan. Moozuffur Shah, for political reasons, gave no decisive answer to this request, but promised to consider the subject. Meanwhile the Prince, impatient of delay, left the King's camp without taking leave, and returning first to Ahmudabad, proceeded, eventually, to the country of Oody Sing, the Raja of Poloh, by whom he was received with marks of attention. From Poloh he went on to Chittoor, where he was received by Rana Sanka, who presented him with splendid offerings; thence he went by Ajmeer to Mewatt, where the governor, Hussun Khan, marched several stages to meet him. After remaining some time there, he went on to Dehly, and was favourably received by Ibrahim Lody, who was at that time preparing to repel the invasion of Babur. Bahadur Khan having on one occasion defeated a detachment of Moguls with a small body of Guzeratties, the Afghan chiefs of Dehly, disgusted with Ibrahim, proposed elevating the Guzerat prince to the throne of Dehly. Ibrahim Lody, however,

* Vide vol. i. p. 394. The Guzerat historian has committed an anachronism in fixing arrival of Julal Khan so late as 1522.

taking the necessary precautions, the Prince found it necessary to fly for safety to Joonpoor.

Moozuffur Shah, hearing of the conduct of his son, wrote to Khoodabunda Khan, who had accompanied him, to entreat the Prince to return to Guzerat, promising to overlook all the events connected with his sudden departure. Shortly after this the King was taken dangerously ill; and his disease daily increasing, factions began to be formed in the army, one party espousing the cause of the Prince Sikundur, and another that of the youngest prince, Luteef Khan. The King was observed to be very anxious to hear of Bahadur Khan's return, and it was generally supposed that he intended to declare him his successor; but on Friday, the 2d of Jumad-ool-Awul, in the year 932, having sent for his eldest son, the Prince Sikundur, he gave him his blessing, and proclaimed him his heir. On the following day he departed this life, in the fifty-sixth year of his age, and in the fifteenth of his reign. Moozuffur Shah was considered a just and upright prince, strictly adhering on all occasions to the tenets of the faith. Among his accomplishments was that of writing a beautiful hand, in which he employed many of his leisure hours. During his lifetime he transcribed several copies of the Koran, which he sent to Mecca to be placed near the holy shrine. He also greatly promoted learning; so that men of letters from Persia, Arabia, and Turkey, found it worth their while to settle in Guzerat during his liberal and auspicious reign.

Jumad-ool-Awul 3. A. H. 932. Feb. 17. A. D. 1526.

SIKUNDUR SHAH.

Moozuffur Shah is succeeded by his eldest son, Sikundur.—The Prince Luteef, the King's younger brother, goes into rebellion—retires to Chittoor, where he finds protection with the Rana.—The Rana defeats the King's army.—The King disgusts his nobles—a plot to assassinate him—his death.

During the painful and protracted illness of Moozuffur Shah, each of the two factions in the army took a decided part to favour its respective leader; but the late King having expressly nominated Sikundur Khan, the eldest son, to the throne of Guzerat, the youngest, Prince Luteef, marched with his adherents towards Nundoorbar and Sooltanpoor. Sikundur Shah, after having buried the late King at Surkech, proceeded to Champanere. Here he learnt that one Shah Sheikhjee, the son of the celebrated Boorhan-ood-Deen Owlia, considered the most holy man of the age, had foretold that his brother, the Prince Bahadur, would eventually succeed to the throne. Sikundur Shah, incensed at this prediction, condescended to vent his indignation in abusing that holy personage in the most gross and indecent terms; he was also so imprudent as to treat with indignity the different nobles of his government, the supporters of his father's throne, and to confer honours and estates on the companions of his youthful follies and excesses. Among those who resented this conduct, by withdrawing from court, was Imad-ool-Moolk Sooltany, an Abyssinian slave of the mother of Sikundur Shah, and a great favourite of the late king. At the same time, also, it became known, that the Prince Luteef Khan had raised a considerable force in the neighbourhood of Nundoorbar and Sooltanpoor, and appeared only to wait for an opportunity of declaring his pretensions to the throne. Under these circumstances, Sikundur Shah deputed one Mullik Luteef, with the title of Shirza Khan, to oppose him; but hearing that the Prince Luteef Khan had gone to Chittoor, the troops were directed to march in that direction, where they sustained a complete defeat. On which occasion the general, with many other officers of distinction, fell, and the remainder of the force was cut off in detail by the Kolies and Rajpoots, having lost no less a number than one thousand seven hundred men.

The inhabitants of Guzerat deeming this an inauspicious omen of the new reign, the nobles of the old government persuaded Imad-ool-Moolk that the King designed to put him to death. Conscious of being ill-disposed towards him, Imad-ool-Moolk readily gave ear to these assertions, and determined to anticipate Sikundur Shah's intentions, by placing another descendant of the house of Moozuffur on the throne, hoping to ensure to himself the superintendence of the affairs of the state. Imad-ool-Moolk therefore prepared a party to attack and put to death the King, in one of his usual rides; but the opportunity passed without the plan succeeding. The King, although warned of the danger, treated it lightly in public; but the circumstance dwelt on his mind so much, that on that very night he dreamed that he was visited by the holy Syud Julal Bokhary, Shah Alum, and Shah Sheikhjee, and also by his father, Moozuffur Shah, who addressed him, saying, "Sikundur, Sikundur, descend from the throne, "for it is the lot of another." This dream weighed heavily on his spirits. He arose early next morning, rode out, and played chowgan; after which he returned, breakfasted, and endeavoured to forget his cares, and drown his thoughts in sleep. Although the plot for the King's death had failed on the preceding day, Imad-ool-Moolk had by no means relinquished it; so that, after the King had lain down, that officer, together with Baha-ool-Moolk, Dar-ool-Moolk Seif Khan, two Turkish slaves, and one Abyssinian, entered the palace with arms. Sikundur Shah, awakened by the noise made by the opposition of his guards, rushed out to ascertain the cause, when the assassins meeting him put him to death. Thus ended the life of Sikundur Shah, on the 19th of Shaban, in the year 932, after a short reign of three months and seventeen days.

Shaban 19. A.H. 932. May 30. A.D. 1526.

MAHMOOD SHAH II.

Nuseer Khan, a brother of the late King, is raised to the throne, and assumes the title of Mahmood Shah II.—The King's elder brother, the Prince Bahadur, arrives from Dehly, and being joined by the nobles, ascends the throne.

After the death of Sikundur Shah, his corpse was conveyed to Halole, in the Champanere district, where it was interred, and Nuseer Khan, the King's younger brother, was raised to the throne by Imad-ool-Moolk, under the title of Mahmood Shah. All the officers went through the usual forms of congratulations to the new monarch, and received honorary dresses from Imad-ool-Moolk, who became regent, and who conferred titles in the King's name on one hundred and eighty persons on the day of the coronation. The complete ascendency obtained by the minister excited the envy of the rest of the nobles, and induced them to write to the Prince Bahadur Khan, who was absent in Hindoostan, to return to Guzerat, and assert his claims to the throne. These letters were despatched by Khoodabunda Khan and Taj Khan, and had the effect of expediting the march of Bahadur, who was already on his journey, having commenced it on the first intelligence of his father's death. Imad-ool-Moolk, hearing of his approach, deputed an officer of rank, charged with presents of jewels and money, to Boorhan

Nizam Shah of Ahmudnuggur, inviting him to march to his aid. The latter accepted the offerings, but took no measures to assist the Guzerat minister. Letters were also written to the Raja of Poloh to occupy the road leading to Champanere, and to the Mogul Emperor Babur of Dehly, promising a crore of rupees if he would lend his aid, by sending a force down the Indus to land at Diù, and co-operate with the Guzeratties. The latter communication never reached its destiny, having been intercepted by the ruler of Dongurpoor.

Bahadur Khan was near Dehly when the letters from Khoodabunda Khan, intimating the death of Moozuffur Shah, reached him; and at the same time he received a deputation from the Afghans of Joonpoor, entreating him to assume the government of that country. In order to satisfy both parties, he promised to pursue whatever direction his horse might take, and throwing the reins upon the animal's neck it took the road to Guzerat. On his arrival at Chittoor he was joined by his two brothers, Chand Khan and Ibrahim Khan, who gave him the first information of the assassination of the late King, Sikundur Shah after which event they had fled, and taken refuge with the Rana. Chand Khan preferred remaining at Chittoor, but subsequently went to Malwa, while Ibrahim accompanied Bahadur Khan. At Poloh he was joined by the Raja Oody Sing, and also by a few of the personal adherents of the late King, among whom were Mullik Survur and Yoosoof Khan.

Bahadur Khan, having now assumed the title

of Shah, sent a confidential officer in advance, with a conciliatory and moderate proclamation to Taj Khan, mentioning that he was thus far on his road to Ahmudabad. This officer, who commanded a force under Imad-ool-Moolk, was absent at Dundooka; but hearing of Bahadur Shah's arrival on the frontier, instantly joined his standard. The Prince Luteef Khan, the second son of Moozuffur Shah, then at Dundooka, raised a sum of money there for his expenses, and marched to join his cousin Futteh Khan. On his arrival at Dongurpoor, Bahadur Shah was joined by Khoorum Khan and many of the Guzerat officers, so that Imad-ool Moolk, finding himself deserted by most of his adherents, began to lavish the royal treasures in raising troops. He succeeded by this means in bringing together a great concourse of people, few of whom were soldiers; and he ordered Azd-ool-Moolk, accompanied by fifty elephants, to march to Mahrasa, and cut off the communication between Bahadur Shah and the Guzeratties. On reaching Mahomednuggur, many officers who were afraid to join him before now went over to Bahadur Shah; and Azd-ool-Moolk was compelled to fall back on Champanere, and to join Imad-ool-Moolk. Bahadur Shah, continuing his march to Mahrasa, received at that place from Taj Khan the royal jewels; after which, proceeding to Nehrwala Puttun, Bahadur Shah was formally crowned on the 26th of Rumzan, A. H. 932, and reached Ahmudabad on the 28th. Imad-ool-Moolk having been joined by the Prince Luteef, attempted to reach Ahmudabad

Rumzan 26. A. H. 932. August 3. A. D. 1526.

before Bahadur Shah ; but finding that the latter was every where acknowledged king, there was an end to further competition. The reign of Mahmood Shah did not exceed four months.

BAHADUR SHAH.

The Prince Bahadur returns from Dehly, and ascends the throne.—A feeble effort is made to create an insurrection by the Prince Luteef Khan, who is severely wounded, and dies.—Imad-ool-Moolk, and the regicides of Sikundur Shah, all suffer death.—Great efforts made by the Portuguese to occupy the island of Diu, in which they are repulsed.—Bahadur Shah is invited to aid the King of Berar against the King of Ahmudnuggur—he proceeds to the south, and causes himself to be recognised King of Ahmudnuggur—makes war with the King of Malwa—conquers his country, and puts the King to death—provokes a war with Hoomayoon, the Great Mogul—is defeated, and loses all his dominions, with the exception of a small portion of Guzerat—is supported by the Portuguese—recovers his kingdom—is killed by the Portuguese in an affray in the harbour of Diu.

On the first day of the following month Bahadur Shah marched to Champanere, at which place Imad-ool-Moolk still continued. He was, however, much impeded by the heavy rain which fell at that season, and was obliged to halt on the Saburmutty; but very soon after continuing his march, he arrived on the banks of the Mehindry, at the Khanpoor ferry. Imad-ool-Moolk, hearing of the King's approach, dispersed his force over the Baroda district, to distract his attention; but this manœuvre had not the effect of diverting Bahadur Shah from his march on Champanere, where Imad-ool-Moolk and the confederates were eventually seized by Taj Khan. Imad-ool-Moolk, his son, and Seif Khan, together with the other regicides taken, were hanged, and their property confiscated; while Rufut-ool-Moolk, an old servant of Moozuffur Shah, received the title of Imad-ool-Moolk. Azd-ool-Moolk, hearing of the fate of his party, fled from Baroda, leaving his property to be plundered by a party of Kolies. Shumsheer-ool-Moolk was despatched in pursuit of Azd-ool-Moolk, and Nizam-ool-Moolk in pursuit of Mohafiz Khan. Both these chiefs sought refuge with Oody Sing, Raja of Poloh; but they were so closely followed, that the little property they had with them fell into the hands of the King's troops. Most of the officers who adhered to the fortunes of Imad-ool-Moolk were in the end seized, and suffered death: some were hanged, and others blown from guns, while the property of all was confiscated. The Prince Luteef Khan, after having remained for some time concealed in the city of Champanere, fled to the country of Poloh, and Azd-ool-Moolk and Mohafiz Khan to Mutwar.*

Zeekad 15. After having gotten rid of all his
A. H. 932. enemies, Bahadur Shah, on the 15th of
August 20. Zeekad, went through the form of being
A. D. 1526. again crowned at Champanere, that city having been considered, during the few last reigns, the capital of the kingdom. The Prince Luteef Khan, who had taken post in the Ahwas hills, was joined by several of the discontented nobles; and Alugh Khan was appointed to the command of an army sent against him. Shortly after the departure

* Mutwar is the tract of country lying between the Nerbudda and Tapty rivers, north and south, and little Oodipoor and Choly Meheswur, east and west.

of these troops, Alugh Khan was represented as being one of the assassins of the late Sikundur Shah. Bahadur Shah was no less enraged than astonished at this information; and having made strict enquiries, and ascertaining that the accusation was false, he ordered the calumniators to be severely punished. In the commencement of the following year, 933, a very serious
A. H. 933.
A. D. 1526.
mutiny broke out among the cavalry; and a large party, headed by nearly two thousand officers, marched to the mosque, and prevented the performance of public worship till they received their arrears of pay. Bahadur Shah, though he could ill brook this conduct, was induced, from motives of policy, to comply with their demands, having good reason for supposing that violent measures would induce them to join the Prince Luteef Khan. Shortly after this event, information arrived, that, in consequence of the advance of the Prince towards Sooltanpoor, the governor Ghazy Khan had marched, attacked, and defeated him, and that although his friends Azd-ool-Moolk and Mohafiz Khan had made their escape, Ray Bheem and his brothers had fallen in the action, and the Prince, being severely wounded, had been taken prisoner. On this news the King deputed Mohib-ool-Moolk and some other noblemen to wait on his brother, in order to see that his wounds were properly attended to, and to administer every comfort to him, till he could be removed to the capital. The Prince Luteef, however, never recovered; but shortly after died, and

was buried at Halole, near Champanere, by the side of the late Sikundur Shah. During this year, Nuseer Khan, who had formerly assumed the title of Mahmood Shah, also died; and a suitable establishment of holy men was maintained to say daily prayers for the souls of these departed princes.

Meanwhile, Oody Sing, Ray of Poloh, with a band of marauders, marched and laid waste the country of Dohud; and most of the public property fell into their hands. This inroad so much incensed the King, that he ordered Taj Khan, with all the cavalry, consisting of nearly one hundred thousand men, to attack and annihilate these bands. The devastation committed by Taj Khan's army induced the Ray to send ambassadors to sue for mercy on any terms. Taj Khan resolved to act up strictly to his orders, and seemed determined to destroy the whole race. Driven to desperation, the Ray at last took up a strong position, and bore the brunt of an action, in which his troops were defeated and himself killed; but it is a remarkable fact, that on this occasion only one Mahomedan of Taj Khan's army is said to have fallen. His force was shortly after recalled, and himself deputed to Cambay, in order to assume the government of that district, as the inhabitants had frequently made complaints against the present governor.

A. H. 934. A. D. 1528. On the following year, 934, Bahadur Shah marched towards the countries of Idur and Wagur, from whence he returned by Champanere to Baroach, for the purpose of superintending the repairs of that fortress; after which he went in person to Cambay, where having heard that a European vessel had been taken and the crew made prisoners off Diù, he repaired to that place, and was met by Kowam-ool-Moolk. All the Europeans taken on this occasion were circumcised, and became Mahomedans.* On his return to his capital, Bahadur Shah received a letter from his nephew, Meeran Mahomed Khan, ruler of Kandeish, stating that Ameer Bereed Shah of Bidur and Boorhan Nizam Shah Bheiry of Ahmudnuggur, having entered into a confederacy, had marched to attack Berar; that in consequence Meeran Mahomed Khan had lent his aid to Imad Shah, King of Berar, and opposed them. He stated also that a severe engagement took place, in which the latter had been drawn into an ambuscade by Boorhan Nizam Shah, and his troops defeated; and, moreover, that a number of Meeran Mahomed Khan's elephants had fallen into the hands of the Deccanies on this occasion; and, lastly, that they had taken the fort of Mahoor by assault, from Imad Shah, so that he begged the aid of Bahadur Shah. Upon this Bahadur Shah desired an answer to be written, stating that during the last year he

* The Portuguese historian states, that they resisted becoming converts, and were eventually released. James de Mesquita was the name of the officer, and his whole crew only consisted of sixteen men in a boat. It is certain that James de Mesquita was with Bahadur Shah afterwards, at the siege of Chittoor, and was employed by him as his envoy to Nuno de Cunha in the year that Bahadur Shah lost his life.

had sent the governor of Nehrwala to the Deccan, in order to accommodate the differences which existed, in conformity with the wishes of Imad Shah, in which he happily succeeded; but that as it now appeared the Deccanies had become the aggressors, he should proceed to that quarter in person.

Mohurrum, A. H. 935. September, A. D. 1528.

In conformity with the intention expressed in this letter, Bahadur Shah moved, in the month of Mohurrum, of the year 935, with a large force towards the Deccan. On reaching Baroda he was overtaken by Jam Feroze, ruler of Tutta, in Sind, who stated that the Arghoons had made a descent upon his country, and taken it. Bahadur Shah gave to the Jam twelve lacks of rupees * for the present, pledging himself to march hereafter and recover his territory from the Arghoons.

The fame of Bahadur Shah by this act of generosity spread far and near. He was welcomed by the inhabitants of all the countries through which he passed in proceeding to the Deccan; and he was joined by the nephew † of the Raja of Gualiar with a body of Rajpoots, as also by Sreeputty Ray, the nephew of Rana Sanka, with many chiefs of distinction, as well as by some of the nobles of the Deccan. The movements of this immense army being very slow, and a large portion having halted for some time at Champanere, Imad

* 144,000*l.* sterling.

† Nursing, the nephew of Man-Sing.—Mirut-Iskundry.

Shah, King of Berar, became impatient of the delay, and sent his son Jafur Khan to Bahadur Shah, informing him that Boorhan Nizam Shah had shut the doors of negotiation, and that nothing could be effected without the King's presence. Bahadur Shah therefore instantly marched on to the Nerbudda, on the banks of which river he was met by Meeran Mahomed Khan, who entreated him to visit Boorhanpoor, where he entertained him in a sumptuous manner, presenting him with elephants, horses, &c. At this place he was joined by Imad Shah, from Gavulgur. The combined armies of Guzerat, Kandeish, and Berar, under Bahadur Shah, now commenced their march through Berar towards Mahoor, against Boorhan Nizam Shah, who gradually retreating, drew the allies after him as far as Jalna, where the King having manifested intentions of occupying the country of Berar for himself, a secret communication was opened with the enemy, and Boorhan Nizam Shah agreed to restore some of the captured elephants, and also consented to read the Khootba in the name of the King of Guzerat, and even promised to pay tribute, if he would return to his own country. Bahadur Shah continued his march till he reached Dowlutabad, and encamped at the Howz Kootloo, where he halted for some time, in order to refresh his army. The enemy, however, contrived to intercept the supplies from the northward and westward, which caused great distress to his followers and cattle, and occasioned a famine in his camp. Notwithstanding which, Bahadur Shah compelled Boorhan

Nizam Shah to acknowledge him King of Ahmudnuggur and Guzerat; in the former of which places proclamations were made, and public prayers read in his name. In the beginning of the year 937 he returned to Guzerat, and remained during the rainy season at Ahmudabad. After the monsoon he marched towards Idur, and despatched Khoodabunda Khan and Imad-ool-Moolk with a large force to Wagur, himself marching to Cambay. Thence he embarked in a vessel, and sailed to Diù; after which he proceeded to Dongurpoor and Banswara, levied the usual contributions, and returned eventually to Mahomedabad Champanere.

A. H. 937.
A. D. 1530.

At this period Oomr Khan, Kootb Khan, and many nobles of the Dehly court, having fled from the Emperor Babur, sought protection with Bahadur Shah. The King now went to Mahrasa, where he was met by Khoodabunda Khan, and many other officers; he then marched to Wagur, and having reduced that province, placed civil and military officers in the different towns to collect the tribute. Pursaram, Raja of Wagur, submitted to the King, while his son became a convert to the Mahomedan faith, and was received into the King's household; but Jugut Ray, the brother of the Raja, first fled to the hills, and then joined Rana Ruttun, the son of the late Rana Sanka of Chittoor, with whom he found a temporary asylum. Shortly afterwards, a messenger arrived in camp at Banswara from Rana Ruttun, begging terms for Jugut Ray. The King having caused a mosque to be built at a village on the larky G'hat, gave it over in perpetuity to Jugut Ray. While the Guzerat army remained encamped there, Bahadur Shah received information that Sooltan Mahmood Khiljy (not withstanding the obligations he had received at the hands of Moozuffur Shah) had sent Shirza Khan, the governor of Mando, to plunder some villages belonging to his ally the Rana of Chittoor, and had proceeded through Oojein to Sarungpoor. At the same time advices were received direct from Rana Ruttun, complaining of the outrage, and requesting the King to take measures to assist him. At this period, also, Silhuddy Rajpoot, and Moyin Khan the son of Sikundur Khan Mewatty, officers of the Malwa court, having intimation of their master's intention upon their lives, fled to Chittoor, and shortly after Bhowput, the son of Silhuddy, arrived in Bahadur Shah's camp. Bhowput was honourably received; and seven horses were presented to him, besides seven hundred gold embroidered dresses to be distributed among his adherents. While the disaffected officers of the King of Malwa sought refuge at the Guzerat court, Sooltan Mahmood himself deputed Duria Khan as envoy to Bahadur Shah; stating, that he had it long in contemplation to pay his respects, but that unforeseen events had occurred to prevent it; that he therefore deputed Duria Khan to ascertain if a visit at present would be agreeable. The King returned a polite answer, saying, that he should halt at Banswara for his arrival. A few days only elapsed before

Ruttun, Rana of Chittoor, and Silhuddy Poorby arrived in the Guzerat camp, where being favourably received, they were presented with thirty elephants, and fifteen hundred gold embroidered dresses, when they returned to Chittoor; but most of the Malwa refugees remained with the King. Bahadur Shah now moved to Tandla, where he had agreed to receive the visit of Sooltan Mahmood, after which he intended to have accompanied him as far as the Dydla pass, on his return to Malwa. At Tandla, the King's nephew, Meeran Mahomed Khan ruler of Kandeish, arrived; and Duria Khan, the Malwa envoy, came to say, that Sooltan Mahmood, having broken his arm by a fall from his horse, was unable to visit Bahadur Shah. The latter, doubting the truth of this assertion, flatly told the envoy that he did not believe him, and obliged him at length to confess the real truth, that the King of Malwa was unwilling to come, owing to his having harboured the Prince Chand Khan of Guzerat, who was living under his protection. Bahadur Shah observed, that he had no enmity towards Chand Khan, and therefore that need not be adduced as a reason, and that he therefore expected Sooltan Mahmood would come to his camp and pay his respects. The King continued his march to Depalpoor, when he learned that Sooltan Mahmood only now waited to place his son in charge of the government of Mando during his absence. The delay which this arrangement involved gave the Guzerat courtiers an opportunity of again misrepresenting the conduct of Sooltan Mahmood Khiljy; so that

Bahadur Shah marched forth with to Mando, to which he laid siege. To Meeran Mahomed Khan of Kandeish was intrusted the post of Shahpoor, on the west face of the fort. Lokmun Sing was ordered to occupy Seetulpoor, and the rest of the Poorbies were sent to Julwara. The head-quarters of the army occupied Mahomedpoor.

Shaban 9. A. H. 937. Feb. 26. A. D. 1531.

On the night of the 9th of Shaban, in the year 937, Bahadur Shah in person, with a small party of select men, escaladed the fort undiscovered, and was soon followed by a considerable body of Guzeratties. Having met with no resistance, the troops, rather than remain quiet till daylight, as had been concerted, proceeded towards Sooltan Mahmood's palace, where the King of Malwa disputed the passage for a time, till being obliged to give way, he was eventually taken prisoner and sent to Champanere, but he died on the road, * while Chand Khan, the Guzerat prince, made his escape during the confusion. The country of Malwa was now partitioned out into districts, and Bahadur Shah occupied Mando. On the following year, the King was prevailed on by his nephew to visit Aseer and Boorhanpoor, where he was met by Boorhan Nizam Shah of Ahmudnuggur, who had not as yet received the royal insignia or title from a sovereign prince. † Bahadur Shah at that period

* The circumstances of the death of Sooltan Mahmood of Malwa will be found fully detailed in the history of that kingdom.

† The order of sovereignty, like that of nobility, appears only to have been considered valid when conferred by the hand of some superior legitimate prince.

conferred on him the white canopy and scarlet pavilion, and addressed him with the title of Shah, which he henceforth assumed, under the name of Boorhan Nizam Shah Bheiry.* Bahadur Shah's object in courting the King of Ahmudnuggur had reference to the aid he expected from him in the attack he then meditated on the kingdom of Dehly. He was, however, disappointed; for Boorhan Nizam Shah not only withheld his assistance in the subsequent war with Hoomayoon Padshah, but, on the contrary, deputed a secret agent to the Mogul court, long before the war in question took place, to obtain assistance, for the purpose of attacking Guzerat. During this interchange of civilities at Boorhanpoor, Bahadur Shah became so pleased with Shah Tahir Jooneidy, the minister of Boorhan Nizam Shah, that he used every means in his power to induce him to quit Boorhan Nizam Shah, and reside in Guzerat, but without effect. Some years afterwards, Shah Tahir succeeded in converting Boorhan Nizam Shah II. to the Sheea persuasion, and induced him to exchange the white canopy and scarlet pavilion for the green standard assumed by the followers of Ally. Bahadur Shah, having returned to Mando, appointed Mokbil Khan to command the fortress of Champanere, and Yekhtiar Khan being sent with the guns and military stores to deposit them in that

* This is the language of the Guzerat historian, in order to gratify the vanity of his master; for, in reality, the kings of Ahmudnuggur assumed the royal titles and insignia several generations anterior to the period in question.

Rubbee-oos-Sany 21. A. H. 938. Dec. 3. A. D. 1531. garrison, he returned to Mando on the 21st of Rubbee-oos-Sany, of which place he was appointed governor. Silhuddy Poorby, the late prime minister of Sooltan Gheias-ood-Deen, within late years had occupied Oojein as his own; and the King wanting some excuse to wrest it out of his hands, charged him with maintaining in his seraglio a number of Mahomedan women. Jumad-ool-Awul 5. Dec. 18. On the 5th of Jumad-ool-Awul the king moved from Mando to Nalcha, when Bhowput the son of Silhuddy, then in Bahadur Shah's service, supposing the king to be on his return to Guzerat, requested permission to go to Oojein and see his father, and to bring him to the presence to pay his respects. The King assented without hesitation, conceiving that Silhuddy could have no intimation of his design. Jumad-ool-Awul 19. Jan. 5. On the 19th of the same month the King encamped at D'har, where having left the army, he proceeded, as if on a hunting-party, towards Bensrode and Shoojalpoor: at the latter place he was met by Silhuddy, who had left his son Bhowput with his family in Ooojein. Ameer Nuseer, the chief who had been sent to accompany Silhuddy, assured the King that the fidelity of the Hindoo chief was not to be depended on, and that, before he could be persuaded to come at all, Ameer Nuseer had ventured to promise him the government of the district of Cambay and a crore of tunkas, previously to which, Silhuddy had made preparations to fly to Seevas. On the King's return to D'har, having consulted his nobles, he caused Silhuddy to be seized and confined with two of his domestics, one of whom made some resistance ; but finding it of no avail, he slew himself with his dagger, and fell dead at his master's feet, after declaring he could not live to witness his disgrace. When this circumstance became known at Oojein, Bhowput, the son of Silhuddy, fled, accompanied by many of his tribe, leaving Oojein to be plundered by the Mahomedans. On the following day Bahadur Shah marched to that city, and having placed Duria Khan, one of the officers of the late Malwa government, in charge, he proceeded to Sarungpoor, the command of which was given to Mulloo Khan, a Guzerat noble, and Hubeeb Khan was made governor of Ashta, which district he soon reduced to subjection. On the King's arrival at Bhilsa, having ascertained that the Mahomedan worship had been discontinued for the last ten years, he caused mosques to be rebuilt, and the exercise of the religion of the true faith to be restored. During his stay at Bhilsa he learned that Bhowput, resolving to resent the disgrace inflicted on his father, had collected troops on the frontier, and had entered into an offensive and defensive alliance with the Rana of Chittoor. The King, anticipating the march of the Rajpoots, deputed Imad-ool-Moolk to attack Bhowput, while himself marched to Raiseen to oppose Lokmun Sing, the brother of Silhuddy, who having raised men in that quarter was waiting the junction of Bhowput and the Rana of Chittoor. On approaching within sight of Raiseen the Rajpoots descended from the hill to attack the King's troops. The advanced guard, consisting of a small body of cavalry, charged the Hindoos without hesitation, and Bahadur Shah with his own hand slew ten men. The main body of the cavalry soon after coming up, the Rajpoots were defeated with heavy loss, and sought safety in flight within the walls of the fort, which was immediately invested, and a regular siege commenced. The Mahomedans, carrying their approaches close to the walls, effected a practicable breach, by means of mines, on the curtain of one face of the fort, and two of the bastions were also levelled by the fire from the batteries. Silhuddy, who was a prisoner in the King's camp, perceiving that it was impossible for the fort to make any longer resistance, offered to become a proselyte to the Mahomedan faith, and then to go to the fort in order to persuade his brother to surrender. The King acceding to the proposal, Silhuddy formally renounced his religion, and being clothed with a dress of honour ate at the royal table, and subsequently accompanied the King with a flag of truce to the walls of the fort, recommending his brother to give up the place. He acquainted him, also, at the same time, of his having become a Mahomedan. Lokmun, the brother of Silhuddy, addressing him in their own provincial dialect, desired him, to obtain a respite for a few days, and to make some excuse for not giving up the fort immediately, acquainting him that the Rana of Chittoor and Bhowput, with forty thousand men, were in full march to raise the siege. Silhuddy, in consequence, made some pretext for allowing the garrison to retain possession of the fort till the next day. This time was granted; but when the period for its surrender arrived further delay was again required; and Silhuddy being permitted to go under the walls in order to enquire the cause, addressed the Rajpoots, saying, that if they remained so blind to their interest, the Mahomedans would, by entering the breaches, put them all to death. This speech was made in the presence of the King's officers, but conveyed a covert reason for holding out, which was sufficiently understood by Lokmun Sing, who, repeating the last words of Silhuddy, showed his countrymen how little they ought to rely on the Mahomedans. He prevailed so far on the troops that, by their exertions, the breaches were repaired during the night; and a party of two thousand men, under Silhuddy's youngest son, then in the fort, marched out to hasten the reinforcements under Bhowput and the Rana of Chittoor. This party being intercepted by the besieged was almost entirely cut off, including the son of Silhuddy who commanded it. The few who escaped death were taken prisoners, and brought in the morning before the King. On the failure of this enterprise, and the death of his son, being related to Silhuddy, he fainted; and the King, now beginning to suspect him, remanded him into confinement under charge of Yekhtiar Khan, to be sent to the fort of Mando.

The force under Bhowput was now approaching rapidly to Raiseen, under the impression that the King had but few troops with him. Bahadur Shah directed Imad-ool-Moolk and Meeran Mahomed Khan of Kandeish to march and attack the enemy. They had not proceeded far when the Mahomedans were met by Poorunmul, another son of Silhuddy, who commanded the advance, consisting of ten thousand cavalry. The King hearing this news, and that Imad-ool-Moolk had halted, left Yekhtiar-ool-Moolk to conduct the siege of Raiseen, and placing himself at the head of the whole of his cavalry, marched in person and encamped at Gungrar. The Rajpoots, hearing of the King's approach, commenced their retreat; and Bahadur Shah being shortly after joined by Aluf Khan from Guzerat, with a reinforcement of thirty thousand fresh troops and a large park of artillery, proceeded towards Chittoor, to which place the enemy had retired. Bahadur Shah resolved, in the first instance, to bring the siege of Raiseen to a close; he therefore deferred any attack on Chittoor till the next year. Upon his return Lokmun, the brother of Silhuddy, perceiving that he could not eventually retain the fort, and that all hopes of succour from Chittoor were at an end, proposed to surrender Raiseen, provided his brother Silhuddy should be released, and again taken into favour. The King acceded to these terms, because he was aware that many Mahomedan females, belonging to Silhuddy, were in the fort, and he knew that in the event of a storm they would all be burnt alive with the Rajpoot women, according to the custom of those people. As a preliminary to the surrender, therefore, Silhuddy was brought to Raiseen, and Taj Khan, who had come to negotiate on the part of

Lokmun, was permitted to return to the fort. Lokmun now brought his own family, to the lower fortifications, leaving Taj Khan with some Poorby Rajpoots in possession of the hill, and sent word to Bahadur Shah that above four hundred females belonging to Silhuddy's seraglio were in the fort. Among these was Silhuddy's wife Doorgawutty, the mother of Bhowput; and he begged, therefore, that he should be permitted to go and escort his own family and females; for that his honour would sustain a blemish, if they were seen by the eye of a stranger, or even by his own brother. Silhuddy, under custody of Mullik Ally Sheer, proceeded to the fort; but upon going to take away his family, his wife, Rany Doorgawutty, the daughter of Rana Sanka, reproached both him and his brother Lokmun for not having defended the place. This woman, with an heroic fortitude, invoking curses on the heads of those who should not revenge her cause, set fire to a pile with which she had caused the female apartments to be surrounded, containing seven hundred beautiful women. She plunged into the flames, and they were all consumed. Silhuddy and Lokmun, with one hundred of their blood relations, now putting on their armour, and calling on their adherents to follow them, rushed impetuously on the Guzerat troops, and bravely met their fate; not one Rajpoot surviving, while the Guzeratties only lost four men.

Alum Khan, the governor of Kalpy, who had rebelled against Hoomayoon Padshah of Dehly, happening to be in attendance on the King of Guzerat at this time, received the governments of

Bhilsa, Raiseen, and Chundery. Bahadur Shah employed the remainder of that year in hunting elephants, and in marching through the country which formerly acknowledged allegiance to the King of Malwa; and having reduced it to obedience, placed his own governors and officers to collect the revenues, and left troops to support their authority. Early in the next year he deputed Meeran Mahomed Khan to march and reduce the fort of Gagrone, wrested from the late Sooltan Mahmood by the troops of the Rana of Chittoor; but as the place had not yet fallen, the King himself moved in that direction, on which the enemy evacuated it without further resistance. From Gagrone the King returned to Mando, leaving Imad-ool-Moolk and Yekhtiar Khan to reduce Runtunbhore, and shortly after he returned to Guzerat to expel the Europeans who had occupied the island of Diù. Upon his approach, however, the enemy fled, leaving their guns upon the island; one of which was the largest ever before seen in India, and required a machine to be constructed for conveying it to Champanere.*

* The Mahomedan historian has treated this success against the Portuguese very slightingly; but Faria-e-Souza (tom i. part iv. chap. iv.) proves that it was one of the greatest efforts his countrymen ever made, and which seems entirely to have failed. The fleet which collected in Bombay harbour consisted of four hundred sail of vessels, on which were embarked three thousand six hundred European soldiers, and ten thousand native soldiers, besides seamen and Lascars. The Mahomedans under Moostufa Khan, the governor of Diù, so completely repulsed this attack, that the Portuguese found it necessary to return to Goa.

In the year 940 Mahomed Zuman Mirza,* a relative of Hoomayoon Padshah of Dehly, who had been confined in the fort of Byana, making his escape, came to the court of Bahadur Shah. Hoomayoon wrote to the King of Guzerat to deliver him up, threatening, in case of refusal, to march and lay waste Guzerat. Bahadur Shah, little accustomed to comply with demands from any potentate, returned an intemperate and haughty reply (which eventually brought upon him his ruin); and in order to show the contempt in which he held the threats of Hoomayoon he conferred the highest dignities on the Mogul prince, thus wantonly irritating the wound which he had already inflicted. The King returned to Champanere from Diù by the route of Cambay and Ahmudabad, and then marched his army to Chittoor, and invested that place for three months. The Rana at last agreed to pay a large sum in specie, to present several horses and elephants, and, among other jewels, the waist-belt† formerly in possession of the Khiljy family, and which had been taken by Sooltan Mahmood of Malwa from the King of Guzerat's pavilion in the battle of Surkech, near Ahmudabad, on the 1st of Suffur, A. H. 856 (A. D. 1452); after which Bahadur Shah returned to his capital. His success in

* Mahomed Zuman was the son of Budee-ooz-Zuman Mirza, descended through Sooltan Hoossein, King of Khorassan, from Tamerlane. Vide Genealogy, vol. ii. p. 1.

† This splendid jewel was sent to Medina, with Bahadur Shah's family; and is mentioned in the Turkish annals as having eventually found its way, in the shape of a present, to the Grand Seignior, Soliman the Magnificent.

compelling the Rana of Chittoor to pay tribute, and the expectation he had formed of being shortly joined by the sons of Bheilole Lody, who had pretensions to the crown of Dehly, induced Bahadur Shah to attempt an attack on the capital of Hindoostan. Alla-ood-Deen, the son of Bheilole Padshah, having reached the court, experienced the most honourable reception from Bahadur Shah, and his son Tartar Khan became enrolled among the nobles of the estate. So confident was Bahadur Shah of success, that he already began to allot to his officers the different districts of Dehly, before he had even marched his army for its subjection. On the following year a sum of three crores of rupees* was furnished to Imad-ool-Moolk, the governor of Runtunbhore, to provide Tartar Khan with a force of forty thousand men; and this prince opened the campaign by reducing Byana, a fortress near Agra. Hoomayoon instantly deputed his brother, Hindal Mirza, to keep Tartar Khan in check till he could come in person; but the Mogul troops had scarcely arrived within a few miles of Tartar Khan's camp at Byana, before the boasting but dastardly Afghans, of which his army was composed, deserted him, leaving him with a force considerably short of twelve thousand men. Tartar Khan, ashamed of the defection of his countrymen (particularly after assuring Bahadur Shah of his confidence in their attachment), refused to retreat before the superior force of Hindal Mirza, but resolved to meet his fate, whatever might be the result. The two

* Three millions sterling.

armies being drawn out advanced slowly to the attack. Tartar Khan made the first charge, with a few confidential retainers, on the centre of the Dehly line, but his troops were defeated, and he fell covered with wounds. The fort of Byana was also retaken, and the army of Tartar Khan was completely dispersed. Hoomayoon, considering this an auspicious commencement of the campaign, followed up his success by declaring war against Bahadur Shah. At this time Bahadur Shah was engaged in the siege of Chittoor, and wrote to Hoomayoon, saying, that as he was employed against an infidel he expected that the Mahomedan king would not oblige him to raise the siege by invading his country. No answer was sent to this communication; but Hoomayoon continued his march unmolested till he reached Sarungpoor in Malwa; and the King of Guzerat, under an infatuation equally preposterous and impolitic, still continued the siege of Chittoor. Having reduced that place, and put to death many of the Rajpoot garrison, Bahadur Shah distributed largesses to his troops, and marched towards Hoomayoon, who, on hearing of his approach, also advanced with the Dehly army, till the two armies met near the town of Mundsoor. The Guzerat army had scarcely taken up its ground when Syud Ally Khan and Khorassany Khan, who commanded the Guzerat pickets, were driven in, and a panic pervaded the troops even on this partial defeat. Bahadur Shah called a council of war on the spot; and Sufdur Khan, the commandant of cavalry, proposed that the army should be led to the attack on the following day; for (said he) having just gained a victory at Chittoor the sooner the troops are again brought into action the better. Roomy Khan, on the other hand, in command of the artillery, proposed that the army should be entrenched, and stand on the defensive, the Guzerat artillery being preferable to any then in India, owing to the excellent Portuguese guns procured from the shipping captured at Diù. The latter advice was adopted; and it was resolved that as the Guzeratties had more fire-arms than the Moguls they should fortify the camp, and in the attempts to storm their lines it was supposed the enemy would suffer so much as to give the Guzerat troops confidence, while it would inspire the Moguls with due respect. At this period the Guzerat army was joined by Alum Khan of Kalpy, who had been invested with the government of Bhilsa and Chundery. Two months elapsed without either army coming to an action, though a few skirmishers daily went forth, and exibited feats of individual courage. The Mogul horse, though unable to make any impression on the intrenchments, managed to invest the Guzerat lines so closely as to cut off their supplies. The forage in the vicinity was completely consumed, and no one dared to quit the lines on account of the Mogul archers. A famine consequently ensued. Bahadur Shah, perceiving that he must eventually be starved into a surrender, suddenly left his camp one night, accompanied by five persons only, among whom were Meeran Mahomed Khan governor of

Kandeish, and Mullo Khan governor of Malwa,* and fled to Mando, without providing, in any way for the troops. On the next morning, the army, discovering that the King had departed, broke up, and the enemy commenced and indiscriminate slaughter and plunder. Bahadur Shah, who had escaped to Mando, was pursued into that place by Hindoo Beg and seven hundred Moguls, who entered the fort at night, along with his followers, and obliged Bahadur Shah to continue his flight, with five or six horsemen, to Champanere, from whence he sent the royal jewels to Diù, and himself went to Cambay. Sufdur Khan, and Alum Khan (the governors of Kalpy and Raiseen) fled also, but some days afterwards they surrendered to the Emperor's troops. Sufdur Khan, who was wounded, entered into the imperial service, but Alum Khan, having before quitted Kalpy, suffered death. Hoomayoon having placed his officers in the fort of Mando proceeded to Champanere, and sacked the city of Mahomedabad, from whence he made forced marches to Cambay, compelling Bahadur Shah to fly to Diù. After which Hoomayoon returned and took the fortress of Champanere,† as has been related in the Dehly history.

A. H. 942.
A. D. 1535.

In the year 942, the farmers of Guzerat deputed agents to Bahadur Shah, assuring him that they were ready and willing to pay him the revenues, notwithstanding

* The Moontukhib-oot-Towareekh, with more probability, states, that his party for the flight consisted of an imperial guard of one hundred officers.

† For an account of the siege of Champanere, vide vol. ii. p. 79.

the occupation of the country by the Moguls. He accordingly sent one of his confidential chiefs with a respectable force to collect money in the different districts. The officer selected for this duty was Imad-ool-Moolk, who encamped at Ahmudabad, and collected about him a force consisting of fifty thousand men. Hoomayoon, hearing this, left Tardy Beg Khan with his division to protect the royal treasury at Champanere, and himself marched to Ahmudabad; at the same time sending a detachment, under Mirza Askurry, accompanied by Yadgar Nasir Mirza and Hindoo Beg, in advance. These troops encountered the Guzerat force near the city of Mahmoodabad, within twelve coss of Ahmudabad, where an obstinate engagement took place. Imad-ool-Moolk was defeated, and his troops suffered severely. Hoomayoon now marched on to Ahmudabad, and made the following distribution of his force: In Ahmudabad, he left Mirza Askurry; in Puttun, Yadgar Nasir Mirza; in Baroach, Kasim Hoossein Sooltan; in Baroda, Hindoo Beg; and in Champanere, Tardy Beg Khan. From Guzerat Hoomayoon marched to Boorhanpoor, and thence returned to Mando. At this period Khan Jehan Shirazy, one of the Guzerat nobles, occupying the town of Nowsary, marched in conjunction with Roomy Khan from Surat towards Baroach, which Kasim Hoossein Sooltan, conceiving himself unable to defend, abandoned, and retired to Champanere. This became the signal for a general revolt, and the subversion of the Mogul authority succeeded. Ghuzunfur Beg, one of Mirza Askurry's officers, disgusted with that prince, went to Bahadur Shah, recommending him immediately to march to Ahmudabad; and Mirza Askurry, perceiving the late arrangements of the King had failed to secure the tranquillity of the conquest, convened a meeting of the Mogul chiefs, and thus addressed them:—"The King is at present at Mando: "the arrangements for the occupation of Guzerat "not having succeeded, our presence here can be "of no use. Sheer Khan Poorby, moreover, is "collecting troops in Bengal, with the intention "of proclaiming himself King of Dehly; and I "think, therefore, we cannot do better than march "to Champanere, secure the treasure, and proceed "to Agra." The officers having agreed to this proposal, resolved to proclaim Mirza Askurry King of Agra, and to make Hindoo Beg minister. The Moguls, therefore, left Ahmudabad (which was immediately occupied by Bahadur Shah), and marched to Champanere, where Tardy Beg Khan refused to join in the confideracy, but retained his ground. The other Moguls, however, marched off to Agra, thus abandoning the kingdom of Guzerat, which had been gained by the valour of the Dehly arms in a few months, without attempting to retain it by risking a single engagement. Bahadur Shah now proceeded to wrest Champanere out of the hands of Tardy Beg, who, perceiving he could not defend the fort alone against the whole force of Guzerat, evacuated it hastily, in hopes of gaining something by following the Mogul army towards Agra.

A. H. 943. In the year 943 the Europeans who
A. D. 1536. had made settlements on the coast, were

in great force at Goa and Choul. It was, therefore, thought expedient to secure the sea-ports of Guzerat; and Bahadur Shah came to Cambay, where he heard that a fleet, in which were between four and five thousand Europeans, had arrived off the island of Diù. He immediately repaired thither with a reinforcement of troops; but the peaceable disposition the Europeans evinced threw him off his guard. The admiral of the fleet complained of severe indisposition as an excuse for not waiting on the King, while he, on the other hand, thought that their services might eventually be of use in his war with Hoomayoon Padshah. Bahadur Shah, therefore, condescended to visit the admiral on board, and was going over the side of the ship on his return, when the boat was shoved off and the King fell into the water. A European, who was leaning over the ship's side at the time, threw a boarding pike at him, which entering his skull he immediately sunk, and was drowned. The Guzerat army, on hearing of the King's death, fled, and left the Europeans in quiet possession of the island of Diù, which they have retained ever since. Thus terminated the life of Bahadur Shah of Guzerat, after a reign of eleven years and three months.

His historian had not time to complete his work, which is to be regretted, as the multiplicity of errors throughout prevents our placing so much reliance on that narrative as a revisal might have ensured.*

* The author of the Mirut-Iskundry says that the work is not intelligible.

NOTE BY THE TRANSLATOR.

The death of Bahadur Shah, who was killed by the Portuguese, is an event at once so remarkable and important that I shall be excused from entering into some detail regarding it. Ferishta, either unwilling to exculpate the Portuguese, or to condemn Bahadur Shah, took little pains to enlighten his readers on a subject which he had the means of investigating, as the circumstance happened within half a century of his own time, and it is certain he had access to the Mirut-Iskundry, because he refers to it in one part of the Guzerat history; but he did not avail himself of it to clear up the very interesting question, as to how Bahadur Shah met with his death.

The Portuguese had for many years been engaged in war with the fleets of the King of Guzerat; and Nuno de Cunha, the governor-general, who arived in India in 1529, carried out from Portugal positive instructions to make himself master of the island of Diù on the Cambay coast, belonging to the King of Guzerat. Accordingly we find that, in the latter end of the next year, he prepared that formidable expedition, consisting of fifteen thousand six hundred soldiers, embarked on board four hundred vessels of all descriptions, which assembled at Bombay, and which was repulsed off Diù, after repeated vigorous assaults, on the 17th of February, 1531. From that day, the efforts of the Portuguese to obtain a footing on Diù were unceasing; and as they found it in vain to negotiate they endeavoured to effect it by force, never ceasing to seize every vessel either belonging to Guzerat or to any of its allies. They landed, and sacked the towns of Tarapoor, Bulsar, and Surat; and at length received under their protection the Prince Chand Khan, a brother of Bahadur Shah, who having failed to support his pretensions to the throne, sought refuge with the Portuguese, through whom, as they assert, their "governor hoped to compass "some considerable advantage." In the following year, the Portuguese under James de Silveira burned the towns of Puttun Somnat, Pent, Mangalore, Tanna, Tolaja, and Moozuffurabad, carrying off four thousand slaves from those places, besides killing a great number.

"All this," observes the Portuguese historian, "encouraged "Nuno de Cunha to straiten Diù and the King of Cambaya "(Guzerat), that he might be obliged to consent to the raising a "fort in that city." In prosecution of this object, the Portuguese took and destroyed Bassein, in which place they obtained four hundred pieces of cannon, and much ammunition. They subsequently landed, and burnt Daman, Tanna, and Bombay.

At this time, Bahadur Shah was engaged in war with Hoomayoon, as we have seen, when the Portuguese governor-general deputed an embassy to wait on the latter, in order to endeavour to obtain a promise of the cession of Diù. The object of Nuno de Cunha was, by this means, to work on the fears of Bahadur Shah, and to induce him to yield to them in his distresses what he was averse to do while his power was unshaken. At last, in the year 1534, Bahadur Shah consented to terms of peace, by which he agreed,

1st, To cede in perpetuity the town of Bassein to the King of Portugal.

2dly, Not to construct any ships of war in his ports.

3dly, Not to combine with the Turkish fleets from the Red Sea, or Gulf of Persia, in attacking the Portuguese.

The historian remarks, "There were other articles in favour of "the King, to sweeten the harshness of these, which were after-"wards moderated, when he gave leave to raise the fort at Diù." Faria-e-Souza, tome i. part iv. chap. v. The following chapter is occupied in giving an account of the history of Bahadur Shah, and of his war with Hoomayoon, which only serves to show how profoundly ignorant the Portuguese were of the interior state of

India, and how little they were informed of events passing almost under their own observation.

We know that Bahadur Shah, after having lost all his dominions with the exception only of the province of Sorut, came to Diú in the utmost distress; and there yielding to the importunities of the Portuguese, he gave them permission to build a factory on the island of Diú, which was constructed in the shape of a strong fort. In consideration of this cession the Portuguese afforded Bahadur Shah the aid of five hundred Europeans, of whom fifty "were of note." This party attended the King on his return to Ahmudabad, when he succeeded in expelling the Moguls, and recovering his throne, which, the Portuguese historian remarks, was effected through their aid *alone*.

It seems likely that the cession made by Bahadur Shah to the Portuguese was for the purpose of raising a mercantile factory; whereas the latter undoubtedly intended to build, as they in fact did, a formidable fortification. From the moment Bahadur Shah discovered of what nature the building was, and having no longer any motive for keeping on terms with the Portuguese, he resolved to wrest it out of their hands. We find the Mahomedan governor of Diú shortly after constructing a wall with a rampart, calculated to place guns on, across the island, on the plea of separating the Guzeratties from the Europeans, but in reality to be used either in defending the town against the fort, or in attacking it if necessary. The construction of this wall led to vast deal of discussion, and created much ill will between the parties, till at last the King of Guzerat desisted from completing it.

This was the situation of affairs when the event occurred which ended in the death of Bahadur Shah. Ferishta, in following the historian of Bahadur Shah, has related it in a manner very unsatisfactory, and wholly unfavourable to the Portuguese. Abool Fuzl, who wrote a very few years after the event took place, has done them as little justice; but fortunately we have the account of Faria-e-Souza, who was himself in India at the time, and that of the author of the Mirut-Iskundry, whose father was an eye-witness, each endeavouring to make out the most favourable story for his own party. It would be unjust, therefore, not to allow them to tell their own stories.

The Portuguese narrative is selected from Captain John Steevens' translation of Faria-e-Souza, published in 1694; that of the Mirut-Iskundry is translated from a collated manuscript copy of the work now in the East-India House.

Extract from Faria-e-Souza's History of the Portuguese in Asia; translated by Captain John Steevens. London edit. 1694. Tome i. part iv. chapter viii.

"The King of Cambaya Badur (Bahadur Shah), who, with only the assistance of the Portuguese, had recovered his kingdom, now studied their ruin; and repenting he had granted leave to raise the fort, endeavoured to take it, and kill the commander and all the garrison. Nuno de Cunha understood his wicked design, and began to prepare to prevent it.

"That brave gentleman, Emanuel de Souza, then commanded at Diù. By him Badur designed to begin the execution. On the eighth of October, at night, a Moor came on the wall, and told Souza the King would send for him the next day to kill him; that he would not tell his name, lest it might be thought an invention to get a reward. Emanuel was long in doubt whether to go or stay; at last he resolved to go. Using at other times to have a numerous retinue well armed, he went now with only one servant, being sent for at the hour he had been before warned. The King, seeing him unconcerned, converted his malice for that time into an honourable reception, and Emanuel returned to the fort. The King's mother endeavoured to dissuade him from this wicked intention; and he thought it was better, by often visiting the Captain in the fort, to take off all suspicion, and so murder him there, and seize upon it. He was of a violent nature, and so began his first visit at an unseasonable hour of the night, not regarding the very unseasonableness was enough to render it suspicious. Souza received him upon his guard: they discoursed of things indifferent. The King went away, believing he had ensnared Souza; and he had given him a sufficient caution.* Nuno de Cunha, being advertised by Emanuel de Souza of the posture of affairs at Diù, thought it strange that he had not secured the King when in his power, and his wicked intentions were known; and that he had given out that ships were come from Portugal with great supplies.

"This invention endangered Nuno; for Badur resolved to murder him first, that he might not come to the relief of the fort when Souza was killed. He writ to him, desiring he would come to Diù about important affairs.

"Nuno, though he knew his wicked designs, made no difficult of going. He set out of Goa on the 9th January, and what with the vessels he carried, and those which followed him, appeared there with near three hundred sail. He put in at Choul, and found that Nizamaluco, induced thereto by Badur, had been there with eight thousand men, pretending it was to divert his women at sea, but in reality with an ill design on that place, which was disappointed by the care of Simon Guedez, who commanded there. At Baçaim (Bassein) he took up his brother-in-law, Anthony di Silveyra, a man of great worth, and left in his place Ruyvaz Pereyra. King Badur was at that time in the mountains hunting. Nuno sent to visit him; but he who let slip no opportunity, now especially, prevented him by sending to him first one John de St Jago, not long before a Christian, but fallen again, and become a favourite of Badur by the name of Frangue Cham. Cunha was indisposed, and feigned himself worse; so lying off of Diù, he sent to excuse himself to the King for not landing immediately.

* This passage ought to be, "though in reality he had put him on his guard."

"The King feigning great friendship presently enters into a boat, in which he had sent Nuno a present of venison. There went with him thirteen men of quality, and Emanuel de Souza, who had carried the last message from Nuno de Cunha to him. He received him on board the galleon in the best manner he could. Being seated, they discoursed of indifferent things; but the King was surprised to see a page whisper Nuno de Cunha: it was a message from Emanuel de Souza, who believing he was to be there secured, or killed, sent word that some captains were waiting his orders. The King was somewhat quieter seeing Cunha did not mind the page, and soon arose and went away. Cunha had thought it strange that Souza did not secure the King when he had him in the fort alone; and now having him aboard the galleon, he did not detain him.* Nuno ordered all the officers to accompany the King first to his palace, and then Emanuel de Souza to the fort, where he proposed to secure the King when he came to visit him, as the King, on the other side, had resolved to seize him at a dinner he had a design to invite him to, and send him to the great Turk in a cage. Emanuel de Souza was going to invite the King to the fort, while Nuno de Cunha got thither. He came up with the King's catur or barge, and made the offer by the means of Rume Cham, who at the same time advised the King not to go, because he suspected they would secure him. He slighted the caution, and bid Souza come into his barge, who stepping over, fell into the sea, but being taken up, the officers who came with him carried him to the King. At the same time came up another of our barges, and some gentlemen, who, seeing Emanuel de Souza, entered hastily into the King's. He suspecting their hasty coming aboard, together with the

* This passage should be, "Cunha thought it strange on a former occasion that Emanuel de Souza did not seize the King when he had him alone in the fort; but it seems more strange that Cunha did not now seize him when on board his vessel."

caution given by Rume Cham, ordered his officers to kill Emanuel de Souza. James de Mesquita understanding it, flew at, and wounded the King, whilst they killed that valiant captain. There was a bloody fray, in which four of our gentlemen were killed, having slain seven of the enemy. Other of our barges coming up, received some damage from a page, who shot several with the King's bow, till killed with a musket-ball. Three of the King's ships (boats) came up to rescue him. He seeing the danger began to fly, but was stopped by a cannon shot, which killed three of his men that rowed. The King thought now to escape by swimming, but being in danger of drowning, carried out, discovering who he was. Tristan de Payva de Santarem coming up, reached out to him an oar to bring him aboard his vessel, when a soldier struck him accross the face with a halbert, and so others, till he was killed. He was a little while above water and then sunk, and neither his nor Emanuel de Souza his body could be found, though Nuno de Cunha caused them to be diligently looked after, to give them the due funeral honours."

Extract from the Mirut-Iskundry.

An Account of the mode in which the Portuguese obtained a footing in Diù by stratagem, and of the martyrdom of the King by the hands of the treacherous captain, or governor, of the Portuguese.

" It is stated, that when Bahadur Shah was compelled to fly, owing to the unfortunate events which have been previously related, he came to the port of Diù. The Portuguese made offers of their assistance, and endeavoured to console him, saying, that the sea-ports along the coast were in their hands, and that they were prepared to afford an asylum to the King in any of them he might select for his residence. Bahadur Shah, owing to his distresses, received these offers with thankfulness. One day the Portuguese represented that their merchants, who were in the habit of trading to Diù, were obliged to find warehouses for their goods in separate remote parts of the town; they requested, therefore, that permission might be granted them to occupy a *hide* of land, on which they might construct an enclosure to contain and protect their goods. This request being acceded to, the King left Diù and proceeded to put down his enemies. The Portuguese, availing themselves of the King's absence, cut the hide of a cow into trips, and measured out a spot equal to the length of the thongs, where they built a strong stone fortification, on which they placed guns, and occupied it with soldiers. The instant the King heard of this, he became much disturbed, and began to consider how he should expel those infidels. He wished, however, to effect it by stratagem, so that the object might be gained with facility. He therefore proceeded from Ahmudabad to Cambay, and thence to Diù. The Portuguese concluded that this step was not undertaken without some treacherous design; and though the King did all in his power to allay their suspicions, they continued to think his conduct was hypocritical. It is stated that when the King arrived at Gogo, on the coast of Diù, he deputed Noor Mahomed Khuleel, one of the confidential officers of his court, to the Portuguese chief, with instructions to use every artifice to persuade him to come and pay a visit to the King. When this envoy met the Captain, he was thrown off his guard by the abundant civilities and attentions shown to him. While they were drinking wine together, the Captain asked Noor Mahomed Khuleel what were the King's real designs? and the envoy communicated that which ought not to have been told, and exposed the King's secret intentions. The night passed away, and on the morning the Captain said, 'I am the King's sincere friend; but owing to indisposition, I find it impossible to wait on him in person.' Noor Mahomed Khuleel returned and delivered the message. The King, supposing that the Captain was deterred from fear, resolved to go on board his vessel, on the plea of enquiring after his health, but in fact to allay his suspicions. He ordered his barge, therefore, and was accompanied by five or six of his fovourite officers: such as

Ameer Nus * Farooky,
Shooja Khan,
Lungur Khan, the son of Kadur Shah of Mando,
Alup Khan, the son of Shooja Gukkur,
Sikundur Khan, the governor of Sutwas, and
Kuns Row, the brother of Medny Row.

He directed that his attendants should not even carry arms with them; and although his ministers and officers represented that it was undignified and imprudent in the King to go, it was of no avail: for it is recorded in holy writ, that 'when death comes, it will not delay for one moment, nor will it be stopped in its progress.' He placed his foot in the barge, and set off. The Captain having laid his plans for seizing the King, proceeded towards the shore to meet him, and attended him on board his own vessel, where he began to exhibit various *apish* attentions and politeness, though treachery was at the bottom. Bahadur Shah was also contriving something of the same nature; but fortune did not second his plans, and they failed.

"During a pause in the conversation, the Portuguese *dogs* made some preconcerted signals to each other. The King perceived that he was betrayed, and that fortune and prosperity had turned their backs on him. His officers addressed him and said, 'Did not we tell you before that we should all be ruined?' He replied, 'If so, fate has ordained it.' The King now arose, and was attacked on all sides by the Portuguese. They say he was near his own boat, when a Portuguese soldier struck him over the head with a sword, and threw him into the water. Those persons who were with him also shared in the honour of martyrdom.

* This name is written the same in three MSS. in the East-India-House library, but it is probably erroneous in all of them.

"This event happened on the 3rd of the month of Rumzan, A. H. 943, (14th of February, A. D. 1537,) and has been commemorated in the following words, comprising the numerals which form the date of the year wherein it occurred; which chronogram was composed by the minister Yekhtiar Khan :—

سلطان البر شهید البحر

" 'The king of the land became a martyr at sea.'

"Bahadur Shah was twenty years of age when he ascended the throne, he reigned eleven years, and was, consequently, thirty-one years old when he was killed."

From these extracts it appears plain, that both Nuno de Cunha and Bahadur Shah were resolved each to seize the other; that the followers of both knew the intentions of their respective masters, and suspected the opposite party; so that nothing was wanting to bring about bloodshed but such an affray as arose, originating entirely out of an accident which blew the embers of suspicion and mistrust into a blaze, and produced the melancholy result which has been related.

The Turkish historian Ferdi, according to Chevalier du Hammer, relates that when Bahadur Shah was compelled to retreat to Diù, he sent his family and the royal jewels to Medina. They consisted of three hundred iron chests, the accumulated wealth acquired from the Hindoo princes of Joonagur, Champanere, Aboogur, and Chittoor, and also of the property of the King of Malwa. These gorgeous treasures never returned to India, but fell into the hands of the Grand Seignior of Constantinople, who from their possession became entitled to the appellation of Soliman the Magnificent. The celebrated waist-belt, valued at three million of aspers, which had been three times taken and re-taken in the wars in India, (vide pp. 39.—83. and 124.) was sent to Soliman by an ambassador whom Bahadur Shah deputed to Constantinople to solicit the aid of the Grand Seignior against Hoomayoon.

MEERAN MAHOMED SHAH FAROOKY.

In default of heirs, Meeran Mahomed Shah of Kandeish is raised to the throne—he dies suddenly.

On the death of Bahadur Shah, his mother, Mukdooma Jehan, left Diù, and repaired to Ahmudabad. On the road she heard of the arrival of Mahomed Zuman Mirza, who had previously proceeded to Lahore for the purpose of causing a diversion on the north-west frontier of Dehly. Having learned the death of the King, this prince put on mourning, and came to condole with the Dowager-queen, for the purpose, as it would appear, of gaining her confidence and plundering the royal treasures. After having been hospitably entertained for several days in the most splendid manner, he one night attacked and defeated the guard over the treasury, and carried away seven hundred boxes of gold, with which he made his escape, and raised a force of twelve thousand men, consisting of Moguls and Hindoostanies. The Guzerat officers, however, convening a meeting, resolved on inviting Meeran Mahomed Khan of Kandeish, nephew of Bahadur Shah, who was then in Malwa, to ascend the throne; and without further hesitation, coins were struck, and public prayers read in his name. Meanwhile Imad-ool-Moolk, at the head of a large force, marched against Mahomed Zuman Mirza, who though sufficiently ambitious, was so devoted to his pleasures, that he was attacked, and his army defeated, himself making his escape to Sind. After which period he never again interrupted the peace of Guzerat. Meeran Mahomed Shah did not long survive his elevation. Having been taken suddenly ill, on reaching Guzerat, he died after a short reign of six weeks, A. H. 943.

MAHMOOD SHAH III.

Mahmood, the son of the Prince Luteef Khan, and who had been confined in Aseer for many years, is raised to the throne—is basely assassinated by his minion Boorhan.

On the death of Meeran Mahomed Shah, there remained no heir to the crown of Guzerat excepting Mahmood Khan the son of Luteef Khan, nephew of the late Bahadur Shah, by whose order he had been confined under Meeran Mahomed Khan Farooky at Boorhanpoor, because during his uncle's reign he once aspired to the crown. In this state of affairs, the Guzerat nobles deputed Mokbil Khan, the brother of Yekhtiar Khan, to Boorhanpoor, inviting Mahmood to the capital, in order to acknowledge him as their sovereign. This measure met with opposition from Meeran Moobarik Khan, the brother of the late King; but the Guzerat chiefs marched to Boorhanpoor, and demanding the release of the Prince Mahmood, Meeran Moobarik Khan was compelled, from motives of policy, to comply with their wishes. He left
Zeekad 10. Boorhanpoor for Guzerat on the 10th of
A. H. 944. Zeekad, in the year 944, and was form-
April 5. ally crowned at Ahmudabad, and Ye-
A.D. 1538. khtiar Khan became prime minister. In the following year, Yekhtiar Khan having lost his life in an affray, Imad-ool-Moolk was created

Ameer-ool-Omra, and Duria Khan was raised to the office of prime minister ; but in the end of the same year jealousy and dissensions arose between these two nobles. Duria Khan persuaded the King to qit Ahmudabad, and proceeded, on the plea of hunting, towards Champanere. Imad-ool Moolk being thus separated from the court, collected troops and followed. The soldiers penetrating the secret object of his much demanded an advance of pay ; after which they left him in the course of three or four marches, and went over to the King. Imad-ool-Moolk, thus abandoned, was glad to compromise matters with Duria Khan, and agreed to retire quietly to his estate of Burungaum in the district of Sorut, and the King returned to

A. H. 947.
A. D. 1540.

Ahmudabad. In the year 947, Duria Khan, on learning that Imad-ool-Moolk, was again raising troops, marched against him, and the latter being defeated fled to Aseer, and placed himself under the protection of Meeran Moobarik Khan Farooky, who espoused his cause. Mahmood Shah Guzeratty now marched into Kandeish, and was opposed at some distance from Boorhanpoor, when Meeran Moobarik Khan was defeated and fled to Aseer, and Imad-ool-Moolk sought shelter with Kadur Khan, ruler of Malwa. Mahmood Shah, availing himself of his good fortune, laid waste the country of Kandeish ; and Meeran Moobarik Khan was induced to come into the Guzerat camp to ask pardon, accompanied by his most respectable nobles. The minister Duria Khan, who had no competitor at court, exercised unlimited control in the Guzerat councils; and in a short time it became apparent that Mahmood Shah had dwindled into a mere pageant.

The King, perceiving his degraded condition, made his escape one night to Dundooka, the jageer of Alum Khan Lody, who espousing his cause, collected a force of four thousand cavalry, while Duria Khan, in concert with Mohafiz Khan and some other of his relations, elevated a poor creature of low origin to the throne under the title of Moozuffur Shah, exercising authority in his name. In order to conciliate the nobility, their estates were enlarged, the salaries of public officers were increased, and the pretender with his minister marched with an army to Dowluka, where they were opposed by Alum Khan, who making a desperate charge on the advance of the enemy dispersed it; but on penetrating to the main body, after a bloody action he was obliged to retreat, not having more than five horsemen left with him. In this dilemma, however, he had presence of mind to escape without notice, and reaching the fort of Dowluka, circulated a report that Duria Khan being defeated had fled to Ahmudabad, but that as part of his army still remained firm, it became necessary to secure the gates of the fort. Duria Khan's officers hearing he had fled, lost no time in going over to the opposite party; and he, who conceived he had gained a victory, was surprised to discover that many of his officers had joined the King. Finding affairs had taken this unfavourable turn, Duria Khan conceived it prudent to retire to Boorhanpoor, from whence he eventually joined Sheer Shah at Dehly. Alum Khan, seeing himself without rivals, thought of nothing else than of usurping the crown of Guzerat; but the King, penetrating his design, obliged him to fly, and he also joined Sheer Shah. The King having now recovered his authority, caused a city to be built within twelve coss of Ahmudabad, and called it Mahmoodabad, but the place was never completed.

In this reign the fort of Surat, on the shore of the sea of Ooman, was completed by Suffy Agha Toork, commonly called Khoodabunda Khan, before which time the Europeans were in the habit of attacking the Mahomedans along that coast. They made several attempts to prevent the building of the fort of Surat, and even brought armed vessels to effect their purpose, but they were generally defeated. The work is strong and well constructed. On the two sides opposed to the land is a ditch sixty feet wide; and the curtain, which is sixty feet high, has a rampart thirty-five yards in width. The whole of the masonry is connected either by bars of iron or lead. Within the town is a beautiful building four stories high, which the Hindoos call Chowkunda, and the Europeans compare it to a Portuguese palace. Finding they could not prevent by force the construction of the fort, the Protuguese offered large sums of money to induce Khoodabunda Khan not to fortify Surat, but their gold was rejected. Mahmood Shah reigned without opposition till the

A. H. 961. A.D. 1553-4.

year 961, when he was put to death by Dowlut, at the instigation of one Boorhan, while reposing on his couch. The cause which led to this transaction will be found in the following account of the life and adventures of Boorhan :—

Boorhan was the Pesh Nimaz (private chaplain) of Mahmood Shah. The King having reason to be offended with him caused him to be built up in a mud-wall, leaving his head only exposed, with the intention of allowing him to be starved to death. Shortly after, the King passing the place, his eyes fell on Boorhan, and being still alive he made a bow, which induced the King to order him to be dug out; but the contraction of the clay and long fasting had reduced him, and bruised him to that degree that it became necessary to preserve him for a considerable time in cotton, during which the King's physicians attended him until he recovered. In spite of the King's mercy, however, Boorhan always bore malice against his sovereign, and secretly sought his life. Sometime after, during a hunting excursion, the King again became offended with Boorhan. As it is customary in the courts of all monarchs to be in favour at one time and in the back-ground at another, Boorhan was again submitted to degradation, and a second time pardoned. On his return from hunting one day the King lay down on a couch, and it, occurred to Boorhan that the present afforded a favourable opportunity for revenge. This officer while in favour at court was intrusted with the command of a band of two hundred men, called the Tiger-killers, no man being embodied in that corps who had not killed a tiger. With this band he hoped to have his revenge, and suggested to his own nephew, Dowlut, that it would be easy to kill the King while asleep, and by that means Boorhan hoped to ascend the throne of Guzerat.

Dowlut assenting to the proposal, and being in the habit of combing the King's hair, which he wore very long, he made preparations for fumigating it according to custom; but finding that the King slept soundly, he tied his locks to the bed-post, and severed his head from his body. The deed being done, Boorhan conceiving he might now reach the throne, took measures accordingly; and having ordered, in the King's name, ten of the tiger-killers into a private apartment, gave them instructions to put to death all who came in. The first persons summoned were Khoodabuanda Khan and Asuf Khan, who the moment they entered were put to death. The executioners supposed they acted by the King's orders, and the nobles imagined they were going to a private audience. Many officers thus fell victims to the snare, till at length Etimad Khan being sent for, he refused to go, as also Afzul Khan, an old nobleman, upwards of seventy years of age. Boorhan pretending that the King was offended with Khoodabunda Khan and Asuf Khan, had ordered them to be executed, and stated that Mahmood Shah had appointed Afzul Khan prime minister. To support this assertion he sent Afzul Khan an honorary dress; but the old man, suspecting treachery, refused to wear it till he saw the King. On this, Boorhan, taking him into the private apartment, where the King lay weltering in his blood, said, "Thus have "I slain him, and thus have I killed many of the "most powerful nobles, but I now appoint you "my minister." Afzul Khan was so affected and shocked at the spectacle, that he burst indignantly into the most virulent curses and imprecations on the head of the wretch who addressed him; and Boorhan, stung with shame, and boiling with rage, drew his sword, and slew that venerable nobleman on the spot. The wretch then addressing the executioners, gave them large presents and titles, and himself sat on the throne, apparently glorying in the bloody scene; after which he continued to lavish large sums of money till the following morning. Next day he gave the elephants and horses of the royal stables to fellows of the lowest description, endeavouring by this means to obtain popularity. The death of the King was no sooner known at the capital than Imad-ool-Moolk, Anwur Khan Abyssinian, and many other officers, assembled a force, and marched to dethrone Boorhan, who came forth to oppose them, having the white canopy borne over his head, and followed by the populace on whom he had bestowed the royal treasures. The conflict was short but sanguinary. On the first charge of the cavalry the mob was dispersed; and the assassin, who styled himself Boorhan Shah, was among the slain; after which his body was dragged through the streets at the foot of an elephant. The reign of Mahmood Shah lasted eighteen years, three months, and some days. In the same year, also, died Sulim, the son of Sheer Shah of Dehly, and Nizam Shah, the King of Ahmudnuggur.

Mahmood Shah was considered a just prince, fond of encouraging literature, particularly punctual in keeping public festivals, and liberal in the distribution of charity.

The most remarkable work of his age is the park wall,* fourteen miles in circumference, on the banks of the Kary, in which was plenty of game, and many pleasure-houses. Mahmood carried his fancy to such lengths, in the embellishments in this park, as to clothe the trunks of many of the trees round the pleasure-houses with green and scarlet velvets. He left no heir, having given positive instructions to all the attendants in the seraglio, that when any of the ladies became pregnant, medicines should be administered to produce abortions, rather than incur the necessity of infanticide after birth ; for he conceived this to be the only means of securing himself from the attacks of his children. It is worthy of remark, that he permitted Etimad Khan, originally a Hindoo slave, who persuaded the King he had destroyed his virility by the use of camphor, to reside within the seraglio without restraint.

The following lines, commemorating the date of the death of the three kings who died in this year, were written by the author's father, Gholam Ally Hindoo Shah :—

* This spot, situated in the neighbourhood of Surat, is particularly mentioned and described by Abool Fuzl in the Ayeen Akburry.

1.

سه خسرو را زوال آمد بیکسال
که هند از عدل شان دار الامان بود

2.

یکی محمود شه سلطان گجرات
که همچون دولت خود نوجوان بود

3.

دگر اسلام شه سلطان دهلی
که اندر عهد خود صاحب قران بود

4.

سوم آمد نظام الملک بحیری
که در ملک دکن خسرو نشان بود

5.

ز تاریخ وفات آن سه پادشه
چه می پرسی زوال خسروان بود

Three kings met with destruction in the same year,
By whose wise rule Hind was the abode of prosperity.
The first was Mahmood Shah of Guzerat,
Who like his own state was in his full prime.
The second was Islam Shah, King of Dehly,
Who in his vast domain was a type of Alexander.
The third was Nizam-ool-Moolk Bheiry,
Who in the territory of the Deccan was an example to other princes.
As to the period when these three sovereigns died,
Why ask it of me? "It was the destruction of kings."*

---

* The words زوال خسروان بود make up the number 961, the date alluded to.

AHMUD SHAH II.

Ahmud is raised to the throne by Etimad Khan—he imprudently betrays his hatred of his minister and benefactor—is found dead one morning in the streets.

MAHMOOD SHAH having left no heir, and there being no relation on whom the succession might devolve, Etimad Khan resolved, rather than see the kingdom in absolute anarchy, to elevate a youth, whom he asserted to be the son of the Prince Ahmud, formerly governor of Ahmudabad, and declared him the legal successor to the crown, Etimad Khan and Meeran Syud Moobarik Bokhary assuming the titles of protectors. The boy remained in this state of tutelage for five years ; after which, having made a friend of the second protector, Meeran Syud Moobarik Khan, he retired to Mahmoodabad, and there, in concert with some military chieftains, put himself at the head of a force, while Etimad Khan and Imad-ool-Moolk,* with several other officers of Ahmudabad, marched to oppose him. The armies met near Mahmoodabad, where Meeran Syud Moobarik Khan being killed, the King was obliged to fly ; but he subsequently

* This title in Guzerat, like Nizam-ool-Moolk and Meer Joomla in other courts, seems to have belonged to the person officiating as minister of state.

returned, and having granted jageers to most of the officers with Etimad Khan, became reconciled to that chief. The power assumed by the minister, however, created jealousy in the mind of the nobles, and a confederacy was formed at the instance of the King, at the head of which was Tartar Khan Ghoory and Imad-ool-Moolk, who one day attacked his palace, and planted cannon against it. Etimad Khan flying, made his escape to the country of Poloh, in the suburbs of the Champanere district, where having collected a force, he returned to Ahmudabad; and through the intervention of some of the officers was again acknowledged prime minister. He received, at the same time, the whole country lying between the sea and Malwa, and the rivers Mehindry and Nurbudda, in jageer. The King could not conceal his animosity against Etimad Khan; and on one occasion drawing his sword he cut a plaintain tree in twain at a blow, and said, "Would to God it had been Etimad "Khan." Shortly after this, the King was found assassinated, lying at the foot of the palace wall; and a report was spread the next day, that he had been carrying on an intrigue under the windows of some nobleman's house at night, when the master of the house, without knowing him ran out, fought him, and put him to death.

A. H. 969. A. D. 1561. The weak and inglorious reign of Ahmud Shah lasted eight years.

MOOZUFFUR SHAH III.

Etimad Khan raises a supposititious son of Mahmood II. to the throne.—The King remains a pageant in the minister's hands.—The kingdom divided among the nobles into seven provinces.—The rulers of each contend for supremacy.—Civil war in Guzerat.—Arrival of the Mirzas, the sons of Mahomed Sooltan Mirza—their extensive power—they are expelled by Chungiz Khan, governor of the southern provinces.—Chungiz Khan dies.—The Mirzas return from Malwa, and re-occupy their estates.—Etimad Khan invites Akbur into Guzerat.—The Mirzas expelled by Akbur.—Their territory occupied.—Moozuffur Shah abdicates the throne, and retires to Agra.—Moozuffur Shah, after nine years, quits Agra, and re-ascends the throne of Guzerat—is expelled, and eventually taken prisoner, and dies.

A. H. 969.
A. D. 1561.

IMMEDIATELY after the death of Ahmud Shah II., in the year 969, Etimad Khan produced a lad named Hubboo,* whom he stated to be the son of Mahmood Shah II.; asserting that his mother had concealed the circumstance of her pregnancy till the fifth month, when the medicines given to produce an abortion having no effect the child was born, but brought up privately; to which facts he procured witnesses to swear. This testimony being received as sufficiently satisfactory, the boy was duly crowned, under the name of Moozuffur Shah III.; and Etimad

* Familiar contraction of Hubeeb.

Khan was appointed sole protector, with the title of Vizier. The kingdom of Guzerat was now subdivided into separate provinces, and allotted to the several officers in the following manner:—

The Puttun district as far south as Kurry was allotted to Moosy Khan and Sheer Khan Folady.

The districts of Radunpoor, Neriad, and Tehrwara, as far as Moonjpoor, were made over to Futteh Khan Buloch.

The districts between the Saburmutty and Mehindry rivers were reserved by Etimad Khan for himself.

The province of Surat, and the districts of Nandote and Champanere, to Chungiz Khan.

The province of Baroach to Roostoom Khan, the nephew of Chungiz Khan.

The districts of Dowluka and Dundooka to Syud Meeran, the son of Syud Moobarik Khan Bokhary.

The province of Sorut, including the fort of Joonagur, to Ameer Khan Goony, who afterwards withdrew from the confederacy. Matters being thus arranged, Etimad Khan retained Moozuffur Shah as a sort of state-prisoner; but he was daily exhibited at court sitting upon the throne; and though the minister went through the form of saluting him, many of the chiefs refused to do so. Things continued for some time in this state, till at length Chungiz Khan governor of Surat, and Sheer Khan Folady of Puttun, came to reside at the capital. Sometime after a dispute arising between the civil officers of the Puttun and Radunpoor divisions, the governors in support of their servants made war on each other; and the latter chief being defeated, Futteh Khan Buloch joined Etimad Khan at the capital, who immediately marched to attack Sheer Khan Folady. Sheer Khan, unable to oppose him in the field, took shelter in the fort of Puttun, and made overtures for accommodation; but these not being attended to, the inhabitants of Puttun finding they had no remedy resolved to fight; and marching out with less than three thousand cavalry, attacked Etimad Khan's army, consisting of thirty thousand horse, with a desperation for which the latter were unprepared. Etimad Khan's army was defeated, and sought safety in flight. Hajy Khan, an officer who had joined Etimad Khan from Delhy, and who command his troops, abandoned his cause, and joined the Foladies. Notwithstanding the defection of Hajy Khan from his party, he demanded to be allowed to enjoy the revenue of his estate, which was in the hands of Etimad Khan. To this the latter refused his assent, till compelled to do so by the Foladies, who marched to occupy it. The Foladies were opposed by Etimad Khan at Chowt'hana, where he was defeated a second time, and fled to Baroach. Etimad Khan now entreated the assistance of Chungiz Khan, through whose mediation a peace was concluded, and Hajy Khan's estate was restored. The reverses which Etimad Khan had sustained induced Chungiz Khan to write to him on the subject of the person whom he styled Moozuffur Shah, saying, "You have placed upon the throne a boy "whom nobody knows, but whom you declare to "be the son of Mahmood Shah: if this be true, "how is it you prevent his communicating with "any one but yourself, and how do you venture "to sit in his presence, which I am informed you "are in the habit of doing? If, on the other hand, "he is not the son of Moozuffur Shah, by what "authority did you impose upon the nation, by "swearing that he was heir to the crown?" Etimad Khan replied, that it was sufficient that he himself knew the circumstances of his birth; observing that Chungiz Khan's father, if alive, could also swear to the facts alleged by him, and to the identity of the King's person; that it therefore behoved him to treat him with the respect which his father had always paid to the late king. Sheer Khan Folady, becoming acquainted with this correspondence, made overtures to Chungiz Khan to seize Etimad Khan, recommending, in the mean time, that no measures of hostility should yet be undertaken. Chungiz Khan, who had now become acquainted with the timidity of Etimad Khan's character, despised him, and merely demanded an increased portion of territory to support the troops which had collected about him. Etimad Khan, unwilling to refuse, pointed out to him the district of Nundoorbar, on the banks of the tapty, which had been usurped by the ruler of Kandeish during the late anarchy in Guzerat; observing that the King was entitled to recover it, either by negotiation or by force. The object of Etimad Khan was to get rid of the importunities of Chungiz Khan, and to direct his attention towards Kandeish instead of Guzerat; hoping that he would be induced, if successful, to attempt the conquest of Kandeish, or if unsuccessful, that he might be subdued: in either of which cases Etimad Khan would get rid of a formidable rival. Chungiz Khan caught at the idea; and having occupied Nundoorbar in the year 974, was tempted to march on to Talnere, where he learned that Mahomed Shah Farooky, the son of Meeran Moobrik Shah, accompanied by Toofal Khan, governor of Berar, was in full march to oppose him. Chungiz Khan occupied a strong position among the broken ground and heights near Talnere, and placed his artillery and his baggage carts in the roads which run along the ravines leading towards it.* Meeran Moobarik Shah Farooky arrived at daylight, but delayed attacking till he had reconnoitred Chungiz Khan's position, whom he could by no means induce to quit his advantageous post. At night, however, he commenced his retreat towards Baroach, and was so closely pursued by the Kandeish troops, that all his baggage and artillery fell into their hands. Nundoorbar was immediately retaken, and a strong garrison placed therein. At this period the sons of Mahomed Sooltan Mirza, five in number, who had been confined in the fort of Sumbhul, by order of Akbur Padshah, when that monarch marched in the year 975 for the purpose of subduing Malwa, now made their escape, and sought an asylum with Chungiz Khan at Baroach. In this history they

A. H. 974.
A. D. 1566.

A. H. 975.
A. D. 1567.

* This accurately describes the approaches to Talnere.

are styled *The Mirzas:** their names are as follow:—

Mahomed Hoossein Mirza,
Ibrahim Hoossein Mirza,
Musaood Hoossein Mirza,
Alugh Mirza,
Shah Mirza.

Chungiz Khan conceived that by receiving among his dependents these fugitives he should add to the respectability of his government, and did not hesitate to enrol them among the number of his officers, assigning to them estates out of his own district; and sometime afterwards he marched, accompanied by the Mirzas, to subvert the power of Etimad Khan at the capital. In the first instance he took possession of Baroda without opposition; and having arrived at Mahmoodabad, within fifteen coss of Ahmudabad, he wrote to Etimad Khan, saying,—

"It is well known to all the world that my "attack on Talnere was in consequence of your "advice, and my defeat on that occasion arose "from your withholding reinforcements. I now "write to inform you, that I am thus far on my "road to pay my respects to the King; and "as it seems likely, if you are in the city "of Ahmudabad on my arrival, quarrels may "ensue between one soldiers even in the streets, "I recommend, in order to prevent the oc-"currence of such an event, that you imme-

* The history of these princes is fully detailed in the reign of Akbur, in the second volume of this work.

"diately quit the capital and retire to your own "estates, permitting the King to retain around "his person such people only as may be most ac- "ceptable to him." Etimad Khan, previously to the receipt of this communication, had collected the army, and marched, with Moozuffur Shah at its head, to the town of Kunoory, twelve miles from Mahmoodabad, where his and Chungiz Khan's troops met; but Etimad Khan is said to have been so dismayed at the appearance of Chungiz Khan's force, that he fled to Dongurpoor before the cavalry had even drawn their swords; and his officers, no doubt approving his conduct, followed his good example, and took different routes. A few only remained with the King, and escorted him back to Ahmudabad. Chungiz Khan marching on encamped at Butwa; and the King on the next day flying from his capital, Chungiz Khan entered and took possession. Sheer Khan Folady, who had formerly concerted with Chungiz Khan the downfall of Etimad Khan, apprehensive that the whole of the latter chief's estates would fall into the hands of the former, insisted on an equal partition, and marched to enforce his demand. Chungiz Khan, deeming it imprudent to dispute the point with Sheer Khan, ceded to him all the country westward of the Saburmutty. Meeran Mahomed Khan, who had defeated Chungiz Khan at Talnere, ventured now to penetrate into the centre of Guzerat, and arrived without opposition within a few miles of the capital. Chungiz Khan, however, having attacked and completely defeated him, compelled him to retreat to Aseer. After this event, Chungiz Khan gave up the territory contiguous to Baroach for the support of the Dehly princes, who were shortly after joined by Shurf-ood-Deen Hoossein Mirza, the son-in-law of Hoomayoon Padshah, and who had lately escaped from the court of Akbur. It was not long before the Mirzas began to complain that the estates allotted to them were insufficient for their support, and seized on other places without consulting Chungiz Khan; and he was obliged to oppose them with ten thousand men. The Mirzas did not hesitate to meet this force; and having defeated it, followed up their success, and took many prisoners, both Abyssinians and Guzeratties. Those who were young and beardless were retained as personal attendants, and the more aged were put to death under the most cruel and indecent tortures; some few only were permitted to depart alive. The Mirzas, however, perceiving that Chungiz Khan was making serious preparations to attack them, marched to Boorhanpoor, and having plundered it, proceeded thence into Malwa. The remaining part of the history of the Mirzas has been related in its proper place.* Shortly after this event, the officers who held the person of the King in subjection delivered him over to Etimad Khan at Dongurpoor, and remained some time with him; but his reduced circumstances having prevented his complying with the demands they made on him, they left Dongurpoor; and Hijaz Khan, Alugh Khan, and Seif-ool-Moolk,

* Vol. ii. reign of Akbur Padshah.

with some others, going to Ahmudabad, joined Chungiz Khan. Some time afterwards, a confidential servant informed these officers that Chungiz Khan intended to invite them to play at chowgan* on the next day, when he proposed to seize and put them to death. "If," said they, "Chungiz Khan should go to the palace, and "send for you there, your cases will be more "desperate, since you will then have no oppor- "tunity to make your escape." The chiefs had scarcely obtained this information, when a servant of Chungiz Khan entering, said that his excellency proposed going out on the following day to play chowgan, and that he requested they would all be of the party. The officers who had lately abandoned Etimad Khan now concerted measures for their own safety; and on the next day, when they attended at the palace to accompany Chungiz Khan to the chowgan plain, Hijaz Khan took the right hand, and Alugh Khan the left, as they entered the play-ground, when giving each other a nod, Hijaz Khan drew his sword, and galloping up to Chungiz Khan, with a single blow struck off his head. The persons engaged in this transaction were, for the most part, Abyssinians. They immediately left the play-ground, and retiring to their own houses, prepared to oppose Chungiz Khan's party; but his nephew, Roostoom Khan, having collected the troops, caused the corpse of his uncle to be raised on his own elephant, and retired to Baroach, while the successful Abyssinians,

* This game has been described, vol. i. p. 199., in a note.

plundering the palace, wrote to Etimad Khan, inviting him to join them from Dongurpoor. Etimad Khan shortly after arrived with the King. The Mirzas, who had taken possession of part of the Malwa territory, on hearing of the death of Chungiz Khan, marched to re-occupy the countries of Surat and Baroach. Roostoom Khan defended the estates for two years, but was at last obliged to come to terms with them. On the first intimation of the advance of the Mirzas, Etimad Khan wrote to Sheer Khan Folady of Puttun, asking his advice; on which it was agreed that an army, consisting of three divisions, should be immediately assembled to expel them: that the first division should proceed in advance under Alugh Khan, an Abyssinian; the second under Etimad Khan, and the reserve under Sheer Khan Folady, to bring up the rear. The first division, under Alugh Khan, marched to Mahmoodabad, but Etimad Khan, with his accustomed cowardice, threw obstacles in the progress of the second corps, which he commanded, and refused to move; and Alugh Khan and the Abyssinians, disgusted at his pusillanimity, resolved to provide for themselves, by seizing on the districts of Cambay and Pitlaud. This measure, however, was frustrated by a quarrel which ensued between Alugh Khan and Hijaz Khan. The crafty Etimad Khan, taking advantage of this circumstance, induced Hijaz Khan to come to Ahmudabad, and to leave Alugh Khan to join Sheer Khan Folady. Amid these dissensions the King fled from Ahmudabad, and joined the Foladies at Gheiaspoor, near

Surkech. Etimad Khan now proposed to Sheer Khan that they should invite the Mirzas, then at Baroach, to assume the reins of government; but Sheer Khan not assenting, Etimad Khan sent an agent to Akbur Padshah of Dehly, inviting him to occupy Guzerat, and add it to the territory of Dehly, as in former times. Akbur having at this period, viz. A. H. 980, reached Nagoor

A. H. 980.
A. D. 1572.

on his march to the southward, detached Peer Mahomed Khan to reduce Sirohy, where he was met by the Guzerat agents, upon which he lost no time in advancing on the capital of that kingdom. Sheer Khan Folady fled, and the Mirzas, who were at Ahmudabad, retired to Baroda and Baroach. Etimad Khan, and Alugh Khan the Abyssinian, alone had the honour of kissing the King's hands, and were enrolled in the list of the Dehly nobility;

Rujub 14.
A. H. 980.
Nov. 20.
A. D. 1572.

while the kingdom of Guzerat was dissolved and re-united to Dehly, as a province of the empire of Hindoostan, on the 14th of Rujub, of the year 980.

Moozuffur Shah abdicated his throne in favour of Akbur, and was sent to Agra in the first instance, but was subsequently given over in charge to Moonyim Khan, to accompany that nobleman on his assuming charge of the government of Bengal. Akbur, however, shortly after, remanded Moozuffur Shah into close confinement; from which he not only effected his escape, but flying into Guzerat, collected a respectable force, attacked the viceroy, Kootb-ood-Deen Khan, and slew him in action; and after an imprisonment of nearly nine years re-ascended the throne of Guzerat. His reign was, however, of short duration; for in the year 991, Akbur having deputed Mirza Khan, Khan Khanan, the son of Beiram Khan, to retake the kingdom of Guzerat, Moozuffur Shah was defeated in a pitched battle, and fled to Joonagur. The checkered and unfortunate reign of Moozuffur Shah lasted for thirteen years and some months (exclusive of nine years' confinement), and his downfall terminated the dynasty of the Mahomedan kings of Guzerat; since which period that kingdom has been considered as a province of Dehly, and the Emperor appoints a governor from his own court.

A. H. 991.
A. D. 1583.

To face page 167. Vol. IV.]

GENEALOGY OF THE GHOORY AND KHILJY DYNASTIES OF MALWA.

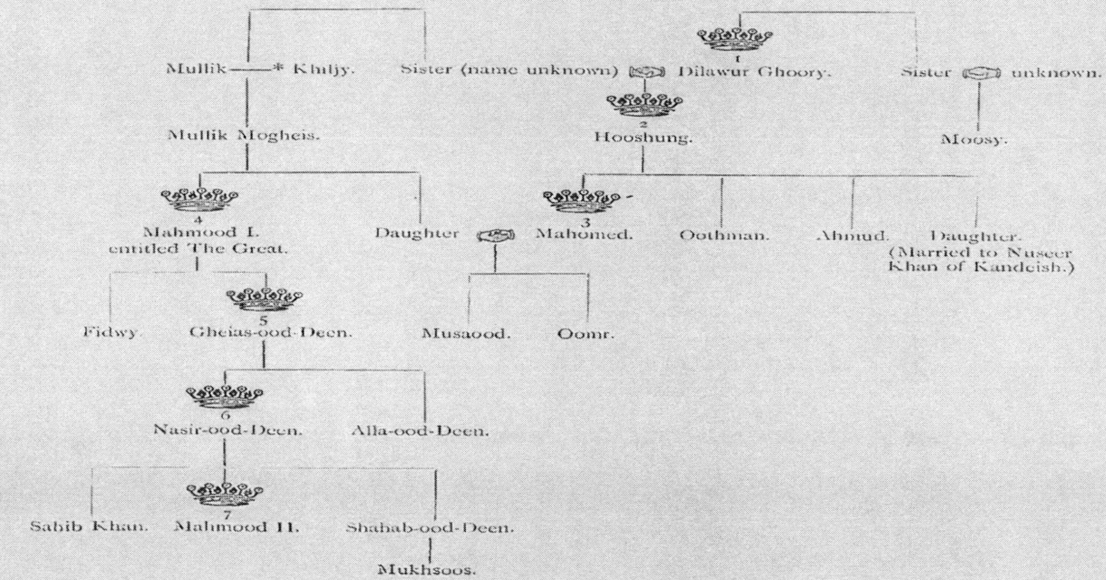

* The name of Mullik Mogheis's father is not mentioned.

CHAPTER V.

HISTORY OF THE KINGS OF MALWA.

SOOLTAN DILAWUR GHOORY.

The origin of his coming to Malwa explained.—He receives Mahmood Toghluk of Dehly after his expulsion by Tamerlane.—Mahmood returns to his capital.—Dilawur assumes the title of Shah, and causes himself to be acknowledged King of Malwa.—Death of Dilawur Shah Ghoory..

THE country of Malwa is extensive, and according to the best authorities has always been governed by independent rajas. It is bounded on the south by the river Nurbudda, on the north it has the Chumbul ;* to the west is Guzerat, and on the east are the districts of Bundelkund and Gurra Mundla. The Hindoo histories go back as far as the reign of Bikramajeet,† after whom reigned

* Ferishta evidently means, that after Guzerat ceases to be the western boundary about Kota, thence the Chumbul running in a north-easterly direction towards the Jumna forms the northern limit of Malwa.

† The accession of this monarch has given rise to an era which commences fifty-six years before Christ.

Raja Bhoj and many others, who are all mentioned among the rajas of Hindoostan. During the reign of Gheias-ood-Deen Bulbun of Dehly, in the year 710, the Mahomedans first invaded
A. H. 710. A. D. 1310 and conquered the province of Malwa; after which it acknowledged allegiance to that crown until the reign of Maho-
A. H. 789. A. D. 1387. med II., the son of Feroze Toghluk, A. H. 789.

At this period Dilawur Khan Ghoory, whose real name was Hussun, a descendant on his mother's side from Sooltan Shahab-ood-Deen Ghoory of Damascus, was appointed governor of Malwa, previously to the accession of Mahomed the son of Feroze, and he subsequently established his independence. After him eleven princes reigned until the time of Hoomayoon Padshah, in the year 977 (A. D. 1569), at which period Bahâdur Shah of Guzerat, and, some years after, Akbur Padshah, made incursions into Malwa; and the latter eventually subdued the kingdom, and attached it again to the Dehly government.

Dilawur Khan on assuming independence took up his residence at D'har, and very shortly afterwards brought under his subjection all the petty rajas of the province; but although he considered D'har as the seat of his government, he frequently visited the city of Mando, remaining there sometimes for months together.

In the year 801, Mahmood Toghluk
A. H. 801. A. D. 1398. being driven from his throne by Ameer Teimoor Korkan, made his escape from Dehly and fled to Guzerat; but not being received

by Moozuffur Shah in the manner he expected, he became disgusted, and sought protection in Malwa. On his arrival at the frontier, Dilawur Khan sent some of his relations, and the most respectable officers of his government, to meet the exiled monarch, and to pay him such attentions as were due to the elevated situation from which he had so lately fallen. On his approach within three marches of D'har, Dilawur Khan himself went forward, and meeting him, accompanied him to his capital, where he proffered for his acceptance all his wealth, both in specie and in jewels; declaring they were much at his service, and that both he and all his family considered themselves his Majesty's subjects. Alp Khan, the son of Dilawur Khan, disapproving of these acts of courtesy, quitted D'har on the first intimation of his father's intentions, and retired to Mando, where he remained during the residence of Mahmood Toghluk in Malwa. It was at this time he laid the foundation of that celebrated fortress which was afterwards completed by him. The work is constructed of solid masonry, and is deemed one of the strongest fortifications in that part of the world.

A. H. 804. A. D. 1401. In the year 804 Mahmood Toghluk, at the instance of the Dehly nobles, quitted Malwa, in order to resume the reins of his own government, taking from Dilawur Khan such a quantity of money and jewels as he deemed requisite. On his departure, Alp Khan returned and joined his father at D'har, after an absence of nearly three years. Dilawur Khan, at the instance of his son, shortly afterwards assumed royal state and titles; such as the white canopy and scarlet pavilion, and coining money: he caused public prayers to be read in his name.

It is said that the grandfather of Dilawur Khan came from Ghoor, and held a high office under the Dehly government; that his father was enrolled among the nobility, and received a title; and that Dilawur Khan himself attained the highest rank in the reign of Feroze Toghluk. During that of his successor, Mahomed, he was nominated to the government of Malwa; and in the reign of Mahmood, in the year 804,
A. H. 804. A. D. 1401. he assumed royalty, and divided his kingdom into estates among his officers, whom he ennobled. Dilawur Khan only survived his assumption of the royal titles four years; for in the year 808 he died suddenly; and
A. H. 808. A. D. 1405. some historians have even asserted that he was poisoned by his eldest son and successor; but the accusation seems unsupported by any well-authenticated proof, and has been, in consequence, generally doubted.

SOOLTAN HOOSHUNG GHOORY.

Ascends his father's throne—is accused of posioning his father—is attacked by Moozuffur Shah I. King of Guzerat—is taken prisoner, and the government placed in the hands of Noosrut Khan.—The inhabitants of Malwa revolt from Noosrut Khan, who is obliged to fly.—Sooltan Hooshung is released, and restored to his throne—he invades Guzerat, and supports a pretender to the crown.—Ahmud Shah invades Malwa.—Battle of Sarungpoor.—Retreat of Ahmud Shah. Sooltan Hooshung besieges Gualiar—besieges Kalpy, and makes the governor submit to his authority—wrests Kehrla out of the hands of the Hindoo raja.—Sooltan Hooshung appoints his son, Ghizny Khan, his successor, and dies.

AFTER the death of his father, Alp Khan assumed the title of King of Malwa, under the name of Sooltan Hooshung Ghoory, and the nobles coming to court, paid their allegiance; but a rumour being prevalent at the time, that his father had been assassinated by him,* Moozuffur Shah of Guzerat, in consideration of the intimacy which had subsisted between him and the late king, marched against Sooltan Hooshung; and in the beginning of the year 810, Moozuffur Shah reached the fort of D'har without resistance, where Sooltan

A. H. 810.
A. D. 1407.

* I have met with no details of this dark event; but the defection of the Malwa officers, and the attack made by the King of Guzerat, on the ostensible ground of deposing the murderer of a father, lead to strong suspicions against Hooshung, although Ferishta states that the accusation against him is generally doubted.

Hooshung opposed him. The armies came to action on the plain in front of the town, and engaged with mutual ardour; on which occasion Moozuffur Shah was wounded, and Sooltan Hooshung was unhorsed; but the troops still continued to fight desperately, till at length fickle fortune, who does not always favour the bravest, turned the scale in favour of Guzerat. Sooltan Hooshung threw himself into the fort of D'har, wherein he was closely besieged by the Guzeratties; but conceiving himself unable to cope with success against Moozuffur Shah, he surrendered at discretion.

Sooltan Hooshung was delivered over in charge to some of the Guzerat nobles, and Noosrut Khan,* the victorious King's brother, was left in charge of the government of Malwa, with a strong detachment from the Guzerat force; and the Malwa troops were directed to obey him as their leader. Moozuffur Shah then retired to Guzerat. Noosrut Khan, extorting large sums of money, and otherwise oppressing the inhabitants, created universal disaffection; so that Moozuffur Shah had scarcely retired from Malwa when Noosrut Khan, apprehensive of remaining longer in D'har, commenced his retreat to Guzerat; while the Malwa army, taking advantage of the circumstance, attacked and destroyed part of his force. The Malwites, however, dreading the vengeance of Moozuffur Shah, abandoned D'har, and took refuge in Mando, where they considered themselves

* He is also called Shums Khan, and appears to have been the possessor of Nagoor, which descended to his children, as appears in the Guzerat history.

safe, and created Moosy Khan, nephew of the late Dilawur Khan, their leader. When this information reached Guzerat, Sooltan Hooshung, although a state-prisoner, wrote a letter with his own hand to Moozuffur Shah, saying, "Considering your Majesty as my father and uncle, I am "induced thus to address you. The insinuations "with which interested persons have assailed "your royal ear, I take God to witness, are false. "It is now reported that the chiefs of Malwa, "forgetting their duty to the respectable Noosrut "Khan, have insulted him by electing Moosy "Khan as their leader, and that having usurped "the control over the territory of Malwa, they "breathe the spirit of defiance. If your Majesty "will condescend to raise me from the dust to "which I have fallen, it is possible that I may "recover the usurped domininon." Moozuffur Shah, after imposing certain conditions on Sooltan Hooshung, released him from confinement, and ordered his grandson, the Prince Ahmud, to reinstate him on his throne. In the

A. H. 811.
A. D. 1408.

year 811, Prince Ahmud, accompanied by Sooltan Hooshung, left Guzerat, and proceeded direct to D'har, which they soon reduced; and having reinstated Sooltan Hooshung in his authority, the Prince Ahmud returned to Guzerat. Sooltan Hooshung remained for some days in the city of D'har, where being shortly after joined by many of the Malwa officers, he sent communications to those in Mando, many of whom rejoiced at his arrival, and were ready to join him; but their families being in the fort they were unwilling to abandon them, and were, therefore, unable immediately to form that junction which they so much desired. Sooltan Hooshung collected a small force and laid siege to Mando; but having lost a number of men without gaining any advantage, he conceived it better to disperse his army into separate detachments, in order to occupy the towns in the different districts.

In the mean time, Mullik Mogheis, the cousin of Sooltan Hooshung, held a private consultation with Mullik Khizr, commonly called Meean Agha, saying, "Notwithstanding Moosy Khan is a fine "young man, and is also my cousin, yet in point "of courage, ability, and good judgment, Hoo-"shung has borne away the palm from the rest of "the family. We have the means of putting him "in possession of the throne, and I am desirous of "promoting the object, both on account of his "character and claims, as well as on account of "my affection for him, for he was brought up "principally under my own mother's charge." Meean Agha approving of the measure, they both quitted the fort during the night, and came direct to Sooltan Hooshung, who appointed Mullik Mogheis his minister and deputy during his absence, if such ever took place again. Moosy Khan having learned what had occurred, and despairing of maintaining his authority, abandoned the fort to Sooltan Hooshung, who assumed the government of Malwa.

A. H. 813. A. D. 1410. In the year 813, Moozuffur Shah of Guzerat dying, his grandson, the Prince Ahmud, succeeded to the throne, according to the will of his grandsire. On this occasion Feroze Khan and Heibut Khan, sons* of the late king, and uncles to Ahmud Shah, having determined to oppose him, raised troops in Baroach, and invited Sooltan Hooshung to march to their assistance. Hooshung, unmindful of the generosity of Moozuffur Shah, and forgetting the personal obligations he owed to Ahmud Shah, recollected only the first cause of the invasion of Malwa, and therefore resolved to march and lay waste part of Guzerat. Ahmud Shah having taken timely precautions, marched with a large force direct to Baroach, where the pretender and his brother were reduced to throw themselves on his mercy, while Sooltan Hooshung returned immediately to D'har. But so restless was the disposition of this prince, or so inveterate his enmity to the King of Guzerat, that he shortly afterwards involved himself in a new war.

A. H. 816.
A. D. 1413.

In the year 816, having heard that Ahmud Shah had marched against the Raja of Julwara, and invested his capital, Sooltan Hooshung, in spite of the gratitude he owed the King of Guzerat, led an army into his territory, and laid it waste. Ahmud Shah for the present postponed the attack on Julwara, and sent his troops to the east, towards Champanere, when Sooltan Hooshung fled with precipitation to Malwa. At this poriod, Mullik Nuseer, the elder son of the late ruler of Kandeish, having seized on Talnere, the hereditary estate of his younger brother, Mahomed Iftikhar, the latter

* It has been explained in vol. iv. p. 12. that these princes were the sons of Noosrut Khan, called also Shums Khan Dundany, and consequently the nephews of Moozuffur Shah.

solicited the aid of Sooltan Hooshung, who sent his son Ghizny Khan with fifteen hundred cavalry to the south, when having secured the fort of Talnere, he proceeded to attack Sooltan-poor, a district of Guzerat; but on the approach of Ahmud Shah, the Prince of Malwa retreated. Ahmud Shah had no sooner gone to Sooltanpoor than the rajas of Guzerat, particularly those of Julwara, Champanere, Nandote, and Idur, taking advantage of his absence, wrote letters to Sooltan Hooshung, saying, that although they had not succeeded in their last attempt, yet if he would now invade Guzerat, they were prepared to assist him with all their forces; promising, at the same time, that they would furnish guides to lead his army by an unfrequented route into the centre of Guzerat, without Ahmud Shah's knowledge. Sooltan Hooshung, resolved to wipe away the stain which his character had sustained in his late unsuccessful invasion of Guzerat, collected his army, and marching in the year

A. H. 821.
A. D. 1418.

821, entered the country by the route of Mahrasa. Meanwhile, Ahmud Shah having reached Sooltanpoor, Ghizny Khan fled precipitately to Malwa, and Mullik Nuseer to Aseer; but Ahmud Shah was surprised to hear that the King of Malwa had in the interim arrived at Mahrasa. Without a moment's delay, Ahmud Shah commenced his return to Guzerat, in spite of the heavy rain which fell at that time; and by rapid marches arrived in the vicinity of his capital, before information of his approach was brought to Sooltan Hooshung by the rajas.

He accordingly sent for those chiefs at whose invitation he had entered into the confederacy, and accused them of treachery in concealing from him the fact of Ahmud Shah's near approach, and made their silence an excuse to retreat by the same route he had advanced, abandoning the rajas, and leaving them to make their way to their different districts, overwhelmed with chagrin and disappointment. On Ahmud Shah's arrival at Mahrasa he halted only a sufficient time to refresh his troops, and then marching into Malwa, he penetrated as far as the town of Calliada near Oojein. Here he was opposed by Sooltan Hooshung, who was defeated, and fled to Mando, pursued by the Guzerat cavalry to the very gates of the fort, while Ahmud Shah followed as far as Nalcha. At this place he halted for some time, sending his light cavalry to scour the country, aware that the fort of Mando was too strong for him to attack with success. Ahmud Shah, therefore, conceived it prudent to confine his operations to D'har, to which place he marched; thence he intended to return to Oojein, but the rainy season setting in, his ministers advised him to defer the conquest of Malwa till the next year, when the campaign might be opened under every advantage; so that he returned to Guzerat in the year 822.

A. H. 822.
A. D. 1419.

Sooltan Hooshung had long evinced great partiality towards Mullik Mahmood, the son of his cousin Mullik Mogheis, and was at this time induced to confer on him the title of Khan, and the office of his father's deputy. He also directed that whenever he should take the field this young man should accompany him, while Mullik Mogheis remained at the capital. In the latter end of the year, Ahmud Shah returned for the purpose of completing the conquest of Malwa; but no Sooltan Hooshung sending ambassadors with magnificent presents to appease his wrath, he accepted terms, and returned to Ahmudabad.

A. H. 823.
A. D. 1420.

In the year 823, Sooltan Hooshung marched to the fort of Kehrla, on the frontier of Berar, and the Raja Nursing Ray, opposed him with an army of fifty thousand men. A severe action ensued, wherein the Mahomedans were victorious; and Nursing Ray being slain, they besieged the fort of Sarungur, and took eighty-four elephants, together with all the Ray's treasures. Nursing Ray's son, being in this fort, signed a treaty, by which he consented to pay an annual tribute to the King of Malwa, after which the latter returned to Mando laden with booty.

A. H. 825.
A. D. 1421.

In the year 825 he left Mando with one thousand chosen cavalry, assuming the character of a merchant, and marched to Jajnuggur, one month's journey from Malwa. In order the better to conceal his object, he took with him horses of different colours; viz. bright bay, bright chestnut, and different shades of grey, such as the Prince of Jajnuggur was known to admire most, and many other kinds of merchandise considered scarce in his country, which the King intended to barter for elephants. The pretended merchants having arrived, the Raja, according to the custom of his country, intimated his intention first of all to inspect the linen goods, and then either to purchase them with money, or to barter elephants for them. The appointed day arrived, and the goods were spread out on the ground; but on account of the heavy appearance of the weather, Sooltan Hooshung told the people that the articles would be damaged if rain came on. The Raja's servants, however, insisted on their remaining exposed till their master came; at the same time, the horses also were all saddled for inspection. The Raja at length arrived, and a thunder-storm coming on shortly after, the elephants of his cavalcade trampled over the merchandise, which was much damaged. Sooltan Hooshung, smarting under the loss he had sustained, ordered his followers to mount, and without hesitation attacked the Raja's escort, many of whom were slain, and the Prince himself taken prisoner; after which Sooltan Hooshung informed him of his real rank. Thus situated, the Raja of Jajnuggur purchased his liberty with seventy-five large elephants; but Sooltan Hooshung obliged him, as a measure of precaution, to accompany him as far as the confines of his country, whence he permitted him to return, but not without having received from him a few more of his finest elephants.* On his

* However romantic the whole of this expedition may appear, the fact of its occurrence is so fully authenticated by all contemporary authors that it can hardly be doubted. Elephants, so important in the warfare of those days, were

approach to Malwa, Sooltan Hooshung, hearing that Ahmud Shah of Guzerat had invaded the kingdom, and was now absolutely employed in the attack of Mando, entertained fears for the fate of the capital. On his arrival at Kehrla he induced the Raja to join him with his troops, after which Hooshung seized his person, and placed him in close confinement, by which means the King secured the fort of Kehrla, and left a garrison of his own troops therein, in order to ensure a position to fall back upon in case Mando should fall. Having taken these steps he marched to Mando, and entered the fort by the Tarapoor gate, on the south face. This fortification being one of the most extraordinary in the world, I think it proper in this place to give some description of it. It is built on the summit of an insulated mountain, said to be nineteen coss in circumference (28 miles). The place of a regular ditch is supplied by a deep ravine, formed by nature round the fortification, which is so deep that it seems impossible to take the fort by regular approaches. Within the forts is abundance of water and forage, though there is not sufficient space for the purposes of cultivation. Any army besieging Mando must confine its operations chiefly to blockading the roads; for it is scarcely possible to invest a place of such extent. Many of the roads from the fort are steep, and difficult of access. That leading to the south,

absolutely necessary to enable Hooshung to oppose the King of Guzerat in the field; and the King of Malwa probably thought no person so fit to select them as himself.

known by the name of the Tarapoor gate, is so rough and steep that cavalry can with difficulty be led up, and on whatever side it is approached a pass must be surmounted; so that the enemy's force, though it occupies the several accessible roads, is necessarily divided, and one party may be cut off without receiving assistance from another. The road on the north leading to the Dehly gate is by far the most easy of access. Ahmud Shah, finding it useless to besiege a fort of this nature, sent out detachments from the army to occupy the surrounding country, himself marching through Oojein towards Sarungpoor. Sooltan Hooshung took advantage of his retreat to make forced marches by a more direct route; and reaching Sarungpoor before him, he sent a communication to the King of Guzerat, in order to delay his approach, saying, "The blood of the "faithful depends on us; let us restrain, then, our "hands from mutually destroying the true believ-"ers. I beseech you, therefore, to desist from this "warfare, and return to Guzerat; meanwhile let "hostilities cease, and receive my ambassador with "the usual offerings, who has power to conclude "an eternal peace between us." Ahmud Shah, relying with confidence on so solemn an appeal, neglected the ordinary military precautions necessary in an enemy's country; and Sooltan Hooshung, availing himself of the circumstance, marched with his army on the 14 of Mohurrum, in the year 826, and made a night-attack upon the Guzerat came; the consequence was,

Mohurrum 14. A. H. 826. Dec. 29. A. D. 1422.

that many of the Guzeratties were killed without opposition. The Malwites penetrated to the royal pavilion of Ahmud Shah, which was guarded by five hundred Rajpoots under the command of Savunt Ray, Raja of Dundooka, afterwards known by the name of the Kurry Raja. These brave men fought desperately, and were nearly all destroyed. Their gallantry alone enabled Ahmud Shah to make his escape under cover of the night; but he remained on the skirts of the camp, actively employed in collecting his dispersed soldiers, and at day-break he led a small but resolute party against the victorious Malwites. Sooltan Hooshung behaved with great bravery, and fought desperately: both he and Ahmud Shah were wounded; but the King of Malwa, on whom the face of victory never smiled, was defeated, and threw himself into the fort of Sarungpoor. Ahmud Shah, by this event, not only recovered all the property he had lost, but in addition took twenty elephants from Sooltan Hooshung, besides seven of those he had lately bor ught from Jajnuggur, and which conveyed his treasure.

Rubbee-oos Sany 4. A. H. 826. March 16. A. D. 1423.

On the 4th of Rubbee-oos-Sany Ahmud Shah commenced his retreat towards Guzerat; and Sooltan Hooshung, elated by this movement, pursued and harassed the rear of his army daily. He compelled him at length to halt, and await the result of an action. The Malwites at first succeeded in breaking one wing of the Guzerat line; but it was so well supported by

Ahmud Shah in person, that he repelled the onset, and was at length victorious, obliging Sooltan Hooshung to fly to Sarungpoor. The Malwa army lost, in killed, wounded, and missing, on this occasion, four thousand nine hundred men; and Ahmud Shah reached his frontier without further molestation. Sooltan Hooshung repaired to Mando, and recruited his defeated army. With respect to the journey of Sooltan Hooshung to Jajnuggur, a different account is given of it by one historian; but as I conceive that narrative not to be so authentic as this, and having given both accounts at length in my Guzerat history, I shall content myself with what has been already said on this subject.

Sooltan Hooshung, having recruited his forces, marched to besiege the fort of Gagrone, which shortly fell into his hands; from thence he proceeded to attack Gualiar, and had closely invested it for one month, when he heard that Syud Moobarik, the son of Khizr Khan, was on his march to the assistance of the Raja, by way of Byana. Having raised the siege, Sooltan Hooshung advanced as far as Dholpoor to meet him, when, after a few days' negotiation, a peace was concluded, mutual presents were exchanged, and both returned to their respective countries.

A. H. 832.
A. D. 1428.

In the year 832, Ahmud Shah Bahmuny, King of the Deccan, made an attack on the fort of Kehrla with a large force. Sooltan Hooshung obtaining information of this event from the late Nursing Ray's son, marched to his assistance; but the Deccanies, hearing of his approach, commenced their retreat, and were pursued by the King of Malwa. Ahmud Shah Bahmuny, however, being hard pressed, caused the army to move on by rapid marches, and remained in the rear with a select body of troops. At length the Deccanies offered Sooltan Hooshung battle. The conflict was not declined; but Ahmud Shah Bahmuny remained in ambush with a select body of cavalry. The King of Malwa (as had been anticipated) attacked the main body with fury, but was steadily received by the Deccanies; and being unprepared for the ambuscade into which he had been drawn by his enemy, was attacked in the rear, and his troops, according to custom, fled in great disorder, leaving in the hands of the enemy all their heavy baggage, and the followers of the army. Among the latter were the females of Sooltan Hooshung's family; to whom, after treating them with every respect, and allowing them a few days' rest, Ahmud Shah Bahmuny gave an escort of five hundred cavalry, with orders to convey them back to Mando.

A. H. 835.
A. D. 1434.

In the year 835, Sooltan Hooshung marched for the purpose of taking the fortress of Kalpy, then in charge of one Abdool Kadur, a Dehly officer. On arriving within a few miles of the place, he heard that Ibrahim Shah Shurky of Joonpoor was also on his march to reduce Kalpy; and conceiving it necessary to defeat him in the first instance, Sooltan Hooshung marched to oppose him. The Malwa and Joonpoor armies were within sight of each other, and a battle was hourly expected, when Ibrahim Shah Shurky (hearing that Syud Moobarik, King of Dehly, was on his march to attack Joonpoor,) commenced his retreat to his capital without delay, leaving Sooltan Hooshung to return to Kalpy, which shortly after surrendered. Having ordered public prayers to be read in his name, and having received homage from Abdool Kadur, Sooltan Hooshung delivered over the charge of the government to him, as before, and returned to Malwa. On the road, he obtained information that a band of daring freebooters from the Jam hills had taken up their abode at the Houz-i-Bheem, and infested the country of Malwa. He consequently marched in that direction; and having destroyed the Houz-i-Bheem, he returned to Mando, from whence he proceeded to Hooshungabad, where he remained during the rainy season.

It is related, that about this period Sooltan Hooshung, being one day on a hunting-party, lost a ruby from his tiara. On the third day it was found and brought to him by a foot-passenger, who received five hundred tunkas for his honesty. Sooltan Hooshung observed, "This circumstance "puts me in mind of a similar event which hap"pened to Feroze Toghluk, King of Dehly, pre"viously to his death. One day that king having "lost a ruby from off his head on a hunting-party, "gave five hundred tunkas to a peasant who "found it. Sometime after, Feroze said, 'This is "a hint to me to prepare for my long journey "into the other world, when I must part with all "the rubies and other jewels which I possess.'" Sooltan Hooshung also remarked, that he was sure this circumstance portended his own dissolution. The courtiers observed, that he should recollect that when Feroze made this speech he was upwards of ninety years of age, and it was not surprising, therefore, that death very shortly verified his prediction. "Your Majesty," they said "is, by the blessing of God, just now in "the prime of life, the circumstances, therefore, "appear altogether different." He was, however, shortly after afflicted with a violent attack of the stone. On the approach of this dangerous disease, he marched towards Mando, having formally proclaimed his eldest son, the Prince Ghizny Khan, his successor; and laying hold of the young man's hand in public durbar, delivered him into the hands of his favourite minister, Mahmood Khan, who promised to support his right to the throne, even to the last drop of his blood. The King then dismissing the durbar, sent for Mahmood Khan, whom he knew to be ambitious, and suspected that he might some day take adantage of the division of interests among the young princes to usurp the government. He told him plainly of his apprehensions, and made him again swear to defend Ghizny Khan, and also to be vigilant in watching the motions of Ahmud Shah of Guzerat, who, he observed, was "an ambitious and enter- "prizing prince, and contemplated the eventual "conquest of Malwa." Mahmood Khan swore the most implicit obedience to Ghizny Khan, and the whole of the present royal family; and the

King, at his instance, consented to release the young Prince, Oothman Khan, from confinement, and to give him an estate on which he might reside, and have no plea for disturbing the reign of Ghizny Khan. The heir-apparent, having heard what was in contemplation, sent for Mahmood Khan, and proposed that his brother should be required to take the oaths of allegiance to him in the King's presence. Mahmood Khan returned to his own house, where he received a secret deputation from Mullik Oothman Julwany and the Prince Oothman Khan. The agents commenced by flattering Mahmood Khan, and observing, that they were surprised at a person of his discretion recommending Ghizny Khan as the King's successor, who, although the elder, was by no means to be compared, either in courage or talents, to his younger brother. Mahmood Khan was not disposed to dispute the qualifications ascribed to Oothman Khan, but was unwilling to have his courage or abilities brought in competition with those plans which he himself meditated on the throne; being fully convinced, that neither the disposition nor ability of Ghizny Khan were calculated to withstand the efforts he had resolved to make to forward his own views for the eventual usurpation of the government. Mahmood Khan therefore replied to the deputies, that it was his business to obey the will of his sovereign, who had declared Ghizny Khan his successor, and remarked that he had never presumed to oppose his wishes.

Zuffur Khan, a person of Prince Oothman's party, despairing of the King's life, fled from camp, in order to induce the keepers of the Prince, then in confinement at Mando, to release him, and give him an opportunity of disputing the crown with his brother. The minister, Mahmood Khan, hearing of this circumstance, informed the heir-apparent, Ghizny Khan, who ordered a party of fifty men of the royal guards to overtake and bring back Zuffur Khan and those who had accompanied him. The officer commanding the guard being well disposed towards the Prince Oothman refused to allow the horses to be saddled without an order from the King himself; and communicating the circumstance to one of the officers of the household, who was also inclined to favour Prince Oothman, he told the master of the horse to speak so loud that the King might overhear him; hoping that he would be provoked with Prince Ghizny Khan, when he heard that even before his death he had usurped all authority over his own household troops. The scheme succeeded; and Sooltan Hooshung, rousing himself, called for his bow and quiver, and swore he would put the Prince Ghizny Khan to death. On this occasion he summoned all the officers into his presence; but they, fearing he was really dead, and that Ghizny Khan had sent for them, in order to seize those who were unfavourable to his views, declined going. When the Prince heard of this he became much alarmed; and not possessing sufficient judgment to act with propriety, he fled to Gagrone, three marches from camp. From whence he deputed Oomdut-ool-Moolk to wait on Mahmood Khan, and to acquaint him with his suspicions of the officers who conspired to raies

Prince Oothman to the throne, at the same time assuring the minister, that excepting himself he believed he had no friend. The message went on to say, that the fact of the King calling for his bow and arrows convinced him that his Majesty intended at least to sieze and confine him, if not to put him to death. Mahmood Khan was obliged to send several persons to the Prince before he could be induced to return to camp. Meanwhile the King's life was despaired of; and the officers of his household, fearing lest Ghizny Khan should succeed to the crown, consulted together, and resolved to remove the King, even in his weak state, to Mando, where they proposed releasing the Prince Oothman, and placing him on the throne.

Zeehuj 9. A. H. 835. Sept. 7. A. D. 1432.

On the following morning, being the 9th of Zeehuj, they carried their purpose so far into effect, as absolutely to place the King (who was quite senseless) in his palanquin, and to take him away from the camp on the road to Malwa; but they had not gone far before he died,—after a reign of thirty years. Mahmood Khan, accompanied by the Prince Ghizny Khan, followed the King's palanquin to bring it back; but the officers of the household declared that it was his Majesty's pleasure that he should be removed towards Mando, and that they had only acted in compliance with his orders. On the King's death, Mahmood Khan issued a proclamation in the name of the Prince Ghizny Khan, setting forth the circumstance, and declaring the nomination of his eldest son to the succession. After which his Majesty, being laid out in state, was conveyed to Mando, where his body was buried in a stone vault, which is still to be seen.* The date of his death will be found in the three last words of the following distich:—

شهي والاقدر سلطان هوشنگ
سوي دار البقا چون كرداهنگ
بپرسيدم زها تف سال تاريخ
ندا امد نما نده شاه هوشنگ

When death had sealed the glorious Hooshung's fate,
And he prepared to tread on Lethe's shore,
I asked a poet to record the date,
Who briefly said, "Shah Hooshung is no more."

The author of his history relates, that water constantly ouses from the sides of his vault, between the apertures of the masonry, which falls in drops; that this phenomenon ceases in the four rainy months, but is unremitting in the dry season; which is absurdly attributed, by the natives of India, to the supernatural intervention of Sooltan Hooshung, for whose death, say they, "the rocks even appear to shed tears."

* His vault and a splendid mausoleum are still to be seen at Mando, though it appears certain he was first entombed at Hooshungabad, a town called after him, lying on the Nurbudda river. The place of interment is still shown by some pious Mahomedans who reside on the spot; and the lines commemorative of his death were legible when the translator visited the tomb in October, 1817.

GHIZNY KHAN,

SURNAMED

SOOLTAN MAHOMED GHOORY.

Ascends the throne—causes the city of Mando to be called Shadiabad—becomes cruel to his brothers and children, as also to his officers—abandons himself to his pleasures—the people are disgusted.—The King accuses his minister of an intention to dethrone him.—The latter pleads his innocence, but resolves to cut off the King.—The King is poisoned by his cup-bearer, at the instigation of the minister, Mahmood Khan Khiljy.

Two days after the death of Sooltan Hooshung, Ghizny Khan was crowned at Mando, and assuming the title of Sooltan Mahomed Ghoory, ordered that his capital might henceforth be called Shadiabad Mando, or "The City of Joy;" and public prayers were read and coin struck in his name. Business was as usual transacted by Mullik Mogheis and his son Mahmood Khan, and no alterations took place in consequence of the death of the late king. Shortly after his accession, Sooltan Mahomed, however, evinced many traits of cruelty in his jealousy towards his brothers. Several persons supposed to favour them were put to death on bare suspicion, without public trials; and he put out the eyes of his nephew and son-in-law, Nizam Khan, and also those of Nizam Khan's three sons by his daughter. These acts excited disgust in the upper classes of society, and terror among the common people; so that the nation appeared ripe for insurrection. About this period the Rajpoots of Nandote having laid waste part of the territory of Malwa, Sooltan Mahomed, by the advice of Mahmood Khan, placing the army under the command of his chief minister, Mullik Mogheis, ordered him to march and punish the enemy, having presented him on the occasion with ten elephants and a robe of honour. Shortly after, it was apparent the King had relinquished all interest in the transaction of public business, leaving it entirely to Mahmood Khan, while he gave himself up to the pleasures of the seraglio, and abandoned himself to drunken excess. The natural consequence of such conduct threw an increased accession of power and influence into the hands of the minister, while respect for the King gradually declined. This state of affairs was by no means pleasing to many of the nobles, who, dreading lest Mahmood Khan should be induced to usurp the crown, and thus put an end to the Ghoory dynasty, sent secret messages to the King, warning him of his danger. Mahmood Khan, who was at this time in the habit of seeing the King daily in private, became aware of his suspicions, and took precautionary measures for his own safety, which did not escape the King's notice, who one day told him that he had heard he intended to usurp the crown; then taking him by the hand, and leading him to his wife, the minister's sister, he conjured him, at all events, to spare his life. The astonished Mahmood disavowed any such motive, saying, that he had never broken the oath which he had sworn to his father, the illustrious Sooltan Hooshung, to support his authority.

Mahmood Khan, however, after he left the seraglio, resolved on the death of the King, which he conceived, having once been suspected of treachery, was now the only means of securing his own life. He in consequence bribed one of the King's private servants to administer poison to him in his wine, from the effects of which he died. The officers about the King's person no sooner ascertained the fact, than they brought forth the Prince Musaood, one of the late king's sons, a boy thirteen years of age, from the seraglio, in order to place him on the throne. One of the officers (Mullik Bayezeed Sheikha) going to Mahmood Khan, and supposing him to be ignorant of the King's death, said that his Majesty wanted to see him, as he wished to send an envoy immediately to Guzerat. Mahmood Khan replied, that having relinquished his office of minister, he intended henceforth to become a sweeper at the tomb of his beloved master Sooltan Hooshung; and that under these circumstances it might be as well that the nobles should come to his house, and make arrangements for the future administration of affairs, as the King appeared to have abandoned himself to wine and women. Mullik-Bayezeed, the more confirmed in his opinion of the minister's ignorance of what had occurred, agreed that those officers who had resolved on placing the Prince Musaood on the throne should go to Mahmood Khan's house, and seize his person. But the minister having obtained timely information of their intentions, previously ordered a body of soldiers to be in readiness in a private apartment, which, when they entered, rushed out and confined them. This bold measure so confounded the rest of the Prince Musaood's party that some fled precipitately out of the city, while others who remained, collecting troops, endeavoured to possess themselves of the canopy over the tomb of Sooltan Hooshung, and placing it on the head of the Prince Musaood, intended to proclaim him King. Mahmood, hearing of their proceedings, mounted his horse, and rode direct to the palace, where he made an attempt to secure the persons of the two young princes, Musaood and Oomr Khan; but meeting with opposition in the courtyard, swords were drawn on both sides, and a fight ensued, which continued till night-fall. On this occasion many persons were killed; but the Prince's party being defeated fled, and Mahmood occupied the palace. On the next day he sent word to his father, inviting him to assume the reins of government; but he declined, saying that he alone was best able to conduct the affairs of the state.

SOOLTAN MAHMOOD KHILJY:

He ascends the throne, confirming to all the nobles their estates and titles.—An attempt is made to assassinate the King, which is frustrated.—The Prince Ahmud Ghoory creates an insurrection.—Ahmud Shah of Guzerat espouses his cause, as well as that of the princes Musaood and Oomr, sons of the late King.—The princes Ahmud and Musaood are cut off by poison, and Oomr is taken prisoner and beheaded.—Pestilence rages in the Guzerat army, which is obliged to retreat.—Sooltan Mahmood invited to Dehly—marches thither, but retreats suddenly—compels Kadur Khan of Kalpy to acknowledge fealty to him—makes war with the Rana of Chittoor—reduces one of the forts of Koombulmere—besieges Chittoor, but is foiled—is engaged in war with the King of Joonpoor.—Treaty of Eerich concluded.—The King besieges Mundulgur—receives tribute from the Raja of Mundulgur, also from the rajas of Kota and Boondy—engages in war with the King of Guzerat.—Battle of Surkech.—Able retreat of Sooltan Mahmood out of Guzerat—is induced to invade the Deccan, owing to the invitation of Julal Khan Bokhary.—War with the Rana renewed.—Takes Ajmere.—Koombulmere capitulates, but is ransomed for a large sum of money.—Boondy taken by storm.—The King invades the Deccan.—Defeats the army of Nizam Shah Bahmuny, and takes the capital.—Is compelled to retreat by the arrival of the King of Guzerat.—Second campaign in the Deccan also unsuccessful.—The fort of Kehrla taken from the troops of Malwa by the King of the Deccan—is restored.—Treaty of Elichpoor, by which Kehrla and the Narnala hills become the boundary of the two kingdoms.—Insurrection in Keechiwara—is suppressed.—Death of the King—his character.

AMONG the several Indian histories, but particularly in the Tareekh Alfy of Moolla Ahmud, we find it related, that the dynasty of the Ghoory family became extinct with Ghizny Khan; and

Shuval 29. A. H. 839. May 16. A. D. 1435.

that on Monday the 29th of Shuval, in the year 839, Mahmood Khan, assuming the title of Sooltan Mahmood Khiljy, ascended the throne, in the thirty-fourth year of his age, and was crowned in Mando with the royal tiara of Sooltan Hooshung. At the same time public prayers were read, and coin was struck in his name; after which, having sent for the officers of the court, and presenting them with robes of honour, he confirmed the grants of the estates and offices which they held under the late king. To some he gave additional titles; among whom was Musheer-ool-Moolk, who received the title of Nizam-ool-Moolk, and was appointed one of his ministers. Mullik Burkhoordar was nominated chief usher, with the title of Taj Khan. In addition to the titles of his father, Mullik Mogheis, who was already denominated Mullik Ashruf, Khan Jehan, he added those of Ameer-ool-Omra, Zoobdut-ool-Moolk, Khoolasut-ool-Malwa, Azim Hoomayoon. He was also permitted to assume the white canopy, and to bear a silver quiver, exclusive marks of royalty, beside being attended by gentlemen ushers bearing golden and silver staves, who perceded him when he appeared in public, proclaiming his titles, commencing "By the grace of God," and so on. The seals of the office of prime minister were also delivered over exclusively into his hands.

Sooltan Mahmood, during his whole reign, gave great encouragement to learned men, and founded several colleges in different parts of the kingdom for the promotion of literature, so that the philosophers and mowlanas in Malwa bore a fair comparison with those of Shiraz and Samarkand. After reorganising the affairs of his government, and having appointed the officers to their respective stations, some of those of Sooltan Hooshung's reign still remained unprovided for, who formed a project to seize the King. And in consequence one night, in pursuance of their plan, Mullik Kootb-ood-Deen Sumnany and Nuseer-ood-Deen Joorjany, with some others, having placed ladders so as to escalade a musjid which commanded Sooltan Mahmood's palace, descended into the court-yard. During this operation, the King hearing a noise, and suspecting treason, came out fully accoutred with his sword, and bow and quiver, and proceeded direct to the spot where the confederates had assembled. He instantly attacked them without hesitation, and wounded many with his own hand; and being soon after joined by Nizam-ool-Moolk and Mullik Mahomed Khizr with the guards, the traitors made their escape, with the exception of one, who being unable to go down the ladder, threw himself off the musjid, and broke his leg. He was, in consequence, taken the next morning. This person discovered the names of all the conspirators, who being seized were punished. But Azim Hoomayoon, the King's father, interceded in behalf of the following persons, who were pardoned, and estates allotted to them :—

The Prince Ahmud Ghoory, son of Sooltan Hooshung, received the estate of Islamabad.

Mullik Yoosoof, entitled Kowam Khan, had Bhilsa.

Mullik Itihad, Hooshungabad; and

Mullik Nuseer-ood-Deen, entitled Noosrut Khan, Chundery.

The Prince Ahmud, taking advantage of his situation, very soon collected a force at Islamabad; and Azim Hoomayoon proposed that remonstrances should be made to him in the first instance; which proving of no avail, the King ordered Taj Khan to proceed with a force to reduce him. On reaching Islamabad, Taj Khan found himself unable to make any impression on the fort, and wrote to court for reinforcements. This delay gave courage to other malecontents; and information was received that Mullik Itihad of Hooshungabad, and Nuseer Khan of Chundery, had both raised the standard of revolt. The King now directed his father to march in person against all the insurgents. His first object was Islamabad, where he was met, at the distance of four miles, by Taj Khan, whose force formed a junction with the minister's army, and measures were taken to commence regular approaches against the fort; but owing to the deference Azim Hoomayoon always evinced towards the descendants of his patron Sooltan Hooshung, he sent some of the most respectable of his officers into the fort, in order to induce the Prince Ahmud to accommodate matters, but without effect. Kowam Khan, who also joined the King's army at this place, but who was secretly in league with the Prince Ahmud, privately furnished the garrison with stores; and the siege might have been protracted indefinitely, had not Azim Hoomayoon bribed one of his servants to administer poison to the Prince in a cup of wine, of which he died. Azim Hoomayoon instantly took possession of the fort without resistance, and marched to Hooshungabad; but Kowam Khan, suspecting that his treachery had been discovered, remained at Bhilsa, while Azim Hoomayoon continued his march. On his arrival at Hooshungabad, Azim Hoomayoon found that Mullik Itihad, afraid to oppose the King's army, had fled to the foot of the Gondwana hills, where the inhabitants seized and put him to death. After having occupied Hooshungabad with the King's troops, and placing a confidential officer in charge, Azim Hoomayoon proceeded to Chundery. On arriving within a few miles of the place he was met by Noosrut Khan, who threw himself on his mercy. Azim Hoomayoon, always inclined to effect his object, if possible, by the most moderate measures, caused Noosrut Khan to go with him to the town, where he established an investigation into his administration; and having ascertained, beyond doubt, that he was constantly instilling insurrection against the government into the minds of the people, he was displaced, and one Hajy Kaloo left in his stead. From Chundery Azim Hoomayoon proceeded to Bhilsa, calling on Kowam-ool-Moolk to account for his conduct; but in spite of the frequent remonstrances sent to him he refused to meet Azim Hoomayoon, or to listen to any accommodation, so that after being closely besieged, and apprehensive that the place must fall, he fled, leaving Azim Hoomayoon to settle the affairs of the district, after which he returned to Mando. On his march thither he learned that Ahmud Shah of Guzerat had espoused the cause of the Prince Musaood Ghoory, and that he was in full march to support his rights at the head of a large force, accompanied by twenty elephants. Azim Hoomayoon made rapid marches towards the capital, and avoiding the Guzerat army by making a detour of twelve miles, he succeeded in throwing himself into the fort of Mando by the Tarapoor gate. Shortly after which the fort was invested by Ahmud Shah. The besieged made daily sallies on the trenches of the besiegers; and Sooltan Mahmood would willingly have marched out and given battle to the Guzerat army in the field, but his intentions were always frustrated by the opposition he met with from those officers who had been in the service of the late Sooltan Hooshung. Sooltan Mahmood, considering that almost the whole of his former adherents were averse to him, resolved to court popularity among the common people, by serving out grain from the public stores gratis. He also held out promises of estates to those Malwa officers in Ahmud's Shah's camp who were at all discontented, so that the Prince Musaood was deserted by many of the old Malwa chiefs, who came over to Sooltan Mahmood, and who at their instigation resolved to lead a night-attack against Ahmud Shah's trenches. Noosrut Khan, the officer who had lately been removed from Chundery, having given private intimation to Ahmud Shah of the intended attack on his lines, the object was, in a great measure, defeated. The assault took place, as was proposed; but Sooltan Mahmood was astonished to find the enemy so well prepared, that even the narrow passes by which he was to advance were stockaded, and the Guzerat troops ready to oppose him. He, however, overcame these obstacles, having stormed and carried the stockades with severe loss; but still finding himself so warmly received on all sides, he was induced to retreat, after having slain a great number of the enemy.

At this period information was received that the Prince Oomr Ghoory, the younger brother of Musaood, who had first fled to Guzerat, had subsequently gone to the country of Rana Koombho of Chittoor. This prince was now at the head of a force; and having entered Malwa, had occupied Chundery, where the inhabitants and soldiers under Hajy Kaloo, revolting from him, had received the Prince with every demonstration of joy. This news having reached Ahmud Shah of Guzerat, he detached his son Mahomed Khan, with a force consisting of five thousand cavalry and thirty elephants, to Sarungpoor to make a diversion in favour of the Prince; and the governor of Sarungpoor, unable to oppose him, joined his standard. Sooltan Mahmood now resolved no longer to remain within Mando; but calling a council of war, it was agreed that Azim Hoomayoon should be left in charge of the fort, and that the King should take the field in person. Sooltan Mahmood marched out, therefore, with the army by the Tarapoor gate, without being opposed, and proceeded towards

Sarungpoor, having sent Taj Khan in advance. This officer falling in with a detachment of Guzeratties under the command of Hajy Ally of Guzerat, who occupied a ford on the Chumbul river, attacked and defeated it. Ahmud Shah, hearing of Sooltan Mahmood's being in the field, directed his son Mahomed Khan to fall back from Sarungpoor on Oojein, to which place he himself proceeded, where the two Guzerat divisions formed a junction. Intimation of the movement of the Guzeratties was afforded to Sooltan Mahmood by Mullik Isak, the late governor of Sarungpoor, who wrote a petition, soliciting pardon for surrendering the place to the Prince Mahomed Khan, and now informed his master of the march of the former to Oojein in order to unite with his father's army: he stated, also, that the Prince Oomr Ghoory was advancing with a force from Chundery to occupy Sarungpoor. Sooltan Mahmood, rejoiced at having obtained this information, pardoned Mullik Isak, and detaching Taj Khan with a party of light cavalry to make forced marches to occupy Sarungpoor, followed with the main body to that place. Upon his arrival he conferred on Mullik Isak the title of Dowlut Khan, and paid him ten thousand tunkas from the royal treasury; he presented him at the same time with a standard and an honorary dress, and increased his pay. He also gave horses and other presents to several other officers, among whom he distributed a donation of fifty thousand tunkas. Intimation was now received that the Prince Oomr, having burned the town of Bhilsa, was advancing to the Sarungpoor frontier, and that Ahmud Shah, with thirty thousand cavalry, and three hundred elephants, had left Oojein, and was in full march to the same place. Sooltan Mahmood, perceiving the object was to hem him in between the Prince Oomr and the Guzerat army, determined to prevent this manœuvre, by attacking the Prince Oomr. He therefore marched the same night, but halted when the army arrived within twelve miles of the enemy, and sent Nizam-ool-Moolk and Mullik Ahmud Silehdar to reconnoitre his position. On the following morning, the two armies moved about the same time to the attack; and as the lines approached, the Prince Oomr, with a select party, took post in the rear of a hill, to fall upon the flanks of Sooltan Mahmood's army. This movement being perceived by the King, he pushed on in person, and suddenly coming upon him, cut-off his division from the main body. The Prince's party fought desperately; but the bold charge made by Sooltan Mahmood in person threw it into confusion. The Prince was taken prisoner, and decapitated. His head was elevated on the point of the royal standard; and the King marched towards the army of Chundery, which had not yet been engaged. The officers of the Prince's army, having learnt his fate, agreed on a truce till next day; but during the night they fled to Chundery, where they placed Mullik Sooliman Ghoory, a relation of the Prince Oomr, on the throne, and saluted him with the title of Sooltan Shahab-ood-Deen. Sooltan Mahmood having detached a force to pursue the Chundery army, marched to attack Ahmud Shah of Guzerat; but a raging disease breaking out in the Guzerat camp, the effects of which were so sudden and fatal that the soldiers had not time to bury the dead, Ahmud Shah was compelled to retreat; and taking the route of Ashta, proceeded to Guzerat in the most expeditions manner, promising the Prince Musaood Ghoory that he would return on the following year and restore him to his rights.

Sooltan Mahmood, on the first intimation of Ahmud Shah's march, supposing it to be directed against his capital, proceeded to Mando, in order to reinforce that garrison; but after halting seventeen days, and finding that Ahmud Shah had retreated to Guzerat, he returned to the attack of Chundery. Here he was opposed by the pretender Mullik Sooliman, who, unable to withstand Sooltan Mahmood's troops, took refuge in the fort, and in the course of two or three days died suddenly. The officers of Chundery, however, still obstinately persisting in resistance, raised another person to the throne; and marching out of the fort, attacked the King, but met with a repulse. The siege of Chundery occupied eight months, when Sooltan Mahmood, becoming impatient, resolved to take it, if possible, by surprise; and heading a party himself, he escaladed the lower town in the dead of the night, and carried it, putting many of the enemy to the sword. Some few made their escape into the hill-fort, but they were closely besieged; and Ismael Khan, under whom the garrison acted, after a few days, sent a flag of truce, offering to surrender, on receiving a promise that the lives of himself and the garrison should be spared. The terms eventually granted were, that the besieged should bring all their private property, and their families, and place them in the public bazar, that the whole army might be witness of their complete subjection, but that their lives should be spared. After which, having put Chundery under the government of Mullik Moozuffur Ibrahim, the King intended to return to his capital, when he heard that Dongur Sing, the Raja of Gualiar, had marched to the southward, and laid siege to the fort of Nurwur. Sooltan Mahmood, notwithstanding the approach of the rains, and the arduous campaign in which his army had just been engaged, marched towards Gualiar, laying waste the Raja's country. The Rajpoots, sallying from the fort, attacked his troops, but they were defeated, and obliged to retreat. Dongur Sing, in consequence, was induced to raise the siege of Nurwur, in order to protect his own capital. The object of Sooltan Mahmood in relieving Nurwur being thus gained, he did not lay siege to Gualiar, but returned to Mando. In the year 843, he commenced the repairs of the palace of the late Sooltan Hooshung, and the musjid built in commemoration of that monarch, near the Rampoora gate. This splendid edifice has two hundred and thirty minarets and three hundred and sixty arches.

A. H. 843.
A. D. 1439.

In the year 844, Sooltan Mahmood received petitions from the chiefs of Mewat and Dehly, stating, that Syud Mahomed, King of Dehly, the nephew and suc-

A. H. 844.
A. D. 1440.

cessor of Syud Moobarik, was totally incapable of supporting the weighty affairs of the government of his vast empire; that the oppressed were calling out on all sides for redress, and that the nation was anxious for Sooltan Mahmood to march to Dehly, and ascend the throne. In consequence of these overtures, in the latter end of the same year, Sooltan Mahmood put his army in motion for that purpose. On his arrival in the neighbourhood of the town of Hindown he was joined by Yoosoof Khan Hindowny, whence he proceeded towards the capital. Syud Mahomed, although he had a large force at his disposal, became alarmed, and proposed to quit Dehly, and fly to the Punjab. He was dissuaded, however, by his officers, and directed, that as there was no occasion for his own presence in camp, the army should march against the enemy under his son. The advance guard, consisting of a select body of archers, was commanded by Mullik Bheilole Lody. Sooltan Mahmood, hearing that the King was not with the Dehly forces, and conceiving it derogatory to proceed in person, retained with him a few thousand of his cavalry, and ordered the rest of his army under his two sons, Gheias-ood-Deen and Fidwy Khan, to oppose the enemy. An engagement took place, in which both armies fought desperately from mid-day till sunset, when the retreat was mutually sounded. On that night, Sooltan Mahmood dreamed that he saw an unknown person placed on the throne at Mando, who afterwards went to the shrine of Sooltan Hooshung, when the officers placed upon his head

the canopy from the tomb of that monarch. Being much distressed in mind on account of this dream, he was deliberating how to act, when on a sudden a messenger arrived from Syud Mahomed, ordering his son to make peace upon any terms. An accommodation immediately succeeded, and the army of Sooltan Mahmood commenced its retreat to Malwa. It is a remarkable coincidence, that on the very night of Sooltan Mahmood's dream an insurrection did take place in the city of Mando, which was put a stop to only by the resolute and timely exertions of his father, Azim Hoomayoon, an account of which reached him on the road to his capital. But I find it stated in some histories, that the cause of Sooltan Mahmood's return originated in his having received intimation of the intended attack of the King of Guzerat; and certainly this appears most probable. At all events, in the
A. H. 845. year 845, he reached Mando, and
A. D. 1441. distributed alms to all the poor in consequence of his safe return after so long a campaign. During the same year he repaired to the town of Nalcha, where he built some beautiful palaces and musjids; but his enterprising mind was ill calculated to indulge long in such pursuits: he assembled his army, and was about to proceed towards Chittoor. At this time he heard that Nuseer, the son of Abdool Kadur of Kalpy, having proclaimed his independence, had assumed the title of Nuseer Shah, and adopted principles in opposition to the tenets of the true faith. Sooltan Mahmood now directed his arms to that quarter. As soon as Nuseer Khan heard

of the movement of the King, he deputed his tutor, Ally Khan, to wait on Sooltan Mahmood with rich presents, which were all rejected, and the ambassador, was not even allowed to enter the camp; till on the arrival of the King of Malwa at Julalpoor, in consequence of the repeated entreaties of his father, Azim Hoomayoon, Ally Khan was admitted to the presence, his offerings were received, and the submission of Nuseer Khan accepted. Sooltan Mahmood, however, marched on within a short distance of Kalpy, before he shaped his course towards Chittoor. After having crossed the Bunas river, he sent on detachments of light troops to lay waste the country. The main body continued to advance slowly, and was engaged every day either in taking prisoners or in destroying temples, and in building musjids in their stead. Sooltan Mahmood now attacked one of the forts in the Koombulmere district, defended by Beny Ray, the deputy of Rana Koombho of Chittoor. In front of the gateway was a large temple which commanded the lower works. This building was strongly fortified, and employed by the enemy as a magazine. Sooltan Mahmood, aware of its importance, determined to take possession of it at all hazards; and having stormed it in person, carried it, but not without heavy loss; after which, the fort fell into his hands, and many Rajpoots were put to death. The temple was now filled with wood, and being set on fire, cold water was throne on the stone images, which causing them to break, the pieces were given to the butchers of the camp, in order to be used as weights in selling meat. One large figure in particular, representing a ram, * and formed of solid marble, being consumed, the Rajpoots were compelled to eat the calcined parts with pân, † in order that it might be said that they were made to eat their gods. Sooltan Mahmood having reduced this fort, which the kings of Guzerat, notwithstanding frequent and long sieges, had never been able to effect, caused public thanksgiving to be made, at which every person in camp was required to attend. From Koombulmere the army marched to Chittoor, and carried by storm the lower fort, in consequence of which the Rana fled to the hills, closely pursued by the King, while his father, Azim Hoomayoon, proceeded to occupy the districts surrounding Mundsoor; on which service he fell sick, and shortly afterwards died at that town. Although from the age of Azim Hoomayoon such an event was to be expected, yet Mahmood no sooner heard the news than he repaired to Mundsoor alone, caused the remains of his parent to be embalmed and conveyed to Mando, and became almost distracted with grief, so that he tore his hair and raved like one bereaved of his senses. In a few days after, having appointed Taj Khan to the command of the force

* If the Mahomedans did not mistake this figure, which was probably that of a bull, and not a sheep, the fact is extraordinary. It is the only instance I recollect of the ram being made an object of worship.

† It is hardly necessary to inform the Orientalist that chunam, or line, is spread between the pân or betel leaf when it is eaten.

at Mundsoor, and conferred on him the title o Azim Khan, the King returned to join his arm at Chittoor. As the rains were now approaching he endeavoured to find some elevated spot o which he might canton during the wet seasor having determined to besiege the fort of Chittoo immediately after. Rana Koombho, however, o
Zeehuj 25. the night of Friday the 25th of Zeehu
A. H. 846. in the year 846, made an attack on th
April 24. Malwa lines, with a force consisting c
A. D. 1443. twelve thousand cavalry and six thou sand infantry. Sooltan Mahmood had taken u an advantageous position, and his advance pickets were strongly posted, so that the lin being enabled to turn out before it could be sur prised, the assault completely failed. The Raj poots suffered severely on this occasion. On th following night, Sooltan Mahmood attacked th Rana's lines, which were destroyed, man Rajpoots killed, immense booty obtained, an the Rana himself obliged to seek shelter in th fort of Chittoor. Sooltan Mahmood, havin ordered public prayers to be read on this occasior determined to defer the siege of Chittoor till th next year, and returned without molestation t Mando, where he built a beautiful pillar seve stories high, in front of a college, which h founded opposite the musjid of Sooltan Hooshung

In the year 847, an ambassador ar
A. H. 847. rived at Mando from Mahmood, th
A. D. 1444. son of Ibrahim Shah Shurky, King c Joonpoor, bringing with him the usual offerings and representing that Nuseer Khan, the son c

Abdool Kadur of Kalpy, having abandoned the doctrines of the true faith, propagated opinions subversive of Mahomedism; and that he had carried this apostasy to such lengths as to make over a number of Mahomedan females to be taught the art of dancing by Hindoos. The ambassador observed, that as the governors of Kalpy, since the time of Sooltan Hooshung of Malwa, had been appointed from that court, the King of Joonpoor had deemed it proper to acquaint Sooltan Mahmood with the circumstances of the defection of Nuseer Khan; stating, that if he had not time to march in person to punish the apostate, Mahmood Shah Shurky begged that he might be permitted to do so in the name of the King of Malwa. Sooltan Mahmood replied, that his own army was at present employed at Mundsoor, in propagating the faith among the infidels, and that he entirely approved of Mahmood Shah's intention: after which the ambassador having received an honorary dress, and some presents for his master, took his leave. Mahmood Shah Shurky was so gratified with the reception his ambassador met with from Sooltan Mahmood, that on the following year he sent to him twenty of his finest elephants.

In the mean time, Mahmood Shah Shurky marched to Kalpy, and assuming the right of a master, expelled Nuseer Khan from the town. The latter addressed a petition to Sooltan Mahmood, stating, that his family had always considered themselves the subjects of Malwa since the reign of Sooltan Hooshung till the present period; that now Mahmood Shah Shurky having penetrated into his district had expelled him without any cause whatsoever, excepting the wish of extending his territory; that Nuseer Khan had accordingly fled towards Malwa, being at present at Chundery, and he requested that Sooltan Mahmood would afford him protection and redress. On the receipt of this letter, the King of Malwa deputed Ally Khan to the court of Joonpoor, requesting that as Nuseer Khan had returned to the right path his estate might be restored to him. Mahmood Shah Shurky remained sulky and sullen during the conference with Sooltan Mahmood's ambassador, and refused to give a direct reply to his communication. The King of Malwa, incensed at this indignity, marched his army on the 2d of Shuval, A. H. 848, to Chundery, where he was met by Nuseer Khan, and thence went towards Eerich and Bhandere. Mahmood Shah Shurky, on hearing this, moved also, and encamped in the neighbourhood of Eerich; where having seized the person of Moobarik Khan, (the son of Jooneid Khan, whose family had held the government of Eerich for many generations,) placed him in confinement, and took up a strong position in the broken ground on the bank of the river Bétwa.* Sooltan Mahmood, desirous of replacing Nuseer Khan in his government, passed Eerich, and marched, in the first instance, direct to Kalpy. Mahmood Shah Shurky followed. Sooltan Mahmood now caused a detachment of his army to make a detour,

Shuval 2. A. H. 848. January 8. A. D. 1445.

* This river forms the boundary between Rajwara and Bundelkund.—*Tod.*

which falling on the rear of the Joonpoor army, cut off its baggage on the line of march, while the King of Malwa halting with the main body brought on a general action, which lasted till sunset, when both armies mutually retreated, and encamped near to each other. The rainy season then approaching, and Sooltan Mahmood having no object to gain by another battle, broke ground, and moved to Futtehabad, where he built a palace seven stories in height. During this occupation the inhabitants of Eerich made complaints against the governor, Moobarik Khan, who had again returned. Sooltan Mahmood in consequence nominated Moozuffur Ibrahim, the governor of Chundery, to attack and reduce him, while Mahmood Shah Shurky, on his part, ordered one Mullik Kaloo to oppose Ibrahim. These two officers met at the town of Rohut, where Mullik Kaloo was defeated, and fled. Moozuffur Ibrahim, however, considering the security of his own district of main importance, returned to Chundery; and Mahmood Shah Shurky, on hearing of Mullik Kaloo's discomfiture, proceeded to Rohut. The war between the Malwa and Joonpoor kings being thus protracted to a considerable length, and many of the faithful destroyed on both sides in several actions, Sheikh Chand of Malwa, one of the most learned and respectable men of the time, engaged to compose the differences; and at the desire of Mahmood Shah Shurky addressed a letter, offering the following terms of peace to Sooltan Mahmood Khiljy:—

"1. That Mahmood Shah Shurky should imme-

"diately evacuate the towns of Rohut and Mahoba, "and deliver them over to Nuseer Khan.

"2. That in four months after the retreat of "Sooltan Mahmood to Mando, the fort and dis- "trict of Kalpy should be restored to Nuseer Khan, "provided he showed contrition for having de- "parted from the tenets of the faith; and con- "ducted himself in every respect like a true "believer.

"3. That the two armies should immediately "withdraw to their respective territories."

Sooltan Mahmood, acceding to these conditions, marched direct to Mando; and in the year 849 founded a large hospital, giving donations for its support, and appointing Mowlana Fuzl Oolla, his own physician, to superintend the whole establishment; which included wards and attendants for all classes of patients, and apartments for maniacs separate from the rest.

A.H. 849. A.D. 1445.

Rujub 20 A.H. 850. Sept. 11 A.D. 1446.

On the 20th of Rujub, in the year 850, Sooltan Mahmood marched to attack the fort of Mundulgur. On reaching Rampoora, he took the government of that place from Bahadur Khan, and gave it to Mullik Seif-ood-Deen; and crossing the Bunass, he moved on to Mundulgur, where Rana Koombho took post. The Rajpoots, sallying from the fort daily, made several desperate efforts in vain to raise the siege, till at length, foiled in all their attempts, Rana Koombho agreed to pay a large amount in jewels and specie, and Sooltan Mahmood concluded a peace and returned to his capital. After his arrival at Mando, he marched towards Byana, and on arriving within six miles of the place, the governor, Mahomed Khan, sent his son Khodawund Khan with a present of one hundred horses and a hundred thousand tunkas of silver. The King, in return, sent to Mahomed Khan an honorary dress embroidered in gold, a tiara of jewels, waistband of gold, and some Arab horses with gold saddles; in consideration of which Mahomed Khan caused the public prayers to be read in the name of Sooltan Mahmood. On returning towards his capital, the King subdued the fort of Anundpoor, situated near Runtunbhore, from whence having detached Taj Khan with a force of eight thousand cavalry and twenty elephants to the attack of Chittoor, himself proceeded to Kota and Boondy; from the raja of which places he levied one hundred and twenty-five thousand tunkas, and eventually retired to Mando.

A.H. 854.
A.D. 1450.

In the year 854, the Raja Gungadas of Champanere, in hopes of receiving aid from Sooltan Mahmood, sent him an offering, and begged his assistance in repelling the attack of Mahomed Shah, the son of Ahmud Shah of Guzerat, who had surrounded and invested his capital. Sooltan Mahmood in consequence marched to his relief; and the King of Guzerat having lost a great number of cattle in the campaign, and being unable to move for want of them, set fire to his camp-equipage, and destroying his military stores, retired to Ahmudabad. Sooltan Mahmood, halting on the banks of the Mehindry, received sixteen lacks of tunkas and a number of horses from Raja Gungadas of Champanere, who came in person to pay his respects; after which the army of Malwa returned to Mando.

A. H. 855.
A. D. 1451.

On the following year, 855, Sooltan Mahmood, with an army consisting of upwards of one hundred thousand men, marched with the determination of conquering Guzerat; and had Mahomed Shah lived, there is reason to suppose he would have succeeded. The Malwa army, on entering Kandeish, laid siege to Sooltanpoor; on which occasion the King was frequently attacked by sallies made from the fort by Mullik Alla-ood-Deen Sohrab Toork the governor; who finding that no reinforcements arrived to his support, not only surrendered the place but joined the army of Sooltan Mahmood, into whose service he entered. He also sent his family as hostages to the fort of Mando, after taking the most solemn oaths of allegiance. Sooltan Mahmood, satisfied of the sincerity of Mullik Sohrab, made him commander-in-chief of the Malwa army, with the title of Moobariz Khan; after which he proceeded towards the capital of Guzerat. On the road news arrived of the death of Mahomed Shah, and of the succession of his son Kootb Shah. In consequence of which event, Sooltan Mahmood wrote a letter of condolence to Kootb Shah on the death of his father, and of congratulation on his own accession, agreeably to the custom of the times; and having ordered a public mourning, he distributed pân and sweetmeats throughout the camp. Notwithstanding these outward forms of respect, Sooltan Mahmood continued his march, laying waste Guzerat as far as Baroda, and making many prisoners, both Mahomedans and infidels, till at length he reached Ahmudabad. At this period Mullik Sohrab, who only waited for an opportunity of making his escape to his own master, left Sooltan Mahmood's camp, and joined the Guzerat army. Sooltan Mahmood on the next day encamped at Surkech, within three coss of Ahmudabad, and Kootb Shah took up ground at the town of Khanpoor, three coss distant from the Malwa camp. The contending armies remained for some days without coming to action, when on the 1st of Suffur, Sooltan Mahmood proceeded with the intention of making a night-attack on the Guzerat lines, but losing his way in the dark, remained till daylight, uncertain where he was. On the morning, putting his troops into order, he directed his eldest son, Gheias-ood-Deen, to take command of the rightwing, composed of the Sarungpoor cavalry, and placed the left wing, composed of Chundery troops, under the command of his younger son, Fidwy Khan, and took command of the centre of the line himself, while the Guzerat army, under Kootb Shah, prepared to receive him. In the commencement of the battle the Guzerat advanced pickets being driven in fell back on the main body. Moozuffur Khan of Chundery, commanding a part of the left wing of the Malwa army, attacked the right of the Guzerat line, and even penetrated to the head-quarter tents, which he plundered, and loaded the elephants with the royal treasury; but

Suffur 1. A. H. 856. Feb. 10. A. D. 1453.

during this movement the left wing, deprived of the services of the Chundery horse under Moozuffur Khan, was defeated, while that officer, who was engaged in conveying away booty, withdrew from the action altogether. Sooltan Mahmood, astonished at seeing his left wing fall back, galloped to its support with only two hundred cavalry, and charging the Guzeratties slew many men with his own hand. At this moment, Kootb Shah of Guzerat, with a select corps, having attacked the King of Malwa, cut off his small party, with the exception of sixteen troopers, with whom the latter made good his way to the royal pavilion; and having secured the crown of Guzerat, carried it off to his own camp, though the main body of his army was by that time completely defeated. During the remainder of the day, Sooltan Mahmood, having collected five or six thousand effective cavalry, caused a report to be publicly spread that he intended to make another attack on the Guzerat lines. The apprehension of which keeping the enemy on the alert enabled Sooltan Mahmood to retreat to Mando during the night; but his army suffered severely from the attacks of the Bheels and Kolies during the march. It is worthy of remark, that Sooltan Mahmood never experienced a defeat before, or afterwards, during his reign. His son, Gheias-ood-Deen, with the right wing of the army, fled to Surat, where he plundered the country, and returned to Mando by the same route he came.*

A. H. 857. In the year 857, Sooltan Mahmood
A. D. 1453. projected an attack upon Mewar; but

* That is, by Nundoorbar, Talnere, and Sindwa.

being apprehensive of the King of Guzerat, he first of all made overtures for accommodation with that monarch, and resolved subsequently to march against Rana Koombho. Having collected his army, he went to D'har, whence he sent Taj Khan to the confines of Guzerat, in order to make proposals of peace; which being acceded to, it was resolved that the two nations should retain whatever they at that moment possessed: that they should enter into an offensive alliance against the Rajpoots of Mewar; by which it was agreed that the parties were to march and attack the Rana of Chittoor's territories; that all the country taken to the southward, and contiguous to Guzerat, should be attached to that kingdom, while that of Ajmere and Mewar, and the country to the northward and eastward, should belong to Malwa, and that the contracting powers should not withhold assistance from each other when demanded.

A. H. 858.
A. D. 1454.

In the year 858 Sooltan Mahmood attacked the Rajpoots of Kerowly, many of whom were killed, and their families taken prisoners, and sent to Mando; after which he marched by way of Gualiar to Byana, and arriving within a few miles of that place, Dawood Khan, the governor, sent a rich offering, and came out to meet him. Sooltan Mahmood retired from the north by Hindown; and having placed his son, Fidwy Khan, in the government of a district embracing Kerowly, Runtunbhore, and Ajmere, he returned to Mando. Shortly after his arrival, he received a communication from Sikundur Khan and Julal Khan Bokhary,* nobles of the court of Alla-ood-Deen Shah Bahmuny of the Deccan, inviting him to take advantage of the moment to march and seize the fort of Mahoor, in Berar. Sooltan Mahmood assembling an army at Hooshungabad marched to the south for that purpose; and on reaching Kehrla, called also Mahmoodabad, he was met by Sikundur Khan Bokhary, who accompanied him to Mahoor. The King of the Deccan also advanced with a considerable force; and Sooltan Mahmood, finding that he could not cope with success against the Deccan army, so far removed from his own resources, retreated to Mando, leaving a part of his army under the command of his favourite general Taj Khan to assist Sikundur Khan Bokhary. Scarcely had he reached Malwa, when he heard that Moobarik Khan Farooky, ruler of Kandeish, had laid hands on the country of Buglana,† lying between the Deccan and Guzerat, and dependent on Malwa. Conceiving this attack as personally concerning himself, Sooltan Mahmood

* The insurrection caused by Julal Khan Bokhary and his son Sikundur Khan, during the reigns of Alla-ood-Deen and Hoomayoon the Cruel, has been detailed at length in the history of the Bahmuny kings. Vide vol. ii. p. 448, &c.

† It is extremely difficult to imagine by what reasoning Buglana could be deemed dependent on Malwa. I do not recollect any previous connection between these two states; and the only inference that can be drawn at this remote period from the assertion of the Malwa historian is, that the Raja of Buglana, being attacked by Moobarik Khan ruler of Kandeish, applied to Sooltan Mahmood of Malwa for aid, with a promise of paying him for it.

marched towards that country, sending Yekbal Khan and Yoosoof Khan in advance. These divisions falling in with the troops of Moobarik Khan of Kandeish put them to the rout, and their chief fled to the fort of Aseer, while the King of Malwa, laying waste many of the towns of Kandeish, returned to Mando; but being informed that the son of Baboo Ray, Raja of Buglana, was prevented from paying his respects at the Malwa court owing to the assaults of the Kandeish troops, Sooltan Mahmood directed his son Gheias-ood-Deen to attack Moobarik Khan, who on the first intimation of his advance again retreated to Aseer. The young raja was thus enabled to proceed to Mando to offer his presents and pay his respects, after which he returned to Buglana. Meanwhile the Prince Gheias-ood-Deen proceeded to Runtunbhore, while the King marched in the direction of Chittoor. Rana Koombho, in order to avert the approaching calamity, met the King on the road, and made a large offering of money coined in his own name.* This

* The cause of Sooltan Mahmood's refusing the offering suggests the idea that Rana Koombho was a subjugated prince, but the fact is certainly otherwise; and we must ascribe the rejection of it to the insufficiency of the amount to appease the insatiable demands of the Mahomedan king. The ranas of Chittoor, though they frequently submitted to exactions from the kings of Guzerat and Malwa, yet they never lost altogether any considerable portion of their territory; and we know that Sanka, the grandson of Rana Koombho, was at the head of that formidable army which made an effort to recover the government from the power of the Great Mogul, Babur, in the battle of Kanwa, fought on the 21st of March, 1526. Vide vol. ii. p. 55.

circumstance so incensed Sooltan Mahmood that he returned the whole sum, and prosecuted his march to Chittoor, having detached Munsoor-ool-Moolk to lay waste the country of Mundsoor. He also threatened, at the same time, to leave his own governor in those provinces, and to build a town to be called after his own tribe, Khiljipoor. Rana Koombho, fearful of losing his country, sent messengers to Sooltan Mahmood in order to appease him, declaring he was willing to pay him any sum he was able rather than relinquish his territory, and promised henceforward to acknowledge himself a tributary of the Malwa crown. The monsoon coming on at this time, the King consented to receive a sum of gold, which he himself named, and then retired to Mando; where having remained some time, in the year 859, he returned to Mundsoor, when dividing the army into detachments, he entirely occupied the whole district.

A. H. 859.
A. D. 1454.

At this period, having understood that the Mahomedan religion no longer prevailed in Ajmere, he marched thither, and laid siege to the fort. The Raja, Gungadhur Ray, attacked the Mahomedan forces on four successive days, fighting on each occasion most gallantly, till at length he was killed; and the Rajpoots retiring in confusion, the Mahomedans followed them so closely that they entered the fort with the fugitives, and by that means obtained possession, but not without sustaining severe loss. The King built a musjid in the fort in commemoration of this event; and creating Khwaja Neamut Oolla governor, with the title of Seif Khan, he fell back on Mundulgur, encamping on the banks of the Bunas river to the south of that fortress. Rana Koombho, at the head of a body of Rajpoots, attacked one flank of the King's army under Taj Khan, and sent another body to attack that of Ally Khan. A severe action ensued in consequence, when the retreat was mutually sounded. On the following morning the Malwa officers persuaded the King of the necessity of his army retiring into quarters, both on account of their reduced numbers and the wretched state of the camp-equipments, now rendered almost useless; which circumstances, together with the approach of the rainy season, induced Sooltan Mahmood to return to Mando.*

Mohurrum 26. A. H. 861. Dec. 23. A. D. 1456. On the 26th of Mohurrum, in the year 861, the King again proceeded to Mundulgur; and after a vigorous siege occupied the lower fort, wherein many Rajpoots were put to the sword, but the hill-fort still held out; to reduce which might have been a work of time; but the reservoirs of water failing in consequence of the firing of the

* Col. Tod, whose authority may be relied on, states that a superb column, which cost 900,000*l.* sterling, built by Rana Koombho about this period, commemorating a great victory obtained by him over Sooltan Mahmood of Malwa, is still standing, and that he copied the inscription from it. This inscription confirms the Hindoo records of the time; and the drawn battle mentioned by the Malwa historian must, therefore, be deemed a defeat, more especially as the ruinous state of camp equipments would hardly justify the abandonment of a campaign, though it might require the army to halt for a season till they were renewed.

cannon,* the garrison was obliged to capitulate, and Rana Koombho stipulated to pay ten lacks of tunkas. This event happened on the 20th of
Zeehuj 20. Zeehuj of the same year, exactly eleven
A. H. 861. months after the King's leaving
Nov. 8. Mando. On the following day the
A. D. 1457. King caused all the temples to be destroyed, and musjids to be erected in their stead, appointing the necessary officers of religion to perform daily worship. Having also provided for the security of the place, he left Mundulgur on
Mohurrum 16. the 16th of Mohurrum of the follow-
A. H. 862. ing year, and proceeded to Mando by
Dec. 4. the route of Chittoor. On the road
A. D. 1457. the King detached his eldest son, Gheias-ood-Deen, to lay waste the country of the Bheels and Kolies. Gheias-ood-Deen having ravaged their districts, and taken many prisoners, returned to his father. Shortly afterwards the King sent his youngest son, Fidwy Khan, to reduce the fort of Boondy,† where the prince was opposed by the Rajpoots, who, after a bloody action, in which they displayed great courage, were defeated, and took refuge in the fort, whither they were pursued so closely, that many threw themselves into the ditch and were taken, after which the fort fell on the first assault. The Prince Fidwy Khan having offered up prayers for his success, and placed an officer of rank in the town of Boondy, rejoined his father at Mando.

* Concussion opens the crevices of the reservoirs, and the water is lost.

† Boondi of Rennell.

A.H. 863. A.D. 1458. Sooltan Mahmood, in the year 863, again marched against the Rajpoots. On arriving at the town of D'har, he detached Gheias-ood-Deen to lay waste the country of the Kolies and Bheels. In this excursion the Prince penetrated to the hills of Koombulmere, and on his return, having given the King some description of that fortress, Sooltan Mahmood resolved to march thither. On the next day he moved for that purpose, destroying all the temples on the road. On his arrival at Koombulmere, having ascended a hill at some distance on the east face of the fort, he was of opinion that nothing but a close siege of several years could effect its reduction, and on the following day, marching towards Dongurpoor, he encamped on the borders of the lake. Sham Das, the Ray of Dongurpoor, fled to Kohtahna, from which place he sent as an offering two lacks of tunkas and twenty-one horses, and Sooltan Mahmood afterwards returned to Mando. Mohurrum, A. H. 866. September, A. D. 1461. In the month of Mohurrum, A. H. 866, having heard that a prince under age had succeeded to the throne of the Deccan, under the title of Sooltan Nizam Shah Bahmuny, and that the officers of the state refused to pay him proper respect, Sooltan Mahmood, at the instigation of Nizam-ool-Moolk Ghoory, marched for the purpose of subduing the Deccan. Having crossed the Nurbudda, he received information that Moobarik Khan of Aseer was dead, and that his son, Adil Khan, who had succeeded him, had commenced his reign by putting to death Syud Kumal and Syud Sooltan, two of the most respectable and holy persons of the age, and plundered their houses of all their property. This information was confirmed by the arrival of their other brother, Syud Julal, who on his knees entreated the interference of the King of Malwa. Sooltan Mahmood, in consequence, marched direct to Aseer, whence Adil Khan addressed a humble petition, accompanied by an offering, which was delivered by one of the descendants of the venerable Sheikh Musaood Gunj Shukr. Sooltan Mahmood considering that even if he proceeded to attack Aseer he might not be able to effect its reduction, which would reflect disgrace instead of honour upon his arms, made a merit of becoming reconciled to Adil Khan Farooky. He therefore accepted his offering, and forgave him, on the plea of his sincere repentance. From Aseer Sooltan Mahmood marched to Elichpoor, and eventually to Balapoor, where his scouts brought him intelligence that the ministers of the young King of the Deccan had distributed two crore of tunkas among the officers and soldiers, and that the Deccan army, besides cavalry and infantry, was accompanied by one hundred and fifty elephants. Sooltan Mahmood, nevertheless, moved directly towards the Deccanies, till within three coss of Bidur, when an action was fought. Khwaja Jehan Toork, entitled Musheer-ool-Moolk, took the command of the Deccan army; and having placed the young king, who was only eight years of age, on an elephant with the white canopy over his head, brought him into the field. Mullik Nizam-ool-Moolk commanded the left wing, and Khwaja Mahmood Gawan, entitled Mullik-oot-Toojar, the right wing. When the armies closed, the latter officer charged the left wing of the Malwa forces, and succeeded in breaking it. On this occasion, both Mahabut Khan, the governor of Chundery, and Zuheer-ool-Moolk, one of the Malwa ministers, were killed, and the right wing giving way shortly after, the Malwa troops fled and were pursued by the enemy for the distance of sixteen or eighteen miles. Sooltan Mahmood no sooner perceived the probability of a defeat than he retired with a party from the field, and waited his opportunity to regain the battle; so that having allowed the Deccanies to be fully engaged in plunder, he suddenly appeared, and charging full on their rear with two thousand cavalry, gave them a complete overthrow. In this dilemma, Khwaja Jehan Toork, who commanded the centre of the army, and had not been engaged, surrounding the young King with a body of troops, carried him off in safety to the fort of Bidur. The face of affairs being thus reversed, Sooltan Mahmood in a few days re-assembled his forces, and invested the capital of the Deccan. Mullik-oot-Tajoor also collected in large force, and marched to raise the siege. The season being excessively hot, and the Malwa army so far from its own resources, Sooltan Mahmood commenced his retreat. During the march, he was greatly harassed by Mullik-oot-Toojar, an annoyance which did not cease till his arrival at Mando. On the following year, having resolved, if possible, to wrest the government of the Deccan out of the hands of the minister, he again marched to the south. For this purpose he ordered the army to assemble at the town of Nalcha, where receiving advices from Siraj-ool-Moolk of Kehrla that Nizam-ool-Moolk, a Deccan officer, with a large force, was on his march to attack that place, the King of Malwa moved in that direction. On the road he learned that the fort having been invested, the governor, who was always in a state of intoxication, had permitted his son to sally with an inadequate force and engage the Deccanies; that he had in consequence been defeated, and that the besiegers pursuing the garrison within the walls, the place had fallen into the hands of Nizam-ool Moolk; but that he, having exercised excessive tyranny towards the inhabitants, had been put to death by a party of Rajpoot infantry.* The instant Sooltan Mahmood heard of these events, he ordered Mukbool Khan with four thousand cavalry to proceed to Kehrla, marching himself to take revenge on the Deccanies towards Dowlutabad. On the road he was overtaken by ambassadors from Surgooja and from Jajnuggur, with presents consisting of five hundred and thirty elephants.† Having bestowed honorary dresses on the envoys, he dismissed them

* The cause of the death of Nizam-ool-Moolk is more satisfactorily accounted for in the Deccan history, vol. ii. p. 486.

† It is clear, from the way in which the historians of the times speak of elephants, as composing part of the Indian armies, their value was highly appreciated. It is probable that Sooltan Mahmood might have sent to the rajas of Surgooja and Jajnuggur, where wild elephants abound, to send some to him, which arrived very opportunely.

to their respective courts, and himself arrived at the town of Khuleefabad, where a messenger met him, conveying a dress from the Ameer-ool-Mominin Moostied Billa Yoosoof, the son of Mahomed Abassy, the Caliph of Egypt, as a token of his friendship and respect, also a letter styling him Defender of the Faithful, Sooltan Mahmood, in return, presented the bearer with several fine horses and other valuable articles. On reaching the Dowlutabad frontiers, news arrived that the King of Guzerat was on full march in his rear, in order to assist the King of the Deccan; on which Sooltan Mahmood taking the route of Malconda* on his return home, plundered that district, and marching through Gondwara arrived at Mando.

The best authenticated history I have seen, however, thus records these events:—"In the "year 870, Nizam-ool-Moolk Toork

A.H. 870. A.D. 1465. "being ordered to attack Kehrla, he "reduced that place by storm" (a detailed account of which has been already given in the history of the Kings of the Bahmuny dynasty of the Deccan); "and on the 1st of Rubbee ool-Awul, of the year 871, the King of Malwa

Rubbee-ool Awul 1. A.H. 871. October 11, A.D. 1466. "despatched Mukbool Khan to the "attack of Elichpoor, and having oc-"cupied that town, he gave it up to "be sacked. During the night the "governor of the town, collecting one thousand five hundred cavalry and all the infan-

* I am not aware of any town in Berar bearing this name; and the Teloogoo termination, *conda*, renders it likely to be an error of transcribers. It may be Mulkapoor, which lies in the direct route of the King's retreat.

" try in the place, resolved on attacking Muk-
" bool Khan, but the latter, hearing of his inten-
" tion, sent off his baggage and part of the army,
" only retaining with himself his best cavalry.
" With this body he took post on the road where
" he expected the assault would be made. The
" enemy, as he anticipated, attacked the army
" for the sake of plundering the camp-equipage,
" &c.; and at the very moment they expected to
" be crowned with victory, Mukbool Khan charg-
" ing with his cavalry on the rear of the assail-
" ants gave them a total defeat, and pursued
" them to the very gates of Elichpoor. The
" Deccanies lost on this occasion twenty officers
" of note killed, and thirty more who were taken
" prisoners. After this success Mukbool Khan proceeded to Kehrla." In the month of Jumad-ool-Awul of the same year, the kings of Malwa and the Deccan concluding a peace, it was agreed, according to some historians, that Kehrla should be retained by Malwa, and that it should be considered as the southern limit of that Kingdom; while others have asserted, that Elichpoor was ceded to Malwa on condition of the King refraining from invading the Deccan in future.

Jumad-ool-Awul, A.H. 871. January, A.D. 1467.

In this year Sooltan Mahmood caused the public accounts to be kept according to the lunar year, abolishing the system of the solar year. In the same year, also, the famous Sheikh Alla-ood-Deen, one of the most holy men of his age, arrived near Mando; on which occasion, Sooltan Mahmood paid him the compliment to go out and meet him at the Howz-i-Rany; and in order to preserve the dignity of each, the parties embraced on horseback. Shortly after, Mowlana Imad having been deputed by the reverend Syud Noor Bukhsh (the founder of a sect of Mahomedans in Kashmeer denominated Noorbukhshies), delivered to the King of Malwa the garment worn by that holy personage. Sooltan Mahmood, considering it a valuable gift, put it on, and in honour of the event distributed alms to all the holy men and the poor of the City. In the month of Mohurrum, information was brought that Mukbool Khan, the governor of Kehrla, having plundered the town, and secured a large booty, had retired to the south, and put himself under the protection of the King of the Deccan. It was, moreover, stated, that he had delivered over all the public elephants and the fort to the young raja of Kehrla, in consequence of which a general massacre of the Mahomedans ensued; and the Raja was joined by the inhabitants of Gondwara, many of whom had entered his service. With these bands he waylaid travellers, and acted the part of a common robber. Sooltan Mahmood, under these circumstances, ordered Taj Khan and Ahmud Khan with their divisions to attack the Raja, while he himself remained to organise the army at Nalcha. The troops under Taj Khan having made rapid marches to Kehrla were opposed on the plain by the young raja, who made a desperate resistance, and fought a severe action; but being defeated in the end, and obliged to fly, he threw himself on the protection of the

Mohurrum, A.H. 872. August, A.D. 1467

Gond zemindars, by one of whom he was seized and delivered up to the King's forces, who in the mean time re-occupied Kehrla. Sooltan Mahmood, on hearing of this success, marched in the direction of Sarungpoor, in order to receive Khwaja Jumal-ood-Deen, ambassador from the court of Aboo Syeed Mirza,* King of Bokhara. Flattered by this mark of attention, Sooltan Mahmood loaded the ambassador with honours and presents, sending his back to his master with a variety of the rarities of India, such as muslins of all descriptions, Arab horses, dancing women, and singers mounted on elephants superbly caparisoned, together with a number of Indian and Abyssinian slaves for the seraglio, and also a few meinas† and parrots which had been taught the Persian language; added to this, the King deputed Alla-ood-Deen as ambassador, to accompany Jumal-ood-Deen on his return to Bokhara. Jumal-ood-Deen was the bearer of a poem composed by himself on the virtues' of Aboo Syeed, written in the Indian language, which he read, and which was translated by Aboo Syeed's ambassador. It is said, this poem gratified the King of Bokhara more than any of the numerous rarities which the ambassador brought.

* Aboo Syeed Mirza, third in descent from Tamerlane, reigned over Transoxania, and held his court at Bokhara. He was the grandfather of Babur, the founder of the dynasty of the Great Mogul in India.

† The meina is, in shape, not unlike the blackbird; but its dark plumage is much intermixed with white and bright yellow, and may be taught to speak more plainly than any other bird. It is supposed, by some persons, to be the same as the mocking-brid of America, though I believe they are different.

In the year 873 advices were brought
A.H. 873. from Ghazy Khan, stating that the ze-
A.D. 1468. mindars of Keechiwara had laid hands on part of the Malwa territory. On this information the King proceeded to punish them, sending a force in advance into the country of the Keechies; but being aware of the difficulty of carrying on operations in the interior, he built a fort which he called Julalpoor, leaving Meer Khan to keep the surrounding zemindars in subjection. After this campaign Sooltan Mahmood returned towards Mando; but having suffered severely from
Zeekad 19. the heat of the weather before he left
A.H. 873. Keechiwara, he fell dangerously ill on
May 27. the road, and died on the 19th of
A.D. 1469. Zeekad, A.H. 873, at the age of sixty-eight.

شهي والاقدر سلطان محمود
چون شد از امر حق رحلت گزيني
بپرسيدم زهاتف سال تاريخ
ندا امد که شد جنت نشيني

"When the illustrious Sooltan Mahmood, according to the will of God, went on his long journey, I asked of a courtier the date of his death, and a voice answered, '*He has a place in heaven.**'"

Sooltan Mahmood of Malwa ascended the throne in the 34th year of his age, and reigned thirtyfour years. It is a remarkable coincidence that this sovereign should have reigned as a king the

* The numerals of the two last words جنت نشيني give the date of his death.

same number of years he lived as a subject, more particularly as Ameer Teimoor Korkan, his contemporary, ascended the throne in the 36th year of his age, and reigned exactly thirty-six years. Sooltan Mahmood was polite, brave, just, and learned, and during his reign his subjects, Mahomedans as well as Hindoos, were happy, and maintained a friendly intercourse with each other. Scarcely a year passed that he did not take the field, so that his tent became his home, and his resting-place the field of battle. His leisure hours were devoted to hearing the histories and memoirs of the courts of different kings of the earth read. He prided himself (not without reason) on his intimate knowledge of human nature, a subject to which he devoted much attention. His justice was so prompt and exact that it frequently happened when a merchant had been plundered during the night in Mando, and the fact was fully established, that he was instantly reimbursed for his losses from the public treasury; and a sum equal to the amount was levied from the police officers whose business it was to trace the robbers, and to protect that part of the city. On hearing that a traveller had been carried off by a tiger, he ordered the governors of the different provinces to send out parties and destroy these wild beasts; proclaiming, that if after the period of two years he ascertained a human being were killed by a wild beast, unless in attacking him, he would hold the governor responsible. The promptitude he observed in making his actions accord with his words was so well understood that for many years after his death wild beasts of any description were scarce throughout the kingdom.*

* Perhaps no part of India so abounds with tigers at present as the vicinity of the once famous city of Mando. This capital, now deserted by man, is overgrown by forest trees; and from being the seat of luxury, elegance, and wealth, has become the abode of wild beasts, and is resorted to by the few Europeans in that quarter of the world for the purpose of enjoying the pleasure of destroying them. Instances have been known of the tigers being so bold as to carry off troopers riding in the ranks of their regiments.

SOOLTAN GHEIAS OOD-DEEN.

Ascends the throne of his father—declares his son, Abdool Kadur, heir-apparent, and places in his hands the entire control of the government, and abandons himself to the pleasures of the haram.—Internal arrangements for the seraglio, containing fifteen thousand females.—His peaceable reign for thirty-three years.—The King's death.

SOOLTAN GHEIAS-OOD-DEEN, the elder son of Sooltan Mahmood, ascended the throne of Malwa on the death of his father. Having conferred on his younger brother, Fidwy Khan, the government of Runtunbhore to be held in perpetuity, he nominated his own son, Abdool Kadur, prime minister, and proclaimed him heir-apparent, with the title of Sooltan Nasir-ood-Deen; conferring on him, also, at the same time, a chutr and palky, an estate for his support, and the command of a body of twelve thousand cavalry. Shortly after his accession the King gave a grand entertainment; on which occasion, addressing his officers, he stated, that as he had during the last thirty-four years been employed constantly in the field, fighting under the banners of his illustrious father, he now yielded up the sword to his son, in order that he might himself enjoy ease the rest of his days. He accordingly established within his seraglio all the separate offices of a court, and had at one time fifteen thousand women within his palace. Among these were school-mistresses, musicians, dancers, embroiderers, women to read prayers, and persons of all professions and trades. Five hundred beautiful young Toorky females in men's clothes, and uniformly clad, armed with bows and quivers, stood on his right hand, and were called the Toorky guard. On his left were five hundred Abyssinian females also dressed uniformly, armed with fire-arms. Each individual within the seraglio was allowed daily two seers of grain and two tunkas of copper. One day having observed a mouse in the royal apartment, he ordered it to receive its daily allowance of rice and money; and this absurdity extended to the tame pigeons, parrots, &c. With all these extraordinary fancies, he was particular in his daily prayers, and gave instructions to his attendants always to wake him at the specified time: if asleep, they were authorised to use every exertion to prevent his missing the hour of prayer; and it is well known that they have even sprinkled water on his face, and pulled him out of his bed before he would rise; but on these occasions he was never known to lose his temper. It is an extraordinary fact that no rebellion among his own subjects, nor invasion of the Malwa territories by an enemy, occurred during his reign until the year 887, when Bheilole Lody, King of

A. H. 887.
A. D. 1482.

Dehly, attacked Runtunbhore. It was with difficulty the circumstance was conveyed to the King's knowledge, though the fact was well known throughout the city, and had become a subject of notoriety and conversation before the minister could have access to the seraglio. On receiving the news, the King directed Sheer Khan of Chundery to collect the forces of Bhilsa, Sarungpoor, and Chundery, and march direct against the invader; and his orders were so promptly carried into effect, that Sheer Khan marched to Byana. Bheilole Lody, rather than risk a battle, retreated, while Sheer Khan pursued him towards Dehly; when Bheilole even thought it advisable to pay a sum of money to induce him to retire without molesting the country. Sheer Khan retreated, and rebuilt the town of Lallpoor, which Bheilole had destroyed; and thence returned to Chundery. In the year 903 Sooltan

A. H. 903.
A. D. 1497.

Gheias-ood-Deen having arrived at an advanced age, his sons anxiously looked for his death, as an event which would secure to one of them the throne of Malwa. The youngest, Shoojat Khan, surnamed Alla-ood-Deen, resolved either to depose his elder brother, Nasir-ood-Deen, after his accession, or to cut him off before his father's death; and this determination becoming known, a jelousy arose between the two brothers, who conspired against each other. The contentions of the princes rose to such a height that the elder brother was obliged to fly from Mando

A. H. 905.
A. D. 1499.

in the year 905. He, however, collected a force, and returned and besieged that fortress. Having during the whole of his father's reign officiated as prime minister, he had great influence, and he gained over some of the officers in the fort who opened the Tarapoor gate, and admitted him on the 24th of Rubbee-oos-Sany, A. H. 906. Upon this occasion Alla-ood-Deen, the younger brother, fled to his father's palace; and Nasir-ood-Deen, following him closely, put him to death, as well as all his children and the whole of his family. Having then assumed the reins of government, he was formally crowned, and in a few days after his father was found dead in the seraglio; and it was supposed that poison had been administered to him by order of his son. Thus died Sooltan Gheias-ood-Deen, after a reign of thiry-three years.*

Rubbee-oos-Sany 24. A. H. 906. October 22. A. D. 1500.

* The possession of uncontrolled power, and the notion that happiness consisted in mere sensual enjoyments, seem to have operated on this prince's mind till it affected it with insanity.

SOOLTAN NASIR-OOD-DEEN.

The King is accused of causing the death of his father. —Distractions in Malwa.—Sheer Khan governor of Chundery, Sikundur Khan of Eerich, and Mahabut Khan of Mundsoor, unite and march against the King.—The rebels are defeated, and Sheer Khan and Sikundur Khan are killed in the action.—The King indulges in scandalous excesses—becomes cruel to his people.—The Prince Shahab-ood-Deen, the King's eldest son, is induced by the nobles to revolt—is defeated, and escapes to Dehly.—The King appoints his third son, Mahmood, his successor, and dies.

Rubbee-oos-Sany 27. A. H. 906. October 25. A. D. 1500.

On the 27th of Rubbee-oos-Sany, of the year 906, Nasir-ood-Deen ascended the throne of Malwa. It was asserted at the time that he poisoned his father; yet considering the animosity of his brother's party, and the number of his personal enemies, it is not just to accuse him of that crime, as no circumstance was ever brought forward to prove the assertion, nor does there appear any motive that should have actuated him to commit such an act, as he had been already crowned by his father's consent, and had long conducted, without restraint, the affairs of the government. His accession, however, was succeeded by a series of domestic feuds, in which many of the nobles were involved; so that it is not a matter of surprise that public affairs fell into a state of disorder.* Sheer Khan of Chundery, taking advantage of these distractions, rebelled, and was joined by Mahabut Khan of Mundsoor, as well as by many other of the malecontent nobles, who assembling a force advanced by the route of Depalpoor towards the capital. Sooltan Nasir-ood-Deen mached to attack them, and was joined by Ein-ool-Moolk and many other of the Malwa chiefs, on which Sheer Khan retreated; but he was reduced to the necessity of fighting a battle near Sarungpoor, where he experienced a total defeat, and fled through Chundery to Eerich; to the former of which places the King pursued him before he returned. The adherents of Sheer Khan now wrote to him, that the King had retreated to Mando on account of the rains, and advised him to repair to Chundery, when by the assistance of the inhabitants he might still collect a sufficient force to oppose the

* The author of the Moontukhib-oot-Towareekh has explained the state of affairs more fully than Ferishta. He states, that after Sooltan Gheias-ood-Deen had placed the administration of his government into the hands of Nasir-ood-Deen, his younger brother, Shoojat Khan, through jealousy, united with Rany Khoorsheed, one of the King's favourite mistresses, to poison the King's mind against him, so that Nasir-ood-Deen was induced to fly from Mando. Shoojat Khan, in concert with the Rany, and without the King's knowledge, raised a force to attack Nasir-ood-Deen, but was defeated, and eventually pursued by the heir-apparent to Mando. Here several officers of rank joined Nasir-ood-Deen, and after a few days admitted him into the fort. Shoojat Khan and the King's mistress were seized and inprisoned, and Sooltan Gheias-ood-Deen became reconciled to his son.

King. Sooltan Nasir-ood-Deen, on hearing that Sheer Khan was again in the field, detached Yekbal Khan and Mulloo Khan against him, who having attacked him within two coss of Chundery, Sheer Khan received a mortal wound, and his colleague Sikundur Khan was killed on the spot. Mahabut Khan of Mundsoor placed Sheer Khan on his own elephant and fled, but he died of his wounds on the road. Sooltan Nasir-ood-Deen arriving at the place where he was interred caused his body to be disentombed, and hung up in the town of Chundery, the government of which place he conferred on Himmut Khan, and after proceeding to Adilpoor he returned to Mando. On his arrival at the capital, he abandoned himself to the most shameless excesses, particularly that of drunkenness. He made it his business to discover and put to death all the adherents of his late brother, whose sins time ought to have buried in oblivion; and his own personal servants also suffered from his cruelty. It is said, that one day while lying in a state of intoxication on the verge of a reservoir of water, he fell in. Four female slaves who were standing by, laying hold of him, at the risk of their own lives, pulled him out, and taking of his wet clothes dressed him again. On recovering from his intoxication he complained of violent head-ache; and the female slaves mentioned the circumstance of his falling into the reservoir in order to account for it; the King, however, was so enraged, conceiving it to be untrue, and that the females only said so by way of reproaching him for his inebriety, he drew his sword, and put them all to death with his own hand, in spite of their cries for mercy, and although they exhibited the wet clothes which they had taken off from him.

A.H. 908.
A.D. 1502.
In the year 908, Sooltan Nasir-ood-Deen marched to attack the Rajpoots of Keechiwara. On arriving at Akburpoor, he built a splendid palace, which was then much admired by all who saw it. Having plundered the whole of the Keechiwara district he returned to Mando, and on the following year

A.H. 909.
A.D. 1503.
(viz. 909) he proceeded towards Chittoor, where having received a large present in money from the Rana, and having procured from Raja Jewundas, one of the subordinate rays, his daughter, he returned to Mando. This lady was afterwards dignified with the title of the Chittoor Queen.

On the road back, news arrived that Ahmud Nizam Shah Bheiry, having declared war against Dawood Khan the ruler of Kandeish, had marched to reduce that province, and compelled the latter chief to take post in Aseer. The ruler of Kandeish owned allegiance to the present King of Malwa, and he considered it his duty to assist him. Yekbal Khan and Khwaja Jehan were therefore ordered to proceed with a large force to the south; but before it reached its destination, Ahmud Nizam Shah commenced his retreat to Ahmudnuggur, and Yekbal Khan, after causing the public prayers to be read in the name of Sooltan Nasir-ood-Deen at Boorhanpoor, returned to Mando.

Sooltan Nasir-ood-Deen during the lifetime of

his father had often opposed his will, and having subsequently revolted, attacked his capital. The King now dreaded lest his own sons might, in imitation of him, rebel also. He in consequence always viewed them with distrust and jealousy. This feeling was so apparent to his son Shahab-ood-Deen, the declared heir to the throne, that he always entered his father's presence with apprehension; and the nobles, in the year 916, wearied and disgusted with the persecution and cruelty of Nasir-ood-Deen, persuaded his son to assume charge of the government at once. For this purpose he left Mando and collected a large force. Sooltan Nasir-ood-Deen, however, having oppossed and defeated the Prince, the latter fled to Dehly, and, in spite of the remonstrances of his father, refused to come back. On the return of Sooltan Nasir-ood-Deen towards Mando, he was siezed with a fever, brought on by excess, at the town of Burtpoor; during which illness, although in the cold season, he bathed, and in a few days after died. He reigned eleven years and four months, having previously declared his third son, Mahmood, his successor.

A.H. 916.
A.D. 1512.

SOOLTAN MAHMOOD II.

Ascends the throne, and secures the person of his brother Sahib Khan.—Sahib Khan is released, and is proclaimed King.—Mahmood retires from Mando, and meets with assistance from Medny Ray, an officer of his government.—The Prince Sahib Khan is defeated, and flies.—The Prince Shahab-ood-Deen dies on his road from Kandeish to Malwa, leaving a son, the Prince Musaood.—The governor of Bhilsa espouses his cause, while the governor of Chundery espouses that of Sahib Khan.—The King of Dehly joins the league in favour of Sahib Khan, but it is dissolved by the ability of Medny Ray, who obtains an entire supremacy in the government.—Sooltan Mahmood retires to Guzerat, and obtains the aid of Moozuffur Shah.—Mando taken from the Hindoos, and Sooltan Mahmood is replaced on his throne.—The Guzerat army retires. Sooltan Mahmood is defeated and taken prisoner by the Hindoos, but is restored to his government.—The King of Guzerat dies.—Contests for the throne.—Sooltan Mahmood of Malwa receives one of the pretenders at his court, where he carries on intrigues against Bahadur Shah of Guzerat.—War ensues.—Mando taken by the King of Guzerat.—Sooltan Mahmood and his family fall into the hands of Bahadur Shah—they are sent to Champanere, and are put to death on the road thither.—Extinction of the race of Khiljy.

On the news of the death of Sooltan Nasir-ood-Deen reaching his son Shahab-ood-Deen, he relinquished the idea of prosecuting his journey towards Dehly, but returning to Malwa, arrived at the capital, while his young brother, Mahmood, still remained at Nalcha. The commandant of

Mando, Mahafiz Khan, having refused him admittance, the Prince fled to Aseer on the approach of his brother Mahmood, who, on entering Mando, was formally crowned with great pomp; upon which occasion no fewer than seven hundred elephants, with velvet housings embroidered in gold, formed part of the procession. Shortly after his accession, a conspiracy was formed against one Buswunt Row, a personal favourite of the King, who had attended him from the period of his birth; and he was put to death by the conspirators, who declared that he had laid a scheme to overturn the government: they also stated, in an address to the crown, that one Nizam-ool-Moolk, another of the King's friends, had trodden in the footsteps of Buswunt Row, and they consequently insisted on his being delivered over to them for trial. The King was alarmed at these desperate encroachments on his prerogative, but thought it advisable to give up Nizam-ool-Moolk to be tried, reserving the punishment in his own hands; but in spite of his wish to spare him, the King was constrained to banish him. Mahafiz Khan, the governor of Mando, presuming on the King's easy temper, had the boldness to address him one day in open durbar in the following words: "Your "elder brother is now in confinement in this fort, "and only waits for an opportunity to put you to "death, and ascend the throne. If you have any "desire to retain your crown, your only chance "of securing it is to order his immediate execu-"tion. If not, you will merit the fate which "awaits you." The King was at first confounded with this language, and asked the governor in an angry tone how he presumed thus to address him? Mahafiz Khan, seeing he had gone too far to retreat, continued to answer the King in a disrespectful tone and manner. The King, unable to restrain himself, seized the sword which lay by his side, and without drawing it from the scabbard stuck Mahafiz Khan two blows on head with all his strength. The blood flowed from the wound, and Mahafiz Khan made his escape home, where collecting all his personal attendants and guards, he marched to the palace. The nobles, who rather promoted than wished to suppress the rebellion, remained quiet in their houses; while the King, collecting his bodyguard, consisting chiefly of foreigners, such as Arabs, Persians, and Abyssinians, made a stand in the palace-yard, and compelled Mahafiz Khan, after having lost many men, to retreat to his own house. The King now used his endeavours to collect a larger force, but in vain; for most of the officers with their retainers had joined Mahafiz Khan. The royal party remained under arms all night, and in the morning, assisted by some of the inhabitants, forced their way out of the fort. The King's departure was the signal for Mahafiz Khan to release the Prince Sahib Khan, and to place the crown on his head. Sooltan Mahmood, having encamped on the plain, summoned the chiefs of provinces to attend him; and the first person of rank who joined his standard was Medny Ray, a Rajpoot chief, accompanied by all his family, and a large force of his tribe. After him came Shirza Khan, governor of Chundery, and subsequently many other nobles of the surrounding districts. The King now issued a proclamation, inviting, with promises of promotion, all persons who should quit the standard of Sahib Khan and Mahafiz Khan, and join the royal army. At the same time he marched towards the capital, and was opposed by the rebel forces. A severe engagement took place, during which the Prince Sahib Khan charged in person at the head of a small body of cavalry, and attacked the King's personal guard, but he was repulsed. The fate of the action was eventually decided by the gallant conduct of Medny Ray and the Rajpoot infantry, who preserved a compact phalanx, and with spears and daggers broke the enemy, and obliged Sahib Khan to take refuge in the fort of Mando, many of his troops being compelled to seek protection in the caves surrounding the hill. Sooltan Mahmood, unwilling to drive his brother to extremity, sent word to him, that notwithstanding what had happened he forgave him on account of their mother, and promised allow him a stipulated annual amount, which he might receive wheresoever he chose, provided he relinquished the idea of ascending the throne, which, the King observed, he considered it his duty to defend with his life. Sahib Khan, relying on the strength of the fort, refused to accede to terms. Sooltan Mahmood now closely invested the place, and received overtures from some of the chiefs within, that they would admit him into the fort by a certain gate. The Prince Sahib Khan, and Mahafiz Khan, discovering the correspondence, and placing no further reliance on their adherents, secured all the jewels they could collect, and made their escape to Guzerat in the month of Shuval, in the year 917; where a dispute having arisen between the Prince Sahib Khan and the ambassador of Shah Ismael of Persia, he was compelled to quit Guzerat* also, and go to Aseer; where having collected three hundred cavalry he went to Gavul, and solicited the assistance of Imad Shah. That prince being on friendly terms with Sooltan Mahmood refused his aid to replace him on the throne, though he assigned to him an estate and the revenue of a few villages. Meanwhile, Sooltan Mahmood, having been re-established on his throne, gave a new form to his government. It is proper to observe here, that at the period when Sooltan Mahmood made his escape from the capital, his eldest brother, the Prince Shahab-ood-Deen, who had taken refuge with the ruler of Kandeish, marched towards Mando, for the purpose of bringing forward his claims to the throne, both as the eldest son of the late Sooltan Nasir-ood-Deen and because he had been originally declared heir-apparent. His constitution, however, being weak, and the heat of the weather excessive, he contracted a fever on the road,† which terminated

Shuval, A.H. 917. December, A.D. 1513.

* For the details, see history of Guzerat, vol. iv. p. 80.

† No other cause seems necessary to account for the sudden death of the Prince than the bare circumstance of his travelling between Kandeish and Malwa in the months of November or December. The experience of several late years has proved that few individuals can traverse those unhealthy regions with impunity at that season of the year.

his existence, leaving his son, Mukhsoos Khan, under the care of his minister, Yekbal Khan, who instantly proclaimed the boy's title to the throne, under the name of Sooltan Hooshung II. Finding, however, on his arrival in Malwa, that Sooltan Mahmood was firmly seated on the throne, after showing some trifling opposition, the Prince and his minister threw themselves on the King's mercy. Shortly afterwards Medny Ray,* who had gained and undue influence in the King's councils, persuaded him that both Yekbal and Mukhsoos Khan were carrying on a treasonable correspondence with the King of the Deccan. Sooltan Mahmood, too easily giving credence to these insinuations, ordered Yekbal Khan to be killed the next day as he came to the durbar, a sentence which was carried into execution before all the by-standers. Sooltan Mahmood, at the instigation of Medny Ray, sent for Bohjut Khan, governor of Chundery, and some other chiefs, to the capital; but they were so much alarmed, both at the influence of Medny Ray and at the sudden execution which had just taken place, that Bohjut Khan, in particular, pleaded

* We must receive with great caution the accusations made by the Mahomedan historian of Malwa against Medny Ray It appears that he first joined the King when the Mahomedan nobles deserted him; that his followers gained the battle of Mando against the Prince Sahib Khan; and it is natural to suppose that the King, whose partiality to Hindoos in the early part of his reign has been recorded, should now give his confidence to one possessed of such power and influence among his relations and cast, and who had evinced an early devotion to the King's cause and to his person.

the near approach of the rainy season as an excuse, for non-attendance at court. The King took no measures against Bohjut Khan, but deputed Munsoor Khan, a nobleman of rank, to reduce Sikundur Khan of Bhilsa, and bring him to court. On hearing of this, Sikundur Khan abandoned Bhilsa, and proceeding to the south, occupied the country lying between Kuhndwa and Shahabad,* where the rays of Gondwana had brought a large force to assist him. Under these circumstances, Munsoor Khan wrote to court that the troops with him were insufficient to oppose the united arms of the rays of Gondwana and Sikundur Khan. Medny Ray, wishing to see the whole of the old officers disgraced, in order to secure to himself all the court influence, answered the letter in the King's name, telling Munsoor Khan that the appearance of the royal troops alone would be sufficient to deter the enemy from attack, and that his application for a reinforcement was merely a subterfuge to avoid fighting. Munsoor Khan, astonished at the tenour and style of this letter, marched instantly with Bukhtiar Khan, and joined Bohjut Khan at Chundery. The King, hearing of the assemblage of troops at that place, took the field in person, and proceeded to D'har having previously sent Medny Ray with his own adherents and one hundred and fifty elephants against Sikundur Khan. Medny Ray soon induced the forces of Sikundur Khan to disperse; and having made

* Probably Shahpoor.

terms with the latter chief, both returned with Medny Ray to Bhilsa, which was again restored to Sikundur Khan. The influence of Medny Ray after this event increased daily. On his return to camp, he heard that a faction at Mando had created one of their party king, and had placed on his head the white canopy, from off the tomb of Sooltan Gheias-ood-Deen; but the kotwal of the city having behaved with much presence of mind and resolution, had put a stop to the commotion, and restored order. Bohjut Khan of Chundery and his party, perceiving the inordinate and increasing power and influence of Medny Ray, were more than ever alarmed; and they accordingly deputed persons to Gavul, inviting the Prince Sahib Khan to return, and to assume the reins of government;* writing, at the same time, a petition to Sikundur Lody of Dehly, stating that the infidel Rajpoots had gained an alarming ascendency over the Mahomedans in Malwa; and that one Medny Ray, a chief of that tribe, had virtually become

* The Moontukhib-oot-Towareekh states, that Sahib Khan reached Chundery, and was met by Bohjut Khan and Munsoor Khan, who proclaimed him King. After a long negotiation, the Prince was induced to forego his title to the whole kingdom, on condition of receiving the fort of Raiseen, the town of Bhilsa, and the district of Dhamony. For his immediate expenses the King sent eleven lacks of tunkas, and presented him with twelve elephants. Bohjut Khan, under the title of Sahib Khan's minister, embezzled the money, and usurped the districts, so that the Prince Sahib Khan was at open war with him. Bohjut Khan, in consequence, fled to the Mogul court.

master of the country and its resources, having persuaded the King to destroy many of the old and confidential officers of the state, while those who were left had taken the alarm, and fled to different parts of the kingdom. The petition proceeded to state, that although Sooltan Mahmood now regretted having exalted Medny Ray, and having placed all his reliance on the Rajpoots, yet he had so given himself up into that chief's hands, that he not only refused to listen to his Mahomedan officers and subjects, but seemed willing, in concert with his Hindoo minister, to cut off the few who remained. That as for the laws of the prophet, and the true worship, they had been wholly abandoned every where, and that the mosques had been converted into receptacles for infidels. It was indeed expected that Ray Rayan, the son of Medny Ray, would in a short time openly declare his accession to the throne. "If, then," says the petition, "your Majesty will con-"descend to send a force, around which the faith-"ful may rally, Sahib Khan, the brother of the "present king, will enter the country, and public "prayers may be read in his name as King of "Malwa in Chundery and in the surrounding dis-"tricts." Mahafiz Khan, the partisan of Sahib Khan, who defended the fort of Mando, and had fled to Guzerat with that prince, was now at Dehly; and a force consisting of twelve thousand cavalry, under the command of Imad-ool-Moolk Lody and Syeed Khan, accompanied by Mahafiz Khan, marched to raise Sahib Khan to the throne of Malwa, with the title of Sooltan Mahomed.

At this period, also, Moozuffur Shah, King of Guzerat, with a large army arrived at D'har, and Sikundur Khan having again raised the standard of revolt, plundered the country. Medny Ray, aware that every thing depended upon his exertions, directed Mullik Lado, the governor of Kuhndwa, to oppose Sikundur Khan, while he himself marched, accompanied by the King, against the forces of Guzerat, which had now arrived within a short distance of Mando; but being attacked and defeated, Moozuffur Shah retreated to Ahmudabad. Mullik Lado defeated Sikundur Khan; but one of his dependents, who had suffered from Mullik Lado, attacked him unawares, and stabbed him to the heart. Sikundur Khan, in consequence, rallying his troops, attacked and defeated the King's forces, who were now without a leader, and having taken six elephants, together with other booty, he returned to Seevas.

Sooltan Mahmood, deferring the punishment of Sikundur Khan for the present, marched against the forces under Bohjut Khan at Chundery. On the road to which place he heard that Sahib Khan had, at the instigation of the Chundery confederates, arrived near his army, and had assumed the title of king, supported by a force from Dehly under Imad-ool-Moolk Lody, and accompanied by Mahafiz Khan. This intelligence occasioned the utmost distress to Sooltan Mahmood; added to which, two parties of cavalry, the one under Suddur Khan, and the other under the Prince Mukhsoos Khan, deserting the royalists, joined the enemy. Sahib Khan now detached a force under one

Mahmood Khan to occupy Sarungpoor; but that officer, alarmed at the approach of the King's army, fled disgracefully. Affairs were in this state when Imad-ool-Moolk and Syeed Khan, at the secret instigation of Medny Ray, recommended Bohjut Khan to read public prayers, and to coin money, in the name of their own master, Sikundur Lody of Dehly; a measure calculated, of all others, to separate the interests of the Dehly and Chundery chieftains. The proposal being made to Bohjut Khan, he spurned the idea of deserting the cause of Sahib Khan, which opened to him no advantage whatsoever, and he accordingly made an excuse to separate himself from the Dehly forces, the object of all others which Medny Ray desired. Meanwhile an order arrived for the recall of the Dehly troops. It is stated that public prayers were actually read, and coin struck, in the name of Sikundur Lody; but on hearing that Sooltan Mahmood of Malwa, with a large army, was on his march to oppose his small detachment, and being unable to spare more troops at the time, Sikundur ordered his army to fall back on Dehly. At all events, Sooltan Mahmood, on the retreat of the Dehly troops, considering it a mark of the intervention of Divine favour, offered up prayers on the occasion, while, in the mean time, Mahafiz Khan and Khwaja Jehan, taking a circuitous route, marched by order of Sahib Khan to invest Mando. The King, obtaining intelligence of this movement, detached Hubeeb Khan with a large force of Rajpoots to oppose the Prince; and in the neighbourhood of Nalcha an action took place, in which Mahafiz Khan was killed, and his force dispersed. The Prince Sahib Khan and Bohjut Khan, deprived of all hopes of assistance, now thought it advisable to make overtures for peace; and one Sheikh Owlia was deputed as envoy to the King for that purpose. Sooltan Mahmood, who prayed for nothing more, gladly ceded the forts of Raiseen, Bhilsa, and Dhamony, to Sahib Khan for his support; at the same time presenting him with ten lacks of copper tunkas and twelve elephants; after which conciliatory letters were written to the different officers who had espoused the cause of Sahib Khan. On the King's return to his capital he was guided entirely by the advice of Medny Ray, who was daily employed in the destruction of one or other of the Mahomedan chiefs. They were frequently put to death without cause, their houses plundered, and their estates confiscated. At last the King evinced his dislike for all the nobles, and for Mahomedans in general, so that most of the officers who held situations under the late Nasir-ood-Deen and Gheias-ood-Deen were put to death, and their offices filled by Rajpoots. The very Mahomedan females who had been educated in the seraglio of Sooltan Gheias-ood-Deen now became the mistresses of Medny Ray and the rest of the Rajpoot officers. The guards at the gates were composed entirely of Hindoos, and the old system of government was completely subverted. Ghalib Khan, the late governor of Mando, became so offended at the ascendency obtained by the Hindoos, that when the King was out on a hunting party with his infidel Rajpoots he shut the gates of the garrison, and refused them admittance. Sooltan Mahmood immediately proceeded to invest the fort. Ghalib Khan, unable to hold out against the royalists, escaped; but the King sent a party of Rajpoots to seize him, by which he was overtaken in a few days and brought into Mando, where he was executed. After this, Medny Ray removed the few remaining Mahomedans from their public situations, so that excepting the personal servants of the King, amounting to about two hundred, the whole of the offices of government were filled with Rajpoots. Affairs had now assumed a very alarming appearance in the mind of the King, who, for the first time, began to reflect seriously on the situation to which he was reduced, and resolved to dismiss all the Rajpoots. It is customary in India, when a servant is discharged, for his master to give him a leaf of pân, as a token that he has received his formal dismissal, and that he bears him no malice; so Sooltan Mahmood having ordered forty thousand packets of pân to be brought him, he sent them in a basket by the hands of Araish Khan to Medny Ray, stating that it was his Majesty's pleasure to discharge the whole of the Rajpoot army, consisting of so many persons; and he directed Medny Ray to distribute the pân amongst them, and to disband them accordingly. The Rajpoots declared to a man that they were prepared to shed the last drop of their blood for the King; that they had always defended his person and kingdom with bravery, and were not aware of what they had been guilty, to be thus discharged at a moment's warning. But they went to Medny Ray, and proposed to remove Sooltan Mahmood and place Ray Rayan, the son of Medny Ray, on the throne. The wily statesman replied, "As to the government of Malwa, it has long been "in my hands; but if I were to usurp the crown, "the kings of Guzerat, of Kandeish, and of the "Deccan uniting, would very soon reduce Malwa "to their subjection, in spite of every effort on our "part: the best thing that can now be done, is to "go and beg the King to forego his intention of "discharging you." Medny Ray succeeded in his wish, which was granted, on condition that the personal offices of the state should be filled by Mahomedans; that the old officers still alive should be replaced in their former situations; that all Mahomedan women should be released from the seraglios of the Rajpoots; and that no Hindoo should hold any civil office at court. These terms being acceded to by Medny Ray, he was more than ever assiduous in gaining the King's good will. But Salb'han,* a Rajpoot officer of rank, provoked him by repeated insults, till at last Sooltan Mahmood, who had only two hundred personal attendants, ordered them to waylay both Salb'han and Medny Ray, and to murder them. They were accordingly attacked: the former was killed, but the latter made his escape to his house, though covered with wounds. The Rajpoots who were devoted to both these officers, on hearing of the death of Salb'han, and the attack made on

* Salivahan.

Medny Ray, proceeded to assault the palace. Sooltan Mahmood, who though a fool in the cabinet, had not his equal in courage in the hour of danger, girt on his sword, and sallying forth with sixteen horsemen and a few infantry attacked the Rajpoots with desperate resolution, many of whom he slew with his own hands, and absolutely beat them back from the palace. After being checked, they collected at Medny Ray's house, and called on him to head them. He replied, that although the king his master had sought his life, he had no right to take up arms against him: he said, moreover, that he was ready, even now, to submit to any punishment which the King chose to inflict, rather than head an army against him. Medny Ray concluded this address by ordering the troops instantly to retire to their quarters; and sent word to the King, informing him that he was out of danger from the wounds which he had received from the King's servants, who had waylaid him for the purpose of putting him to death; that he was ready, for the good of the state, to lay down his life; and that if his Majesty was of opinion that his death was necessary for the promotion of that object, he was prepared to submit himself to execution. Sooltan Mahmood, convinced of Medny Ray's fidelity, again received him into favour; but the latter being ever after suspicious of the King's intentions, went in future to the palace attended by an escort of five hundred men. This measure so greatly disturbed the King's mind, that one night leaving the fort of Mando with one horseman and a few foot-attendants, he did not draw rein till he arrived on the confines of Guzerat.* The officers on the frontier, after hearing his story, received him with the utmost respect, and wrote to Moozuffur Shah, who immediately despatched Keisur Khan and Taj Khan to put themselves under his orders for the present; and after his army was collected, the King of Guzerat marched thither himself, and placing Sooltan Mahmood on his right hand on his own throne treated him in every respect as an equal. In the year 923, the two kings proceeded at the head of the Guzerat army towards Malwa.

A. H. 923.
A. D. 1517.

Medny Ray having left his son Bhew Ray † in the fort of Mando, collected twelve thousand cavalry and a large force of infantry, and marched to occupy D'har, and to repair its fortifications. On the near approach of the two kings, he reconnoitred their forces, and conceiving he could not oppose them with success in the field, sent five or six thousand cavalry, and about ten thousand infantry, consisting of bowmen, musketeers, and artillery-men, to reinforce the garrison of Mando, and quitting D'har left Malwa, and went to Chittoor, in order to obtain assistance from Rana Sanka. The Guzerat army having arrived before D'har, it instantly opened its gates, after which the two kings marched to Mando, and laid siege to that fortress, which had hitherto proved impregnable. At the same time

* He was accompanied by his favourite mistress and the master of the horse.—*Moontukhhib-oot-Towareekh.*

† The title of this young man was Ray Rayan, or the Prince of Princes.

the King of Guzerat detached Adil Khan, ruler of Aseer, at the head of his own troops and a detachment of Guzerat cavalry, to watch the movements of Medny Ray. After a close siege for some months, in the year 924, the fort of Mando was taken by assault, and nineteen thousand Rajpoots were slain, including those who were destroyed in the performance of the Jowhur, a ceremony involving the sacrifice of their women and children on a funeral pile. Sooltan Mahmood, who entered in rear of the storming party, after the capture of the fort went up to Moozuffur Shah, and having congratulated him on his victory, asked what was to become of him. He answered in the most noble manner, "I congratulate you on the acquisition of your "kingdom, which I have now restored to you," and immediately quitting the fort, the King of Guzerat returned to his own camp. On the following day he communicated to the King of Malwa, that as the latter might require some time to arrange his affairs in the fort, he would march on to Oojein, and reduce the Rajpoots in that quarter. Moozuffur Shah proceeded, however, in the first place, to D'har, where he received information that Adil Khan's detachment was still at Depalpoor; for the Rajpoots, having heard of the fall of Mando, had dispersed. Moozuffur Shah now halted for some time at D'har, till joined by Sooltan Mahmood, who requested him to return and spend a few days with him at his capital, to which he assented. On his arrival, a magnificent festival

A. H. 924.
A. D. 1519.

was prepared, upon which occasion the King of Malwa brought in a tray, and waited on the King of Guzerat. After which, having accompanied him as far as the borders, and having received from that monarch an auxiliary force of three thousand cavalry, under Asuf Khan Guzeratty, to be stationed at Mando, Sooltan Mahmood returned to his capital. The forts of Chundery and Gagrone being in possession of Medny Ray's soldiers, and those of Bhilsa, Raiseen, and Sarungpoor in that of Silhuddy Poorby, it was resolved to wrest them out of their hands; for which purpose the King marched to Gagrone against Medny Ray, who being joined by Rana Sanka now returned with an immense army. The Malwa force had marched several miles, and had but just arrived at its ground, when the King was surprised to hear that he was close to the enemy; on which he immediately ordered the line under arms, and insisted on bringing on an action, a measure to which Asuf Khan, the Guzerat general, objected, representing that both horse and foot* were fatigued, and had been long without food, so that it would be better to delay the action till they were

* Those persons whose experience has not led them to observe the difference in the conduct of the same troops being brought into action at one time hungry and jaded, and at another time when in full strength, can hardly understand the importance of studying this object; nor is the effect of physical capacity on animal spirits at all times sufficiently considered. One of the most valuable lessons which a general can learn is to know precisely to what his soldiers are equal, and by neglecting this knowledge the best troops may be defeated even when opposed to inferior numbers.

refreshed. The King, whose temper was impatient and sanguine, and himself as brave as a lion, insisted on engaging the enemy, which remained steady and ready to receive him, while the forces of Malwa were neither properly drawn up nor in a condition to attack. The Guzerat cavalry, headed by the King in person, commenced the attack by charging the Rajpoot horse, estimated at nearly fifty thousand men. On this occasion Asuf Khan's son and almost the whole of the Guzeratties were killed, after behaving in the most gallant manner.* The King's life was saved only by the strength of the armour he wore, and he was left on the field with only ten horsemen. With these few men, whom he addressed and exhorted to die as martyrs against the infidels, he again charged and fell into the hands of the enemy covered with wounds, the whole of his small party being killed. The astonished Rajpoots, surrounding him as they perceived him weltering in his blood, looked on him as more than mortal. His enemy, Rana Sanka of Chittoor, caused him to be brought into his own tent, dressed his wounds, attended him in person, and showed him every mark of attention; and after his recovery, he furnished him with an escort of one thousand Rajpoot horse, and sent him to Mando, where he re-assumed the reins of government.† During the commotion which of late had

* Thirty officers of rank in the Malwa army lost their lives.

† Sooltan Mahmood was conveyed, in the first instance, to Chittoor, where the place of his confinement is still shown; but he was released on recovering from his wounds. It is impossible not to contrast the chivalrous conduct of the Hindoo

shaken the very foundation of the Malwa monarchy, many of the districts had been occupied and retained by the different chiefs, who appropriated the revenues to their own use. Of these especially were the following:—Sikundur Khan of Seevas; Medny Ray, who held possession of Gagrone, Chundery, and other places; Silhuddy, who occupied Bhilsa, Raiseen, and Surungpoor, besides many others holding small jageers; so that by this means the finances of the state were reduced to a low ebb.

Sooltan Mahmood, contrary to the practice of the other kings of glorious memory, without exercising his reason or judgment, conceived kingdoms were to be ruled by the edge of the sword;* and in the year 926, he marched against

A. H. 926.
A. D. 1519.

Silhuddy of Sarungpoor, but miscalculating his strength, he was attacked by the Rajpoots, by whom he was completely defeated. In this situation, rallying a few troops, while the enemy were engaged in plunder, he again charged and dispersed them, and pursued the

---

princes, in their behaviour to Mahomedans in general, with the sordid, cruel, and bigotted conduct of the latter towards Hindoos. It seldom happened that a Hindoo prince, taken in battle, was not instantly beheaded; and life was never spared but with the sacrifice of a daughter delivered up to a sort of honourable prostitution, or by the payment of vast sums of money and jewels.

* Ferishta alludes here to the impolicy of relying on force only to reconcile factions, and of the King's treating all his nobles as enemies, without securing friends, or permitting any one to remain neutral and inactive.

fugitives so closely into the fort of Sarungpur, that he obtained possession of it as also of twenty-four elephants. Silhuddy made his escape; and without attempting to regain Sarungpoor was content to occupy Bhilsa and Raiseen. The King now returned to Mando.

A. H. 932.
A. D. 1525.

In the year 932, the government of Guzerat, on the death of Moozuffur Shah, devolved on his son, Bahadur Shah, whose younger brother, Chand Khan, fled, and sought protection with Sooltan Mahmood at Mando; who, on account of the personal obligations he owed to his father, received him with kindness, and paid him the utmost attention. At the same time, also, Ruzy-ool-Moolk, one of the Guzerat nobles, having gone to Dehly to induce Babur Padshah to dethrone Bahadur Shah, and to place Chand Khan on the throne, now arrived at Mando; and being permitted to have a private and secret conference with that prince, returned to the Mogul Court at Agra. Bahadur Shah, hearing of these circumstances, wrote to Sooltan Mahmood, reproaching him for giving countenance to the intrigues carrying on by Ruzy-ool-Moolk; who subsequently arriving a second time at Mando, and communicating with the Pince Chand Khan, after the remonstrances of Bahadur Shah, again returned to Agra. Bahadur Shah, though he took no immediate steps, resolved to be revenged on the King of Malwa for supporting these treasonable proceedings against him. The fall of the house of Khiljy appearing now to be inevitable, Sooltan Mahmood did not adopt measures to prevent its occurrence, or even to ward off the impending destruction which seemed to threaten him. Rana Sanka of Chittoor dying about this period was succeeded by his son, Rana Ruttun See;* and Sooltan Mahmood, without any provocation, deputed Shirza Khan with a force from Mando to attack that prince; for which purpose the Malwa troops marched and laid waste some of the Chittoor districts. Ruttun See, fully aware of the dissensions which existed between the Malwa and Guzerat sovereigns, proceeded towards the former kingdom; and Sooltan Mahmood made a movement, by the route of Oojein and Sarungpoor, to oppose him. On reaching the latter place, the King summoned Silhuddy of Bhilsa and Moyin Khan, the adopted son of the late Sikundur Khan of Seevas, to join his army, to oppose the Chittoor forces under Ruttun See. On their arrival, he conferred the title of Musnud Ally on Moyin Khan, and presented him with the scarlet pavilion, only used by kings. Moyin Khan was the son of a butter-man, but adopted by Sikundur Khan. The King also conciliated Silhuddy, by giving over to him in perpetuity some villages contiguous to Raiseen and Bhilsa. These honoures, so unexpectedly bestowed upon two persons who so little deserved them at Sooltan Mahmood's hands, were followed by circumstances which roused their suspicious; and they concluding the gifts were only intended to lull them into security, deserted the King's camp, and joined the forces of Ruttun

* In the Guzerat history he is simply styled Ruttun.

See; after which Silhuddy, with his son Bhowput, Moyin Khan, and Ruttun See, all went and paid their respects to Bahadur Shah of Guzerat, then encamped on the banks of the river Gurchy.* Sooltan Mahmood, hearing of the circumstance, deputed Duria Khan Lody to wait on the King of Guzerat; acquainting him, that owing to the obligations conferred on him by the late Moozuffur Shah of Guzerat, he wished to show the respect he owed to his family, by going to pay his personal respects to his son, and to congratulate him on his accession to the throne. Bahadur Shah received the messenger with great coolness, but said that he should be glad to see the King of Malwa. Rana Ruttun See returned to Chittoor; but Silhuddy continued in the Guzerat camp till the meeting between the two kings should take place. Sooltan Mahmood, however, ashamed to visit Bahadur Shah after his conduct in giving countenance to the intrigues carried on between Ruzy-ool-Moolk and the Prince Chand Khan against the King of Guzerat, evaded the meeting, under the plea of the necessity of his proceeding against Seevas. Having marched thither, and being out on a hunting party, his horse fell, and he broke his right arm; † on which he sent an excuse to the King of Guzerat for his non-attendance, and returned to Mando, where he

* This is certainly a mistake in the original.

† It has been already seen, in the Guzerat history, vol. iv. p. 114., that his arm was not broken; and that the accident, of whatever nature it was in reality, need not have prevented his visit to Bahadur Shah.

employed himself in repairing the fortifications. Bahadur Shah now plainly perceiving it was the intention of Sooltan Mahmood to avoid a meeting, marched towards the capital. On his entering Malwa, he was daily joined by deserters from Sooltan Mahmood's army, and among those of note was Shirza Khan, governor of D'har. Bahadur Shah having reached Mando surrounded it; and making his observations, marked out the ground for the mines and batteries. Sooltan Mahmood with three thousand men defended the place; but they were much harassed by the attempts made night after night by the besiegers to carry the fort by escalade; and though invariably repulsed, the garrison was worn out by incessant watching, till on the 9th of Shaban, in the year 932, the banners of Guzerat appeared at daylight waving on the battlements. The Prince Chand Khan, the brother of Bahadur Shah, fled to the Deccan, and Sooltan Mahmood retired to his palace, which he resolved to defend till the last, but was at length induced to surrender. Bahadur Shah was disposed to treat him kindly, and even to restore to him his government; but the irritability of Sooltan Mahmood's temper and his pride combined hurried him away so far, that he abused Bahadur Shah grossly to his face. He was in consequence ordered into confinement with his seven sons, and sent to the fort of Champanere under Asuf Khan,* who attended them with an

Shaban 9. A. H. 932. May 20. A. D. 1526.

* This was the same officer who commanded the Guzerat auxiliaries in the battle of Gagrone.

Shaban 14. A. H. 932. May 25. A. D. 1526. escort. Five days afterwards, viz. on the 14th of the same month, the detachment was attacked by two thousand Bheels and Kolies in camp at Dohud; and Asuf Khan, supposing this formidable assault was made for the purpose of effecting the release of the Malwa royal family, ordered the King and his sons to be put to death;* so that (excepting Sahib Khan, who had been formerly created Sooltan Mahomed, and was then in attendance on Babur Padshah,) not a single male of the house of Khiljy remained; and the kingdom of Malwa, in the year 941, A. H. 941. A. D. 1534. became incorporated with that of Guzerat, until it was eventually conquered in the year 978, by Akbur Padshah, Emperor of Dehly.†

* During the confusion that occurred in the night-attack, Sooltan Mahmood disengaged the chains from his feet, and the sentries, fearing he might effect his escape, put him to death without orders. He was buried in the vicinity of the tank at Dohud; and his children, with the remainder of his family, were conveyed to Champanere.—*Moontukhib-oot-Towareekh.*

† Here the Malwa historian ceases: the remaining part of the narrative Ferishta collects from the histories of Guzerat and Dehly.

CONCLUSION OF THE HISTORY OF MALWA.

Bahadur Shah of Guzerat distributes Malwa among several chiefs.—Malwa subdued by Hoomayoon.—Hoomayoon is expelled from India, and Kadur Khan, an officer of the Khiljy government, occupies the country.—He provokes an attack from Sheer Shah Soor, who places his minister and relative, Shooja Khan, in charge of the government.—Shooja Khan dies, leaving three sons, Dowlut, Moostufa, and Bayezeed.—The two former are murdered by the latter, who assumes the title of Baz Bahadur.—Akbur, Emperor of Dehly, attacks him.—Baz Bahadur defeated, and the government of Malwa is given to Peer Mahomed Khan.—Baz Bahadur attacks Peer Mahomed Khan, who is slain, and the former recovers his country.—Malwa reconquered by Akbur, and Baz Bahadur expelled.—He eventually enters the service of Akbur, as an officer of two thousand horse.

ON the death of Sooltan Mahmood, and the subsequent occupation of Malwa by Bahadur Shah, that monarch gave over to Silhuddy Poorby, who had been the first person to join his standard, the districts of Oojein, Sarungpoor, and Raiseen; but we find in the Guzerat history, that some time afterwards he gave offence to Bahadur Shah, and being attacked in the field, he fled to Raiseen, where he put himself to death, and his son Bhowput made his escape from Malwa. Bahadur Shah then appointed Alum Khan of Kalpy governor of Raiseen. Budr Khan of Malwa was created governor of Oojein, and Yekhtiar Khan governor of Mando; after which the King returned to Champanere. At a subsequent period, when Hoomayoon Padshah of Dehly seized Guzerat, he previously occupied Mando, and ordered public prayers to be read in his name, leaving his own officers in the government of Malwa; but shortly after his return to Agra, Mulloo Khan, one of the officers of the late Khiljy government, retook all the country lying between the Nurbudda and the town of Bhilsa after a struggle of twelve months against the Dehly officers; whom having eventually subdued, he caused himself to be crowned in Mando, under the title of Kadur Shah of Malwa. At this period, also, Bhowput and Poorunmul, sons of the late Silhuddy, marching from Chittoor, obtained possession of the fort of Raiseen, but acknowledged allegiance to Kadur Shah, and paid him tribute. Shortly after his accession, Kadur Shah received a firman,* with a seal on the face of it, from Sheer Shah Poorby Afghan, King of Bengal, stating that Hoomayoon Padshah was on the march to attack him, and that he desired the King of Malwa would make a movement towards Agra, which would distract the operations of the King of Dehly, and give the former an opportunity of acting with effect on that monarch's territory. On the receipt of this firman or order, Kadur Shah was so incensed that he insisted on his secretary writing a firman in return

* Communications between equals are sealed on the back; of inferiors, at the foot of the writing; and of superiors and masters, on the top, and on the face of the letter, where, in Europe, we frequently affix the date,

with the seal upon the face of it. When Sheer Shah received the answer, he tore off the seal, and putting it on the point of his sword said, "If it "please God that I should ever meet with Kadur "Shah, I will then put him in mind of his "impertinence in putting his seal on the face of a "letter to my address;" and in consequence, when that monarch ascended the throne of
A. H. 849. Dehly, he marched in the year 849 to
A. D. 1445. conquer the kingdom of Malwa. On his arrival near Sarungpoor, Kadur Shah, whose military resources were incapable of resisting those of Sheer Shah, determined to throw himself on his mercy. Accordingly, without the knowledge of any of Sheer Shah's officers, he suddenly made his appearance in durbar; and after having a secret conference with that monarch, received from him the greatest honours, was allowed to sleep in his private tent, and was presented with the dress which Sheer Shah wore at their meeting. On the next day Sheer Shah marched to Oojein, where he required his minister and relative, Shooja Khan, to pay obedience to Kadur Shah as King of Malwa. But this kindness was not to last: for on the following day he told Kadur Shah that he conferred on him the district of Luknow as a residence, of which he made him governor, and said that he expected him to remove with his family in a few days. Kadur Shah, astonished at this resolution, which he considered equivalent to perpetual banishment, fled with his family to Guzerat. Sheer Shah then made over the country around Oojein and Sarungpoor to Shooja Khan, and created him governor of Malwa, himself marching to Runtunbhore. Kadur Shah

having made his escape, it became politic to secure the persons of the other Malwa nobles, to prevent their forming a junction with him at some future period. Shooja Khan first seized the person of Moyin Khan of Seevas, who was at that time in camp. This measure induced his son Nuseer Khan to revenge his father's cause; but Shooja Khan being joined by the Raja of Gualiar defeated Nuseer Khan in an action near Sarungpoor, whence he fled into the Gondwana hills. Subsequently to this event, information was received from Hajy Khan, the governor of D'har that Kadur Shah, with a large force, had arrived in his vicinity from Banswala, and that he expected an action to take place in a day or two. Shooja Khan no sooner heard the news than instantly proceeding in his palanquin to D'har, he arrived there in the evening, in time to make dispositions for a night-attack on Kadur Shah, which completely succeeded. Shooja Khan's activity enabled him in a few months to possess himself of the whole of Malwa without fighting another action. Having ruled Malwa for many years, an Afghan named Oothman Khan came one day into the Deevankhana, or Hall of Audience, of Shooja Khan, in a state of intoxication, and began to spit about on the carpets. The servants rebutted, and said they would be spoiled, but he took no notice, till at last they desired him to go out; on which he was so imprudent as to strike one of them in the face, and beat him severely. Shooja Khan, hearing of this circumstance, ordered Oothman Khan's hands to be cut off. Oothman survived the operation, and carried his complaint to Sulim Shah* of Dehly at Gualiar, who told him that he might, if he chose, take revenge on Shooja Khan, who would soon be at that city. When Shooja Khan heard this, he merely observed "Sulim Shah is a fool for his pain." Some days after, when going to the durbar, he saw Oothman Khan sitting in the corner of a shop wrapt up in an old mantle. Shooja Khan ordered his palanquin to stop, and was going to ask if he wanted any thing, and intended to relieve his distress; but Oothman Khan, who only waited such an opportunity, jumped up, and with the blade of a sword, which was fastened round his arm, made a blow at Shooja Khan, whose servants immediately attacked the ruffian, and put him to death. Sulim Shah was much vexed to hear that this affray had ended in the death of Oothman; not only because he had sanctioned the attack on his part, but his indignation had been roused against Shooja Khan for having called him a fool. Sulim Shah drew upon him the curses of the whole of Shooja Khan's family and servants, when they learned that their master had received a dangerous wound in the side from the hand of the ruffian Oothman Khan, who had been instigated to the act by the King himself. The irritation produced on account of this affair induced Shooja Khan to quit Gualiar without taking leave, and to march towards Sarungpoor; on which Sulim Shah ordered a detachment in pursuit; and in a few days after he marched himself to seize Shooja

* It is to be recollected that Sulim Padshah was himself of the tribe of Afghan.

Khan's person and family, although that nobleman was one of thirty-six persons who were personally engaged in placing his father, Sheer Shah, on the throne. On the arrival of Sulim Shah near Sarungpoor, Shooja Khan declared that he never would suffer any one over whom he had power to draw his sword against the son of his old master, and he therefore fled to Banswara, leaving Sulim Shah at liberty to place Eesy Khan in the government of Malwa; after which he returned to Gualiar. But some time after, when Sulim marched towards Lahore,* he reinstated Shooja Khan in the government of Malwa. On this occasion the latter divided the country into the following districts: Oojein and its dependencies were placed in charge of his son, Dowlut Khan. Raiseen and Bhilsa were made over to Moostufa Khan, his youngest son. Hundia, Seevas, and its dependencies to Mullik Bayezeed, his elder son, himself retaining the government of Sarungpoor. Some time elapsed before the government of Dehly was completely subjected by Hoomayoon Padshah, on his return from Persia; and during that period Shooja Khan, as well as the other chiefs of the empire, were on the point of declaring themselves independent, and of coining money, when cruel fate snatched the cup of prosperity from his lips, and death presented him with the potion of mortality. He died in the year 962; and his eldest son, assuming the title of Baz Bahadur, took the reins of government into his hands.

A.H. 962.
A.D. 1554.

* Vide vol. ii. p. 141. Sulim died in 1547, and Hoomayoon regained the empire of Dehly in 1555. Vide vol. ii. p. 176.

The administration of Shooja Khan in Malwa, from first to last, was twelve years. Among the public works which do credit to his memory is the town of Soojalpoor, near the city Oojein, independent of which are many other memorials of his reign in different parts of the kingdom of Malwa.

After the death of Shooja Khan, his eldest son, Mullik Bayezeed, marched from Hundia to Sarungpoor, and assumed charge of the government, taking possession of all his father's effects. His brother, Dowlut Khan, who had been a great favourite of Sulim Shah, and had the Sarungpoor division of troops to support him, asserted his claim to a partition of the kingdom; and after some negotiation, the districts contiguous to Oojein and Mando, together with some villages, were ceded to him. The districts of Sarungpoor, Seevas, Bheelwara, and the private estates of Shooja Khan, were considered as belonging to Bayezeed, and the districts of Raiseen and Bhilsa, with their dependencies, were left in the hands of Moostufa Khan. After this arrangement, Bayezeed marched to Oojein, on pretence of paying a visit of condolence to Dowlut Khan, on the occasion of their father's death. The latter, unsuspicious of any other motive, was put to death by his elder brother. The head of Dowlut Khan was sent to Sarungpoor, and hung up on one of the gates of that town; after which, having taken possession of many towns in Malwa which were previously almost independent, in the year 963 Bayezeed was crowned, under the title of Sooltan Baz Bahadur. After this

A. H. 963.
A. D. 1555.

event he marched to Raiseen to expel his remaining brother, Moostufa Khan, who, after sustaining several actions, was eventually completely defeated, and his army dispersed. Moostufa Khan fled from Malwa, leaving Baz Bahadur to take possession of the forts of Raiseen and Bhilsa.

About this period, having met with opposition from some of his officers, Baz Bahadur caused them to be seized and thrown into deep wells alive, where they were either drowned or starved to death. Some time after this he marched to invade Gondwara, in which campaign his uncle, Futteh Khan, was killed; after which he returned to Sarungpoor, and made preparations to reduce the fortress of Gurra. On his arrival in that vicinity, he was opposed by the troops of the Rany Doorgawutty, the widow of the late Ray Krishn Sing, who governed the country. Baz Bahadur was opposed by the Gonds, on the submit of a pass where their infantry were strongly posted, and having been drawn into an ambuscade, his troops were so completely routed that he was compelled to make his escape singly to Sarungpoor; but his army was completely surrounded and made prisoners, most of whom were put to death. Baz Bahadur was so much affected with this disgraceful termination of the war, in which his army had been destroyed, without being able to make resistance, that in order to drive away care he abandoned himself to sensual pleasures. At this period the science of music had attained considerable perfection in Malwa, and Baz Bahadur devoted himself entirely to its cultivation and encouragement; and his attachment to Roop Muny, a celebrated courtesan of that age, became so nortorious, that the loves of Baz Bahadur and Roop Muny have been handed down to posterity in song. Akbur Padshah of Dehly, taking advantage of the state of Malwa under Baz Bahadur, ordered an army commanded by Adhum Khan, in the latter end of the year 968, to march and occupy that country. Baz Bahadur heard nothing of the movement of this force until it arrived within a short distance of his capital, when he collected his troops around Sarungpoor, but they had hardly time to join, before the Moguls were within two miles of the place. His eyes were now opened to his situation; and entering on the field of action with as little concern as if going into the company of females, he advanced impetuously, though without order, into the battle. He personally behaved with great gallantry; but his troops deserting him, he was obliged to fly, leaving Adhum Khan to occupy Sarungpoor. After some time Adhum Khan being recalled, Peer Mahomed Khan Sheerwany was sent in his stead to the government of Malwa. In the year 969, Peer Mahomed Khan marched to oppose Baz Bahadur on the frontier, who had collected and force in conjunction with Toofal Khan, regent of Berar, and Meeran Moobarik Khan of Aseer. Peer Mahomed Khan advanced, in order to lay waste the country of Boorhanpoor; but the confederates so distressed him, that he was obliged to retreat to Malwa, whither they pursued him,

A. H. 968.
A. D. 1560.

A.H. 969.
A.D. 1571.

and driving the Mogul troops out of Malwa, re placed Baz Bahadur on the throne. He had scarcely time to draw breath, when in the year

A. H. 970.
A. D. 1562.

970 Abdoolla Khan Oozbuk, anothr of the officers of Akbur Padshah, occupied Malwa. Baz Bahadur fled to the hills of Gondwara, from whence he made occasional sallies, and for a time took and retained possession of some small districts; but what he gained by force of arms he very soon lost again, owing to the indolent habits in which he indulged: at length he thought it best to deliver himself up to Akbur Padshah. In consequence he left

A. H. 978.
A. D. 1570.

his retreat in the year 978, after a reign of seventeen years. He sometimes lived in the luxuries of a court, and at other submitted to the privations of a camp; and frequently wandered and begged assistance from one state to another, abiding in the woods and hills for whole months together, from an apprehension of being seized. In this year, having joined Akbur Padshah at Dehly, Baz Bahadur received a commission as an officer

A. H. 1018.
A. D. 1609.

of two thousand cavalry. From that period till the present year, being 1018, the kingdom of Malwa has been included among the provinces of the empire of Dehly.

CHAPTER VI.

HISTORY OF THE KINGS OF KANDEISH.

MULLIK RAJA FAROOKY.

Origin of this chief.—Accidental circumstance of his being first brought to the King's notice—is raised to the rank of a noble of two thousand horse, and receives the districts of Talnere and Kuronde in jageer—compels the Raja of Buglana to pay tribute—invades the districts of Sooltanapoor and Nundoorbar, belonging to the King of Guzerat, but is obliged to retire to Talnere—concludes peace with the King of Guzerat—assigns Talnere to his youngest son, and leaves the rest of his territory to his eldest son, Nuseer Khan Farooky.—Death of Mullik Raja—his pedigree derivable from Oomr Farook.

The first person who assumed independence in the province of Kandeish was Mullik Raja, the son of Khan Jehan Farooky, whose ancestors were among the most respectable nobles at the Dehly Court, in the reigns of Alla-ood-Deen Khiljy and Mahomed Toghluk.

On the death of Khwaja Jehan, his son Mullik Raja was very young, and inherited only a small patrimony. He was diffident in his disposition, and, at the same time, too proud to thrust himself

To face page 280. Vol. IV.]

GENEALOGY OF THE KINGS OF KANDEISH,

ENTITLED FAROOKY.

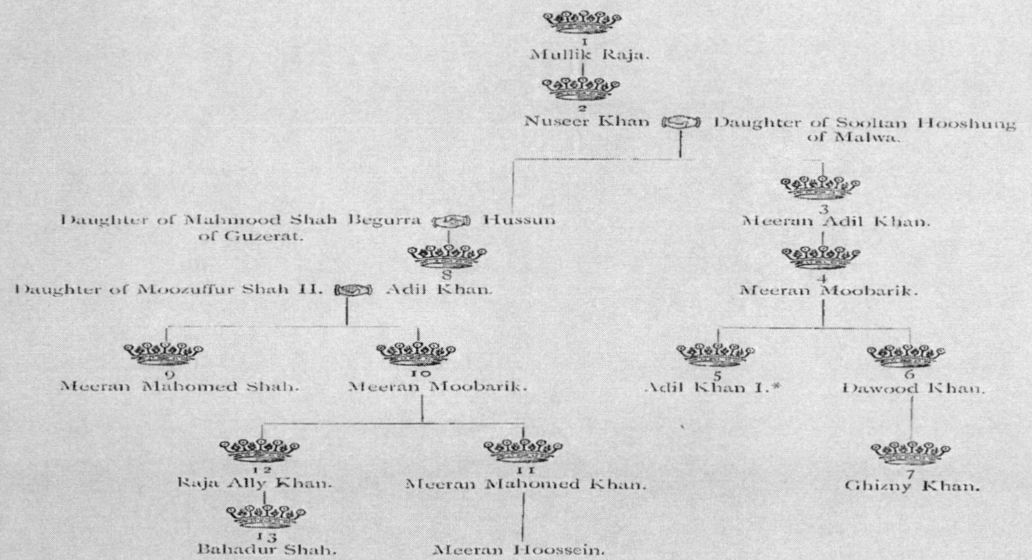

* Adil Khan is supposed to have had a son called Azeez, from whom Shah Shums-ood-Deen Farooky of Boorhanpoor claims descent. Vide note, vol. iv. p. 299.

into notice through the throng of abject courtiers who usually attend on monarchs. When he arrived at a certain age, he found he had expended the little property which he inherited, and he therefore entered the King's army as a private horseman. He was excessively addicted to the chase; and one day having attracted the notice of some of the courtiers on a hunting party, while he attended the King, he was admitted into the *gholam khas*, or the life-guard of Feroze Toghluk. Some time after this, it happened when the King was on a sporting excursion in Guzerat that his Majesty followed an antelope thirteen or fourteen coss (from twenty-six to twenty-eight miles), and his attendants, excepting one or two, were all left behind. The King and his steed were completely exhausted. Far removed from the camp, and with his horse jaded, it appeared improbable that he could reach it for many hours. At this moment a horseman was descried at a distance, leading a brace of greyhounds, whom the King's party beckoned towards them. Upon his arrival he was asked if any thing could be procured to eat. He replied, pointing to his steed, which carried some game, that he had some venison, and if his Majesty pleased he would instantly strike a light and dress it. The King, upon learning that his host was Mullik Raja, the son of the late Khan Jehan, an officer of respectability, resolved to promote him; and at the very first durbar raised him to the rank of an officer of two thousand horse, and shortly afterwards conferred on him the districts of Talnere and Kuronde, situated on the borders of the Deccan.

A.H. 772.
A.D. 1370.

In the year 772, Mullik Raja marched with a force to his frontier, and not only took peaceable possession of his own small district, but reduced Bharjy, Raja of Buglana, to consent to the payment of an annual tribute to the King of Dehly. In this first expedition he received a tribute of five large elephants and ten small, besides a quantity of pearls and jewels as well as specie. On his return, he caused the elephants to be covered with velvet housings, embroidered with gold; and having laden several camels with muslins, and other manufactures of Kandeish, and also some pearls, he sent them as an offering to the King. Feroze Toghluk observed, that the very duty which the governor of Guzerat ought to have performed long ago had been fulfilled by Mullik Raja. He was, in consequence, honoured with the title of *Sipah Salar** of Kandeish, and raised to the rank of a commander of three thousand horse. In the course of a few years he could muster twelve thousand horse, and levied contributions from the rays of Gondwana as far as Gurra Mundla; and such was his fame, that the Ray of Jajnuggur, notwithstanding the distance, established a friendly intercourse with him.

After the death of Feroze, when Dilawur Khan Ghoory assumed independence in Malwa, an intimate connection took place between the latter and Mullik Raja, so much so, that Dilawur Khan gave his daughter in marriage to Mullik Nuseer, the son of the governor of Kandeish. At this

* Sipah Salar, Commander-in-chief.

period, Moozuffur Shah of Guzerat declared himself independent; and some internal commotions subsequently arising, Mullik Raja, relying on the support of Dilawur Khan, invaded the Guzerat provinces, and laid waste the districts of Sooltanpoor and Nundoorbar. Moozuffur Shah, though engaged in reducing the infidel Hindoos in his kingdom, on hearing of this inroad, made rapid marches to Sooltanpoor, from whence Mullik Raja was glad to retreat, and to seek protection in the fort of Talnere, wherein he was closely invested by the King of Guzerat. On this occasion Mullik Raja employed the most accomplished and learned men about him to negotiate a peace; and as Moozuffur Shah hoped to obtain assistance from the governors of Kandeish and Malwa, in reducing the infidels, he consented to terms. After which period, Mullik Raja confined his military operations entirely to his own country, and was indefatigable in promoting the arts of civilisation and of agriculture during the rest of his life. Before his death, he sent for his two sons, Mullik Nuseer and Mullik Iftikhar. To the former he gave the "garb of "desire and assent," which he received from his preceptor and tutelary saint, Sheikh Zein-ood-Deen of Dowlutabad, and nominated him his successor. On his younger son, Mullik Iftikhar, he bestowed the fort and district of Talnere; and on the 22d of the month of Shaban, A. H. 801, Mullik Raja died, and was buried at the town of Talnere, after a reign of twenty-nine years.*

Shaban 22. A.H. 801. April 28. A.D. 1399.

* Several of the tombs of the early Farooky kings, con-

In the year 1013, (A.D. 1604,) when the author attended the palanquin of the daughter of Ibrahim Adil Shah from Beejapoor to Boorhanpoor, he asked Mirza Ally Isfahany, after the capture of Aseer, if any history existed of the Farooky family. The Mirza replied, he knew of none; but said that he once saw a genealogy of the family down to Mullik Raja, which he copied and had by him, which contains the descent of the Farooky family. It is as follows:—

Mullik Raja, the first Mahomedan ruler of Kandeish, is descended from the Caliph Oomr Farook, and traces his pedigree thus: Mullik Raja, the son of Khan Jehan, the son of Ally Khan, the son of Oothman Khan, the son of Simeon Shah,* the son of Ashab Shah, the son of Armian Shah, the son of Ibrahim Shah of Bulkh, the son of Adhum Shah, the son of Ahmud Shah, the son of Mahmood Shah, the son of Mahomed Shah, the son of Azim Shah, the son of Asghur, the son of Mahomed Ahmud, the son of the Imam Nasir Abdoolla, the son of Oomr-ool-Farook, entitled Khuleefa, or representative of the last of the prophets.

Mullik Raja became the disciple of the holy

---

structed in a peculiar style of architecture, are still in tolerable repair at Talnere, but there are few, if any, inscriptions legible on them.

* The word Shah, in its original signification, means Saint, and was first adopted by the Sofy kings of Persia, who engrafted the sacred title on that of royalty when they ascended the throne; and the kings of India subsequently assumed the title, without reference to its sanctified origin.

saint Zein-ood-Deen of Dowlutabad, and from him received the "garb of desire and assent," which he delivered to his son Nusser, who in like manner transmitted it to his son, and in this way it was handed down from father to son for nearly two hundred years; and Bahadur, the son of Raja Ally Khan, the last of the independent rulers of Kandeish, possessed this precious relic when he lost his kingdom.

MULLIK NUSEER.

ENTITLED

NUSEER KHAN FAROOKY.

Treacherously obtains possession of Aseer—deprives his brother of the fort of Talnere, and attacks the districts of Sooltanpoor and Nundoorbar, belonging to Guzerat—is compelled to sue for terms—builds the city of Boorhanpoor, and fortifies Aseer—gives his daughter in marriage to the heir-apparent of the Bahmuny kingdom—supports the fugitive Raja of Julwara against the King of Guzerat, and induces the King of the Deccan to do so likewise.—The Guzerat King proves victorious.—Nuseer Khan supports some rebellious chief of the Deccan in Berar against their King—he is compelled to fly from Boorhanpoor.—The battle of Lulling, in which he is defeated.—His death.

IN the reign of Mullik Nuseer this family greatly extended its power. Mullik Nuseer Khan also assumed the ensigns of royalty. Learned men were invited from all parts, and literature was much promoted. He received from the King of Guzerat the title of Khan, and caused the public prayers to be read in his name, realising the wish that his father carried with him to the grave, namely, that of assuming the royal pavilion and canopy. He also seized the fort of Aseer from Asa Aheer.*

* The word Aheer signifies cow-herd. It is worthy of note that many of the most ancient hill-forts in India have reference to the pastoral live of their possessors; and when the Indians are at a loss to fix an era for any ancient

As the story relative to the family of the original possessor of Aseer is interesting, I shall give it at full length. On the summit of a high hill in Kandeish lived a herdsman who possessed much agricultural wealth. He was, in reality, one of the principal landholders in that country. His ancestors had for nearly seven hundred years retained the estates, and at an early period built a wall round the hill of Aseer, in order to protect their numerous herds of cattle from the bands of robbers which infested the mountains. Asa succeeded to his father's property: being a thrifty person, his herds increased to the number of five thousand buffaloes, five thousand cows, twenty thousand sheep, and one thousand brood mares, independently of which he had two thousand retainers, who were employed in all purposes of husbandry, as well as for his protection. The farmers, both of Gondwana and Kandeish, whenever they were in distress, always found relief by applying to Asa Aheer, or the herdsman, for so he continued to be called, inspite of his wealth and power. It happened that a short time before the arrival of Mullik Raja at Talnere famine raged in Kandeish and in Gondwana, and not more than two or three thousand individuals of the Koly or

---

structure or sculpture they invariably refer it to the period of the shepherd kings. Among the most remarkable instances of hill-forts which occur to me at present are the following: Aseer, the cow-herd; Asa's dwelling; Gavulgur, the cow-herd's fort; Golla-conda (Golconda), the shepherd's hill; Yenna-conda (Inaconda), butter hill; and Gualiar, which has probably reference to the same origin.

Bheel tribes escaped its effects. Asa had at this time many storehouses, both in Gondwana and Kandeish, which his agents opened in order to sell the corn; but his wife, who was of a charitable disposition, prayed her husband to allow the grain to be served out to the poor without payment, and by that means secure to himself a good name in this world, and eternity in the next. It was to assist them, also, that he was induced to have the old walls of the town of Aseer levelled, and to cause a fort to be built a masonry, by which means he employed many labourers. He also distributed food to the aged and decrepid, who were unable to perform manual labour. This work went by the name of the fort of Asa Aheer, and was afterwards celled Aseer.*

Upon the assumption of the authority of all Kandeish by Mullik Raja, Asa, being a peaceable and unambitious man, was the first of all the landholders to acknowledge fealty to him; and, moreover, presented him with many things which he required on the establishment of his family. Mullik Raja very soon saw that a fortification like that of Aseer, in the hands of an ambitious chief, in the centre of his province, would enable such a person to shake the very foundation of his government; but he felt himself under too many obliga-

* The temple of Aseer is mentioned as the residence of Aswathama many centuries before this period. Whatever might have been its condition under the Hindoos, the mosque and battlements made to receive canon, with other modern improvements, attest that it owes much of its present efficiency to the Mahomedans.

tions to Asa to wrest it by force out of his hands.* Mullik Nuseer, also, when he succeeded to the government, received many personal favours from Asa, and knew from his peaceable disposition that he never would give him a plea to attack him. He, however, resolved to seize Aseer, and to make it his capital, and adopted the following plan to carry his scheme into effect :—He sent a letter to Asa, saying, that the Rajas of Buglana and Antoor had collected large forces, and that they did not conduct themselves to him in the manner they had done to his father, the late Mullik Raja. The Raja of Kehrla also threatened him. The fort of Talnere, he said, agreeably to his father's will, was in the possession of his brother, Mullik Iftikhar, and that of Lulling was situated too near his enemies to offer him a safe retreat ; he begged, therefore, that his family might be received into Aseer. Asa willingly consented; and ordering suitable apartments to be fitted up for the reception of Mullik Nuseer's ladies, directed that every attention should be paid to them. On the first day several dolies † with women came into the

* Asa was, probably, one of the hereditary provincial governors of the court of Dewgur (Dowlutabad) before the conquest of the Deccan by the Mahomedans. On the extinction of the royal race at Dewgur the dependent chiefs became emancipated from all allegiance, and resisted the arms of the invaders as long as they could. Many of the provincial chiefs, in that case, would naturally become independent ; but we have no certain accounts of the fate of those of the Deccan, and, therefore, much must be left to surmise.

† Covered litters, like palanquins, for the conveyance of females and sick persons. Vide vol. ii. p. 115.

place, and were visited by Asa's wife and daughters. On the second day a report arrived that two hundred dolies, filled with the wife, mother, and the rest of Mullik Nuseer's family, were coming. Asa accordingly ordered the gates to be thrown open to receive them, and went with all his sons a considerable way from the female apartments to meet them; but what was his astonishment, when, instead of women, he found the dolies filled with armed soldiers, who leapt out and murdered him with the whole of his family, not leaving a male child of his race. The inhabitants of the fort were so dismayed that they fled with their families from a scene of such horror. Mullik Nuseer, who was at this time in the fort of Lulling, on hearing of the success of his plan, repaired to Aseer, and employed himself in strengthening the fortifications. It is, however, a well authenticated fact, that the property of Asa was never appropriated by any of the Farooky dynasty to their own use; and all the money and jewels taken on this occasion fell into the hands of Akbur Padshah, when he marched to the southward, and took the fortress of Aseer, two centuries afterwards. *

The moment that this news reached Sheikh Zein-ood-Deen of Dowlutabad, the tutelary saint of the family, he proceeded towards Kandeish to congratulate Mullik Nuseer on his success against

* Ferishta's Mahomedan feeling is quite absorbed in his indignation towards Nuseer Khan and his race. The observation regarding the property of Asa is meant to imply that Providence prevented Nuseer Khan's family from enjoying the benefit of its possession.

the infidels; and the latter, with all his family, marched to meet the holy personage, and encamped on the western bank of the river Tapty. Sheikh Zein-ood-Deen arrived with a number of his disciples, and they pitched their tents on the eastern bank. Mullik Nuseer went over the river, and endeavoured to persued the Sheikh to return with him to Aseer; but he declined doing so, as he said he had not permission to cross the Tapty. After remaining some time in their respective encampments on the western and eastern banks, the Sheikh desired to take his leave; but Mullik Nuseer begged that he would condescend to accept of an estate in Kandeish. The Sheikh answered, that dervishes had no occasion for estates; but begged of Mullik Nuseer to build a town on the eastern bank of the river, and call it after himself, Zeinabad,* and a city on the western, where he was himself encamped, to be called Boorhanpoor, in honour of the famous Sheikh Boorhan-ood-Deen† of Dowlutabad; and he recommended, also, that he should make the latter his capital: both of which towns were accordingly built; and Boorhanpoor afterwards became the capital of the Farooky dynasty.

There is an old but a very true saying, that "a rug will contain ten dervishes, but a kingdom "is too small for two rulers." So was it with that of Kandeish; for as soon as Mullik Nuseer

* Jehanabad of the maps.

† These two holy personages are buried at the town of Roza, near Dowlutabad, and their names are still held in great veneration in the Deccan.

obtained possession of Aseer he cast a jealous eye upon his brother's estate of Talnere; and in order to secure it he induced the King of Malwa to assist him. To this end, Mullik Nuseer marched, in the year 820, towards Talnere with a force, and procured the aid of his brother-in-law, Sooltan Hooshung of Malwa. Mullik Iftikhar, astonished at the approach of his brother's army, remonstrated with him, and wrote, but in vain, to Ahmud Shah of Guzerat for assistance. Ghizny Khan, the son of Sooltan Hooshung, and nephew to Mullik Nuseer, arrived with a force of five thousand horse from Malwa, to support Mullik Nuseer; and by their united efforts, in a short time the fort of Talnere fell, and Mullik Iftikhar was taken prisoner, and sent to the fort of Aseer. After the capture of Talnere, it was agreed that the allied forces of Kandeish and Malwa should march and occupy Sooltanpoor in the name of the King of Malwa; for which purpose they absolutely moved and invested the fort of Sooltanpoor. On this, Ahmud Shah of Guzerat marched the whole of his army to the south, and sent a very considerable detachment under Mullik Mahmood Toork in advance. On hearing this, Ghizny Khan of Malwa fled to Mando, and Mullik Nuseer retreated to Talnere, wherein he was closely besieged by Mullik Mahmood Toork. Meanwhile, Ahmud Shah arrived at Sooltanpoor. Mullik Nuseer, thus deserted by the Prince of Malwa, was reduced to the extreme of distress in Talnere; and made overtures to some of Ahmud

A.H. 820.
A.D. 1417.

Shah's ministers with such success, that that monarch not only accepted the presents which he sent him, but in return bestowed on him the white canopy and scarlet pavilion, and honoured him with the title of Khan, which he assumed ever afterwards.

Some years after this event, Ahmud Shah Bahmuny of the Deccan, desirous of forming a respectable connection for his son, deputed ambassadors to Nuseer Khan, soliciting the hand of his daughter in marriage for the Deccan prince, Alla-ood-Deen. Nuseer Khan, who perceived that this connection would strengthen his power, readily assented; and the Kandeish bride was conveyed by the ambassadors in great state from Boorhanpoor to Ahmudabad Bidur.

A.H. 833.
A. D. 1429.

In the year 833, Raja Kanha, Ray of the district of Julwara, fled from the power of the King of Guzerat, and arrived at Aseer, where he presented to Nuseer Khan some elephants and other valuables, begging of him to assist him in recovering his country. Nuseer Khan replied, that he really had not the means to cope with the King of Guzerat; but that if he chose to apply to the King of the Deccan he would perhaps exert himself in his favour, and Nuseer Khan promised to give him a letter to that monarch on the subject. Ahmud Shah Bahmuny, at the instance of Nuseer Khan, put a small force at the disposal of the Raja to recover his country. When this detachment arrived at Nundoorbar it plundered the district, and the King of Guzerat ordered a force to oppose it. An engagement ensued in consequence, in which the Deccanies were entirely defeated, and many slain. This disaster naturally involved the King of the Deccan in a war with Guzerat; for he conceived it necessary to retrieve the character of his arms. He accordingly deputed a large force to march under the command of the Prince Alla-ood-Deen for that purpose. When this army reached Dowlutabad it was joined by Raja Kanha and Nuseer Khan, and the whole proceeded towards Guzerat. Another battle* ensued, and the Deccan troops were again defeated, and Raja Kanha was compelled to take refuge in the Kandeish hills.

A.H. 840.
A.D. 1436.

In the year 840, Nuseer Khan received accounts from his daughter that she experienced ill treatment from her husband, Alla-ood-Deen Shah; in consequence of which her father suspended all amicable intercourse with him; and in the year 841, at the instance of the King of Guzerat, invaded his country. He first entered Berar; and being supported by many malecontent Deccany chiefs caused the public prayers to be read in his name. He next invested the fortress of Narnala; but Alla-ood-Deen Shah having deputed Mullik-oot-Toojar with a large force to oppose him, Mullik Nuseer, accompanied by the Deccan officers, was compelled to fly. He was pursued by Mullik-oot-Toojar as far as Boorhanpoor, which city he completely sacked. Nuseer

A.H. 841.
A.D. 1437.

* This battle took place on the plain above the Manukpoonj pass, vide vol. iv. p. 27.; but the Deccan historians have omitted to mention it.

Khan then took refuge in the fort of Lulling, and solicited the assistance of the kings of Guzerat and Malwa. Mullik-oot-Toojar, determining to attack Nuseer Khan before reinforcements could arrive, pushed on by forced marches to Lulling, and reached that place with a select body of archers, amounting to about three thousand men. Nuseer Khan had with him only two thousand soldiers, but he attacked Mullik-oot-Toojar. After a severe action he was compelled to retreat, and with difficulty reached the fort. In this engagement he lost about twenty elephants and all his baggage; which disaster weighed so heavily upon his mind that he died in a few days after, on the 20th of Rubbee-ool-Awul, in the year 841, after a reign of forty years. Nuseer Khan was buried by his son in the family-vault at the Talnere by the side of his father, Mullik Raja.

Rubbee-ool-Awul 20.
A.H. 841.
Sept. 19.
A.D. 1437.

MEERAN ADIL KHAN FAROOKY.

Succeeds his father, and obtains the aid of the King of Guzerat to expel the Deccan troops from Kandeish— is assassinated in Boorhanpoor.

NUSEER KHAN was succeeded by his son Meeran Adil Khan, who instantly wrote pressing letters to the Kings of Malwa and Guzerat for aid. The Guzerat army shortly after arriving at Sooltanpoor compelled Mullik-oot-Toojar to raise the seige of Lulling, and to retreat into the Deccan. After this, Meeran Adil Khan reigned for about three years, and suffered martyrdom* in the city of Boorhanpoor, on Friday the 8th of Zeehuj, in the year 844. As I have never been able to procure any satisfactory account of the manner of his death, I can give no information on the subject: he lies buried, however, at Talnere by the side of his father.

Zeehuj 8. A. H. 844. April 28. A. D. 1441.

* The expression implies assassination.

MEERAN MOOBARIK KHAN FAROOKY

Ascends his father's throne, and dies, after a reign of seventeen years.

MEERAN ADIL KHAN was succeeded by his son Meeran Moobarik; and all that we know of his history is, that he reigned without undertaking any foreign conquest, or drawing upon him-
Rujub 12. A.H. 861. May 17. A.D. 1457.
self the hostility of his neighbours, for a period of seventeen years. He died on the 12th of Rujub, A.H. 861, and was buried at Talnere.

MEERAN GHUNY,

COMMONLY CALLED

ADIL KHAN FAROOKY I.

Ascends his father's throne—compels the neighbouring rajas to pay him tribute—refuses to acknowledge the supremacy of the King of Guzerat, or to pay him tribute.—A Guzerat army marches to Kandeish, and exacts the arrears due—Death of Adil Khan Farooky.

AFTER the death of Meeran Moobarik Khan he was succeeded by his eldest son Adil Khan; and the province of Kandeish, under his government, attained a degree of prosperity which it had never known under any of its former rulers. Adil Khan obliged the neighbouring rajas to pay him tribute, compelling those of Gondwana and Gurra Mundla to acknowledge fealty to him; and neither Kolies nor Bheels in his days infested the roads, nor disturbed the peaceable inhabitants of towns. This prince added considerably to the fortifications of Aseer, and constructed the strong outwork called Mallygur; he also built the ark, or citadel, of Boorhanpoor, and raised many magnificent palaces in that town. It was in consequence of the great strength which he had acquired that he assumed the title of Shah-i-Jharkund (King of the Forests), and was induced, contrary to the practice of his ancestors, not only to withhold the annual tribute from the King of Guzerat, but openly declared that he owned no allegiance to that monarch. This was no sooner made known to Mahmood Shah Begurra than he directed his army to march into Kandeish, and not to return without having received all the arrears of the annual tribute which Adil Khan had so long withheld. For this purpose, in the year 904, the Guzerat army marched, and that of

A. H. 904.
A. D. 1498.

Kandeish also moved to oppose it; but the latter was glad to effect its retreat within the walls of Talnere and Aseer, which places were both invested. Adil Khan was unable to cope with the power of Mahmood Shah, and in order to preserve his personal safety and government was compelled to pay the arrears of tribute before the Guzerat forces retired into their own country. Five years after this event, on

Rubbee-ool-Awul 14.
A.H. 909.
April 8.
A.D. 1503.

Friday the 14th of Rubbee-ool-Awul, of the year 909, Adil Khan died, after a reign of forty-six years. His body was buried at his particular request near the palace of the Dowlut Meidan* in Boorhanpoor.

* The Dowlut Meidan, or Royal Circus, is a level spot of ground lying about a mile to the north of Boorhanpoor. The palace grounds extended over several acres, and a portion of it, like a park, was used to exercise and train the King's chargers. The place still preserves its name; but I had great difficulty, in the year 1821, when I visited Boorhanpoor, in finding the King's tomb, now situated in a wilderness of pomegranates, custard apples, guavas, and other fruit-trees, once the choicest of the land, and which served to grace the royal banquet. The trees and their scions have grown into an almost impenetrable shrubbery; and this edifice, together with other ruins with which the Dowlut Meidan is covered, has become the retreat of venomous serpents and wild beasts.

DAWOOD KHAN FAROOKY.

Provokes a war with the King of Ahmudnuggur—solicits aid from the King of Malwa, which is granted.—The King of Ahmudnuggur declines the contest, and retires.—The Malwa general causes his master to be acknowledged King of Kandeish, and after exacting valuable presents from Dawood Khan he retires to Malwa.—Death of Dawood Khan Farooky.

MEERAN ADIL KHAN leaving no male child to inherit his dominions, they devolved on his younger brother Dawood.* Immediately after his

* Ferishta, in concluding the reign of Mullik Raja, states, that when he visited Boorhanpoor, in 1604, he failed in procuring any history of the Farooky kings of Kandeish; but that he copied a genealogy of the family, which he obtained from Mirza Ally of Isfahan, who had somewhere seen it, and copied it also. That document only gives sixteen generations for a period of seven hundred and thirty years, which requires forty-five years seven months and fifteen days to each generation; an allowance far too great, according to Sir Isaac Newton and other chronologists.

The translator visited Boorhanpoor in 1821, more than two centuries after Ferishta, and was equally unsuccessful in procuring any historical materials beyond a chronology preserved in the family of a highly respectable person (Shah Shums-ood-Deen), who claims to be a lineal descendant of Adil Khan I. through his son Azeez Khan, whose right to the throne was set aside by his uncle Dawood. As Azeez Khan is not mentioned by Ferishta, the authenticity of Shah Shums-ood-Deen's pedigree rests at present on his assertion. Certain it is, however, his family is entitled Farooky; and his accession, two brothers, Hoossein Ally and Yar Ally, Moguls, began to acquire great influence about the person of the Prince; so much so that he created the elder his prime minister, with the title of Hissam-ood-Deen. At the instigation of this person, in the latter end of the year 909, the King declared his intention of attacking some of the frontier towns of the kingdom of Ahmudnuggur. Ahmud Nizam

A. H. 909.
A. D. 1503.

---

hereditary landed property at Boorhanpoor has descended to him through a line of ancestors beyond the period of any records at present in that city.

The genealogy preserved by Shah Shums-ood-Deen is more complete than that of Ferishta, and furnishes thirty-seven generations for a period of eight hundred and nineteen years, which allows of twenty-two years one month and about nineteen days for each generation. The genealogy runs thus:—

The caliph Oomr Farook
Abdoolla
Oobeid Oolla
Nasir
Mahomed Ahmud
Azim
Mahomed
Mahmood
Ahmud
Adam
Ibrahim
Armian
Zoolkuful
Asheea
Daniel
Khwaja Tilla
Sikundur
Shaeeb
Simeon
Oothman
Ally
Khan Jehan
Mullik Raja, the first king of Kandeish
Nuseer Khan
Meeran Adil Khan
Meeran Moobarik Khan
Adil Khan I.
Azeez Khan
Keisur Khan
Raja Feroze Khan
Raja Kasim Khan
Meeran Moobarik Shah
Sahib Khan
Mohbut Khan
Mahomed Hoossein Khan
Mahbut Khan, entitled Baba Sahib
Shah Shums-ood-Deen, the possessor of the estates, and head of the family, at present residing in Boorhanpoor.

Shah Bheiry, anticipating his movement, marched an army into the province of Kandeish. Dawood Khan retreated within the fortress of Aseer, and sent an envoy to Malwa, soliciting the assistance of Sooltan Nasir-ood-Deen. The King of Malwa, viewing him as a neighbour and relative, sent a force under Yekbal Khan to assist him; when Nizam Shah Bheiry, unwilling to become involved in a war with Malwa, retreated to Ahmudnuggur. Yekbal Khan, however, continued his march to Boorhanpoor, where he required Dawood Khan to cause the public prayers to be read in the name of Sooltan Nasir-ood-Deen; and having exacted from Dawood Khan two elepants, and sundry articles of value, the Malwa general returned to Mando. Some years after, Dawood Khan died on Wednesday, the 1st of Jumad-ool-Awul, in the year 916, after reigning eight years. Mullik Hissam-ood-Deen and the rest of the officers placed Ghizny Khan, the son of the late King, on the throne; but after two days, for what cause God only knows, Mullik Hissam-ood-Deen caused the young king to be poisoned.

Jumad-ool-Awul 1. A. H. 916. August 6. A. D. 1510.

ADIL KHAN FAROOKY II.

ENTITLED

AZIM HOOMAYOON.

Alum Khan, a relative of the late King, residing at Ahmudnuggur, is elevated to the throne.—Mullik Larun, governor of Aseer, refuses to acknowledge him.—Adil Khan Farooky of Talnere puts forward his claim—is supported by his grandfather, the King of Guzerat, and his title is every where acknowledged.—Alum Khan, supported by the King of Ahmudnuggur, makes a second effort to ascend the throne, but is defeated.—Adil Khan Farooky attends his father-in-law, Moozuffur Shah II., in the campaign in Malwa—his death.

On the death of Ghizny Khan, there being no other male relations living in Kandeish, the nobles sent a deputation to Ahmud Nizam Shah, requesting him to permit the Prince Alum Khan, a descendant of the Farooky family, then residing at Ahmudnuggur, to assume charge of Kandeish. At a council held by Nizam Shah Bheiry and Imad-ool-Moolk, King of Berar, those princes resolved to acknowledge Alum Khan* heir to the vacant throne of Kandeish; but Mullik Larun, an officer the latter government, who had command of the fort of Aseer, refused to acknowledge the new king. At the same time, Adil, the son of Hussun, and grandson of Nuseer Khan, by the daughter of Mahmood Shah of Guzerat, and who

* It is no where explained whose son Alum Khan was, or on what grounds his claim to the throne rested.

was then residing at Talnere, wrote a petition to that monarch, supported by one from his mother, begging to be placed in the government of his ancestor. Mahmood Shah, perceiving that the country of Kandeish was about to be involved in civil war, resolved to assume a right of interference in favour of his grandson, Adil Khan. For this purpose he marched in person to Kandeish, and Hissam-ood-Deen, becoming alarmed, wrote petitions to the kings of Ahmudnuggur and Berar to support Alum Khan. Both the latter kings sent detachments of troops, consisting of four thousand horse; but the Kandeish officers, perceiving themselves unable to cope with the Guzerat army, dispersed. Hissam-ood-Deen, seeing the course affairs had taken, despatched Alum Khan to the Deccan, and himself joined the King of Guzerat, as did also Larun Khan, who had previously secured the fort of Aseer. Mahmood Shah therefore placed Adil Khan in the government of Boorhanpoor, with the title of Azim Hoomayoon, and gave to him in marriage the daughter of Moozuffur Shah, sister by the same mother of Bahadur Shah of Guzerat, presenting him, at the same time, with a sum of three hundred thousand tunkas of silver.*

Mullik Larun received the title of Khan Jehan and the jageer of Ahwas, while Hissam-ood-Deen became ennobled under the title of Shehr-yar Khan, received the town of Danwur as an estate, and was placed in charge of Talnere. Titles and small jageers were also conferred on several other nobles; and Mahmood Shah Begurra returned to Ahmudabad.

* 20,000*l.*

When Adil Khan had, by the assistance of his maternal grandfather, been placed in the government of Kandeish, he removed his family and property from Talnere to Boorhanpoor, and Hissam-ood-Deen proceeded from the latter to the former place; the whole of which district he received as a jageer. Some time after this, the Prince, discovering that Hissam-ood-Deen was intriguing at the court of Ahmudnuggur, in order to replace Alum Khan on the throne, order him to appear at court. Hissam-ood-Deen, aware of the cause of this summons, determined neither to give umbrage by disobeying the order, nor to go so slightly attended as to render his imprisonment a matter of easy accomplishment. He in consequence went, at the head of four thousand horse, to Boorhanpoor, and was met at some distance by Adil Khan, who had only a small retinue of three hundred men with him. Hissam-ood-Deen received every attention, and the following was the day fixed for him to pay his visit in state; on which occasion the King gave instructions to have him murdered by his servants the moment he left the hall of audience. Hissam-ood-Deen, as was expected, came to the levee attended by all his officers, while the whole of his cavalry remained drawn up on the outside, with a view of overawing the King. After a long and formal visit, the King took Hissam-ood-Deen aside into a private apartment, under the plea of communicating something important, and on his return he was cut down by the royal guards. Mullik Boorhan, a Guzerat chief, who had been left by

Mahmood Shah Begurra as the King's minister, immediately attacked Hissam-ood-Deen's officers, who were most of them put to death; while almost at the same moment a select body of Guzerat horse fell upon the Talnere cavalry, and completely dispersed them. This vigorous though sanguinary measure restored to the King the whole of the Talnere district, which formed nearly half of his territory, and also removed an ambitious and powerful rival.

Some time afterwards, the King visited the fort of Aseer, where he found that Sheer Khan and Seif Khan, two Guzerat officers, had been intriguing with Nizam Shah Bheiry of Ahmudnuggur; and that monarch, accompanied by Alum Khan, actually arrived on the frontier for the purpose of again placing the latter in the government. The King immediately despatched a messenger to Moozuffur Shah II. of Guzerat, detailing the whole circumstances, and begging that he would send a force to his assistance. On receipt of this communication, Moozuffur Shah directed a sum of twelve lacks of tunkas to be sent to Adil Khan, to enable him to raise troops, and also despatched a large force under Dilawur Khan and Sufdur Khan to his aid; writing to him at the same time to say, that if it were necessary he would himself march to protect his rights. "As for Nizam-ool-"Moolk Bheiry," said he, "who styles himself "king, he is one of the slaves of the household of "the kings of the Deccan: he shall suffer for "daring to march against the lineal descendant "of the house of Farook, and a prince who is my "son-in-law." The same language was also made use of to the ambssador of Ahmud Nizam Shah, resident at the Guzerat court, who was informed of the King's determination to support Adil Khan even at the risk of his crown. Ahmud Nizam Shah, seeing the turn affairs had taken, thought it prudent to retreat, while Sheer Khan and Seif Khan were permitted to retire to Gavulgur. After the arrival of Guzerat army Adil Khan employed it to levy the tribute from the Raja of Galna, a dependent of the Ahmudnuggur government, from whom he raised a large sum of money; after which he returned to Boorhanpoor, and permitted the Guzerat army to proceed home-wards.

A.H. 923. A.D. 1517. In the year 923, Adil Khan II. accompanied his father-in-law, Moozuffur Shah, with a force to Mando, and assisted greatly in the Malwa campaign; but as the events of that war are detailed both in the Guzerat and Malwa histories, I have not thought it necessary to repeat them in this place.

A. H. 926. A. D. 1520. In the year 926, Adil Khan, falling dangerously ill, died at Boorhanpoor, after a reign of nineteen years. He was succeeded by Meeran Mahomed, his eldest son, by the sister* of Bahadur Shah of Guzerat.

* This relationship is mentioned, because Moozuffur Shah of Guzerat had several children by different wives; but the Queen of Kandeish was by the same mother as Bahadur Shah of Guzerat, which accounts for her son, Meeran Mahomed Shah, being elevated to the throne of Guzerat After Bahadur Shah's death.

MEERAN MAHOMED KHAN FAROORY,

ENTITLED

MEERAN MAHOMED SHAH.

Ascends his father's throne—assists the King of Berar to wage war with the King of Ahmudnuggur—is defeated, with the loss of all his military train, including elephants—obtains the aid of his uncle, Bahadur Shah of Guzerat—attends Bahadur Shah throughout the campaign against Ahmudnuggur.—Termination of the war.—Meeran Mahomed Khan assists Bahadur Shah in the campaign in Malwa—is present at his final overthrow at Mundsoor—retires to Kandeish—assists the governor of Malwa to recover that country from the Moguls.—Bahadur Shah of Guzerat dies.—Meeran Mahomed Khan is raised to the throne of Guzerat, under the title of Meeran Mahomed Shah—his death.

After the death of Adil Khan II. he was succeeded by his son Meeran Mahomed Khan. Shortly after his accession to the government, Imad Shah, King of Berar, and Boorhan Nizam Shah of Ahmudnuggur, were engaged in war with each other; and the former having lost his country, came to Boorhanpoor; when both Imad Shah and Meeran Mahomed Khan of Kandeish wrote to Bahadur Shah of Guzerat, requesting his interference in adjusting the differences with the King of Ahmudnuggur. Bahadur Shah, in consequence, deputed Ein-ool-Moolk, the governor of Puttun, to proceed to Boorhanpoor, and endeavour to mediate a peace. Boorhan Nizam Shah consented to an amicable adjustment of affairs for the present, in order to meet the wishes of the court of Guzerat; but shortly after the return of Bahadur Shah's ambassador, he attacked and took the fort of Mahoor, and reduced several other districts in Berar. In consequence of this, in the year 934, Imad-ool-Moolk entered into a league with Meeran Mahomed Khan of Kandeish, who marched with all his army and elephants to the assistance of Imad-ool-Moolk, and joined him near the Godavery river. In a few days after and action took place with Boorhan Nizam Shah, in which the latter was defeated; but Imad-ool-Moolk, elated with his success, permitted his troops to disperse in search of plunder. This afforded the enemy an opportunity to rally; and Boorhan Nizam Shah, charging with a body of three thousand cavalry among the confederates, not only recovered the public property he had formerly lost, but captured several of the Kandeish elephants. Many of the Kandeish troops, too, were killed; and the late victorious army of Imad-ool-Moolk being routed, was closely pursued for upwards of eight miles. Meeran Mahomed Khan took the route of Aseer, while his ally, Imad-ool-Moolk, fled to Gavulgur, from whence they both wrote an account of their disaster to Bahadur Shah of Guzerat. After repeated solicitations, the King of Guzerat marched in person to

A. H. 934.
A. D. 1527.

Boorhanpoor, and from thence, accompanied by Meeran Mahomed Khan and Imad-ool-Moolk, entering the Deccan, penetrated as far as Jalna without resistance. On arriving there Bahadur Shah took measures for occupying Berar for himself, and threatened, by removing Imad-ool-Moolk, to place his own officers in the government. Imad-ool-Moolk, on discovering his intentions, consulted with Meeran Mahomed Khan what was to be done. The latter said, "This is the natural consequence of "calling in foreign aid at all; and the only remedy "to be now pursued is to read the prayers, and to "coin money, in the name of the King of Guzerat, "and to style yourself a tributary and servant of his "government." However humiliating the proposal, Imad-ool-Moolk did not hesitate to adopt Meeran Adil Khan's advice. He therefore proposed it to Bahadur Shah, and recommended him to march immediately to Ahmudnuggur for the same purpose. This pleased Bahadur Shah so much that he agreed to the whole arrangement, and proceeded, accompanied by the Berar and Kandeish troops, towards Ahmudnuggur, where (as has been formerly related in the Guzerat history) the public prayers were read in the name of the King of Guzerat. After this campaign Bahadur Shah proceeded to Baroach, and Meeran Mahomed Khan and Imad-ool-Moolk retired to their respective capitals.

A. H. 939.
A. D. 1532.

In the year 939, Bahadur Shah marched towards Malwa for the purpose of subjugating that kingdom, in which campaign Meeran Mahomed Khan was present at the reduction of the fort of Mando; after which he returned to Boorhanpoor. Boorhan Nizam Shah of Ahmudnuggur, alarmed at the occupation of the kingdom of Malwa, deputed an ambassador to Meeran Mahomed Khan, professing great regard for him, and requesting his interference with the King of Guzerat, to reconcile some differences which existed between them.*

Bahadur Shah, in the following year, marched to Boorhanpoor, where he was met by Boorhan Nizam Shah, on whom he conferred the white canopy and scarlet pavilion; after which the latter returned to Ahmudnuggur and the former to Malwa. Meeran Mahomed Khan also accompanied the King of Guzerat in his expedition against Chittoor, and was with him in his retreat before the arms of Hoomayoon Padshah to Mando. After the occupation of Guzerat by Hoomayoon, that monarch sent one of his principal officers, called Asuf Khan, to levy contributions in the Deccan, and was himself on his march towards Boorhanpoor, which he no doubt intended to occupy: but the sudden irruption of Sheer Shah from Bengal into the Dehly territory obliged Hoomayoon to return through Malwa towards Agra. At that time Bahadur Shah made an effort to recover Guzerat, and requested Meeran Mahomed Khan to invade Malwa at the same time, and expel the Dehly officers. Meeran Mahomed Khan did so; and in concert with Mulloo Khan, the late Guzerat governor of Malwa, took possession

* This passage alludes to a transaction mentioned in the Deccan history, vide vol. iii. p. 222.

of Mando. While Meeran Mahomed Khan was there, information reached him that Bahadur Shah* had sipped of the cup of martyrdom from the hands of the infidel Portuguese at Diù, and that his mother, in concert with the nobles of Guzerat, had proclaimed Meeran Mahomed Khan of Kandeish king. A deputation shortly after arrived at Mando for the purpose of escorting him to Guzerat. Meanwhile he was formally crowned at Mando, and assumed the title of Meeran Mahomed Shah; but his reign was of short duration; for on the journey to Ahmudabad he was taken
Zeekad 13. dangerously ill, and died suddenly on
A. H. 942. the 13th of Zeekad, A. H. 942. His
May 4. body was conveyed to Boorhanpoor,
A. D. 1535. and interred in the vault of his father, Adil Khan II.

* Vide history of Guzerat, vol. iv. p. 131.

MEERAN MOOBARIK KHAN FAROOKY.*

Succeeds his elder brother on the throne—refuses to deliver up the Prince Mahmood of Guzerat, then confined in Aseer, to the nobles of that kingdom—is compelled to do so—puts forth pretensions to the throne of Guzerat, and marches an army to Ahmudabad—is defeated—procures the cession of Sooltanpoor and Nundoorbar by the King of Guzerat.—Baz Bahadur, King of Malwa, is expelled from his throne by Peer Mahomed Khan, an officer of Akbur Padshah.—The Moguls Pursue Baz Bahadur to Boorhanpoor, and sack the town—they retreat, and are closely pursued by Meeran Moobarik Khan and Baz Bahadur.—The Moguls routed near the Nurbudda, and Peer Mahomed Khan loses his life.—Death of Meeran Moobarik Khan.

At the period of the death of Meeran Mahomed Shah, none of his children were of an age to take the reins of government; and his brother Moobarik, hearing of his decease at Boorhanpoor, immediately assumed the title of Shah. Shortly after his accession the nobles of Guzerat deputed Yekhtiar Khan, an officer of that kingdom, to demand the Prince Mahmood, son of Luteef Khan,† nephew of the late Bahadur Shah, whom

* Although the assumed the title of Shah, or King, it was a dignity to which he had no right, as he did not succeed to the government of any kingdom. I therefore call him Khan, to prevent the confusion which might otherwise arise.

† The efforts made by the Prince Luteef Khan, the brother of Bahadur Shah, to ascend the throne of Guzerat, have been

that monarch had, during his lifetime, sent to Meeran Mahomed Khan of Kandeish, to be confined in a hill-fort during his life. Meeran Moobarik, who himself aspired to the throne of Guzerat, and to which his brother had been so lately elevated, threw obstacles in the way of the enlargement of the Prince Mahmood; but the Guzerat officers resented his detention so wormly, that Meeran Moobarik Khan was compelled, from motives of policy, to permit Yekhtiar Khan to take charge of him, and he was accordingly crowned at Ahmudabad in the year 943.

A.H. 943.
A.D. 1536

At this period, also, Imad-ood-Moolk of Guzerat fled, and sought protection at Boorhanpoor. He was hospitably received by Meeran Moobarik Khan, who encouraged him to collect a body of twelve thousand Guzerat horse. With this force they both marched for the purpose of placing Meeran Moobarik Khan on the throne. On the other hand, Duria Khan, accompanied by Mahmood Shah III., opposed them. The armies met, and a sanguinary contest ensued, in which the Kandeish troops were defeated. Moobarik Khan fled to Aseer, and Imad-ool-Moolk to Mando,

---

fully detailed in the Guzerat history, vide vol. iv. p. 113. Mahmood could not have been more *conveniently* disposed of than in the hands of a foreign prince, between whom and the succession to Guzerat he alone intervened. Indeed, considering the times, it reflects some credit on the memory of Meeran Mahomed Shah that Mahmood was suffered to outlive him.

where he sought protection with Sooltan Kadur of Malwa. The Guzeratties under Duria Khan, following up their success, plundered and laid waste the country of Kandeish, through which they passed, and compelled Meeran Moobarik Khan to pay a very heavy fine. Mahmood Shah, when in confinement in the fort of Aseer, promised, if ever he succeeded to the government of Guzerat, to give to Meeran Moobarik Khan the district of Nundoorbar; and upon this occasion he formally yielded it up to him.

A.H. 969. A.D. 1572.

In the year 969, Sooltan Baz Bahadur, King of Malwa, was compelled to fly before the Mogul forces, and sought protection with Meeran Moobarik Khan. Peer Mahomed Khan, the Mogul chief, who had driven him from his seat of government, pursued him into the very centre of Kandeish, penetrating as far as Boorhanpoor, when he devastated the country, sacked the city, dishonoured the females, and committed enormities unfit to relate. Meeran Moobarik Khan wrote to Toofal Khan, governor of Berar, begging his assistance in this momentous crisis, who with the alacrity proportionate to the emergency marched the whole of his force to Kandeish, and joined Meeran Moobarik Khan and Sooltan Baz Bahadur. The ferocious bands of Peer Mahomed Khan had been so glutted by debauch, and so enriched by spoil, that they had little inclination to risk their booty in action; and their leader, contrary to his own will, was compelled to retreat to Malwa. Many of the soldiery were so desirous to reach their quarters, that they went off even before Peer Mahomed Khan, and left him to follow with a small force and all the heavy baggage and military stores. The allied forces under Toofal Khan pursued the Moguls; and having intimation of their dispersed state, made rapid marches, and overtook Peer Mahomed Khan on the banks of the Nurbudda. The allies immediately charged the enemy, who, overpowered by numbers, sought safety in flight. Many were drowned in the river; and Peer Mahomed Khan himself, who ordered his elephant to be urged into the stream, was among the number. The confederates, following up their success, marched on to Mando, where Sooltan Baz Bahadur again assumed the reins of government; after which the allies returned to their respective countries. Meeran Moobarik Khan died, some years afterwards, on the night of Wednesday the 6th of Jumad-ool-Akhur, A.H. 974, after a reign of thirty-two years.

Jumad-ool-Akhur 6. A.H. 974. Dec. 24. A.D. 1566.

MEERAN MAHOMED KHAN FAROOKY.

Succeeds his fathar.—Kandeish invaded by Chungiz Khan of Guzerat, who takes Sooltanpoor and Nundoorbar—besieges Talnere—is opposed by Meeran Mahomed Khan and Toofal Khan of Berar.—The siege of Talnere relinquished, and Chungiz Khan flies to Guzerat.—Meeran Mahomed Khan raises an army of thirty thousand men—invades Guzerat, and claims the throne—is defeated in the battle of Ahmudabad—is closely pursued by the Mogul Mirzas in Guzerat—they plunder Kandeish, and retire to Malwa.—Meeran Mahomed Khan aids Toofal Khan of Berar against the King of Ahmudnuggur.—Toofal Khan loses his territory, and eventually his life, in the struggle.—Boorhanpoor sacked by the Deccan army.—Meeran Mahomed Khan pays a large sum to obtain peace.—Death of Meeran Mahomed Khan.

MEERAN MOOBARIK KHAN was succeeded by his son Meeran Mahomed. In the same year Chungiz Khan of Guzerat, instigated by Etimad Khan, the prime minister of Moozuffur Shah III., invaded the district of Nundoorbar, and having compelled the Kandeish officers to retreat, boldly pushed on to the fortress of Talnere. Meeran Mahomed Khan, hearing of this inroad, called on Toofal Khan for assistance; and the combined forces of Kandeish and Berar marched to the western frontier. On their arrival at Talnere, they found Chungiz Khan strongly posted with ravines on his flanks, and his artillery and carriages of all descriptions forming a barrier in his front. Meeran Mahomed Khan used every effort in vain, during the day of his arrival, to induce Chungiz Khan to quit his position; but during the night Chungiz Khan fled singly to Baroach, leaving his army and all his artillery in the hands of Meeran Mahomed Khan, who, on the following day, occupied the ground which the enemy had quitted. At this time the Guzerat government was in a state of the utmost confusion, and a civil war prevailed. Most of the nobles were of opinion that Moozuffur Shah III., who was merely a pageant in the hands of Etimad-ool-Moolk, was not the son of Mahmood Shah, and they refused to acknowledge his right to the throne. Meeran Mahomed Khan, therefore, conceiving himself to be the only rightful heir, and hearing that he might expect support from the Guzerat nobles, if he boldly asserted his claims, collected a force of thirty thousand horse, and marched to Ahmudabad. Chungiz Khan, who had, in the mean time, been successful in the civil war, was at the capital, whence he had expelled his rival Etimad-ool-Moolk and the King. On gaining information that Meeran Mahomed Khan, with a large force, had arrived near Ahmudabad, Chungiz Khan marched to oppose him with only seven thousand men, supported by the Dehly Mirzas (who are mentioned both in the Guzerat and Dehly histories), and gained a complete victory. Meeran Mahomed Khan was glad to effect his retreat in safety to Aseer, leaving in possession of the Guzeratties his elephants, artillery, and all the royal equipage which the rulers of Kandeish assumed. A short time after this event, the Mirzas, having plundered great part of southern Guzerat, invaded Kandeish also; and before Meeran Mahomed Khan could collect an army sufficient to oppose them, they laid waste and levied contributions on several districts, and quitted the province.

A. H. 982. A. D. 1574. In the year 982, Moortuza Nizam Shah Bheiry of Ahmudnuggur invaded and subdued the country of Berar, and seized and confined Toofal Khan. One of the officers of his government came to Kandeish, and styling himself Imad-ool-Moolk, the representative of Toofal Khan, begged the assistance of Meeran Mahomed Khan. The latter was so deceived by this impostor that he actually sent a force of five thousand men to accompany him, in order to recover Berar. The impostor marched and laid waste the country; but Moortuza Nizam Shah, at the instance of Chungiz Khan* Isfahany, his prime minister, returned, and having dispersed the Kandeish troops like sheep, turned his attention towards Meeran Mahomed Khan, who had been the means of this invasion. In consequence of which the King of Ahmudnuggur sacked Boorhanpoor, and moved on to Aseer, where after a close siege of considerable length Meeran Mahomed Khan was compelled to sue for peace, and paid to Moortuza Nizam Shah the sum of six hundred

* It is a curious coincidence that both the ministers at Ahmudnuggur and Guzerat should bear the name of Chungiz Khan at the same time; but it is sufficient to bear in mind the distinction between the two kingdoms, and the reader will be prepared not to confound them.

thousand moozuffuries,* a sum nearly equal to three hundred thousand siccas of silver, besides two hundred thousand moozuffuries to the minister Chungiz Khan.

A.H. 984.
A.D. 1576.

In the year 984, Meeran Mahomed Khan was seized by a fever, and after lingering some months, died. His only heir was his son Hoossein Khan, then a minor.

* According to this statement, a moozuffury was eqnal to half a rupee, fifteen-pence English money. It was a base silver coin, struck in the reign of Moozuffur Shah III. of Guzerat, which became current at this time in Kandeish; but has long since been extinct.

RAJA ALLY KHAN FAROOKY.

Succeeds his brother—writes to Akbur, acknowledging his supremacy.—Character of Raja Ally Khan.—A body of revolted chiefs from Ahmudnuggur arrive at Boorhanpoor—they plunder the town, and are pursued by Raja Ally Khan—they return, with a force of Moguls, into Berar—are again defeated by Raja Ally Khan.—The Prince Moorad Mirza, the son of Akbur, invades the Deccan—he is joined by Raja Ally Khan, who eventually loses his life at the battle of Peitun, on the Godavery.

On the first intimation of the illness of which Meeran Mahomed Khan subsequently died, his brother Raja Ally, then at Agra, proceeded direct to Boorhanpoor, and arrived at the latter city three days after his death. The nobles went out to meet him; and in consequence of the minority of Hoossein Khan they deposed that prince, and placed Raja Ally on the musnud. At this period, the princes of Hindoostan, from Bengal to Sind, including Malwa and Guzerat, had been subdued by the victorious arms of Akbur Padshah; and Raja Ally Khan, in order to avoid so unequal a contest, dropped the title of king, which his brother had assumed, and wrote a letter to Akbur, begging that be might he considered as his vassal and tributary; and in order to convince him of his sincerity, sent him many rich and valuable presents. He also maintained a friendly intercourse for a period of years with the Kings of the Deccan. Raja Ally Khan was a person of superior talents: just as a governor, wise and prudent as a statesman, brave and intrepid as a warrior, and possessing a high spirit and a laudable ambition. He was the idol of his people, and neither engaged in wars of conquest nor patiently permitted his country to be invaded. He employed his time in reading with doctors of the Hunefy sect, and in the cultivation of the arts, until the year 1002, when (during the secession of Moortuza Nizam Shah of Ahmudnuggur from public affairs) a dispute arising between Sulabut Khan, the Ahmudnuggur regent, and Syud Moortuza, the governor of Berar, a battle took place at the distance of twelve miles from Ahmudnuggur; wherein Syud Moortuza was defeated, and retreated with twelve thousand men, accompanied by some of his officers, to Elichpoor. On being closely pursued, these chiefs directed their march towards Boorhanpoor, and requested the assistance of Raja Ally Khan, who neither gave them encouragement nor a direct refusal. Meanwhile, impatient of delay, Syud Moortuza's soldiers sacked the city, and directed their march towards Agra. Raja Ally Khan pursued and defeated this mutinous body on the banks of the Nurbudda, taking all its baggage and carriage-cattle; among the latter of which were one hundred elephants. Syud Moortuza, however, was enabled to cross the river, and proceeded to join Akbur Padshah, to whom he complained of the ill usage he had experienced

A. H. 1002.
A. D. 1593.

from Raja Ally Khan, but more particularly from Sulabut Khan. Akbur, who had long been desirous of invading the Deccan, thought the present a good opportunity to carry his project into effect. For this purpose he received the Deccan refugees into his service, and gave them high military stations. Raja Ally Khan, on hearing of their elevation, foresaw the future destination of the Dehly arms, and therefore deputed an envoy to Akbur, to whom he presented all the elephants he had taken from the Deccanies, as also a considerable sum of money. The offering was accepted; and on the following year, viz. 1003, Syud Moortuza and the rest of the Deccan chiefs were directed to proceed to Mando, whence Mirza Azeez Koka furnished a considerable force for the purpose of invading Berar, while Mirza Mahomed Tuky was deputed by the King of Ahmudnuggur to oppose them. When the Dehly force arrived at the town of Hundia, on the Banks of the Nurbudda, the commander sent a person to wait on Raja Ally Khan, in order that he might mediate an accommodation between the Ahmudnuggur and Berar officers; while, on the other hand, Mahomed Tuky, the Nizam Shahy general, was empowered to make overtures to Raja Ally Khan, to induce him to join the Deccan army. After the most mature deliberation, Raja Ally Khan thought fit to join the Deccanies, with whom he proceeded towards Hundia; and having arrived within two miles of the Moguls, intended to attack them on the following day. During the night, however,

A.H. 1003.
A.D. 1594.

the Mogul general, leaving his tents standing and lights burning, decamped, and taking the road to Berar, plundered the country, and sacked the towns of Elichpoor and Balapoor. Raja Ally Khan and Mirza Mahomed Tuky, on hearing of this manœuvre, countermarched, but the Mogul rejoined the force he had left at Hundia* without encountering opposition; and the Deccan allies, having secured themselves from attack, returned to their respective governments of Ahmudnuggur and Kandeish.

A. H. 1004.
A. D. 1595.
After the death of Boorhan Nizam Shah II., in the year 1004, the Prince Moorad Mirza, son of Akbur Padshah, and Khan Khanan, the son of Beiram Khan, marched for the purpose of subduing the Deccan. Raja Ally Khan of Kandeish accompanied them, and was killed, with many officers of distinction, by the explosion of a powder tumbril, in the famous battle fought between Khan Khanan and Soheil Khan, general of the Ahmudnuggur forces.†

A. H. 1005.
A. D. 1596.
The reign of Raja Ally Kahn lasted for a period of twenty-one years; and his body was carried to Boorhanpoor, where he was buried with due honours.

* The Mogul historian relates, that they retired out of Berar by the route of Sooltanpoor and Nundoorbar, which must be, I think, erroneous. They probably returned through the hills along the same route by which they entered Berar.

† Vide vol. ii. p. 274., and vol. iii. p. 308.

BAHADUR KHAN FAROOKY.

Ascends his father's throne—defies the power of Akbur.—Aseer besieged, and taken by capitulation; and Bahadur Khan, the last of the kings of Kandeish, becomes a state-prisoner in Gualiar.

A.H. 1005. A.D. 1596. AFTER the death of Raja Ally Khan in the year 1005 he was succeeded by his son, Bahadur Khan, who was supported by Khan Khanan, the general of Akbur Padshah. This prince soon abandoned himself to the pleasures of the seraglio, and neglecting altogether state-affairs, diverted himself with minstrels and dancers. At the period of the death of the Prince Moorad Mirza, in the town of Shahpoor, the Prince Daniel Mirza succeeded him. Bahadur Khan neither sent condolence on his brother's death nor congratulations on his accession to the command of the forces in the Deccan, as is customary; and when Akbur Padshah, a few years afterwards, arrived at Mando with the avowed intention of invading the Deccan, Bahadur Khan, instead of adopting the policy of his father in relying on the honour of Akbur, and going with an army to co-operate with him, shut himself up in the fort of Aseer, and commenced preparations to withstand a siege. To this end he invited fifteen thousand persons, including labourers, artisans, and shop-keepers, into the place, and filled it with horses and cattle, in order that they might serve for work, and eventually for food and other purposes. When Akbur Padshah heard of these proceedings, he sent orders to Khan Khanan, and to the Prince Daniel Mirza, to continue the siege of Ahmudnuggur, while he himself marched to the south and occupied Boorhanpoor, leaving one of his generals to besiege Aseer. The blockade of this fortress continued for a length of time till the air from filth became fetid, and an epidemic disease raged, caused by the number of cattle which daily died. At this period a prevalent report was spread, and generally believed in the garrison, that Akbur had the power of reducing forts by the art of necromancy, and that magicians accompanied him for that purpose. Bahadur Khan, believing that his misfortunes arose from the above-mentioned cause, took no means to counteract the evils by which he was surrounded. He neither gave orders for the removal of the dead cattle, for the establishment of hospitals, nor for sending out useless persons, till at length the soldiers, worn out, became quite careless on duty; and the Moguls stormed and carried the lower fort called Mallygur. Nothing could exceed the infatuation of Bahadur Khan, who, although he had then ten years' grain, and money to an enormous amount, still kept the troops in arrears; and they, seeing that no redress was to be expected, resolved to seize him, and to deliver him over

to Akbur Padshah. Before this project was carried into effect Bahadur Khan discovered the plot, and consulted his officers, who all agreed it was too late to think of a remedy. The pestilence raged with great fury, the troops were completely exhausted, and nothing remained but to open negotiations for the surrender of the fort, on condition that the lives of the garrison shold be spared, and that they should marched out with their property. The terms were acceded to, with the exception of the last proposition regarding the Khan's private property, all of which fell into the King's hands; and Bahadur Khan, the last of the Farooky dynasty, humble himself before the throne of Akbur Padshah, in the year 1008:
A.H. 1008. A.D. 1599. while the impregnable fortress of Aseer, with ten years' provisions, and countless treasures, fell into the hands of the conqueror.

The town of Bahadurpoor, near the city of Boorhanpoor, was built by Bahadur Khan.

CHAPTER VII.

SECTION I.

HISTORY OF THE KINGS OF BENGAL AND BEHAR, COMMONLY CALLED POORBY.

FUKHR-OOD-DEEN POORBY.

Mullik Fukhr-ood-Deen slays Kuddur Khan, the governor of Bengal, and proclaims himself King—he is slain by Alla-ood-Deen.

THE first Moslem chief who invaded the kingdom of Bengal was Mullik Mahomed Bukhtyar, in the reign of Kootb-ood-Deen Eibuk,
A. H. 587.
A. D. 1191.
King of Dehly, in the year 587. After whom, the several governors of that country were appointed from the capital, as is mentioned in the Dehly history. When Mullik Fukhr-ood Deen put to death Kuddur Khan, the governor of Bengal, in the reign of Toghluk, he proclaimed himself king, and declared his independence from the throne of Dehly.*

Mullik Fukhr-ood-Deen was originally a soldier in the service of Kuddur Khan, governor of

*Vide vol. i. p. 423.

To face page 401. Vol. IV.]

GENEALOGIES OF THE SEVERAL DYNASTIES OF THE KINGS OF SIND.

I. HEREDITARY MONARCHS OF THE SOOMUNA RACE.

1 Jam Afra.

2 Jam Chowban.

4 Jam Timajy.

3 Jam Bany.

5 Jam Sulah-ood-Deen.

6 Jam Nizam-ood Deen.

7 Jam Ally Sheer.

8 Jam Giran.

ELECTIVE KINGS OF THE SOOMUNA RACE.

9 Jam Futteh Khan.

10 Jam Toghluk.

11 Jam Sikundur.

12 Jam Sunjur

13 Jam Nunda.

14 Jam Feroze.

DYNASTY OF ARGHOON.

15 Shah Beg Arghoon.

16 Shah Hoossein Arghoon.

DYNASTY OF TURKHAN.

17 Eesa Turkhan.

18 Mahomed Baky Turkhan.

Khan Baba

19 Jany Beg Turkhan

Bengal; but after slaying his master, he proclaimed himself king, and appointed his servant, Mokhlis Khan, to the command of an army, which he sent to enforce obedience among the inhabitants of the surrounding country. This officer was opposed by Mullik Ally Moobarik, who slew him in action; and having defeated his troops, proclaimed himself king, under the title of Alla-ood-Deen, in the year 739. As Mullik Fukhr-ood-Deen was only just seated in his government, and by no means confident of the attachment of his subjects, he thought it imprudent to quit the capital. Alla-ood-Deen marched to Luknowty; and establishing a force in that place, resolved to attack Fukhr-ood-Deen, for which purpose he proceeded towards Bengal. Fukhr-ood-Deen, being now compelled to fight, met his opponent; and in a pitched battle, which took place in the year 741, the former was defeated, taken prisoner, and put to death, having only survived his elevation two years and five months.

A. H. 739.
A. D. 1338.

A. H. 741.
A. D. 1340.

ALLA-OOD-DEEN POORBY.

Alla-ood-Deen assassinated.

AFTER the death of Fukhr-ood-Deen, Alla-ood-Deen succeeded to the government, and returned to Luknowty; where having firmly established his authority, he went to South Bengal. On his return, he found that Mullik Hajy Elias Mullahy* had succeeded in tampering with his army; and Alla-ood-Deen was shortly after assassinated, after a reign of one year and some months.

* The sailor.

HAJY ELIAS,

ENTITLED

SHUMS-OOD-DEEN POORBY.

Hajy Elias assumes the title of Shums-ood-Deen—invades the territory of Jajnuggur in order to procure elephants—is attacked by Feroze Toghluk of Dehly.—The King of Dehly retreats.—Peace concluded.—Death of Shums-ood-Deen.

On the death of Alla-ood-Deen, Haji Elias assumed the title of Shums-ood-Deen Poorby Bhungera, and caused the public prayers to be read, and money to be coined, in his name, as King of Bengal. After his accession he did all in his power to gain the esteem of his subjects, and to secure the attachment of his troops. Shortly after, he led an expedition to Jajnuggur, in order to obtain elephants,* and returned to Luknowty. For thirteen years Shums-ood-Deen Poorby resisted with success the forces of the King of Dehly, who could never succeed during the whole of that period in making any impression upon him. At

* The fact of Sooltan Hooshung of Malwa and Shums-ood-Deen of Bengal both having gone to Jajnuggur to procure elephants is very remarkable, and proves that those animals must have been excellent, as well as numerous, in that province.

Shuval 10. A. H. 754. Oct. 14. A. D. 1353. length, on the 10th of Shuval, in the year 754, Feroze Toghluk marched from Dehly towards Luknowty. On the approach of the enemy, Shums-ood-Deen retreated from his capital to the strong fortress of Yekdalla,* whither Feroze Toghluk advnced. On arriving in the suburbs, Shums-ood-Deen sallied from the fort, and gave the royal army battle; on which occasion, after many men were slain on both sides, he was defeated, and obliged to retreat into Yekdalla, leaving all the large elephants, which he had brought from Jajnuggur, in the hands of the enemy. At this period, fortunately for Shums-ood-Deen, the rainy season having commenced with violence, Feroze was compelled to raise the siege of Yekdalla, and to retreat to Dehly. In the year

A. H. 755. A. D. 1354. 755, he sent an ambassador to Dehly with magnificent presents, and begged forgiveness for opposing the King's army. The ambassadors were honourably received, and dismissed with courtesy.

In the year 759, another ambassador,

A. H. 759. A. D. 1357. Mullik Taj-ood-Deen, was again sent with magnificent offerings to Dehly. The ambassador was treated with distinguished honours; and in return, the King of Dehly deputed Seif-ood-Deen, kotwal, with a number of Arabian and Tartar horses, an elephant, and many valuable gifts, to Luknowty; but before the

* This place is not to be found in the modern maps, though Major Rennell, in his Bengal Atlas, placed it near Dacca.

ambassador crossed the frontier, Shums-ood-Deen died, after a reign of sixteen years. Seif-ood-Deen, however, delivered over his horses and presents to Mullik Taj-ood-Deen to carry to Bengal, and returned in person to Dehly.

SIKUNDUR POORBY.

Sikundur, the son of Shums-ood-Deen, raised to the throne—is attacked by Feroze Toghluk of Dehly, but purchases a peace by the presentation of several elephants—his death.

On the death of Shums-ood-Deen, the nobles of the state elevated his eldest son to the throne three days afterwards. He had not
A. H. 760. A. D. 1358.
long entered on his rule before his country was again invaded, in the year 760, by Feroze Toghluk of Dehly. When the Dehly army arrived at Pundwa, Sikundur Poorby, following his father's example, took refuge in the fortress of Yekdalla, from whence he sent an agent to offer his submission, and to promise annual tribute; which induced Feroze to retreat, after having received twenty-seven elephants* and many other valuable presents. Sikundur
A. H. 769. A. D. 1367.
Prooby reigned in peace for a period of nine years, and then died, A.H. 769.

* Major Stewart, in his History of Bengal, whose information is probably better than that obtained by Ferishta, enumerates forty-eight elephants, besides money. He also states, that Sikundur Poorby was killed in action, in repulsing the troops of his rebellious son who succeeded him.

GHEIAS-OOD-DEEN POORBY.

Reigns seven years, and dies.

A.H. 775. A.D. 1374. GHEIAS-OOD-DEEN succeeded his father, and reigned for a period of seven years and died in the year 775.

SOOLTAN-OOS-SULLATEEN POORBY.

Reigns ten years, and dies.

ON the death of Gheias-ood-Deen, the nobles elevated his son to the throne, under the title of Sooltan-oos-Sullateen (or the King of Kings). This prince was benevolent, merciful, and brave; and after a reign of ten years he died, in the year 785. A.H. 785. A.D. 1383.

SHUMS-OOD-DEEN POORBY II.

Reigns three years, and dies.

On the vacancy of the throne, by the death of Sooltan-oos-Sullateen, it was filled by his son, Shums-ood-Deen II.; who after an inglorious reign of three years quitted this world of vanity for that of eternity, in the year 788.

A.H. 788.
A.D. 1386.

RAJA KANS POORBY.

Raja Kans, a zemindar of Bangl, becomes the founder of a new dyanasty—reigns seven years, and dies.

Subsequently to the death of Shums-ood-Deen II. a zemindar of the name of Kans made head against the Mahomedan power, and succeeded in placing himself on the throne of Bengal; but the Almighty withdrew his favour from him, and after a reign of seven years he died, A.H. 795.

A.H. 795.
A.D. 1392.

JEETMUL,

ENTITLED JULAL-OOD-DEEN.

Jeetmul, the son of Raja Kans, voluntarily renounces the Hindoo religion, and embraces the Mahomedan faith —reigns seventeen years, and dies.

After the death of his father, Jeetmul called together all the officers of the state, and said, so strong a desire to become a convert to the Mahomedan faith had seized him, that he was resolved to embrace that religion; observing, at the same time, if the chiefs would not permit him to succeed to the throne, he was prepared to cede it to his brother. His officers declared they were disposed to accept him as their king, without any reference to the religion he might choose to adopt. So that several learned men among the Mahomedans of that country were summoned to witness Raja Jeetmul renounce the Hindoo religion, and profess that of the Moslems. He was at the same time entitled Julal-ood-Deen; and after ascending the throne, he ruled with such justice, that he became entitled to the appellation of the Nowsherwan of the age. He reigned with great spendour for a period of seventeen years, and died in the latter end of the year 812.

A.H. 812.
A.D. 1400.

AHMUD POORBY.

Succeeds to his father's throne—reigns eighteen years, and dies.

A.H. 830. A.D. 1420. THE Prince Ahmud, as heir-apparent, succeeded his father on the throne; and after reigning eighteen years, died A.H. 830.

NASIR-OOD-DEEN GHOLAM POORBY.

Nasir, a slave, usurps the throne; but is shortly after deposed.

ON the death of Ahmud, one of his personal attendants had the audacity to usurp the place of his sovereign, and seizing the king's property, distributed it among his fellow-servants, in order to obtain their support; but the nobles of the state having discovered one of the descendants of Shums-ood-Deen Bhungera I., placed him on the throne, and deposed the usurper; who is stated by some historians to have reigned several days; others, only a few hours.

NASIR POORBY.

Reigns for two years, and dies.

AFTER Nasir-ood-Deen Gholam was put to death, he was succeeded by Nasir Shah, a lineal descendant from Shums-ood-Deen Bhungera. This prince reigned to the satisfaction of
A. H. 832. all classes of his subjects for a period
A. D. 1428. of two years, when he died, A.H. 832.

BARBIK POORBY.

Reigns peaceably for a period of seventeen years, and dies.

NASIR was succeeded by Barbik, who
A. H. 849. reigned peaceably for a period of seven-
A. D. 1435. teen years, and died A.H. 849.

YOOSOOF POORBY.

Reigns for eight years, and dies.

BARBIK was succeeded by Yoosoof,
A. H. 866. who reigned between seven and eight
A. D. 1457. years, and died in the year 866.

SIKUNDUR POORBY.

Is elevated to the throne, and instantly deposed.

YOOSOOF was succeded by Sikundur; but he gave such offence to his nobles that they deposed him, and on the same day placed in his stead Futteh.

FUTTEH POORBY.

Enlists a large body of Hindoo infantry called Paiks, whom he employs as his household troops—he is murdered, after a reign of seven years.

THIS prince, after his accession, gave proofs both of his judgment and justice, and his liberality kept pace with his other good qualities. He raised the court of Bengal to a more respectable footing than it had hitherto attained. During his reign, he enlisted a corps composed of Paiks,* whom he retained as his personal guard. It was the custom in Bengal, at that time, for five thousand Paiks to mount guard daily over the palace, and for the King to see them every morning before they were relieved. On one occasion, one of the eunuchs of the palace having gained over the guard, murdered the King. This event happened in the year 886, after the King had reigned seven years and five months.

A H. 886.
A.D. 1401.

* A description of Hindoo infantry.

THE EUNUCH SHAHZADA.

Ascends the throne—requires the officers of the government to swear allegiance to him—is put to death.

When the eunuch had succeeded in putting his sovereign to death, he assumed the title of Shahzada (Prince), and collected together all the eunuchs in the place, as also men of low station and desperate fortunes, who are ever ready to join in the cause of usurpers, with the hope of preferment. The chief officers and nobles of the state, however, resolved to depose this insolent upstart. Among these was Mullik Andeel, an Abyssinian chief who was at that period on the frontier. This chief was contriving the means of punishing the usurper, and of reaching the capital in safety to carry such a plan into execution, when the eunuch ordered him to the presence, for the purpose of seizing and putting him to death. Mullik Andeel, however, considered this order as fortunate, as it afforded him an opportunity to cover his design, and he accordingly proceeded to the capital. On his arrival, he found his own party so strong that the eunuch was deterred from any attempt on Mullik Andeel's life. In the mean time, the eunuch placing the Koran before him in durbar, made Mullik Andeel sweer that he would not put him to death. Mullik Andeel solemnly swore, that since he had ascended the throne he would never lay hands on him while he "*filled that seat.*" He, however, determined to revenge the death of his master, and for this purpose secured the good will of the eunuch's personal servants. One night, after a debauch, Mullik Andeel entered the eunuch's hall of audience, and found him sleeping. He was then laying upon "*the throne*," and recollecting his pledge, Mullik Andeel refrained from hurting him; but the eunuch, at the same moment turning on his side, fell from the throne. Mullik Andeel, who now felt himself released from his vow, drew his sword, and made a cut at Shahzada. The sword only wounded him slightly, but roused him; and seeing a naked weapon opposed to him, he rushed (though unarmed) on Mullik Andeel, and as he was the stouter man of the two, threw the latter. In the struggle the lights were extinguished. The eunuch had hold of Mullik Andeel by the throat, and the latter, who was undermost, held the eunuch by the hair. Mullik Andeel called on his accomplices for aid. Yoghrish Khan Toork ran in, and discovering that they were both on the ground, hesitated what to do, till Mullik Andeel contrived to call out, "Cut away: the hog is up-"permost; and you cannot cut through him so "as to hurt me." Yoghrish Khan made three or four cuts, when the eunuch lay as if lifeless; but after the conspirators had left the room, he ran and hid himself. On discovering that he had fled, search was made, and he was betrayed by his door-keeper, and killed by Mullik Andeel's own hand. On the death of the eunuch Mullik

Andeel sent for Khan Jehan, the prime minister to the late king; and having related to him the whole of the affair, he said it was now proper for the nobles to elect a regent, as the son of Futteh Shah was only two years old. The minister and the other officers went to the late king's palace, and asked the Dowager-queen whom she chose to appoint regent. She replied, that she had sworn to support the claims of that person alone to the succession who should put to death the eunuch, the murderer of her husband. Mullik Andeel for a long time withstood her entreaties; but the rest of the nobles having unanimously declared that there was no one so fit for the situation as him, he at length consented, and ascended the throne under the title of Feroze. The eunuch reigned for a period of two months.

FEROZE POORBY.

Mullik Andeel ascends the throne, under the title of Feroze Poorby.

The nobles having elevated Mullik Andeel, with the title of Feroze Poorby, to the throne of Bengal, he repaired to the city of Gour, where he gave universal satisfaction to all class-

A.H. 899. es of his subjects for a period of

A.D. 1493. thirteen years, and died A.H. 899.

MAHMOOD POORBY.

Surrenders his government into the hands of his slave, who puts him to death.

UPON the death of Feroze, Mahmood succeeded to the dignity of his father. He, however, yielded up the reins of his government into the hands of his slave, Hubbush Khan, who at length acquired such an ascendency, that the King retained nothing but the name. Siddy Budr Dewana (or the Madman), another slave, jealous of his fellow-servant, slew Hubbush Khan; and having got into his hands all the power of the state, bribed the commandant of the body-guard, who connived at his entering the palace unperceived one night, when he put his sovereign, Mahmood, to death.

Siddy Budr ascended the throne on the next morning, and calling together all the nobles, declared to them his intention of
A. H. 900.
A. D. 1492.
proclaiming himself King. Mahmood Poorby reigned only during the space of one year.

Hajy Mahomed Kandahary states, that Mahmood was the son of Futteh Shah Poorby, and not of Feroze, and that Hubbush Khan was the slave of Barbik Khan, who, at the particular desire of

Feroze before his death, placed Mahmood on the throne; but scarcely six months had elapsed before Hubbush Khan determined to usurp the throne. His project being discovered by Siddy Budr, he put Hubbush Khan to death, and subsequently slew his sovereign, and succeeded to the government, under the title of Moozuffur.

MOOZUFFUR HUBSHY.*

Ascends the throne—raises one Syud Shureef of Mecca to the office of minister.—Syud Shureef goes to war with his Prince, who is assassinated by one of the body-guard.

THIS slave proved a cruel and sanguinary monarch, putting to death great numbers of learned men and others, whose principles induced them to adhere closely to the tenets of the orthodox faith. At length, having headed his army against the infidels of Bengal, he slew many of them. He promoted Syud Shureef, an inhabitant of Mecca, to the office of minister, when the King eventually became subject to the will of that subtle statesman. Syud Shureef induced his master to disband the greater part of his standing army, and to reduce his force to so low a state, that many of the chiefs quitted the court. At length, in the

A. H. 903.
A. D. 1496.

year 903, the disbanded officers, headed by the minister, collected a force and seized Moozuffur in the fortress of Gour, in which were five thousand Hubshies, and thirty thousand Bengalies and Afghans. The siege continued, according to some writers, only four days, while others asserted it lasted as many months, during which time several sallies were made from the fort, in which both parties lost many men. All the

* Abyssinian.

prisoners taken by the besieged were brought before Moozuffur, and put to death with his own hand. It is asserted that he slew in this way four thousand men. At last, making a desperate attack on the besiegers, among whom was his late minister, Syud Shureef, a general action ensued, and the loss on both sides amounted to twenty thousand men. Victory declared in favour of the Bengal nobles, and Moozuffur with many of his relatives were killed in the battle. Hajy Mahomed Kandahary relates, that during the reign of Moozuffur upwards of one hundred and twenty thousand persons, both Mahomedans and Hindoos, lost their lives. He also states, that the nobles of the government first revolted from Moozuffur, when Syud Shureef, taking advantage of the moment, gained the commandant of the Paik body-guard, and having one night entered the apartment of
A. H. 904. A. D. 1497. Moozuffur, attended by sixteen men, he put him to death, after a short but sanguinary reign of three years.

ALLA-OOD-DEEN POORBY II.

Syud Shureef ascends the throne under the title of Alla-ood-Deen II.—his promptitude in restraining his soldiers from plunder—he disbands the Paik guards—his death.

On the following morning, after the death of Moozuffur, Syud Shureef ascended the throne, and assumed the title of Alla-ood-Deen. During his administration he imputed to his sovereign every vice, particularly that most unpopular one, of penury combined with avarice; but there is no doubt the minister not only encouraged these feelings, but he may be said to have fed his propensity to amass treasure, through the unpopular measure he recommended of disbanding his army. It was by these insinuations that this crafty politician managed to obtain the ascendency over his king, while at the same time he stimulated the military chiefs to revolt, by exposing him to their hatred, and succeeded in securing their good will towards himself. Moozuffur being removed, Syud Shureef met with no difficulty in assuming the lead in the government, and in subsequently obtaining the crown. On his accession he found himself obliged at first to permit the besiegers to sack the town of Gour, but in a day or two he commanded all plunderin to cease; which order not being obeyed, he put to death twelve thousand of the marauders. By this means he not only stopped its further progress, but appropriated to his own use the property these people had secured for themselves. Amongst this booty were many golden vessels, out of which the people of Bengal of large property were accustomed to eat. This luxury was carried in those days to such excess, that whoever could produce most solid gold plate at an entertainment was considered the greatest man. This species of vanity is even at this period prevalent throughout Bengal.*

Alla-ood-Deen, who was a sensible man, shortly after his accession disbanded the Paik body-guard, which had been of late years the cause of the death of so many princes. He also dismissed the Abyssinians; and as this latter class had acquired the character of regicides, no town in Bengal, after their dismissal, would permit them to domicile therein, so that they were constrained, though reluctantly, to retire Guzerat and the Deccan. Alla-ood-Deen, in a short time, established such an excellent system of government as had not been witnessed in Bengal for many years. This prince ruled with justice for a considerably longer period than any of his predecessors, until the
A. H. 930. year 930, when he died a natural death,
A. D. 1523. after a reign of twenty-seven years.

* Ferishta speaks of 1609. The taste for expense in Bengal and Behar does not seem to have diminished greatly even up to the period of our connection with that country. The splendour and munificence of Asuf-ood-Dowla, the Nabob of Luknow, within the last forty years, astonished Europeans, and have acquired for him among his countrymen the title of Lukbukhsh, the Bestower of Millions.

NUSEEB POORBY.

Succeeds his father on throne—he affords an asylum to the princes and officers of the house of Lody, expelled from Dehly by the Moguls.—The King becomes cruel and tyrannical—his death—his government usurped by his minister.—Sheer Shah conquers Bengal.—Hoomayoon attacks Sheer Shah, but is repulsed.—Sheer Shah ascends the throne of Dehly, and nominates Mahomed Khan Afghan to the government as his lieutenant.—Mahomed Khan assumes independence, under the appellation of Bahadur Afghan.

On the death of his father, Nuseeb (the eldest son of Alla-ood-Deen) succeeded to the throne. Instead of confining or putting to death his brothers, as is often the practice, this young prince, with a manly generosity permitted them to retain their respective governments, and increased the comforts of their situations. When Babur Padshah slew Ibrahim, the son of Sikundur Lody, and ascended the throne of Dehly, many of the adherents of the Lody dynasty sought protection at the court of Bengal, and, among others, the Prince Mahmood (brother of Ibrahim Lody the late king) also took refuge there. These refugees were hospitably received, and estates were allotted to each; and in the end the daughter of Ibrahim Lody became the wife of the King of Bengal. In the year 930, when Babur Padshah marched and conquered the province of Joonpoor, he intended also to have subdued the whole kingdom of Bengal. Anticipating the demand for submission, Nuseeb sent an ambassador with magnificent presents to Babur which satisfied him, and induced him to return to Dehly; but when that monarch abdicated his throne in favour of his son Hoomayoon, the latter marched to conquer the kingdom of Bengal.

At this time, A. H. 939, Nuseeb
A.H. 939. sent an embassy with presents to
A.D. 1532. Bahadur Shah of Guzerat, who gave audience to the envoy in the fort of Mando. Some years afterwards, this prince's disposition appears to have undergone a complete change; for departing from that mildness of manner and suavity of temper, which procured for him, in the first instance, the esteem of his subjects, he pursued a system the most sanguinary and cruel; but the Almighty did not long suffer him to tyrannise over his subjects, for he died in the
A. H. 945. year 945, after a reign of eighteen years.
A. D. 1538. I was never able to ascertain whether he was murdered or died a natural death: be that as it may, after his death, Mahmood, one of his ministers, succeeded in usurping his throne.

About this period, Sheer Khan, who afterwards ascended the throne of Dehly, attacked and defeated Mahmood in action, and eventually expelled him from Bengal; whence he fled to the court of Dehly, where representing his grievances, Hoomayoon Padshah marched with an army and took the kingdom of Bengal from Sheer Khan, whom he defeated in a general action. On this occasion,

Hoomayoon caused the public prayers to be read in his name in the city of Gour, the name of which he changed to Jumalabad, Sheer Khan, rallying his defeated troops, in the

A.H. 949.
A.D. 1542.

year 949 succeeded in reconquering Gour. On his death, and after the accession of his brother Sulim Shah to the throne of Dehly, the province of Bengal was made over to Mahomed Khan Afghan, one of the officers of his court, on the death of whom his son declared his independence, and proclaimed himself king, under the title of Bahadur.

BAHADUR AFGHAN:

He reigns five years, and dies.

THIS Prince reigned for five years;
A. H. 956. but being deposed in the year 956, he
A. D. 1549. was succeeded by another of the nobles of Sulim Shah.

SOOLIMAN KIRANY.

Sooliman Kirany Afghan appointed governor by the King of Dehly—he assumes the title of King—reigns for twenty-five years, and dies.

AFTER the death of Sulim Shah, in
A. H. 961. the year 961, Sooliman threw off his
A. D. 1553. allegiance from the throne of Dehly, without assuming the title of king. During his rule, he subdued the province of Orissa; and, notwithstanding he was virtually independent, he used frequently to send valuable presents to Akbur Padshah. Sooliman having reign-
A. H. 981. ed in Bengal for a period of twenty-
A. D. 1573. five years, died in the year 981.

BAYEZEED AFGHAN.

Ascends his father's throne; but is murdered by a relation, who also suffers death.

Sooliman was succeeded by his eldest son Bayezeed, who after a reign of one month was murdered by his first cousin Hansoo, who also fell a victim to his own treachery, having been killed by the servants of the king out of revenge.

DAWOOD KHAN.

Dawood succeeds his brother Bayezeed—is attacked by Moonyim Khan, the general of Akbur Padshah of Dehly.—Battle of Moonere, in which Dawood Khan is defeated, and flies to Orissa, where, after several actions, he is permitted to reside.—Moonyim Khan, governor of Bengal, dies.—Dawood Khan recovers Bengal; but is eventually defeated, and slain in battle.

On the murder of Bayezeed he was succeeded by his younger brother Dawood Khan. This prince was much addicted to sensual excesses; and the propensity was rendered more degrading by his inclination to associate with persons of low origin and mean connections, by whom he was induced to attack the frontiers of the kingdom of Dehly. Moonyim Khan, entitled Khan Khanan, governor of Joonpoor, was ordered to punish this audacity; but, in the first instance, he only sent a detachment of his army against Dawood, which was opposed by the advanced guard of the latter under Lody Khan Afghan. Several skirmishes ensued; but at length a truce was concluded, and both parties resolved to return to their respective head-quarters. Akbur Padshah, hearing of the result of the campaign, was much dissatisfied, and again directed Moonyim Khan to invade Behar. At this period, a dispute arose between Lody Khan and his master, Dawood Khan; on which the former wrote letters to Moonyim Khan, the Mogul chief, promising to assist him in the capture of Behar. Dawood Khan, obtaining secret intimation of this correspondence, succeeded, by flattering promises of reconciliation, in inducing Lody Khan to come to the capital, where he was put to death. After which, Dawood Khan marched to oppose the Mogul army. A severe engagement took place in crossing the Soane near the village of Moonere, where that river and the Suroo fall into the Ganges. Dawood Khan was defeated, and a hundred of his boats fell into the hands of Moonyim Khan, who, having crossed the Soane, marched on to Patna, to which place Dawood Khan fled for protection. Moonyim Khan immediately invested the place, and was subsequently joined by Akbur Padshah; upon whose approach Dawood Khan fled to Bengal, and the forts of Patna and Hajypoor fell to the Mogul army. On this occasion, four hundred elephants, the property of Dawood Khan, came into Akbur's possession. Moonyim Khan followed up the fugitive as far as Gurhy, from whence Dawood Khan fled in Orissa, whither he was also pursued by a small field-detachment of the Mogul army, which was defeated by Jooneid Khan, Dawood Khan's son. This detachment was pursued by Moonyim Khan, who was opposed by Dawood Khan in person, when a severe battle took place, wherein the latter was defeated, and retired to a fort on the borders of Cattack. Here he was also attacked; and finding escape impracticable, he marched out to oppose the Moguls. Moonyim Khan now proposed a truce, which ended in a solemn peace, by which Dawood Khan was invested with the government of Orissa and Cattack; and the other provinces of the Bengal kingdom were occupied by Moonyim Khan in the name of Akbur Padshah. After Moonyim Khan's death, Akbur placed the government of Bengal in the hands of Khan Jehan Toorkman; on which occasion Dawood Khan retook the province of Bengal from the nobles of the Dehly government. In the year

A. H. 993.
A. D. 1584.

993, Khan Jehan was appointed governor, and Dawood Khan attacked him on a spot between the villages of the Gohey and Nunda; when after a severe engagement the latter was taken prisoner, and suffered death as a rebel, while his son, who was severely wounded in the action, died a few days afterwards. From that period, the kingdom of Bengal, including the districts of Orissa and Cattack, was subdued, and fell under the subjection of Akbur Padshah. Thus ended the rule of the Poorby or independent eastern kings of Bengal. On the death of Akbur, an Afghan chief, by name Oothman Khan, made head against the Dehly government, and collecting a force of twenty thousand of his countrymen, proclaimed himself king; after which he attacked the country belonging to Jehangeer Padshah of Dehly, who ordered Islam Khan, the son of Sheikh Budr-ood-Deen of Futteh-poor, to march and subdue the usurper;

A. H. 1018.
A. D. 1609.

and in the present year, being 1018, the war still continues.

To face page 359 *Vol. IV.*]

GENEALOGY OF THE KINGS OF JOONPOOR,

ENTITLED SHURKY.

1
Khwaja Jehan,
entitled Mullik-oos-Shurk.

2
Moobarik.

3
Ibrahim.

Hussun.

5
Hoossein.

4
Mahomed.

Julal.

CHAPTER VII.

(CONTINUED.)

SECTION II.

HISTORY OF THE KINGS OF JOONPOOR, DENOMINATED SHURKY.

KHWAJA JEHAN SHURKY.

Is appointed governor of the provinces east of Dehly—proclaims his independence—compels the rulers of Bengal to pay him tribute—his death.

THE different rulers who have governed in the provinces of Joonpoor and Anturbede* are styled by historians the Shurky kings.

It appears from the Towareekh Moobarik Shahy, that Mahomed, the son of Feroze Toghluk, created one of his eunuchs (Mullik Survur) his prime minister, and honoured him with the title of Khwaja Jehan; that upon the death of Mahomed, and on the accession of his son Mahmood Toghluk, that monarch, in the month of Jumad-ool-Awul, A.H. 796, conferred on his minister the additional title of Mullik-oos-Shurk,†

Jumad-ool-Awul, A.H. 796. March, A.D. 1394.

* The territory south of Dehly, lying between the rivers Jumna and Ganges, is denominated Anturbede.

† The title signifies Chief of the East.

and appointed governor of the eastern provinces of the empire, and Joonpoor became his capital. The governor soon succeeded in bringing all the neighbouring zemindars to acknowledge his authority, and recovered various forts and strong holds which the infidels had of late years wrested from the Mahomedans, and placed his own garrisons therein. The reign of Mahmood Toghluk was interrupted by serious internal commotions; and Khwaja Jehan took advantage of these circumstances to assume the title of Sooltan-oos-Shurk;* and having reduced Gorukpoor and Bheiraich, proceeded to subdue the provinces of Anturbede and Behar. The Poorby kings, who reigned at Luknowty in Bengal, instead of sending the accustomed presents to the King of Dehly, propitiated the Shurky monarch by sending them to him. His power was therefore daily

A.H. 802. increasing, when an untimely death

A.D. 1399. snatched him from his worldly dignities. He died, A.H. 802, after a short reign of six years.

* King of the East.

MOOBARIK SHAH SHURKY.

Assumes the regalia, and causes coin to be struck in his name as King.—Mulloo Yekbal Khan invades country.—Peace concluded.—The death of Moobarik Shah Shurky.

On the death of Khwaja Jehan he was succeeded by his adopted son, Mullik Kurrunful, who realised the wish that his predecessor carried with him to the grave; and, accordingly, on his accession, perceiving that the kingdom of Dehly was thrown into disorder and anarchy, he, with the consent of the officers of his government, assumed the regal canopy, and caused coin to be struck, and prayers to be read, in his name, under the title of Moobarik Shah Shurky.

No sooner did this information reach Dehly than Mulloo Yekbal Khan (who had lately usurped the throne, and expelled Mahmood Toghluk from his government,) marched, in the year

A. H. 803. 803, with an army to attack Joonpoor.
A. D. 1400. On reaching Kunowj, he found Moobarik Shah, with a force consisting of Moguls, Afghans, and Rajpoots, encamped on the eastern bank of the Ganges to oppose him. Mulloo Yekbal Khan halted on the western shore, and there the respective chiefs, as if apprehensive of each other, remained stationary for upwards of two months. At length, being distressed for

forage and provisions, they came to an accommodation, by which they agreed to return quietly to their respective capitals. News arrived some time after, that Mahmood Toghluk, emerging from his concealment in Malwa, whither he had fled, had now resumed the government of Dehly; and that Mulloo Yekbal Khan, accompanied by him, was again preparing to attack Joonpoor.
A. H. 804.
A. D. 1401.
In the mean time Moobarik Shah died, in the year 804, after a short reign of eighteen months.

IBRAHIM SHAH SHURKY:

His country invaded by Mulloo Yekbal Khan, attended by Mahmood Toghluk.—Peace concluded.—Ibrahim takes Kunowj from the King of Dehly; also takes Sumbhul, which is retaken—encourages literature in his country—proceeds to besiege Byana; but concludes a peace with the King of Dehly.—Death of Ibrahim.

On the death of Moobarik, his younger brother, Ibrahim, was elevated to the throne. He was famous during his reign for the encouragement he afforded to literature; and we find that in those times of anarchy and confusion which prevailed in Hindoostan, Joonpoor became the seat of learning; as appears from several works now extant, dedicated to Ibrahim Shah.

In the early part of his reign, his kingdom was threatened by the invasion of Mulloo Yekbal Khan; who, having obtained possession of the person of Mahmood Toghluk, marched a second time to attack the eastern provinces. Ibrahim Shah assumed the same position his brother had taken up before, on the banks of the Ganges, and Yekbal Khan encamped also on the opposite side, near the city of Kunowj. Mahmood Toghluk, though nominally king, was not only virtually deprived of all authority, but the semblance even of respect was denied him; and being disgusted more than ever with Mulloo Yekbal Khan, he one day took advantage of the circumstance of being on a hunting party to make his escape. He withdrew to Ibrahim Shah Shurky, in hopes that the latter would assist him either in regaining his power, or, at any rate, in subduing Mulloo Yekbal Khan; but Ibrahim Shah, dreading the effect of his presence among his troops, refused him support; and Mahmood, covered with disgrace, returned to Kunowj, in which city he succeeded in establishing his authority; so that both Mulloo Yekbal Khan and Ibrahim Shah Shurky, leaving him in quiet possession, returned to their respective capitals without fighting a battle.

In some histories it is related that Mahmood Toghluk went over to the Shurky court during the reign of Moobarik Shah, and that the latter prince died while Mahmood was with him; but that on the accession of Ibrahim, who was then at Joonpoor, Mahmood Toghluk occupied Kunowj, which he was permitted to retain. God only knows which account is correct.

A.H. 808. A.D. 1405. According to the Dehly historians, Mulloo Yekbal Khan was killed in the year 808, and Mahmood Toghluk recovered his authority. On that occasion he evacuated Kunowj, and on the following year, A.H. 809. A.D. 1406. 809, Ibrahim Shah Shurky marched to retake it. Mahmood Toghluk, however, appearing at the head of his troops, opposed him. The two armies encamped as before, on either side the Ganges, within their own boundaries, where having remained some time, they each returned to their respective capitals. Mahmood Toghluk now returned to Dehly, and disbanded his army, when Ibrahim Shah availed himself of the circumstance to invest Kunowj, and he took it after a siege of four months. Having halted at that city during the rains, he afterwards marched to the northward, for the purpose of making encroachments on the territory of Dehly. On being joined by many of the nobles of that kingdom, who deserted Mahmood Toghluk, he proceeded to the province of Sumbhul, which was evacuated without resistance, and Tartar Khan was nominated governor. On the arrival of Ibrahim Shah Shurky on the Jumna, he heard that Moozuffur Shah of Gurzerat, having invaded Malwa, had defeated and taken prisoner Sooltan Hooshung,* and that he was at that time on his march to assist Mahmood Toghluk. Reports even went so far as to say that he intended to attack Joonpoor itself. Ibrahim Shah, in consequence, retreated hastily to his capital, while Mahmood Toghluk, instead of pursuing him with the Dehly army, contented himself with re-occupying the province of Sumbhul, and Tartar Khan returned to his master at Joonpoor.

A.H. 816.
A.D. 1413.

In the year 816, Ibrahim Shah again marched towards Dehly, but after a few days returned to his capital, where he led a peaceful life in the prosecution of literary pursuits, and in the promotion of the arts of civi-

* Vide vol. iv. pp. 9. 172.

lisation, till, in the year 831, Mahmood
A.H. 831. Khan of Mewat induced him to march
A.D. 1427. his army to attack the fort of Byana, where he was opposed by the forces of Syud Moobarik, King of Dehly. The two armies lay entrenched at the distance of eight miles from each other for twenty-two days, during which period some trifling skirmishes ensued; when Ibrahim Shah Shurky, marching out from his entrenchments towards the Dehly army, brought on an action, which, though it lasted from noon till night, proved indecisive, the forces having mutually retreated in good order. On the following day, the two sovereigns concluded a hollow peace, and retreated to their respective capitals.

In the year 839, Ibrahim Shah Shurky
A.H. 839. proceeded to reduce Kalpy, where he
A.D. 1435. was opposed by Sooltan Hooshung of Malwa; but on receiving intimation that Syud Moobarik of Dehly was in full march to attack Joonpoor, he countermarched without risking an engagement, and Kalpy fell into the hands of the King of Malwa.

In the year 844, Ibrahim Shah Shur-
A.H. 844. ky, being taken dangerously ill, died,
A.D. 1440. after a long reign of upwards of forty years. He was equally beloved in life, as he was regretted by all his subjects.

MAHMOOD SHAH SHURKY.

Attacks Kalpy, which is evacuated by its governor.—The King of Malwa resents the injury.—Peace concluded,—Mahmood Shah attacks Dehly—is compelled to retreat, and loses a great portion of his baggage and elephants during the operation.—War continued with Bheilole Lody, King of Dehly.—Death of Mahmood Shah Shurky.

A.H. 847.
A.D. 1443.

AFTER the death of Ibrahim Shah, he was succeeded by his eldest son Mahmood. In the year 847, he sent an envoy to the court of Malwa to inform Sooltan Mahmood Khiljy that Nuseer Khan, the son of Kadur Khan of Kalpy, had, within the last two or three years, disgraced the Mahomedan name by encouraging the Hindoo faith, and had carried his views of toleration so far as to permit Mahomedan females to dwell with infidels. He deemed it (he said) necessary to inform him of these proceedings, considering Nuseer Khan a dependent of Malwa since the reign of Sooltan Hooshung. In conclusion, he observed, that the scandal to Mahomedism was such, that if the King of Malwa did not deem it politic or convenient to send troops in order to restore the religious observances of the faithful at Kalpy, he would himself march to effect that object. Sooltan Mahmood replied, that he had heard of the proceedings of Nuseer Khan; but that his armies being at present employed against the infidels of Mewar and Kota, he was unable to spare them to operate against Nuseer Khan, and sanctioned the advance of Mahmood Shah Shurky to bring Nuseer to a due sense of his obligations as a true believer. Mahmood Shah, pleased with the reception of his envoy, immediately put his army in motion, having, in the mean time, sent twenty-nine elephants as a present to the King of Malwa. On his approach towards Kalpy, Nuseer Khan wrote petitions to Sooltan Mahmood Khiljy, soliciting his protection; and on ascertaining the plea for the attack of the Shurky troops, he promised to cause a reform in his administration, and to afford no reason for further complaint; reminding Sooltan Mahmood that his predecessor, Sooltan Hooshung, had made over the estate of Kalpy in perpetuity to his father, Kadur Khan, from whom it had descended to him. Sooltan Mahmood, moved by the penitence eveinced by Nuseer Khan, wrote to Mahmood Shah Shurky, saying, that as Nuseer Khan had promised in future to conduct himself in a more cautious manner, he trusted that the King of Joonpoor would abstain from adopting any measures against him. Which communication was sent by an express courier. In the mean time, Mahmood Shah Shurky having reached Kalpy, sacked the town, and obliged Nuseer Khan to fly to Chundery, to which place Sooltan Mahmood of Malwa proceeded, in the year 848, with his army.* On his approach, Mahmood Shah Shurky marched to Eerich, where a partial engagement

A.H. 848.
A.D. 1444.

* These events ate fully detailed in the Malwa history. Vide vol. iv. pp. 210—214. They are only adverted to in this place in order to render each of the local histories complete within itself.

took place; when, through the mediation of Sheikh Jumal-ood-Deen Sudda, a peace was concluded, by which it was agreed that Nuseer Khan for the present should occupy the towns of Eerich and Rahut, and that four months after the return of the respective forces the district of Kalpy and its dependencies should be restored to him. Mahmood Shah Shurky, having recruited his army, took the field again for the purpose of reducing some refractory zemindars in the district of Chunar, which place he sacked, and from thence he proceeded into the province of Orissa, which he also reduced; and having destroyed the temples and collected large sums of money, returned to Joonpoor.

A.H. 856.
A. D. 1452.

In the year 856, Mahmood Shah besieged the city of Dehly; but Bheilole Lody returning from Depalpoor, whither he had proceeded for the purpose of conquest, Mahmood Shah was compelled to retire, as he discovered that Duria Khan Lody, who had formerly deserted the King of Dehly and joined him, was now prepared to abandon him also. The retreat, however, was delayed till the last moment, which enabled Bheilole Lody to pursue the King of Joonpoor so closely, as to intercept and destroy his baggage; on which occasion Futteh Khan Hirvy, who commanded the Shurky rear-guard, was killed, and seven war-elephants were taken.

A. H. 861.
A. D. 1456.

In the year 861, Bheilole marched to reduce Etawa, where he was opposed by Mahmood Shah Shurky; a particular account of which transaction has been given in the

Dehly history. The two armies having encamped near the town of Shumsabad, Kootb Khan Lody, first cousin to the King of Dehly, made a night-attack on the Shurky lines, which failed, and he was made prisoner. Affairs remained in this state, when, in the year 862, Mahmood Shurky was seized with severe illness, and died in camp, after a reign of twenty years.

A. H. 862.
A. D. 1457.

MAHOMED SHAH SHURKY.

War continued with the King of Dehly.—Mahomed Shah becomes very cruel—puts his brother Hussun Khan to death.—His mother and his other brothers conspire against him.—A civil war prevails.—Mahomed Shah loses his life.—A truce concluded with the King of Dehly for four years, and an exchange of prisoners takes place.

MAHMOOD was succeeded by his eldest son Bheekun Khan, who caused himself to be proclaimed King, under the title of Mahomed Shurky. On his accession he formed a treaty with Bheilole Lody, which stipulated that each should retain what they then possessed. On his return to Joonpoor Mahomed Shah disgusted all ranks by his cruelty and irritable temper; which no one felt more severely than his mother, the Dowager-queen. He had not long been crowned, when Bheilole Lody marched towards Joonpoor, in order to effect the release of his cousin Kootb Khan, who was made prisoner during a night-attack on the Shurky lines at Shumsabad, and who had not been released. On this occasion one Purtab Sing, a zemindar, who owned allegiance to the Dehly government, dreading the power of Mahomed Shah Shurky, joined him.

Mahomed Shah now proceeded towards Soorsutty, and was opposed at Rabery by the light troops of Bheilole Lody. During this campaign, Mahomed Shah Shurky wrote to the kotwal of Joonpoor to put to death his brothers, Hussun Khan and Kootb Khan. That officer replied, that the Dowager-queen, Beeby Rajy, was so careful lest any one should approach the princes, that he found it quite impossible to carry the project into effect. Mahomed Shah, therefore, requested that his mother might join him in camp, on the plea of consulting her as to the expediency of settling an estate for life on Hussun Khan, his younger brother. The Dowager no sooner left Joonpoor than the kotwal carried his instructions into effect, by murdering the Prince; and the Queen, Beeby Rajy, halted at Kunowj to perform the *matum*, or mourning ceremony for her son, where she remained in spite of Mahomed Shah Shurky's solicitations for her to proceed to camp.

During this time, the princes Hoossein Khan and Julal Khan resolved to become independent of their brother the King; and they spread a report in the camp, that the Dehly army, then in their vicinity, proposed to make a night-attack on the Shurky lines. Mahomed Shah directed the Prince Hoossein Khan, accompanied by Sooltan Shah and Julal Khan Ajoodhuny, two of the Shurky generals, to proceed with a force composed of thirty thousand cavalry and one thousand elephants, to intercept the enemy. Hoossein Khan marched only to a short distance, and encamped; when Bheilole Lody, taking advantage of his separation from the army, sent a force to attack him. Hoossein Khan, conceiving himself unable to resist the Dehly troops, retreated towards Kunowj, and wrote to his brother, Julal Khan, to join him there. In attempting to effect this, Julal Khan was taken prisoner by the Dehly troops, and Bheilole Lody resolved to detain him till the release of his cousin, the Prince Kootb Khan. Mahomed Shah, perceiving his army thus divided into factions, was induced to retire on Kunowj also, whither he was pursued by Bheilole Lody; after which the latter returned to Dehly. The Prince Hoossein Khan was received at Kunowj by his mother with open arms; and assumed the title of King before the arrival of Mahomed Shah, whom he opposed at the Rajgeer passage of the Ganges. Mahomed Shah, deserted by his officers, was compelled to seek safety in flight; he was, however, overtaken, and would no doubt, from his well-known prowess, have slain many of his pursuers, but that his mother, having gained over his armour-bearer to her interest, persuaded him to take off the points from all the arrows in his quiver. It was in this defenceless condition that he was killed by an arrow entering his throat. A peace was soon after concluded between Hoossein Khan, who assumed the title of Shah, and Bheilole Lody; when it was agreed that a suspension of hostilities should take place for four years; after which, if it were found necessary, another treaty might be formed. Purtab Sing, who formerly joined Mahomed Shah Shurky on his march from Joonpoor, was induced by Kootb Khan to join the army of Bheilole Lody; and on the arrival of Hoossein Shah Shurky at the Howz-i-Burma, he sent for Kootb Khan from Joonpoor, and equipping him in handsome style, permitted him to return to Dehly. On his arrival there, the Shurky prince, Julal Khan, was also released, and joined his brother at Joonpoor. The reign of Mahomed Shah lasted only for the short period of five months.

HOOSSEIN SHAH SHURKY.

Ascends his brother's throne—leads a vast army into Orissa—compels the Raja of Gualiar to pay him tribute—lays claim to the throne of Dehly, and engages in war with Bheilole Lody—is defeated, and quits his kingdom, which henceforth is incorporated with that of Dehly.

THIS prince ascended the throne of the Shurky kings immediately after the death of his brother Mahomed Shah. One of the first acts of his government was to put to death several officers, who after his succession had headed a party against him. Shortly afterwards he led an army, consisting of thirty thousand horse and a hundred thousand infantry, besides four hundred elephants, for the purpose of conquering Orissa. On reaching that province he caused his troops to disperse in detachments, in order to lay waste the country. The Ray of Orissa, unable to oppose this sudden inroad, perceived no remedy but submission ; and in order to conciliate the invader, the Ray sent thirty elephants, a hundred horses, and various articles, including silken and other cloths ; with which Hoossein Shah being satisfied, he returned to Joonpoor.

A. H. 870. A. D. 1465. In the year 870, Hoossein Shah sent a considerable army to reduce the fortress of Gualiar; which was invested, and after some time the Ray made peace, and consented to pay tribute. Hoossein Shah had now attained such power, that he was prevailed on by his wife, a princess of Dehly, to lay claim to that throne. For this purpose he marched, in the year 878, with an army composed of one hundred and forty thousand horse and foot, and one thousand four hundred elephants. On information of the movement of the Shurky army, Bheilole Lody deputed an embassy to Sooltan Mahmood of Malwa, promising to him the cession of the district of Byana for the services of his army, in order to oppose Hoossein Shah; but the envoy had scarcely reached the Malwa capital before the Shurky troops were already in possession of the suburbs of Dehly. Bheilole Lody, conceiving himself unable to withstand the army of Hoossein Shah, made overtures for peace, and agreed to cede the whole of the territory of Dehly, retaining for himself the city and a tract of country lying within a circuit of eighteen coss of the capital. Hoossein Shah, elated with pride, rejected these terms; and Bheilole, who repented of his offer the instant it was made, became glad of the opportunity of retracting. He therefore left the city with eighteen thousand cavalry, and encamped on the banks of the Jumna, opposite the Shurky troops. As the river was between the two camps, some time passed before any action occurred, till one day Bheilole Lody, taking advantage of the Shurky cavalry being absent on a foraging party, led his cavalry into the Jumna, and attacked the enemy at noon. The Shurky line, wholly unprepared for this assault, had no time to form, but fled, and the whole of the family of Hoossein Shah Shurky was taken; the ladies of which were treated with every mark of respect, and shortly after sent to Hoossein Shah. In the following year

A.H. 879.
A.D. 1474.

Hoossein Shah was again induced by his wife, Mullika Jehan, to march against Dehly, and having reached the vicinity of that capital, he was met by an envoy who offered terms; but the prosperity of the Shurky dynasty having arrived at its zenith, its decline commenced from this moment. Hoossein Shah mistaking for pusillanimity the overtures of Bheilole for reconciliation rejected them, and boldly asserted that he would be content only with the possession of Dehly. Bheilole, in consequence, marched forth, and opposed the Shurky army in three successive actions. In the first battle, Hoossein Shah was defeated, as also in the second; when being followed by the Dehly troops he sustained a third defeat, and was individually so closely pursued that he left his horse and escaped on foot. The details of these circumstances have already been related in the Dehly history. The Dehly army advanced without any other check to Joonpoor, which fell to the arms of Bheilole Lody; while Hoossein Shah, abandoning his capital, was obliged to content himself with a small tract of country, yielding only a revenue of five lacks of rupees.* Bheilole Lody having delivered over Joonpoor and its kingdom to his son Barbik, enjoined him not to deprive Hoossein Shah of the small tract to which he was confined, terming it his family estate. On the death of Bheilole Lody, and on the accession of his eldest son, Sikundur Lody, Hoossein Shah Shurky incited the Prince Barbik of Joonpoor to march against his brother, and wrest the government out of his hands; but Barbik was defeated in the first action, and retired to Joonpoor, to which place he was pursued by Sikundur Lody. Joonpoor fell shortly after, and it was added to the kingdom of Dehly. Hoossein Shah was now induced to seek refuge with Alla-ood-Deen Poorby of Bengal, by whom he was treated with the respect due to his station till his death. The subversion of the Shurky dynasty may be dated therefore from the subjugation of that principality by Sikundur Lody,

A. H. 881.
A. D. 1476.

an event which occurred in the year 881. The reign of Hoossein Shah Shurky lasted for a period of nineteen years.

* 50,000*l*.

To face page 379. Vol. IV.]

GENEALOGY OF THE KINGS OF MOOLTAN,

OF THE AFGHAN TRIBE OF LUNGA.

1
Kootb-ood-Deen Lunga.
|
2
Hoossein.
|
Feroze.
|
3
Mahmood.
|
4
Hoossein II.

CHAPTER VIII.

THE HISTORY OF THE KINGS OF MOOLTAN.

SHEIKH YOOSOOF.

Some account of the first conquest of Mooltan—reverts to the Hindoos—is again subjected to Mahomedan rule by Mahomed Ghoory.—In the fallen condition of the Dehly empire, the Mooltanies elect Sheikh Yoosoof to be their governor—he is treacherously seized by Ray Sehra Lunga, an Afghan chief, who usurps the throne.

The introduction of the Mahomedan faith into Mooltan first took place in the latter end of the first century of the Hijra, by the conquest of that country by Mahomed Kasim; after whom, until the reign of Mahmood of Ghizny, no account is to be traced of its history. It is mentioned in the Ghizny annals that Mahmood conquered Mooltan from the infidels; but that on the decline of the Ghizny power, the inhabitants, taking to arms, succeeded in expelling the Mahomedans, and in establishing a separate government. From the period of its subjugation by Moyiz-ood-Deen Mahomed Ghoory, it remained
A.H. 847. tributary to Dehly until the year 847,
A.D. 1443. when the governor of that province,

like most others of the kingdom at the same period, declared his independence; after which time several princes reigned in succession.

When the sceptre was transferred from the hands of Alla-ood-Deen, the son of Mahomed, the son of Feroze Toghluk, into those of Syud Khizr Khan, the Dehly empire fell into anarchy and disorder, and the province of Mooltan, wholly unprotected, became open to invasion from the contiguous kingdoms of Ghoor, Ghizny, and Kabul. Without a regular governor, and having suffered severely from these predatory inroads, the inhabitants of Mooltan, seeing the necessity of having a leader to direct their exertions, and to protect the country from their troublesome neighbours, as-embled in the year 847, and selected

A. H. 847. A. D. 1443.

Sheikh Yoosoof, a man of learning, one wisdom, and high character, of the tribe of Kooreish, to be ruler over the people of Mooltan and Oocha, when the public prayers were read, and money coined, in his name. This prince fully repaid their confidence by re-organising the government, and gaining the esteem and friendship of the surrounding zemindars. Among other persons, was one Ray Sehra,* the chief of the town of Seevy and its neighbourhood, who sent a message of congratulation to Sheikh Yoosoof Kooreishy, stating that his ancestors and those of the Sheikh had known each other for many generations, and he therefore courted his

* My enquiry has failed in fixing the proper name of this Afghan chief: that in the text is probably an error in the manuscripts to which I have had access.

friendship. He represented, also, that as Bheilole Lody had taken advantage of the distracted condition of the Dehly kingdom, and proclaimed himself king, it was but just of Sheikh Yoosoof to take into favour the tribe of Lunga, which was in his neighbourhood, and by enrolling himself and followers among his most faithful servants, afford them an opportunity of showing their attachment. As a proof of his regard, Ray Sehra offered to give his daughter to Sheikh Yoosoof, who having consented to the match, the marriage was celebrated according to the custom of kings. After this the Afghan chief frequently came from Seevy to Mooltan to visit his daughter, and generally brought some presents with him. On these occasions he used to occupy some spot outside of the town, where he pitched his tents, and came in to see his daughter and son-in-law without attendants. At last he came to Mooltan with a number of his tribe, having made up his mind to endeavour to seize Sheikh Yoosoof, and to usurp the government. On coming into the neighbourhood, he sent word to his son-in-law that he had brought the whole of his tribe to Mooltan, in order to give the Sheikh an opportunity of seeing, and of allowing them to pay their respects to him. The simple Sheikh, unacquainted with the artifices and subtlety of the world, agreed. The Afghan arrived in the evening; and having remained in his tents some time after prayers, three separate messages were sent by his daughter for him to go into the town. He at length complied; and desired his servant, when he called for something to drink at dinner, to give him, instead of water, a cup full of fresh duck's blood, which the Afghan drank off. During the evening he complained of severe pains in his bowels; and on an emetic being administered he threw up the blood which he had just drank. This circumstance so alarmed the Sheikh that he sent for the Afghan's doctor from his camp, as also for several of his kinsmen and clansmen, who were admitted with their arms without suspicion. After a certain number had entered Ray Sehra threw off the mask, and seized the Sheikh. Sheikh Yoosoof only reigned for a period of two years.

KOOTB-OOD-DEEN LUNGA.

Ray Sehra, entitled Kootb-ood-Deen Lunga, ascends the throne—he expels his predecessor and son-in-law from Mooltan—his death.

Ray Sehra, having secured the person of Sheikh Yoosoof, caused the public prayers to be read in his name, under the title of Kootb-ood-Deen Mahmood Lunga; and the inhabitants of Mooltan submitted to his government without murmur or discontent. After ascending the throne, he sent his predecessor, Sheikh Yoosoof, out of the city under a guard to Dehly by the south gate; and in commemoration of that event, he caused that entrance to be built up with brick and mortar; and I understand it is to be seen in the same state at this day, being the year 1018 (A. D. 1609).

Sheikh Yoosoof on arriving at Dehly was met by Bheilole Lody, and was received with respect; afterwhich such an intimacy arose between those two great personages, that the King of Hindoostan gave his daughter in marriage to Sheikh Abdoolla, the son of the deposed ruler of the province of Mooltan.

A. H. 874.
A. D. 1469.

Kootb-ood-Deen Lunga reigned for a period of sixteen years, and died, much lamented, in the year 874.*

*Some difference occurs between this narrative and that given by Sheikh Abool Fuzl in the Ayeen Akburry, who, in speaking of the sovereigns of Mooltan, assigns seventeen years for the reign of Sheikh Yoosoof instead of two. Kootb-ood-Deen Lunga in that work is styled Mahmood Shah, and is simply called a foreigner.

HOOSSEIN LUNGA.

Succeeds his father—gives encouragement to learned men, and establishes colleges in Mooltan under their superintendence—raises troops, and invades the Punjab—takes Kotgirvur and Dhunkote.—Mooltan besieged in his absence by the Prince Barbik and Tartar Khan.—The besieged are repulsed.—Enlists in his army a large body of Bulochies from Mikran—sends an envoy to Dehlv, and makes peace—deputes an ambassador to Guzerat-abdicates his throne in favour of his son Feroze, who is assassinated.—Death of Hoossein Lunga.

After the death of Kootb-ood-Deen Lunga, the principal nobles in Mooltan elected his son Hoossein to succeed him, and the public prayers were read in his name. This prince was not only a great promoter of literature, but himself a very learned man. He erected colleges, in which were some of the most eminent scholars of the time. In the beginning of his reign he marched to reduce the fort of Sheevur, at that time held by Ghazy Khan, who on hearing of the approach of the Mooltanies advanced to oppose them, to the distance of twenty miles from his capital; and although he behaved with great bravery in the war which ensued, he was compelled to fly, and before he could reach the fort of Sheevur was reduced to seek protection in Bheemra. The members of his family who were in the fort of Sheevur, however, made a gallant resistance, and held out under the expectation of receiving aid from the town of Khooshab, then under Ameer Syeed Khan. Disappointed in these hopes, they eventually surrendered the fort of Sheevur, but obtained permission to proceed to Bheemra. Hoossein Lunga having remained some time to recruit his army, marched towards the fortress of Hoot. Mullik Kazy Gukkur, who was nearly related to Ameer Syeed Khan, was governor of the place; and, for form's sake, having defended it for a few days, gave it up to Hoossein Lunga, who after remaining there a short period returned to Mooltan; and from thence he marched against Kotgirvur and Dhunkote, both of which places he reduced to subjection. Meanwhile Sheikh Yoosoof persuaded Bheilole Lody to assist him in recovering his country. At this time, when Hoossein Lunga had advanced so far to the eastward as Dhunkote, Bheilole Lody deputed his son, the Prince Barbik (who is mentioned both in the Dehly and Joonpoor histories), with an army to reduce Mooltan. Barbik having been joined by the forces of Tartar Khan Lody in the Punjab, proceeded towards Mooltan. The brother of Hoossein, who had been left in the fort of Kotgirvur after its fall, had proclaimed himself king, under the name of Shahab-ood-Deen. On receipt of this information, Hoossein Lunga marched to reduce the place; and having confined his rebellious brother in fetters, was on his return, when he heard that the Prince Barbik and Tartar Khan had arrived near the city of Mooltan, which they were on the point of attacking. Hoossein Lunga moved his camp without delay; and making rapid marches, crossed the Indus, and threw himself into the fort, before the arrival of the Dehly army; and drawing up his soldiers, he thus addressed them:—"My "brethren and fellow-soldiers, I do not suppose "that every man in my army is necessarily "a hero, nor do I expect too much from any "of you. Some there are, however, who, seeking "preferment, and ambitious for fame in the field "of battle, lay aside all other considerations; "while there are others whose attachment to their "families will induce them to hold back, and "merely keep their situations in the service, by not "positively flying before the enemy. Both these "classes have their value: the former are useful "for foreign conquest, and the latter for protecting "our homes. All those of the latter class will be "required on the present occasion for the defence "of the garrison, while those of the former, I trust, "will be ready to join me at daylight to-morrow "morning under the walls." On the following day at sunrise twelve thousand men prepared to follow Hoossein, whom he led out against the invaders. After having brought his front opposite the Dehly forces, he directed his cavalry to dismount, himself showing the example, and then ordered the whole to discharge three rounds of arrows in rapid succession into the enemy's lines. This discharge shook the Dehly army, who were prepared only for skirmishing; and the Mooltany horse having mounted again, broke the enemy's ranks, and completed the defeat. Barbik Khan and Tartar Khan fled, passing by the fort of Sheevur, which they did not venture to attack; but proceeding direct to Hoot, they succeeded in obtaining possession of that fort by promising advantageous terms to the garrison, in the first place, after which they inhumanly put them to the sword.

At this period, one Mullik Sohrab Duvally with his two sons, Ismael and Futteh Khan, arriving from Mikran, engaged in the service of Hoossein Lunga, who gave over to them the country lying between Kotgirvur and Dhunkote, for the support of himself and tribe. Many other Bulochies, also, hearing of the reception of Mullik Sohrab, flocked in great numbers to Mooltan, and were also received into his service, and a portion of the country of Sind, lying contiguous to Bulochistan, was also given up to them; till at length all the country lying between Setpoor and Dhunkote was occupied by Bulochies. It was at this time, also, that Jam Bayezeed and Jam Ibrahim, of the tribe of Sahna, being offended with the treatment they experienced from Jam Nunda, King of Sind, came to the court of Hoossein Lunga of Mooltan.

The tribe of Sahna appears to be of obscure origin. The Sahnas seem originally to have occupied the tract lying between Bhukkur and Tutta, in Sind, and pretend to trace their pedigree from Jam Jumsheed,* King of Persia. Being a warlike

* The ruins of the city of Persepolis, which was destroyed by Alexander, are, at this period, called the Tukht Jumsheed, or the Throne of Jumsheed, King of Fars.

race, Jam Nunda used to boast he was also descended from Jumsheed, though he was at variance with the tribe of Sahna. A dissension arising among the Sahna tribe, Jam Nunda took advantage of it to instigate them against Jam Bayezeed and Jam Ibrahim, two brothers, who being eventually compelled to seek safety in flight, found protection in Mooltan. Hoossein Lunga afforded them an asylum, and conferred the district of Sheevur on Jam Bayezeed, and that of Oocha on Jam Ibrahim.

Bheilole Lody of Dehly dying, and being succeeded by his son Sikundur, Hoossein Lunga deemed the opportunity favourable to gain the alliance of that court; and consequently deputed an ambassador with rich presents to Dehly, conveying letters of condolence and congratulation: the former, on account of the death of Bheilole, and the latter, on Sikundur Lody's accession to the throne.

On the arrival of the Mooltan ambassador, Sikundur Lody received the presents, and entered into a treaty of alliance, by which it was agreed that the respective armies of Mooltan and Dehly should keep within their present limits, but that, if required, they should assist each other in case of external invasion. It is related that Hoossein Lunga also sent ambassadors to Moozuffur Shah of Guzerat, the particular object of which was to procure architects, and to bring a plan and model of the several buildings at Ahmudabad. The envoy, Kazy Mahomed, having returned, the

King questioned him as to the King's palace at Ahmudabad, and asked if such a one could be built at Mooltan. The envoy replied, "It be-"hoves servants, when required to answer, to "speak the truth; and I am, therefore, constrained "to acquaint your Majesty, that I really cannot "even describe the magnificence of the palace of "Ahmudabad; and I doubt if the whole revenue "of Mooltan were set aside for a year, whether it "would defray the expense of such a building." Hoossein Lunga was offended at this blunt speech; and although he made no observation, he was evidently stung at the contemplation of his own relative insignificance. The prime minister, Imad-ool-Moolk, perceiving the King's dejection, remarked, that his Majesty had no cause to lament, since, though India might be the country of riches, yet Mooltan could boast of being a country of men, some of whom were famed in the field of battle, while others were as renowned for their literary acquirements. Among the latter he enumerated Sheikh Yoosoof Kooreishy, Sheikh Baha-ood-Deen Zacharia, and others brought up in the philosophic school of Hajy Abdool Wahab; besides Futteh Oolla and his disciple Azeez Oolla, both inhabitants of Mooltan, and who had each thousands of disciples. The King was pleased at the ingenious turn which his minister had given to the conversation; but it is evident it had an effect on his mind; for very shortly afterwards he abdicated his throne in favour of his son Feroze, asserting as a reason that he was old, and found his faculties failing him. After this he retired from public life; and living in a humble style, contented himself by having about him holy personages, who expounded the laws of the prophet, and explained the tenets of the faith.

On the accession of the Prince Feroze to the throne, Imad-ool-Moolk still held the office of prime minister; but the young king becoming jealous of the great popularity of Beilal, the prime minister's eldest son, he resolved on that youth's destruction, and employed one of his own servants to assassinate him, by shooting an arrow through his heart in the public streets. The minister, unable to obtain redress, and bent on revenge, caused poison to be administered to the young king, of which he died. On the death of Feroze, the old king Hoossein was again prevailed on to ascend the throne, and proclaimed his grandson, Mahmood, the son of the late Feroze, heir-apparent, and successor to the government. Imad-ool-Moolk continued to hold the office of prime minister, nor did Hoossein Lunga openly profess to consider him the murderer of his son; but in due time he intimated to Jam Bayezeed, the Sahna emigrant, that he would confer on him the office of vizier, if he could get rid of Imad-ool-Moolk, who was accordingly seized the next day, and put in irons.

Suffur 26. A. H. 908. Aug. 29. A. D. 1502.

A few days after which, on Sunday, the 26th of Suffur, A. H. 908 (but according to some 904), Hoossein Lunga, King of Mooltan, quitted this perishable state of existence for that of eternity, after a reign of thirty or of thirty-four years. I regret that the Towareekh Banadur Shahy,* which contains the history of this prince, is so full of errors; to detail which would be useless, and only tend to lengthen the work to no purpose.

* This is the work which Ferishta also speaks of in the same strain, vol. iv. p. 131.; and which the author of the Mirut Iskundry declares to be absolutely unintelligible.

MAHMOOD LUNGA.

Is elavated to the throne by the minister Jam Bayezeed.—The King abandons himself to low company.—The minister quits the town, and employs his son to receive the King's orders.—The young king attempts to murder the minister's son in court, but himself receives a wound.—The minister and his son fly from the capital—they occupy Sheevur, and claim the protection of the King of Dehly.—Civil war between the King and his minister—they agree to divide the empire.—The King is attacked by Shah Hoossein Arghoon, who marches to Mooltan.—Death of Mahmood Lunga.

On the day after the death of Hoossein Lunga, Jam Bayezeed, the prime minister, in concert with the other nobles, placed Mahmood Khan, the heir-apparent, on the throne; but this youth being very young, and silly withal, chose the society of low fellows, who administered to his foibles and vicious propensities, and prevented the approach of respectable people to his person, so that they withdrew from court, leaving him to his own favourites. These profligates resolved to displace Jam Bayezeed, the minister, from office; and he, having obtained intimation of their plan, feigning indisposition, confined himself to his house, built on the banks of the Chunab, where he transacted the public business. Jam Bayezeed having one day sent for some of the revenue collectors of the neighbouring towns, they behaved disrespectfully, and even insolently, to the minister, who ordering their heads to be shorn, caused each of them to be mounted on an ass, with his face to the tail, and to be exposed in this state through the city of Mooltan. The minister's enemies, exaggerating the circumstance, represented that he had disgraced some of the King's personal servants, and had, without any cause, for some time transacted public business at his own house, without consulting the King, excepting through the means of his son Alum Khan. They said that such conduct was degrading to his Majesty, and that the minister was in reality assuming the entire control of the state. Some days after this, when Alum Khan, the minister's son, was at the durbar, a few of the King's associates attacked him in the most abusive language, regarding the conduct of his father. Alum Khan, the most elegant young man of the times, unaccustomed to such usage, stood in amazement, without uttering a word. From abuse they proceeded to threats, and at length commenced kicking and beating him in the presence. The King rose, and though he did not actually assist yet did not check them. Alum Khan, recovering himself a little from his surprise, drew his dagger, and in brandishing it to clear his way it came in contact with the King's head, and in tered the skin just over a vein, which bled profusely. The sight of the King's blood, fortunately for Alum Khan, withdrew the attention of the assailants from him to the monarch, who in a minute or two fainted, and Alum Khan effected his escape to his father's house. Jam Bayezeed directed him immediately to fly to Sheevur, and collect the army at that place; while he, assembling all his Mooltan adherents, also left the city to join him. Mahmood Lunga now deputed a force after the minister, who being overtaken, halted to give battle, in which he defeated the royal army. He then proceeded to Sheevur, and caused the public prayers to be read in the name of Sikundur Lody of Dehly. At the same time he addressed a petition to that throne, giving in detail an account of the whole of the late proceedings. Sikundur Lody sent an honorary dress, and appointed him his governor of Sheevur. He also directed Dowlut Khan Lody, governor of the Punjab, to aid him in case he required his assistance.

Mahmood Lunga having collected his army marched towards Sheevur, to reduce his revolted minister; but the latter, and his son Alum Khan, quitting Sheevur, proceeded to the Ravy,* and applied to Dowlut Khan. Before he arrived, however, the contending armies were absolutely engaged. Dowlut Khan, on reaching the ground, sent some respectable officers to Mahmood Lunga; and it was eventually agreed that the river Ravy should from the boundaries between the country of Jam Bayezeed and Mahmood Lunga. After which, Dowlut Khan having accompanied Mahmood Lunga to Mooltan, also visited Jam Bayezeed at Sheevur, from whence he returned to Lahore. Notwithstanding this treaty, to which such a person as Dowlut Khan became guarantee,

* Hydroates.

it was not long before some of the principal articles were broken, the origin of which was as follows :— One Meer Jakur* Zund, with his two sons, Meer Sheheed and Meer Shahida, came from Solypoor to Mooltan. Nizam-ood-Deen Bukhshy states, that Meer Shahida was the first person who disseminated the principles of the Sheea faith in India; but he leaves us quite in the dark as to who this Meer Jakur Zund was, from whence he came, or what was his origin, his family, or connections. Mullik Sohrab Duvally having great influence with Mahmood Lunga, prevented the reception of Ameer Jakur in Mooltan, who out of revenge went over to Jam Bayezeed, by whom he was graciously received, and who gave him a jageer in the district of Oocha, to the great vexation of Mahmood Lunga. Jam Bayezeed was a man of strong mind, exceedingly learned himself, and a liberal patron of literature. Some ignorant writers have stated that he used to send provisions ready cooked, as daily food, from Sheevur to Mooltan, down the river Chunab, for the holy persons residing in the latter city; but such idle stories are too absurd to merit belief.

A.H. 930. A.D. 1523. In the year 930, Babur Padshah having conquered the country of Punjab proceeded to Dehly; from whence he wrote an order to Hoossein Arghoon, governor of Tutta, informing him that he intrusted him henceforward with the direction of affairs in Mooltan.

* The name of Jakur occurs before among the Suljook Toorks. Vide vol. i. p. 107.

That chieftain, in consequence, crossed the Indus, near the city of Bhukkur, with a large army. Mahmood Lunga of Mooltan no sooner heard of this circumstance than he deputed Sheikh Baha-ood-Deen Kooreishy to wait on Hoossein Arghoon, accompanied by Mowlana Bheilole, one of the most learned men of the age. The ambassadors, on reaching Hoossein Arghoon's camp, were received with all possible politeness. He replied to their remonstrances against his approach, by assuring them that he was only going to Mooltan to carry into effect some new regulations ordered by Babur Padshah, and also to pay his devotions at the shrine of Sheikh Baha-ood-Deen Zacharia. Mowlana Bheilole replied, that there appeared no necessity for his going in person to enforce his regulations; for he had only to express them, and his master would carry them into effect; and that with regard to his visit to the shrine of Sheikh Baha-ood-Deen,* he himself had come to anticipate his steps. Hoossein, however, was not to be thus averted from his purpose, but continued his march, and the ambassadors returned. Shortly afterwards, Mahmood Lunga, being seized with the cholic, died, A. H. 931, after a reign of twenty-seven years.

A. H. 931.
A. D. 1524.

* It will occur to the reader that the ambassador's name was Sheikh Baha-ood-Deen, and the descendant of Zacharia: the evasion of the Mowlana was a play upon his name.

HOOSSEIN LUNGA II.

Hoossein, the son of the late King, is placed on the throne.—Mooltan is besieged and taken by Shah Hoossein Arghoon, and becomes a dependency of Dehly.

On the death of Mahmood, one Lushkur Khan, at the head of the tribe of Lunga, deserted to Hoossein Arghoon, having previously laid waste the small villages surrounding the city of Mooltan. The rest of the army, left without leaders, sought protection in the fortress; and the ameers raised the son of the late King, although a minor, to the throne, under the name of Hoossein Lunga II. Notwithstanding the title which the boy received, he was only a pageant in the hands of his sister's husband, Shooja-ool-Moolk, who assumed the office of protector, under the appellation of vizier; and although he had not a month's provisions in the fort, he was so fool-hardy as to prepare to stand a siege; and Shah Hoossein Arghoon, conceiving the capture of the city as already accomplished, marched to invest it. The place had been attacked but a very short time, when provisions becoming scarce, the cavalry officers went to the protector, proposing that they might be led out against the enemy while their horses had yet strength, and adopt the only method of raising

the siege. Shooja-ool-Moolk gave no answer to this proposition at the moment; but afterwards, having sent for the officers, rejected their offer, by stating that the King was not yet firmly seated on his throne; that the army had no personal attachment to him; and that it was probable many of the soldiers would go over to the enemy, while the few who did fight would fall victims, without conferring any good on their country. From a document in my possession in the hand-writing of Mowlana Sad-oolla of Lahore, who was himself in the city during the siege of Mooltan, I have made the following extract:—
"After the garrison had been besieged for some "months, and the place so closely invested that it "was impossible for any one either to enter or "quit it, the distress for provisions was so great, "that if one of the garrison could catch a dog or "cat he killed it, and hoarded up the flesh as a "treasure. Besides this, Shooja-ool-Moolk pro-"moted a vagabond by the name of Jooma to the "command of the fort, and placed him at the head "of three thousand militia infantry. Wherever "this monster heard of any grain, he used to "march down with a party and seize it; so that "the inhabitants were driven to the alternative "either of submitting to die by famine, by the "sword of the enemy, or, by throwing themselves "over the walls, attempt, if possible, to escape. "At length, at midnight, in the year 932, Mooltan "was carried by escalade, and many "poor creatures were killed. On the "following morning all the inhabitants

A.H. 932.
A.D. 1525

"between the ages of seven and seventy years "were imprisoned, among whom were my father "and myself. When our situation became known "we were released from fetters, but the treatment "we experienced brought my poor father's grey "hairs to the grave. The city of Mooltan thus "fell into the hands of Hoossein Arghoon. The "young prince was kept a state prisoner; and the "place so completely sacked, and the habitations "so destroyed, that no one could then suppose it "would ever regain its former splendour; but "Hoossein Arghoon left one of his ameers, called "Shums-ood-Deen, in charge, with orders to "rebuild it; and having nominated Lushkur Khan "Lunga his deputy, he returned to Tutta. Lushkur "Khan was the means of rebuilding Mooltan; after "which, having procured a party to assist him, "he expelled Shums-ood-Deen, and assumed the "title of governor."

When Babur Padshah abdicated the throne in favour of his son Hoomayoon, the latter prince gave the country of Punjab in jageer to Mirza Kamran. On his arrival at Lahore, he sent for Lushkur Khan, and appointed a place for him to reside in, which is now included in one of the mohullas or wards of Lahore, and is called after him. At the same time he made over the district of Kabul to him, in lieu of that of Mooltan; since which time the kingdom of Mooltan has continued a province of the empire of Dehly.

GENEALOGIES OF THE SEVERAL DYNASTIES OF THE KINGS OF SIND.

I. HEREDITARY MONARCHS OF THE SOOMUNA RACE.

- 1 Jam Afra.
  - 4 Jam Timajy.
    - 5 Jam Sulah-ood-Deen.
      - 6 Jam Nizam-ood Deen.
        - 7 Jam Ally Sheer.
          - 8 Jam Giran.
  - 3 Jam Bany.
- 2 Jam Chowban.

ELECTIVE KINGS OF THE SOOMUNA RACE.

- 9 Jam Futteh Khan.
  - 11 Jam Sikundur.
    - 12 Jam Sunjur
      - 13 Jam Nunda.
        - 14 Jam Feroze.
- 10 Jam Toghluk.

DYNASTY OF ARGHOON.

- 15 Shah Beg Arghoon.
  - 16 Shah Hoossein Arghoon.

DYNASTY OF TURKHAN.

- 17 Eesa Turkhan.
  - 18 Mahomed Baky Turkhan
    - 19 Jany Beg Turkhan
  - Khan Baba

CHAPTER IX.

THE HISTORY OF SIND AND TUTTA.

MAHOMED KASIM.

Invasion of Sind by Mahomed Kasim.—Deebul, called Tutta, taken.—The Arabians proceed up the river Indus.—Sehwan taken.—Mooltan taken.—Mahomed Kasim recalled—account of his singular death.—Subversion of the Mahomedan power in Sind and Mooltan.

It is related in several histories, such as the Kholasut-ool-Hikayat, the Huj-Nama, and the history of Hajy Mahomed Kandahary, that the first establishment of the Mahomedan faith in the country of Sind occurred under the following circumstances:—

Hijaj (the son of Yoosoof Shukfy), governor of Bussora at the time when Wuleed, the son of Abdool Mullik, was ruler of the provinces of both Iraks, resolved on invading India. Accordingly, in the year 87, he deputed Mahomed Haroon with a select force into Mikran, who subdued that country, and made converts of many of the inhabitants called

A.H. 87.
A.D. 705.

Bulochies; and having there established a regular government, the Mahomedan faith may be said to have prevailed in that country from the period alluded to.

We are told that in those days, also, the inhabitants of the island of Selandeep (Ceylon) were accustomed to send vessels to the coast of Africa, to the Red Sea, and to the Persian Gulf, a practice prevailing from the earliest ages; and that Hindoo pilgrims resorted to Mecca and Egypt for the purpose of paying adoration to the idols, to which they looked with the utmost veneration. It is related, also, that the people trading from Selandeep became converts to the true faith at as early a period as the reign of the first caliphs, and that having thus had intercourse with Mahomedan nations, the King of Selandeep despatched a vessel laden with various rare articles, the produce of his country, to the caliph Wuleed at Bagdad.*

*I have been unable to procure the original works quoted by Ferishta at the head of this chapter; but it is to be hoped they are attainable in Europe, and that on consulting them some light may be thrown on the intercourse said to prevail between India and Egypt previously to Mahomedism. This subject is full of interest, and opens an extensive field of investigation for the Oriental antiquary, as leading to the developement of the history of a period at which India and Egypt were closely connected, as must once have been the case, from the identity which seems to pervade the mythology, astronomy, and the calculation of time, of both nations. The travels of Ibn Batoota, a learned Mahomedan of the fourteenth century, is now in the hands of Mr. Professor Lee of Cambridge, who is about to publish an English translation, with copious annotations. From a hasty view of this work, I am led to suppose a vast deal of valuable information on the intercourse carried on between the

On this vessel arriving at the entrance of the Persian Gulf it was attacked and captured by orders of the ruler of Deebul,* together with seven other boats, in which were some Mahomedan families going on pilgrimage to Kurbula. Some of the captives making their escape carried their complaint to Hijaj, who addressed a letter to Raja Dahir, the son of Sasa, ruler of Sind, and sent it to be forwarded from Mikran by Mahomed Haroon. Raja Dahir replied, that the act of hostility was committed by a powerful state, over which he had no control.

On the receipt of this letter Hijaj obtained the consent of Wuleed, the son of Abdool Mullik, to invade India, for the purpose of propagating the faith; and at the same time deputed a chief of the name of Budmeen, with three hundred cavalry, to join Haroon in Mikran, who was directed to reinforce the party with one thousand good soldiers more to attack Deebul. Budmeen failed in his expedition, and lost his life in the first action. Hijaj, not deterred by this defeat, resolved to follow up the enterprise by another. In consequence, in the year 93, he deputed his cousin and son-in-law, Imad-ood-Deen Mahomed Kasim, the son of Akil Shukhfy, then

A.H. 93.
A.D. 711.

early Arabians and the coast of India will be found; and it is to be hoped that such gentlemen as Professor Lee, who devote themselves exclusively to literature, will, in time, develope the rich materials of Oriental history and science that lie hidden in the depths of languages so little cultivated, so vaguely understood, and so meanly appreciated.

* Modern Tutta, on the Indus.

only seventeen years of age, with six thousand soldiers, chiefly Assyrians, with the necessary implements for taking forts, to attack Deebul. This army proceeded by the route of Shiraz and Mikran. On reaching the towns of Deboon and Dursila, on the confines of the Sind territory, Mahomed Kasim halted; and having taken the necessary steps for advancing he marched on to Deebul, situated on the banks of the Indus, which town is now called Tutta.

On reaching this place, he made preparations to besiege it, but the approach was covered by a fortified temple, surrounded by a strong wall, built of hewn stone and mortar, one hundred and twenty feet in height.* After some time a bramin, belonging to the temple, being taken, and brought before Kasim, stated, that four thousand Rajpoots defended the place, in which were from two to three thousand bramins, with shorn heads, and that all his efforts would be vain; for the standard of the temple was sacred; and while it remained entire no profane foot dared to step beyond the threshold of the holy edifice. Mahomed Kasim having caused the catapultas to be directed against the magic flag-staff, succeeded, on the third discharge, in striking the standard, and broke it down. In a few days after which the place fell.

* The Mahomedan historians seem to have confounded Deebul, properly Devul, meaning *the Temple*, with the town of Tutta. The defence of which Hindoo temples are capable has been frequently exemplified. The reader of modern Indian history will find several instances mentioned by Orme in the wars of the Carnatic, particularly those of Chilumbrum, and of Seringham at Trichinopoly.

Mahomed Kasim levelled the temple and its walls with the ground, and circumcised the bramins. The infidels highly resented this treatment, by invectives against him and the true faith. On which Mahomed Kasim caused every bramin, from the age of seventeen and upwards, to be put to death: the young women and children of both sexes were retained in bondage; and the old women being released, were permitted to go whithersoever they chose.

The booty of the temple amounted to a large sum, one fifth of which was sent to Hijaj, together with seventy-five female slaves. The rest of the plunder was distributed among the soldiery. Mahomed Kasim, having come for the purpose of propagating the faith, proceeded to invest the town of Deebul, from whence Foujy, the son of Dahir, with a party of soldiers, forced his way to the fort of Braminabad*; to which place he was pursued by Mahomed Kasim, who having closely invested it for some time, the lives of the besieged were spared, and they were allowed to retain their private property, on condition of surrendering.

Mahomed Kasim marched thence into Seevustan, to a place called Sehwan, the inhabitants of which country, being bramins, represented to their chief, Kucha Ray, the cousin of Dahir, governor of Sind, that as the spilling of blood was contrary to the tenets of their religion, it appeared to him advisable to submit quietly to the payment

* The Hindoo name of Bamunwasy is evidently sunk, and the Mahomedan appellation is given by the author.

of the tribute required by Kasim. Kucha Ray, despising the idea of this compromise, refused compliance, and the Mahomedans proceeded to invest Sehwan. After a week's siege, a party from the garrison, making their escape by night, fled to the Ray of Sulim,* in order to gain reinforcements; but the bramins gave up the place on the following morning, and Mahomed Kasim distributed the property among the troops, reserving one fifth for Hijaj. From hence he marched to the fortress of Sulim, which he also reduced, and divided the spoils according to the practice of those times.

At this period, Hully Sa, † the eldest son of Raja Dahir, having collected a large force, marched to oppose Mahomed Kasim; and the latter took up a strong position, and entrenched himself. In this situation his resources being contracted, and many of his carriage-cattle dying, the soldiers became discontented, and at length broke into open mutiny; Mahomed Kasim, however, encouraging his troops with the hope of aid, wrote to Hijaj Bin Yoosoof, who having heard of his situation before his letters arrived, had already despatched a reinforcement of one thousand horse, with other requisites, to Sind. On receiving this seasonable assistance, Mahomed Kasim again took the field, and attacking the young Ray, several battles ensued, though neither party appears to have obtained any advantage of consequence. Raja Dahir

* The early Mahomedan writers have so mutilated the Indian names, that they are frequently not to be recognised.

† Perhaps Hurry Sa.

having consulted his astrologers and bramins on the present crisis of his affairs, they declared that it was written in the ancient books,* that "at a "certain period a prophet would arise from among "the people of Arabia, who would succeed in con-"verting many nations to a new persuasion: after "which, in the lunar year 86, the Arabian forces "would invade the borders of Sind, and in the "year 93 they would subdue all those countries." Raja Dahir having in many instances found the predictions of his astrologers verified placed great reliance on them, but resolved to defend himself with a courage becoming his rank and family. The cup of his life being now filled to the brim, he joined his son's army, of which he assumed the

Rumzan 10. command in person; and on Wednes-
A. H. 93. day the 10th of Rumzan, in the year 93,
A. D. 711. with a force consisting of fifty thousand
men, composed of Rajpoots, Sindies, and Mooltanies, he marched to attack the Mahomedans.

Mahomed Kasim, with barely six thousand troops, mostly Arabian cavalry, waitd the onset. Raja Dahir at first took up a position near the Mahomedan lines, and endeavoured by skirmishes and manœuvres to entice the enemy from the strong position which he occupied; but failing in every attempt he resolved to storm it. Part of the Arab cavalry quitting the entrenched camp galloped fort and engaged the Indians singly; a mode of warfare in which the Arabians had the

* In this prophecy the flimsy veil of the Mahomedan historian is easily penetrated.

advantage, from the superior management of their horses, and their skill in the use of the sword. At length the action became more general, and Dahir with his relations led on the Indians into the centre of the enemy. On this occasion, one of the Arab firemen threw a naphtha ball* on the white elephant of Dahir, which became so alarmed at the terrible effect of the liquid flame, that he ran off to the river, in spite of the efforts of his driver, and plunged into the stream. The temporary absence of the Raja communicated a panic to his army, which instantly followed. Mahomed Kasim pursued the fugitives; but the elephant having come out of the water Raja Dahir again drew up his troops, and made a resolute stand on the banks of the Indus. when receiving an arrow wound he fell. He, however, insisted on being placed upon a horse; and although the wound was very severe, he charged in the most gallant manner into the midst of the Arabian horse, where he died like a hero. On his death, the Hindoo troops fled in confusion towards the fort of Ajdur. The Mahomedans gained a vast quantity of plunder by this victory. Mahomed Kasim now proceeded to Ajdur.† Hully Sa, the son of Dahir, after leaving a suffi-

* Naphtha balls thrown from engines, and arrows to which lighted tow dipt in naphtha was affixed, were used for the purpose of setting fire not only to the linen trappings of the enemy but also to thatched houses, barns, and stacks of corn and straw. The naphtha, or petrolium, is a substance not unlike tar floating on the surface of water. The translator saw several pits of this resinous oil in Persia, where it abounds.

† This may perhaps have been Oocha. The Persian or Arabic letters would admit of the words being mistaken by copyists.

cient garrison in that fort, proposed to meet the Mahomedan forces in the field; but his counsellors dissuading him, he retired to the fort of Braminabad.

The widow of Raja Dahir resolved to adopt the measure abandoned by her son; and with a truly masculine spirit, placing herself at the head of fifteen thousand Rajpoots, prepared to meet the Mahomedans. Mahomed Kasim, however, giving orders to his troops not to attack, they merely stood on the defensive; and the Rajpoots quietly withdrew with their female chief into the fort of Ajdur, which was now closely invested. The siege being protracted to a great length of time, the garrison were nearly starved out, when they came to the final alternative of performing the Jowhur, a ceremony which requires the Hindoos to sacrifice their women and children on a burning pile; and the men, after bathing, rush on the point of the enemy's lances sword in hand. This dreadful step being taken, the gates of the fortress were thrown open, and a body of Rajpoots, headed by the widow of Dahir, attacked the Mahomedans in their camp, and all lost their lives.

The heroes of Assyria having repulsed this attack forced their way into the fort, where they slew six thousand Rajpoots, and took prisoners three thousand more. Among the latter were the two daughters of Raja Dahir. These princesses were sent by Mahomed Kasim to Hijaj, to be received into the seraglio of Wuleed; and after having placed all the towns of Sind under Arab governors, Mahomed Kasim proceeded to reduce

Mooltan, which was also subject to the authority of Dahir. On reaching Mooltan, Mahomed Kasim also subdued that province; and himself occupying the city, he erected mosques on the site of the Hindoo temples.

When the two daughters of the King of Sind arrived at the court of Hijaj at Bussora, he forwarded them to the seraglio of the Caliph Wuleed at Damascus, where they remained until the year 96, when having sent for

A.H. 96. A.D. 714. them into his presence, he enquired their names. The elder replied that she was called Surpa Devy, and the younger Burreel Devy. The Caliph becoming enamoured of the elder, wished her to submit to his embraces, when she burst into tears, and told him that she was unworthy of him, since she had been disgraced on three successive nights by Mahomed Kassim. The enraged Caliph, whose will was the law, wrote with his own hand an order to Mahomed Kasim, requiring him to clothe himself in a raw hide, and embrace that death which he so richly merited. The faithful Kasim submitted to this unjust decree; and caused himself to be sown up in a raw skin, which produced his death. After which his body was sent to the Caliph. Upon the arrival of the corpse, the Caliph, sending for Surpa Devy, said, "Behold Mahomed "Kasim in his shroud: it is thus I punish the "sins of those servants who insult the deputy of "the prophet of God." Surpa Devy replied, with a smile full of triumph and of sarcasm, "Know, oh Caliph, that Mahomed Kasim respect-"ed my person as that of his own sister, and

" would no more have polluted my bed than that " of his mother. He, however, put to death my " father, my mother, my brother, and my country- " men, and in his death, indifferent to my own " fate, I have gratified that revenge which has so " long been consuming me."* The Caliph became much disconcerted; and having dismissed the damsel, he lamented over the body of his faithful and innocent servant.

On the death of Mahomed Kasim, a tribe who trace their origin from the Ansaries established a government in Sind; after which the zemindars, denominated in their country Soomura, usurped the power, and held independent rule over the kingdom of Sind for the space of five hundred years; but neither the names nor the history of these princes are, I believe, at present extant, since I have failed in my endeavour to procure them. In the course of years (although we have no account of the precise period), the dynasty of Soomura subverted the country of another dynasty called Soomuna, whose chief assumed the title of Jam. During the reigns of these dynasties in Sind the Mahomed kings of India Proper, such as those of Ghizny, Ghoor, and Dehly, invaded Sind, and seizing many of the towns, appointed Mahomedan governors over them.

* It is difficult to give credence to this romantic tale; but the gratification of revenge in Indians, where their honour is concerned, is so strong, the fortitude of Hindoo females so gteat, and the devotion of the servants of the caliphs so pure and disinterested, that the story may be allowed to hold its place among others not less remarkable in the annals of the world.

Among these rulers, Nasir-ood-Deen Kubbacha asserted his independence, and caused the public prayers to be read in his name as King of Sind. I shall therefore introduce my reader to him as the first Mahomedan king of Sind of which we have any authentic account. With respect to the first invasions of the Ghizny, Ghoory, and Dehly troops into Sind, accounts of them have been already given in their proper place. I shall record, therefore, this history of Sind from such scanty materials as I have been enabled to collect of the Soomura and Soomuna dynasties, though they be imperfect and unsatisfactory.

NASIR-OOD-DEEN KUBBACHA.

Obscure origin of Nasir-ood-Deen—his character—is made governor of Mooltan—becomes independent—extends his conquests over the Punjab, and nearly to Dehly—his power is gradually circumscribed by the Gukkurs, aided by Julal-ood-Deen Khwaruzm Shah—is attacked by Shums-ood-Deen Altmish.—Oocha taken.—Bhukkur besieged.—He attempts to fly with his family down the Indus—perishes in a storm.

NOTWITHSTANDING that former historians have ranked Nasir-ood-Deen among the servants of the kings of Dehly, and denied him a place in the list of Indian monarchs, probably on account of his low origin, the compiler of this work, deviating in this instance from the practice of his predicessors, has elevated him to that station in history to which, as the ruler of a considerable empire, he appears justly entitled. His pedigree is obscure, and all that seems known of him is, that he was one of the Toorky slaves of Shahab-ood-Deen Mahomed Ghoory; from which situation, having risen to the dignity of a throne, he proved himself wise, brave, generous, and polite. The greater part of his life was spent in the service of Shahab-ood-Deen; and when that monarch engaged the Suljooks, Nasir-ood-Deen Kubbacha was left in charge of the government of Oocha. Previously to this period, however, he espoused the daughter of Kootb-ood-Deen Eibuk, viceroy of India, and after the death of his first wife he married her sister. Subsequently to taking possession of his new government, he frequently came to Dehly, in order to pay his respects to his sovereign and father-in-law, Kootb-ood-Deen; after whose death, having seized many of the towns subject to the Sind government, he reduced the territory of the Soomuras, whose subject were a mixture of Mahomedans and Hindoos, to the small tract of country around Tutta, bounded by the desert. At first the inhabitants fled to the hills, but his proclamations of protection soon brought them back to their respective homes; after which he declared himself King of Sind, and caused public prayers to be read, and money to be coined, in his name, thus relinquishing his allegiance to the throne of Dehly. Besides Sind, his kimgdom embraced the provinces of Mooltan, Kohram, and Soorsutty. He was twice attacked by Taj-ood-Deen Yeldooz of Ghizny, but he successfully repelled both these invasions.

A. H. 611.
A. D. 1214.
In the year 611 the armies of Khwaruzm and Khulij, having reached Ghizny, made some impression on the Seevustan frontier; on which occasion Nasir-ood-Deen Kubbacha opposing them slew many of the Tartars; but he was at length compelled to fly before the army of Ghizny, commanded by the minister Mooveiud-ool-Moolk Sunjurry.

A. H. 614.
A. D. 1217.
In the year 614, Nasir-ood-Deen having marched for the purpose of subduing Lahore, conquered in that campaign the province of Surhind; but being pursued

by Shums-ood-Deen Altmish of Dehly, the successor of Kootb-ood-Deen Eibuk, Nasir-ood-Deen fled through the Punjab to the banks of the Neelab; which river not being fordable, the Dehly monarch dashing his charger into that rapid stream, was followed by part of the army. Many were drowned; but the King, with a few of his troops, gained the opposite bank, and gallantly attacking the Sindies, completely defeated them, compelling Nasir-ood-Deen to retreat, and make the best of his way to Mooltan; on which occasion his standard and kettledrums fell into the hands of the conquerors.

On the invasion of Chungiz Khan into Tooran, the nobles of Khorassan, Ghizny, and Ghoor having fled to the court of Nasir-ood-Deen Kubbacha at Mooltan, found honourable employment in his service; till at length Julal-ood-Deen, the son of the King of Khwaruzm, having been expelled from his own country by the resistless forces of Chungiz Khan, marched to the south, and attacked the country of Nasir-ood-Deen.

The following seems a correct account of this event:—Julal-ood-Deen having been driven from Khwaruzm retreated towards India, and arrived on the banks of the Attock, where he was overtaken by the forces of Chungiz Khan. In this situation there appeared no alternative but to perish in the waters or repel the enemy. He chose the latter resource, and gallantly opposed the infidel Tartars, many of whom he slew with his own hand; but at length his army being broken, he retired with seven hundred horse. He was again pursued, and again defended himself for several hours in the most gallant manner; but was at last compelled to seek safety in flight, his horse being scarcely able to support him. In his retreat he joined his sons, and mounting a fresh charger, once more checked the pursuing enemy; at last, on being quite overpowered by numbers, he retired fighting desparately till he reached the bank of the river Indus, where, having taken off his armour and secured his royal canopy, he swam the stream with only seven followers; and on the opposite bank he caused his canopy to be erected in sight of the Tartar army. It is said Chungiz Khan came to the bank of the river to witness the spectacle, and expressed his admiration of his character, saying, "Julal-ood-Deen is indeed the "the lion of battle, and the crocodile of the waves." Some of his troops having volunteered to cross and seize him, Chungiz Khan rebuked them, and said, "No! such a hero should only "fall in the heat of action." He remained concealed in the neighbourhood of the river for two or three days; and having collected between fifty and sixty of his followers, who had escaped without their arms, he attacked a post consisting of about two hundred men, who, unconscious of any enemy near, were regaling themselves with a feast. The attack made on them is thus represented:— Julal-ood-Deen having ordered each of his people to cut a good large stick from the jungle, he dispersed the party of soldiers who were feasting, and plundered them of their arms and property. He then mounted his own men on their horses, and was enabled next day to muster a troop of one hundred and twenty men. In a few days after, hearing of a guard composed of three thousand men being near him, he suddenly assaulted them, and obtained so large a quantity of money as enabled him, in a short time, to appear in considerable force, and make several successful attacks on the troops in the Punjab, driving them before him like sheep, till at length his army amounted to four thousand cavalry. When Chungiz Khan heard of these successes he detached some of his best officers accross the river to attack Julal-ood-Deen; but the moment the Tartars advanced, he fled before them towards Dehly, plundering the country as he proceeded. On his arrival near Dehly, he deputed one of his principal officers to wait on Shums-ood-Deen Altmish, relating his misfortunes, and requesting a small tract of country to reside on; unless, indeed, he thought fit to furnish him with a sufficient force to oppose Chungiz Khan, and enable him to regain his crown.

Shums-ood-Deen determined not to permit so dangerous a person to remain in his dominions; and it is even said he caused his ambassador to be privately murdered. He however sent some valuable presents to Julal-ood-Deen: but declared that the air of India was so unwholesome to strangers, that he could not recommend any spot on which he might take up his residence. Julal-ood-Deen, comprehending the purport of this message, retired towards the Gukkurs, among the hills of Bilala and Nikala, from whence he sent Taj-ood-Deen Khiljy, one of his officers, to plunder in the Jood hills.

Julal-ood-Deen, having collected about twelve thousand men, deputed an ambassador to proceed to the court of the Gukkur chief, who had some time before been converted to Mahomedism, soliciting the hand of his daughter in marriage. To this the Gukkur readily assented; and deputed his son to escort the Princess to Julal-ood-Deen, at the same time stipulating for his assistance in repelling the frequent attacks of Nasir-ood-Deen Kubbacha, King of Sind. Julal-ood-Deen at this time conferred on his wife's brother the title of Khullij Khan, and shortly after deputed his Barbik (Usher), one of the most distinguished of his officers, with a body of seven thousand men, to accompany the Gukkur prince. This force proceeded to the banks of the Indus, and encamped near the city of Oocha, where it was opposed by Nasir-ood-Deen with twenty thousand men. A sanguinary conflict ensued, wherein the latter was defeated, and compelled to seek safety in a small boat, in which he crossed the Indus, and retired to the fort of Nuggur.* On this news being transmitted to Julal-ood-Deen, who had just learned that an army from Dehly was on its march to attack him, he left the hills of Bilala, and marching to Oocha occupied Nasir-ood-Deen's palace. From thence he wrote, desiring him to deliver into his hands one Anwur Khan and his family, who had deserted him on the day of the battle of Attock with Chungiz Khan.

* I am not aquainted with any town of the name in that part of India. Colonel Tod says there were seven towns, or nuggurs, called Oocha; this may, therefore, be one of them.

Nasir-ood-Deen complied with his request, and also sent to Julal-ood-Deen some valuable presents, himself retiring to Mooltan; in consequence of which, the latter returned to the country of Bilala, whence he had come. On the march he attacked a small fort, where he received an arrow wound in his arm; and his troops became so irritated at the event, that upon the capture of the place they indiscriminately slaughtered men, women, and children. At this period Julal-ood-Deen heard that Choghtay, the son of Chungiz Khan, was on his march to seize and convey him to the presence of the Tartar conqueror; but as he was unwilling to cope with his former enemies, and conceiving that Nasir-ood-Deen bore no ill will towards him, he marched to Mooltan, and there demanded some mules for the transport of his baggage. Nasir-ood-Deen, who expected the Tartar forces would invade his country on Julal-ood-Deen's account, refused his assistance, and he returned from Mooltan to Oocha; where not meeting with the support he expected, he laid that city in ashes, and marched to the south towards Tutta; and whenever he arrived at one of Nasir-ood-Deen's villages on the route, he either laid it under heavy contributions or destroyed it. On reaching Tutta, the Ray, whose name was Jeisee, of the dynasty of Soomura, fled; and putting all his baggage and family in boats on the Indus, departed for some of the contiguous islands. Julal-ood-Deen now occupied Tutta, destroyed all the temples, and built mosques in their stead; and on one occasion detached a force to Nehrwala (Puttun), on the bor-

A. H. 620. A. D. 1222. der of Guzerat. In the year 620, having heard that his brother Gheias-ood-Deen had established himself as King of Irak, Julal-ood-Deen abandoned his views in India, and proceeded through Mikran to Persia; and as the acts of the subsequent part of his life are related in the Persian histories, I shall leave them to furnish the reader with any further account of this prince, and returned to Nasir-ood-Deen Kubbacha. The Prince Choghtay Khan having reached Mooltan, laid siege to that place; but Nasir-ood-Deen conducted himself with such bravery, that he compelled the Tartars to withdraw. The Tartar prince marched to the south, and invading both Mikran and Kech laid waste those countries, and wintered at Kalinjur, a place situated on the borders of Sind; but finding provisions scarce in his camp, he put to death ten thousand Indians of all classes, whom he had taken prisoners, rather than liberate them. Notwithstanding this barbarous act, famine and plague both raged shortly afterwards, which compelled him to move; and having heard no more of Julal-ood-Deen, he returned to Tooran.

A.H. 622. A.D. 1224-5. In the year 622, Shums-ood-Deen Altmish, King of Dehly, made several attempts to remove Nasir-ood-Deen from his government, and even marched for that purpose as far as Oocha; but Nasir-ood-Deen having made preparations for a siege, took post with a respectable force in the town of Bhukkur. The King of Dehly sent his general, Nizam-ool-Moolk Mahomed, (the son of Aby Syeed

Jooneidy, to whom the Jama-ool-Hikayat is dedicated,) to attack the latter place, while he engaged in the attack of Oocha, which fell to the Dehly arms after a siege of two months and twenty days. On receipt of this intelligence, Nasir-ood-Deen deputed his son, Alla-ood-Deen Beiram, to Oocha, to treat for peace; but before it was concluded the garrison of Bhukkur became so straitened for supplies, that Nasir-ood-Deen, accompanied by his family, embarking in boats, proceeded down the Indus for the purpose of taking possession of one of the islands. During the voyage he was, however, unfortunately drowned. Another, and probably the most authentic, account of this invasion states, that when Shums-ood-Deen Altmish arrived at Oocha, he left the army with his minister, Nizam-ool-Moolk Jooneidy, to besiege that place, which after two months he succeeded in reducing; that from thence the King proceeded to the attack of Bhukkur, to which place Nasir-ood-Deen had retreated; but having no hopes of eventually repelling the arms of the Dehly monarch, he placed his family and personal attendants, with his treasure, in boats, and endeavoured to occupy a contiguous island; but a storm coming on, the boat in which he had himself embarked foundered, and every person perished. This monarch reigned in Sind and Mooltan for a period of twenty-two years.

ACCOUNT OF THE DYNASTY OF SOOMUNA,*

ENTITLED JAM.

Jam Afra reigns for three years, and is succeeded by his brother Choban, who reigns fourteen years, and is succeeded by his nephew Jam Bany—attempts to throw off his allegiance from Dehly, but is attacked by Feroze Toghluk, and taken prisoner—he is carried to Dehly, but is subsequently restored to his government—is succeeded by Jam Timmajy.—The Soomunas embrace Mahomedism.—Jam Sulah-ood-Deen ascends the throne—is succeeded by his son, Jam Nizam-ood-Deen, who is succeed by Jam Ally Sheer—he is succeeded by his son Giran, in whom the lineal descent becomes extinct.—The people elect Jam Futteh Khan as king—he is succeeded by his brother Jam Toghluk.—The chiefs raise Jam Sikundur, the son of Futteh Khan, to the throne.—Jam Sungur is elected by the people.—Jam Nunda is elected.—Sind invaded by the troops of Shah Beg Arghoon, ruler of Kandahar.—The fort of Sewly taken.—Bhukkur taken.—Sind overrun by the Arghoons, who quit the country.—Death of Jam Nunda—is succeeded by Jam Feroze.—Contests between Jam Sulah-ood-Deen and Jam Feroze.—Sulah-ood-Deen is supported by an army from Guzerat.—Feroze calls in the aid of the Arghoons.—Sulah-ood-Deen is killed.—The Guzeratties are expelled, and the Arghoons seize the country.

THE zemindars of Sind were originally of two tribes or families, the one denominated Soomuna and the other Soomura, and the chief of the former

* Colonel Tod observes, that this race of Jam was of Rajpoot origin, and of the Jureja branch of Yadoo, descended from Shama or Sama, the black god Krishn.

was distinguished by the appellation of Jam. In the latter end of the reign of Mahomed Toghluk of Dehly, Sind owned allegiance to that monarch; nevertheless, occassionally taking advantage of local circumstances, the Sindies contrived, for a considerable period, to shake off their allegiance. The first of the family of which we have any account was

JAM AFRA.

A. H. 740.
A. D. 1339.
OF this prince we have no further notice than that he died a natural death, after a reign of three years and six months.

JAM CHOBAN.

JAM CHOBAN was nominated by his predecessor to succeed him in the government of Sind. We are told he was famed for his forbearance and moderation, and reigned peaceably for a period of fourteen years.
A. H. 754.
A. D. 1353.

JAM BANY.

ON the death of Jam Choban, his nephew Jam Bany, the son of Jam Afra, having set up his claims to the government, established them, and succeeded his uncle Jam Choban. During his reign he publicly asserted his independence from the throne of Dehly, and refused to pay the accustomed tribute. Owing to this, in
A. H. 762.
A. D. 1360.
the year 762, Feroze Toghluk of Dehly marched with an army to Sind. Jam

Bany, incapable of making resistance, fled, but having previously secured a large quantity of provisions and forage for his cattle, he laid waste by fire for many miles the surrounding country. By this stratagem his enemies were reduced to the utmost distress for forage, and compelled to fall back on the cultivated plains of Guzerat, where Feroze remained during the rainy season. After which the grass having grown, and being too green to be burned, Feroze was enabled to prosecute his march into Sind. Jam Bany was now reduced to submit to the Dehly arms, and threw himself on the mercy of Feroze Toghluk, who appointed his own governor over the provinces of Sind and Tutta, and returned to Dehly accompanied by Jam Bany, and other principal Sind chieftains in his train. Being some time after perfectly satisfied of their fidelity, he reinstated Jam Bany in his govrnment, which he resumed with all his former dignities. Shortly after this he died having

A.H. 769. A.D. 1367. reigned for a period of fifteen years.

JAM TIMMAJY.

ON the death of Jam Bany he was succeeded by his brother Timmajy, who after

A. H. 782. A. D. 1380. having passed a peaceable reign of thirteen years died. It appears from the foregoing few names that the Sind princes were hitherto bramins.*

* By bramins, Ferishta, perhaps, simply means Hindoos.

JAM SULAH-OOD-DEEN.

AFTER the death of Timmajy, he was
A. H. 793. succeeded by Jam Sulah-ood-Deen,
A. D. 1391. who reigned for a period of eleven years, and then died.

JAM NIZAM-OOD-DEEN.

ON the death of his father, Jam
A.H. 796. Nizam-ood-Deen succeeded to the go-
A.D. 1393. vernment; but after a short reign of two or three years he died.

JAM ALLY SHEER.

JAM ALLY SHEER succeeded his father, Nizam-ood-Deen, and from the first period of his reign to its close, we are told that his government assumed a shape more respectable than any of his predecessors; but his reign, like that of the world, was of comparatively short duration, and he was snatched from his affectionate subjects
A. H. 812. after the short space of six years,
A. D. 1409. when he died, universally and deservedly lamented.

JAM GIRAN.

ALLY SHEER was succeeded by Jam Giran, the son of Jam Timmajy; but fate being jealous of his good fortune deprived him of his dignities on the second day of his accession.

JAM FUTTEH KHAN.

Upon the death of Jam Giran, a consultation of the chiefs of the Sind tribes was held; and we find they elected Futteh Khan
A. H. 827. Soomuna, the son of Iskundur Khan,
A. D. 1423. to the government. He ruled over that country for a period of fifteen years, and died.

JAM TOGHLUK.

Futteh Khan was succeeded by his younger brother, Toghluk, who was universally beloved. During his reign, the empire of Dehly being reduced to a state of anarchy, and the King obliged to fly from his throne, Jam Toghluk looked towards Guzerat, that had lately declared its independence, for support. To obtain this end, he opened a friendly intercourse with that kingdom, which continued during the period of the Soomuna dynasty. Jam Toghluk died,
A.H. 854. after a reign of twenty-seven years,
A.D. 1450. and was succeeded by his kinsman, Jam Moobarik, who was deposed, after a short reign of three days.

JAM SIKUNDUR.

The chiefs of the tribes having deposed Moobarik on the third day after his accession, placed in his stead Sikundur, the son of Jam Futteh Khan, and nephew to the late Jam Toghluk; but his reign was also of short duration, for he died in the space of eighteen months after his elevation.

A. H. 856.
A. D. 1452.

JAM SUNJUR.

SIKUNDUR was succeeded by Sunjur, a descendant of the former kings of Sind, who was elected from among the people as their ruler, not only on account of his descent, but from his personal virtues. He reigned with justice for a period of eight years, and was succeeded by Jam Nizam-ood-Deen, commonly called.

A. H. 864.
A. D. 1460.

JAM NUNDA.

NIZAM-OOD-DEEN NUNDA was a prince who promoted the prosperity of his country. He was contemporary with Hussun Lunga, King of Mooltan. We find that in the year 890 Shah Beg Arghoon made a descent from Kandahar, and besieged the fort of Sewly, then commanded by Bahadur Khan Sindy, which he took by assault; and having left his younger brother, Mahomed, in charge, he retreated to Kandahar. Jam Nunda deputed one Moobarik Khan to retake Sewly. Upon his approach he

A. H. 890.
A. D. 1485.

was opposed by Mahomed Beg Arghoon; and several engagements took place, in one of which the latter was killed, and the fort of Sewly again reverted to the government of Sind. The moment the King of Kandahar heard this, he appointed Mirza Eesy Turkhan to occupy the post of his brother; and Jam Nunda collected an army, and sent it, under the command of Moobarik Khan, to oppose him. A severe engagement occurred on the frontier, in which the Sindies were defeated with great loss, and Moobarik Khan, who was himself wounded, fled to the fortress of Bhukkur. Shah Beg Arghoon, hearing of the success of his general, collected a still larger force, and marched in person to Bhukkur, where he was opposed by Kazy Kavun, who was at last obliged to submit, and Fazil Beg Gokultash was left in the government of that province. Shah Beg then proceeded to Sehwan, which he also reduced; and having placed Khwaja Baky Beg in charge, and deeming these conquests sufficient for his first campaign, he returned to Kandahar.

Jam Nunda expended large sums for the purpose of collecting a force in order to recover the fortress of Sewly, but was unsuccessful in every attempt. Indeed the Sindies, who had once been defeated by Eesy Turkhan, could never be brought to face the Toorkmans again. Such was the dread which prevailed at that time among the Sindies, that one day a Toorkman having dismounted for the purpose of fastening the girth of his saddle, was surrounded by a party of forty Sindies. The astonished Toorkman mounted his

horse in dismay, in order to effect his escape; but the Sindies imagining it was to attack them, the whole troop dispersed over the face of the country, and the Toorkman rode up quietly to his comrades, who were at a considerable distance. Historians relate that this circumstance, connected with others equally disgraceful to the credit of his subjects, broke the heart of Jam
A. H. 894. Nunda, who died after a reign of
A. D. 1492. thirty-two years.

JAM FEROZE.

On the death of Jam Nunda, he was succeeded by his son Feroze, who appointed his relation, Duria Khan, to the office of prime minister; shortly after which, Jam Sulah-ood-Deen, a distant relative, set up his pretensions to the government, when, after several engagements with Jam Feroze, he fled to Guzerat. Moozuffur Shah of Guzerat espoused a first cousin of the Sind pretender, and was induced to send troops to assist him in deposing Jam Feroze. On reaching the confines of Sind, Sulah-ood-Deen gained Duria Khan over to his interest, and took many of the towns on the confines. Jam Feroze, however, eventually succeeded in repelling these attacks; and although Duria Khan, in the first instance, joined Sulah-ood-Deen, he subsequently returned to his allegiance to Feroze, and compelled the pretender to retreat to Guzerat, covered with shame and confusion.

Moozuffur Shah of Guzerat, notwithstanding his

late disappointment, again assisted
A. H. 926. A. D. 1519. Sulah-ood-Deen with a force, in the year 926, with which he marched, and succeeded in expelling Jam Feroze, and himself occupied Sind. Reduced to the utmost extremity, Jam Feroze applied to Shah Beg Arghoon for assistance, who deputed one Soombul Khan with a respectable force to expel the usurper, and re-establish Jam Feroze in his father's government. The two armies met near Sehwan, where a bloody engagement took place, in which, though Sulah-ood-Deen distinguished himself by his valour, he fell, and the government of Sind reverted to Jam Feroze. Shah Beg Arghoon having long contemplated the entire subjugation of Sind, availed himself of the present moment to accomplish it; and considering that no one would be more interested in wresting it out of the hands of Sulah-ood-Deen than Feroze, he permitted the troops to act in his name, but after his success he determined to seize the country for himself. This period had now arrived; and, accordingly, in the following year, 927, Shah Beg march-
A. H. 927. A. D. 1520. ed to conquer Sind, and occupied the whole country, even to the possession of Tutta itself.

On the re-assumption of the government by Jam Feroze, Duria Khan was restored to the office of prime minister, and subsequently fell in action against the troops of the King of Kandahar, while his master, who attempted for sometime to collect a force to recover his throne, was eventually compelled to fly his country and seek safety in Guzerat; but upon his arrival, finding that

Moozuffur Shah had died, and had been succeeded by Bahadur Shah, he returned to Sind; when seeing no chance of recovering his government, he resolved to enter into the service of Bahadur Shah of Guzerat. From this period may be dated the downfal of the Soomuna dynasty, and the establishment of that of Arghoon.

SHAH BEG ARGHOON:

His origin—expulsion from Kandahar by Babur—invasion and occupation of Sind—his death.

THE founder of this dynasty was the son of Mirza Zoolnoon Beg Arghoon, the commander-in-chief and head of the nobles at the court of Sooltan Hoossein Mirza, King of Khorassan,* his family having always been considered, since the invasion of Chungiz Khan, as the first in the empire. Sooltan Hoossein Mirza, in the year 884, (A.D. 1479), nominated Zoolnoon Beg Arghoon to the government of Kandahar, and the provinces of Zemeen-Dawur, Samira, Lowluk, and Ghoor, notwithstanding one of the princes of the blood-royal was styled Prince of Kandahar, and sometimes, for form's sake, went to visit his principality. Zoolnoon Beg, at length taking advantage of circumstances, declared himself independent. On this occasion he nominated his son Shooja Beg, commonly called Shah Beg, to the government of Kandahar. The provinces of Samira and Lowluk were given in charge to Abdool Ally Turkhan, and the government of Ghoor

* Sooltan Hoossein Mirza is the fourth descendant of Tamerlane by his son Oomr Sheikh, King of Khorassan, vide Genealogy of the Great Mogul, vol. ii. p. 1.

to Ameer Fukhr-ood Deen, while he himself spent the remainder of his days in the government of Zemeen-Dawur. About the period when he established his independence, a lucky incident occurred which secured it for him. The Prince Budee-ool-Zuman Mirza having quarrelled with the King, retired in disgust to his old friend, Mirza Zoolnoon Beg, who not only received him with hospitality, but even gave him his daughter in marriage; and on the reconciliation of the father and son, Zoolnoon was not only forgiven, but the interest obtained through the marriage of his daughter procured for him confirmation in his government. Mirza Zoolnoon Beg was subsequently killed in action; and after his death the province of Kandahar devolved on his son Shah Beg, who after having first reduced the towns of Sewly and Bhukkur, as before mentioned, resolved to extend his conquests over Sind. At this period, Babur Padshah having invaded the province of Kandahar, Shah Beg, in spite of his efforts, was unable to resist him, he therefore availed himself of the opportunity that occurred, in the differences between Jam Feroze and Sulah-ood-Deen, to carry his favourite project into effect; and having subdued Sind, settled himself as king in that country. His reign was, however, but of short duration, for he died two years after the conquest, in the year 930.

A.H. 930.
A.D. 1523.

Shah Beg was exceedingly well read, and is mentioned as the patron of literature by many authors in their works. His courage was so fierce as to be nearly allied to rashness: he always led his own troops into battle. He has been often heard to say, after an action, that he was as much astonished at himself, as others who related his conduct, and constantly confessed that he lost all self-control after the first charge.*

* How many instances of this temporary frenzy do we meet with among men who can form plans of attack with coolness, precision, and judgment, yet when they go into battle are bereaved of all reflection, and who, instead of attending to their troops and to the events passing before them, seem wholly devoted to the exercise of their own personal prowess. As such men seldom survive many actions, they are usually to be found among the junior ranks of the army Some of my military readers, however, may be able to bring to their remembrance individuals, in whom this courageous frenzy prevailed, who had been so fortunate as to attain high rank in the army.

SHAH HOOSSEIN ARGHOON.

Shah Hoossein ascends his father's throne—completes the subjugation of Sind—takes Mooltan, which is retaken by the inhabitants.—Hoomayoon Padshah takes refuge in Sind, where he continues for two years and a half.—Conduct of Shah Hoossein—promises his daughter in marriage to Yadgar Nasir Mirza, and proclaims him King.—Hoomayoon quits Sind.—Shah Hoossein expels Yadgar Mirza.—Kamran Mirza comes to Sind—receives in marriage the daughter of Shah Hoossein.—Death of Shah Hoossein Arghoon.

AFTER the death of Shah Beg, he was succeeded by his eldest son Hoossein, who, following in the path of his father, reduced those towns in Sind which had not yet been subdued by his predecessor. He also rebuilt the fort of Bhukkur, and strengthened that of Sehwan.

A.H. 931.
A.D. 1524.

At the period that Babur Padshah directed his generals to reduce Mooltan, in the year 931, Mahmood Lunga deputed some officers to wait on him, entreating him to forego the conquest of his country; to which Babur consented, on his acknowledging fealty, and paying tribute. But Mahmood dying suddenly, was succeeded by his son Hoossein Lunga. Shah Hoossein Arghoon of Sind scarcely gave him time to ascend his father's throne, when he invested his capital; and after a close siege of fifteen months took it by storm, putting to death some of the inhabitants. Many, however, were taken prisoners, among whom was Hoossein Lunga himself. Having placed the fort of Mooltan in the hands of Khwaja Shums-ood-Deen, he returned to Tutta. After quitting Mooltan, an insurrection of the inhabitants occurred in favour of one Shumsheer Khan, a noble of the Lunga government, who expelled Shums-ood-Deen, and Shah Hoossein did not find it convenient at that time to take revenge for the revolt.

A. H. 947.
A. D. 1540.

In the year 947, when Hoomayoon Padshah was driven from India by Sheer Shah, and endeavoured to collect troops from all quarters, he marched from Lahore into Sind, and halted near the city of Bhukkur. Thence he sent an order to Shah Hoossein Arghoon to assist him. Shah Hoossein, doubtful of the sincerity of Hoomayoon, delayed his visit for six months, and then returned an answer sufficiently indicative of his determination not to visit him at all. Hoomayoon, incensed at this neglect, invested his uncle, Yadgar Nasir Mirza, with the government of Bhukkur, and proceeded himself to Tutta. Shah Hoossein promised his daughter in marriage to Yadgar Nasir Mirza, and also offered to assist in rendering him king of Sind; in proof of which, he caused the public prayers to be read in the name of Yadgar Mirza. At the same time, Shah Hoossein, having embarked in a boat, landed near the royal army, and succeeded in cutting off Hoomayoon's supplies, owing to the influence he possessed among the inhabitants.

Hoomayoon, thus situated, was compelled to sue for peace, and deputed as his ambassador Beiram Khan Bharloo, a Toorkman chief. Affairs being amicably adjusted, Hoomayoon procured from Shah Hoossein camels, boats, and other necessary equipments for his journey. After having remained two years and a half in those countries, he marched towards Kandahar, Shah Hoossein, having gained his point, by separating the interests of Hoomayoon and Yadgar Nasir Mirza, did not hesitate now to drive the latter out of Bhukkur, and compelled him to retreat to Kabul.

A H. 952. A.D. 1545. In the year 952, Kamran Mirza, the son of Babur Padshah, having separated from Hoomayoon, joined Shah Hoossein, by whom he was treated with every attention. He even gave him his daughter in marriage; and presenting him with a large casket of jewels Kamran proceeded to Kabul, in order to establish his claims in that province.

A. H. 966. A. D. 1554. Shah Hoossein, after having reigned for a period of thirty-two years, died A. H. 962.

On the death of Shah Hoossein, the government of Sind was divided between two rivals, Mahmood the governor of Bhukkur, and Mirza Eesy Turkhan governor of Tutta; who both assumed the title of king, and between whom frequent dissensions arose, and battles were fought.

Mahmood of Bhukkur was either mad, or such a monster of iniquity and cruelty as we seldom read of; such, at least, is the character given of him by historians. Akbur padshah, on coming to Lahore, deputed Mohib Ally Khan to conquer Sind, and that officer reduced the whole province of Bhukkur, exclusive of the fort; till at last Mahmood being reduced to extremities, wrote a petition to Akbur Padshah, saying, that he was ready to give up his only remaining fortress to any other officer, but would not surrender it to Mohib Ally Khan. Akbur Padshah in consequence deputed Geesoo Khan to receive it; but Mahmood died before his arrival, in the year 982, after a reign of twenty years. Bhukkur thus fell without farther opposition, by which Akbur Padshah became possessed of Upper Sind, and put an end to the hopes of the race of Mahmood.

A. H. 982.
A. D. 1572.

MIRZA EESY TURKHAN.

Succeeds to the government of Sind after the death of Shah Hoossein Arghoon.

A. H. 975.
A. D. 1470.

MIRZA EESY TURKHAN also died, after a reign of thirteen years, A. H. 975; but as we have no account of the transition of the dynasty of Arghoon to that of Turkhan we cannot form any probable conjectures on that head. It appears to me, from all I have read, and from what I can learn on the subject, that Mirza Eesy Turkhan was a Toorkman, and commander-in-chief of Shah Beg's army.

MIRZA MAHOMED BAKY TURKHAN.

Contests between Mirza Mahomed Baky and Khan Baba, the sons of Mirza Eesy Turkhan.—Mirza Mahomed Baky is successful.

AFTER the death of Mirza Eesy Turkhan, his two sons, Mirza Mahomed Baky and Khan Baba, both set up as rivals for the government; but the elder brother, Mirza Mahomed Baky, having collected the more numerous force, succeeded in establishing himself; and during his rule he always maintained a friendly intercourse with Akbur Padshah of Dehly, frequently sending presents, and acknowledging fealty to that monarch; but during the life of Mahmood of Bhukkur, like his predecessor he was sometimes engaged in war, and sometimes at peace. He died, after a reign of eighteen years, in the year 993.

A. H. 993.
A. D. 1584.

MIRZA JANY BEG TURKHAN.

Mirza Jany Beg, the grandson of Mirza Mahomed Baky, succeeds him—is attacked by Mirza Khan, the son of Beiram Khan Toorkman—concludes peace—gives his daughter in marriage to Mirza Eerich, the son of Mirza Khan.—Mirza Jany Beg attends the Mogul army to Dehly—is enrolled among the nobles.—Sind attached to Dehly.

Upon the death of Mirza Mahomed Baky, he was succeeded by his grandson, Mirza Jany Beg. Akbur Padshah, who before the death of Mirza Mahomed Baky had gone to Lahore and remained there for some years, expected a personal visit from the ruler of Tutta; but being disappointed, and having already taken Bhukkur, he proceeded to take measures for the subjugation of Tutta, the remaining province of Sind. In the year 999, therefore, he presented the government of Mooltan and Bhukkur to his commander-in-chief, Mirza Khan, the son of Beiram Khan, directing him to proceed and occupy it in his name.

A. H. 999.
A. D. 1590.

This officer, in the first instance, attacked the fort of Sehwan; on which occasion Mirza Jany Beg collecting a large force, and being aided by the zemindars, embarked in boats and vessels, and went up the river towards Sehwan. Mirza Khan raising the siege, proceeded to attack Jany Beg's forces. On reaching Nuseerpoor, within eight coss of the Sindian army, he found that Mirza Jany Beg had with him upwards of one hundred large vessels, exclusive of two hundred boats filled with archers, musketeers, and artillery, though he had only twenty-five vessels. With these he boldly bore down to engage the Sindy fleet, himself taking up a commanding position on the bank of the river Indus, whence he not only surveyed the events of the action, but erected a battery on shore to act against the enemy. A shot having struck one of the Sindy boats, it caused coufusion, which enabled the Mogul fleet to capture seven of the Sindy vessels, in which they put to death two hundred men. The action occurred on the 26th of Mohurrum, A. H. 1000, and lasted for a whole day and night, when the Sindies were eventually defeated. After this, Mirza Jany Beg taking up a position flanked on each side by a marsh on the bank of the river, strengthened it by throwing up a breast-work all round. Mirza Khan now proceeded to invest this entrenched camp; and daily skirmishes took place between the two armies, in which neither gained any apparent advantage, though many lives were lost. The Sindians, however, having cut off the supplies from Mirza Khan's camp, reduced it to a state of absolute famine, and compelled him to desist from the attack. Mirza Khan now marched to the south, and encamped at Ahwan (near the city of Tutta), detaching a force to renew the siege of Sehwan. Mirza Jany Beg, conceiving himself able to cope

Mohurrum 26. A. H. 1000. November 3. A. D. 1591.

with that detachment, marched to intercept it. Mirza Khan, hearing of this movement, detached Dowlut Khan with reinforcements to join the Sehwan division; and Jany Beg gave battle, but was defeated, and taking to his boats fled to Arnool, where he prepared for another attack. The victorious army pursuing him, invested Arnool, where they were shortly afterwards joined by Mirza Khan in person. The besieged held out obstinately, though reduced to eat their horses and camels. But eventually Mirza Jany Beg offered to acknowledge fealty to the King of Dehly, to surrender the place, and to proceed to the presence in three months from the date of the peace, while it was agreed by Mirza Khan, on the other hand, to refrain from all hostile measures till orders could be received from court. Mirza Khan shortly after celebrated the nuptials of his son Mirza Eerich with the daughter of Mirza Jany Beg.

A. H. 1001.
A. D. 1592.
After the rainy season of the year 1001, having occupied the forts of Bhukkur, Sehwan, and Tutta, Mirza Khan accompanied Mirza Jany Beg to the presence Akbur Padshah, who created him a noble of the realm, and his dignities were enrolled in the public records, while Mirza Khan received great honours, also, from his sovereign; and from that date the whole kingdom of Sind reverted to the sovereignty of the empire of Dehly, as it continues at this day.

CHAPTER X.

THE HISTORY OF KASHMEER.

Some account of the situation, the climate, and the productions of Kashmeer, from the histories of Mirza Heidur Doghlat and from the Zufur Nama.

THE following brief account of Kashmeer is extracted from an interesting and authentic work on that country, written by Mirza Heidur Doghlat, who is himself mentioned in the course of this history :—

Kashmeer lies to the N. E. of the district of Pugly, in the Punjab : it is almost surrounded by mountains ; and the valley called Kashmeer is one hundred coss in length, and from ten to twenty in breadth. The soil is in general rich, and produces fine crops both of grain and saffron, the latter of which his particularly good ; but the meadows on the banks of rivers being in general too moist for the purposes of cultivation, they are allowed to lie waste, and are covered with fine grass, interspersed with shamrocks, violets, and iris. The climate of Kashmeer, different from that of Hindoostan, is divided in to four seasons as in northern countries. In summer the artificial aid of fans is not requisite, as a cool refreshing breeze constantly blows over the valley from the moun-

To face page 444, *Vol. IV.*]

GENEALOGY OF THE KINGS OF KASHMEER.

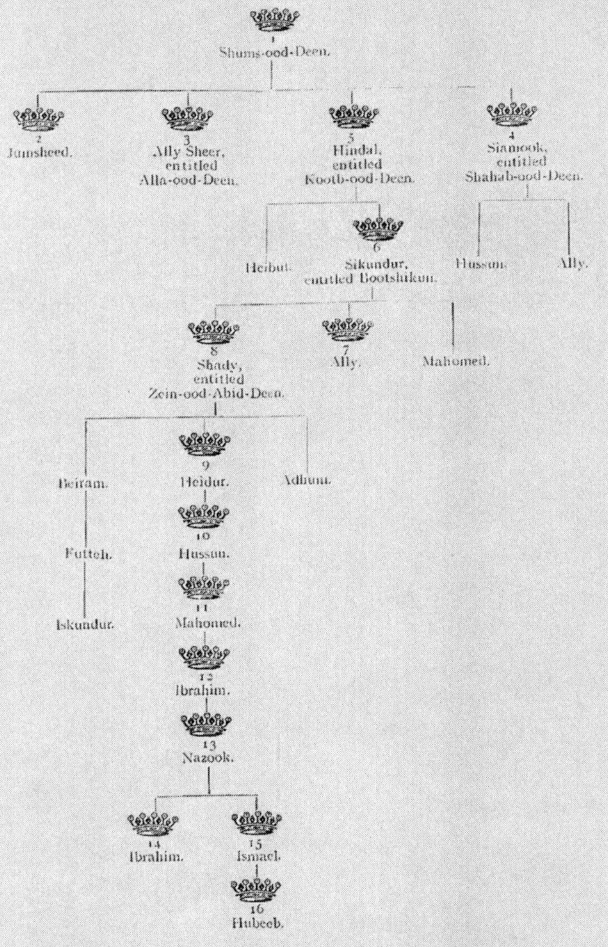

GENEALOGY OF THE DYNASTY OF CHUK.

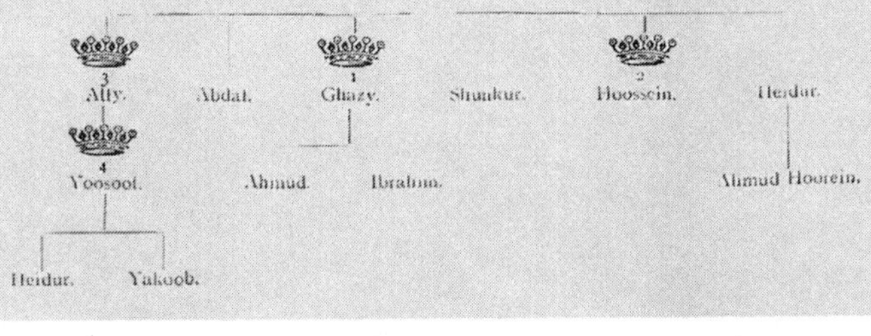

tains; while the piercing cold of winter is tempered by its proximity to those hills covered with snow, which shield this favoured spot from the bleak blasts that prevail in the neighbouring steppes of Thibet and Tartary. Fires are commonly used in houses in winter, and are often absolutely necessary.

The houses in Kashmeer are high, most of them having five stories: they are commonly built of ebony. The streets are paved with cut stone. They have no bazars as in India; and there appear to be no open shops, except those of money-changers and linen-drapers. The butchers, cooks, bakers, and grocers, used not to expose their goods as in other countries; and even now the artisans take in work and execute it in their own houses. Since the invasion of the Choghtay Tartars (Moguls), the people expose their articles for sale. Kashmeer has always been famed for its fruit: it abounds with mulberries, cherries, and other fruits of the north, all of which are of excellent quality. The former, both large and small, are in great plenty, but seldom eaten by the natives; as the trees are cultivated for the sole purpose of feeding the silk-worm, the produce of which is in great demand for exportation. Among the curiosities of Kashmeer are the Hindoo temples, the walls of which are composed of blocks of hewn stone laid so even upon each other, that they look, at a short distance, as if entirely one solid slab; they are neither cemented by mortar nor connected with leaden bars: many of the stones are from forty to sixty feet in length, and from three to fifteen feet in thickness and in width. Most of these eddifices are surrounded by square walls from five to six hundred feet in length, and in many parts nearly one hundred feet in height. The temples are situated within these squares, and generally erected upon a stone terrace supported massive solid columns, each of a single stone: the apartments within are small, being in general only about twelve feet square, and on the walls are sculptures of human figures, some representing mirth, others grief. In the middle of one of the temples is a throne cut out from the solid rock, on which is a minaret with a dome.* The temples in Kashmeer are, on the whole, so magnificent, that I find myself unequal to give an adequate idea of them; and I imagine there are no such buildings of the kind in the known world. Near to Kashmeer is a district called Tirma,† wherein, at the foot of a hill, are some hot springs; which, though dry all the year round besides, gush out from the rock boiling hot when the sun enters the sign Taurus; and during that period two or three mills are kept in motion by the rapidity of the stream; but after a certain time this phenomenon ceases, and the spring dries up.‡ The mouth of the cavity from whence it takes its rise has been frequently built up with hewn stones

* These appear to have been like the Cyclopeian cities of which we read, and which are occasionally discovered even in modern times.

† It is celebrated for its shawl-manufactory. The best are called Tirma shawls.

‡ Bernier visited the spring, and ascribes the phenomenon of its running only in the hot months to the melting of the snow at its source, which he conceives to be remotely situated within the mountains.

cemented with lead; but the force of the water has in the ensuing year invariably expelled them. There is a remarkable willow in the district of Nakm, which has grown to such a height that it would be difficult to shoot and arrow over it; notwithstanding which, if you shake one of its branches, the whole of the tree is put in motion. Among other curiosities in Kashmeer, is the reservoir of hot water at Dewsur. This piece of water is about sixty feet in length, around which are five shady trees overhanging it. The natives consider the spot sacred, and say that when one wishes to know if any undertaking will prosper, he must take an earthen vessel, fill it with rice, and having secured the mouth so that water may be excluded, throw it into the holy font: if on coming up the rice is boiled, it is deemed a fortunate omen, but unpropitious if otherwise. The vessel has been known not to appear for five years, but never longer; though it sometimes appears in five days, five weeks, or five months; but it usually gives the decision on the same day on which the person consulting the oracle throws in the vessel.

In the town of Alwur is the palace of Zein-ool-Abid-Deen, one of the kings of Kashmeer. This building is elevated on a terrace thirty feet high, and six hundred feet long. The edifice was originally built of the lapis lazuli, and is situated in a garden which has perhaps never been surpassed for beauty. This monarch also built a handsome palace in his capital of Serinuggur, twelve stories high; in some of which stories are fifty different apartments. The whole is of wood, and considered more beautiful than the Husht-Behisht at Tabreez (Tauris), or the Bagh-i-Ragh, the Bagh-i-Sufeed, or the Bagh-i-Shehry of Hirat, the Ray-Afzay, the Dilgoosha, or the Tuvuloody of Samarkand; all of which are reckoned magnificent of their kind. The author of the Zufur Nama gives the following account of this province:—Kashmeer being seldom visited by travellers is, consequently, but little known. It is, however, a beautiful valley situated in 33°54′ north latitude. It is bounded on the south by Hindoostan, on the east by Little Thibet, on the north by Kashghar, and on the west and south-west by the country of the Afghans. The plain in which it is situated is, from the best of my information, in length, from east to west, one hundred coss; and in breadth, from north to south, twenty-five coss. It is entirely surrounded by mountains, and is said to contain one thousand villages. In consequence of the coldness of the climate at one season of the year, none of the tropical fruits, such as dates, limes, or oranges, will flourish, but they are imported from the warmer countries contiguous. The town of Serinuggur, the capital of Kashmeer, like Bagdad, is situated on a river which flows through it, and is larger than the Tigris. This river takes its rise in the Kashmeer hills, at a spot called the spring of Deebur. Three bridges of boats, as at Bagdad, are thrown across, by which people pass. The river changes its name when it leaves Kashmeer, and in some places is called the Dundana, in others the Jumna, till passing through the Punjab it falls into the Chunab; which rolling under the walls of Mooltan joins the Indus, and eventually reaches the sea of

Ooman (the Indian ocean), near Tutta in Sind. This fortunate valley, situated in the midst of mountains, is by nature almost impregnable to an invading army. There are three roads which lead out of it. The first, towards Khorassan, is exceedingly difficult, and almost inpassable for cattle; but where these obstacles present themselves there are porters,* whose business it is to transport goods and merchandise on their backs to a spot where cattle may be laden and procured. The road to India is equally bad, but the best and most practicable is that towards Thibet. On this road, however, is a plain, on which no other vegetable grows but a poisonous grass that destroys all the cattle which taste of it, and, therefore, no horsemen venture to travel that route. The inhabitants of Kashmeer, at the period of the Mahomedan invasion, were worshippers of the sun, adoring it as the emanation of an invisible Deity. In the reign of Futteh Shah, King of Kashmeer, one Shums-ood-Deen arrived from Irak, and began to disseminate doctrines different from those of any other known sect. His followers assumed the title of Noorbukhsh (Illuminati), but the holy men of the Mahomedan faith succeeded in putting down these sectarians; so that at the present period, the author of this history, Mahomed Kasim Ferishta, having been at some pains to ascertain what religion the inhabitants of Kashmeer now profess, has reason to think that the common people are Mahomedans of the Hunefy persuasion, though the sol-

* Franklin describes the porters, and their mode of expediting travellers over the mountains and chasms in the rocks.

diery are commonly Sheeas, as well as some few of the learned men. The King of Little Thibet, contiguous to Kashmeer, is so prejudiced in favour of Sheeas that he allows no man of any other faith to enter his towns. The tribe of Chuk, in Kashmeer, contends, that Meer Shums-ood-Deen of Irak was a Sheea, and that he converted many thousands of people, after which he was crowned in the name of the twelve Imams; and that the Ahowita, the book containing the tenets of the Noorbukhsh religion, is not the composition of that venerable personage, but the production of some ignorant infidel. God only knows on whom we are to depend.

SHUMS-OOD-DEEN.

Shah Meer, a Mahomedan of the Hunefy persuasion, becomes minister to Raja Sena Dew of Kashmeer—he usurps the government.—The Raja dies.—The ministers marries his widow, and proclaims himself King under the title of Shums-ood-Deen—revises the laws—fixes the assessment on land at seventeen per cent. on the gross produce—resists the attacks of the Tartars of Kashghar—abdicates the throne.

In the compilation of this history of Kashmeer, I pass over the series of years during which the infidels reigned over that country, the details of which are neither interesting nor authentic.* I shall, therefore, proceed to the period of the first establishment of the Mahomedan faith, which only took place within the last two or three centuries. The original inhabitants of Kashmeer appear to have been followers of Bramha, until the year 715, during the reign of Raja Sena Dew, when a person called Shah Meer, coming to Kashmeer, was admitted into the service of that prince. This man traced his pedigree thus: Shah Meer,

A.H. 715.
A.D. 1315.

* Ferishta wrote to enlighten his countrymen on the progress of the Mahomedans in India. To him, therefore, the Hindoo histories, which are usually mingled with mythology, would not only have been uninteresting but for the most part unintelligible. We have no reason to believe the Mahomedans ever studied Sanscrit. Sheikh Feizy, in the time of Akbur, appears to be the only exception of whom we have any account.

the son of Tahir, the son of All, the son of Koorshasp, the son of Neekodur, a descendant from Arjoon an infidel; an account of whom is to be found in the Mahabharut, a work translated by order of Akbur Padshah.*

Shah Meer remained some time in the service of the Raja, and so entirely gained his confidence, that upon the death of Sena Dew he was appointed prime minister to his son and successor, Raja Runjun, and also succeeded to the high and responsible situation of governor to the next heir, Chundur Sein. Shortly afterwards, on the death of Raja Runjun, one Raja Anund Dew came from Kashghar,† and asserted his claim to the throne, as the nearest relation who had attained the age of manhood. Anund Dew also made Shah Meer his minister, and provided handsomely for his two eldest sons, Jumsheed and Ally Sheer. Shah Meer had also two other sons, called Siamook and Hindal. The whole of this family not only gained great ascendency over the Raja but also over the minds of the people, till the Raja, becoming jealous of their power, forbade them the court.

* Shah Meer, a Persian, is the son of Tahir, an Arab, the son of All (of whom it would be difficult to trace an origin), who is the son or Koorshasp, a fire-worshipper, the son of Neekodur, another fire-worshipper, a descendant from Arjoon Pandoo, one of the Hindoo princes of Hustnapoor (Dehly), who lived at a period beyond historical research. It is surprising that a person of Ferishta's sagacity should have overlooked the evident absurdity of this pedigree.

† It is probable this Hindoo prince had been compelled to seek safety in Kashghar, being the nearest heir to the crown of Sena Dew.

This exclusion drove Shah Meer and his sons into rebellion, when having occupied the valley of Kashmeer with their troops, most of the officers of the Raja's government also joined them. This insurrection soon brought the Raja to the grave, who died of a broken heart, in the year 727. His wife, Rany Kowla Devy, who wished to take the reins of government out of the hands of the stranger, wrote to Shah Meer, entreating him to place Chundur Sein, the son of Raja Runjun, on the throne; and Shah Meer not assenting, the Rany collected an army, and marched to oppose him; but she was defeated, and taken prisoner. It appears, however, that she afterwards consented, though reluctantly, to become the wife of Shah Meer, and to embrace the mahomedan faith; an event which secured to him the country which he had before nearly usurped. The second day after his marriage Shah Meer imprisoned his wife, and proclaimed himself King, under the title of Shums-ood-Deen, causing coin to be struck, and public prayers to be read, in his name, and he established the Hunefy doctrines of the Mahomedan religion throughout Kashmeer. On his accession, he took off the heavy imposts under which the people laboured, protected them from the annual exactions of Diljoo, chief of Kashghar, and fixed the assessment on land at seventeen per cent. on the gross produce.* The inroads and predatory incursions of the surrounding nations, especially

A. H. 727.
A. D. 1326.

*Would that Shums-ood-Deen's assessment had extended throughout India!

those of Diljoo, which during the reign of Sena Dew had laid waste the whole valley, were now checked by the valour of Shums-ood-Deen, who, upon one occasion, marched in to Kashghar, and severely retaliated on the Tatars for their former incursions.

During the reign of Shums-ood-Deen, he divided the inhabitants of Kashmeer into two classes, the one called Chuk, the other Makry, and would not entertain any man as a soldier who was not of one or other of these tribes. After having established certain other rules and regulations, he abdicated his throne in favour of his two elder sons, Jumsheed and Ally Sheer, and in the same year died, after a reign of twenty-three years, A. H. 750.

A. H. 750.
A. D. 1349.

JUMSHEED.

The elder son of Shums-ood-Deen, ascends the throne —his younger brother, Ally Sheer, puts in his claim to a share in the government.—Civil war, in which Jumsheed, the elder brother, is expelled, and shortly after dies.

On the death of Shums-ood-Deen, his eldest son, Jumsheed, aided by many of the nobles, ascended the throne; but shortly afterwards the soldiery being attached to his younger brother, Ally Sheer, induced him to proclaim himself at the town of Mednypoor. Jumsheed immediately marched with an army against his rival, and proposed to negotiate a peace rather than draw his sword against his brother; but Ally Sheer, aware he could gain nothing by an amicable settlement, made a night-attack on Jumsheed's army, and completely defeated it. After his retreat Jumsheed again returned to the charge, and took the town of Mednypoor, which was carried by storm, after a desperate resistance by the garrison, which was almost entirely cut to pieces. Ally Sheer, who had previously left Mednypoor, now returned with his army, and compelled Jumsheed to fly to Gujraj; while Siraj-ood-Deen, his prime minister, having invited Ally Sheer to Serinuggur, he was

there received as King. Jumsheed made no further efforts to regain his government,
A.H. 752. A.D. 1351. but shortly afterwards died, after a reign of fourteen months, A.H. 752.

ALLA-OOD-DEEN.

Ally Sheer is proclaimed King, under the appellation of Alla-ood-Deen.—A severe famine prevails.—He seizes several bramins, who endeavour to quit the kingdom.—A new law enacted, by which a wife who has been false to her husband forfeits all claim on his estate.—The town of Bukhshypoor built.—The King dies.

On the death of Jumsheed, Ally Sheer was proclaimed King, under the title of Alla-ood-Deen; and he appointed his younger brother, Siamook, to the office of minister. During his reign a severe dearth was experienced in Kashmeer, to which many people of both sexes fell victims. About the same period, some bramins endeavoured to emigrate to Kashghar; and the King, supposing it to be for the purpose of creating a revolt, caused them to be seized and confined for life. A law was enacted during this reign, by which no woman convicted of being false to her husband could inherit his property. Alla-ood-Deen founded the city of Allapoor, near the town of
A. H. 765. Bukhshypoor, where he died, after a
A. D. 1363. reign of thirteen years, A. H. 765.

SHAHAB-OOD-DEEN.

Siamook succeeds his brother, under the title of Shahab-ood-Deen—he marches an army into the Punjab, and invades Sind—on his return, he invades Pishawur—is met in the Punjab by the Raja of Nagrakote—returns to Kashmeer—builds the towns of Lutchmynuggur and Shahabpoor—his sons rebel against him, and are expelled the kingdom.—The King relents, and sends for his eldest son, Hussun, from Dehly; but dies before his arrival.

On the death of his elder brother, Siamook succeeded to the government, with the title of Shahab-ood-Deen. He was the first of the Kashmeer monarchs who appears to have marched for the purpose of making foreign conquests; for shortly after his accession he proceeded with an army through the Punjab, and encamped on the banks of the Indus, where he was opposed by the Jam of Sind, whom he completely defeated. The fame of this event reached even the provinces of Kandahar and Ghizny, whose governors were apprehensive he would next make a descent upon them. Having passed through the city of Ashnuggur, he invaded Pishawur, where he put to death many of the inhabitants who opposed him, and thence marched to the Hindoo Koosh; but finding those mountains inaccessible, he retraced his steps, and encamped on the banks of the Sutlooj. Here he was met by the Raja of

Nagrakote, who had returned from a plundering excursion into the Dehly country; and having come back laden with spoils, he placed them at the feet of Shahab-ood-Deen, and acknowledged fealty to that monarch. On his return to Kashmeer he was met by an envoy from the King of Little Thibet, who begged that he would not invade his country. Shortly after which he created his younger brother, Hindal, heir-apparent. His own two sons, Hussun Khan and Ally Khan, being outlawed and expelled the kingdom at the instigation of his second wife, fled to Dehly. And although he recalled the former before his death, Alla-ood-Deen died previously to his arrival at Jummoo.

The towns of Lutchmynuggur and Shahabpoor were built by this prince. He reigned for a period of twenty years, and died A. H. 785.

A. H. 785.
A. D. 1386.

KOOTB-OOD-DEEN.

Hindal succeeds his brother, and assumes the title of Kootb-ood-Deen—engages in war with the Raja of Lohkote. —The Prince Hussun, the eldest son of the late king, joins the Raja ; but they are both betrayed into the King's hands.—The Raja of Lohkote suffers death.—The Prince Hussun Khan is imprisoned.—The King's death.

On the death of Shahab-ood-Deen, his brother Hindal ascending the throne, assumed the title of Kootb-ood-Deen. This prince was remarkable for his extreme attention to public business, which he transacted in person, and generally with justice and moderation. In the latter part of his reign he deputed an officer with a force to reduce the fort of Lohkote, then in a state of revolt. After some severe actions on both sides the Kashmeer officer was killed; and Kootb-ood-Deen shortly after recalled his nephew, Hussun Khan, who, upon the news of his father's death, retired from Jummoo to Dehly. Hussun Khan having reached Kashmeer became so popular as to excite the King's jealousy, who resolved to secure his person ; but the Prince being warned of his danger by Ray Rawul, fled to Lohkote, and gave additional confidence to that rebellious garrison. Kootb-ood-Deen now seized the person of Ray Rawul, but he effected his escape, and joined Hussun Khan, with whom he concerted additional plans of revolt; but in their attempt to gain the surrounding zemindars, they were betrayed, seized, and sent to the King, who ordered Ray Rawul to be executed, and his nephew, Hussun Khan, to be imprisoned. In the latter part of his reign, it pleased God to give to the old King two sons, the one called Sugga and the other Heibut Khan. After having reigned for a period of fifteen years, Kootb-ood-Deen died in the year 799.

A.H. 799.
A.D. 1396.

SIKUNDUR BOOTSHIKUN,

OR,

ALEXANDER THE ICONOCLAST.

Subverts the Hindoo religion in Kashmeer, compelling all those bramins who refuse to embrace the Mahomedan faith to quit the country – encourages Mahomedan literature—prohibits the sale of vinous liquors, and exempts all manufactures from export duties.

KOOTB-OOD-DEEN was succeeded by his son Sugga, who assumed the title of Sikundur, and subsequently acquired the surname of Bootshikun, or the Iconoclast. In consequence of his tender years, his mother, the Dowager-queen, whose name was Soorut Rany, exercised the supreme control for a considerable period; during which time she caused her own daughter and son-in-law to be put to death, because she discovered they had entered into an intrigue against her son, the young king. The prime minister, Ray Makry, secretly poisoned the King's younger brother, Heibut Khan, for which, when the King heard of it, he swore he would take revenge at some future period, for the minister had too great power at that time to admit of his attempting it. Ray Makry, perceiving that he was suspected as the cause of Heibut Khan's death, proposed to the King to permit him to lead an army against Little Thibet, in order to evade his master's vengeance, and the latter, not without hopes that he might fall a victim in the expedition, allowed him to march. So far from it, however, Ray Makry succeeded in reducing the kingdom of Little Thibet, and added to his reputation and strength, so that he actually marched against Kashmeer to subvert the government. He was opposed on the Thibet frontier by the King in person, and sustained a total overthrow at the town of Nere. Ray Makry sought temporary safety in flight, but being subsequently seized, he was kept in confinement; in which situation he put an end to his existence by poison, while the King was occupied in making the proper arrangements for settling the newly acquired province of Thibet.

At this period, Ameer Teimoor (Tamerlane), being about to invade India, sent an ambassador with a present of an elephant to Sikundur in Kashmeer, who, on ascertaining the future intentions of that conqueror, sent word that he was ready to join him with his army at any place he might appoint. Ameer Teimoor replied, that he should require his services and assistance in the Punjab, after his return from the conquest of Dehly. On Ameer Teimoor reaching the Punjab, after having crossed the Sewalik mountains, Sikundur of Kashmeer marched to meet him; but on learning that he expected him to bring three thousand horses and one hundred thousand pieces of gold as an offering, he returned to his capital; and a serious offence might have been taken by Teimoor, had he not early explained himself, by denying his having ever entertained any such expectations. Sikundur now proceeded to pay his respects ; but in the mean time Teimoor crossed the Indus, and being in full march to Samarkand, the King of Kashmeer returned to Serinuggur. Sikundur gave great encouragement to literature, and rendered his capital as famous for learning as Irak and Khorassan.

In these days he promoted a bramin, by name Seeva Dew Bhut, to the office of prime minister, who embracing the Mahomedan faith, became such a persecutor of Hindoos that he induced Sikundur to issue orders prescribing the recidence of any other than Mahomedans in Kashmeer; and he required that no man should wear the mark on his forehead, or any woman be permitted to burn with her husband's corpse.* Lastly, he insisted on all the golden and silver images being broken and melted down, and the metal

* The consequence of prohibiting the marks on the forehead of Hindoos was deeply felt by our own government in the year 1806; that of prohibiting suttees has yet to be tribed. It is useful to have had experience of the effects produced in the one instance ; and a knowledge that the abolition of the latter practice was one of the measures adopted by a powerful Mahomedan king, in the midst of a Mahomedan population, by way of striking a death-blow at the Hindoo religion, is not without its value. In the progress of knowledge in India, every rational advance towards what we term civilisation in Europe may be fairly anticipated; but woe to the hand that ventures to tear aside with violence the veil of superstition, in that or in any other country, before its people are prepared to remove it through the efforts of reason, and the effects of liberal education !

coined into money. Many of the bramins, rather than abandon their religion or their country, poisoned themselves; some emigrated from their native homes, while a few escaped the evil of banishment by becoming Mahomedans. After the emigration of the bramins, Sikundur ordered all the temples in Kashmeer to be thrown down; among which was one dedicated to Maha Dew, in the district of Punjhuzara, which they were unable to destroy, in consequence of its foundation being below the surface of the neighbouring water. But the temple dedicated to Jug Dew was levelled with the ground; and on digging into its foundation the earth emitted volumes of fire and smoke,* which the infidels declared to be the emblem of the wrath of the Deity; but Sikundur, who witnessed the phenomenon, did not desist till the building was entirely rased to the ground, and its foundations dug up.

In another place in Kashmeer was a temple built by Raja Bulnat, the destruction of which was attended with a remarkable incident. After it had been levelled, and the people were employed in digging the foundation, a copper-plate was discovered, on which was the following inscription :—

"Raja Bulnat, having built this temple, was "desirous of ascertaining from his astrologers how

* The spontaneous fire-pits of Badkoo, or Bakou, on the western shores of the Caspian, will probably be in the recollection of most of my readers; and the same phenomenon at Kashmeer, in nearly the same parallel of latitude, ought not, therefore, to surprise us.

" long it would last, and was informed by them, " that after eleven hundred years, a king named " Sikundur would destroy it, as well as the other " temples in Kashmeer." The King was surprised, though vexed, that the Hindoo prophet should have predicted the truth, and declared, if they had placed the plate against the wall, he would have preserved the temple to belie the prophet. Having broken all the images in Kashmeer, he acquired the title of the Iconoclast, " Destroyer of Idols." Among other good* institutions of Sikundur was the prohibition of vending wine, and the relinquishment of all export duties. At length, in his old age, having contracted a violent fever, he sent for his three sons, Ameer Khan, Shady Khan, and Mahomed Khan, to whom he gave his blessing; and declaring Ameer Khan his successor, with the title of Ally Shah, he died A. H. 819, after a reign of nearly twenty years.

A. H. 819.
A. D. 1416.

* The civilised European will not very readily allow that the prohibition of the sale of fermented liquors could possibly be considered a *good* institution.

ALLY SHAH.

Succeeds his father on the throne—resolves to travel in foreign countries, and places his brothers, Shady and Mahomed, in charge of the government—is dissuaded from his intention, and endeavours to re-assume the throne—is opposed by his brothers, whom he defeats—is subsequently attacked, and overpowered by Shady Khan.—Death of Ally Shah.

In consequence of the veneration for the memory of Sikundur, his eldest son, Ameer Khan, was acknowledged King of Kashmeer, under the title of Ally, although as yet a minor. In the beginning of his reign, the whole of the affairs of the state devolved upon Seeva Dew Bhut, the prime minister. That statesman, with all the zeal of a convert, persecuted the few bramins who still remained firm to their religion; and by putting all to death who refused to embrace Mahomedism, he drove those who still lingered in Kashmeer entirely out of that kingdom. Shortly after the King's accession, the minister, being seized with a spitting of blood, died. Ally immediately appointed his younger brother, Shady Khan, to transact the business of the state in his stead; and in a very short time took the resolution of travelling in foreign countries. He, in consequence, associated his youngest brother, Mahomed Khan, with Shady Khan, and went to visit his father-in-law, the Raja of Jummoo,

This prince strongly dissuaded Ally Shah from prosecuting his design, and advised him by all means to re-assume charge of his government. His two brothers, however, flatly refused to acknowledge him. The Raja of Jummoo, therefore, in conjunction with the Raja of Rajoory, collected troops for the purpose of reinstating Ally Shah. Shady Khan was obliged to fly and take refuge at Seealkote, with Jusrut, the brother of Sheikha Gukkur, who had made his escape from Teimoor, and settled in the Punjab. Jusrut, espousing the cause of Shady Khan, attacked Ally Shah and defeated him; on which occasion it is asserted by some, that he fell into the hands of the conqueror, while others affirm, that having fled from the scene of action he was pursued by Shady Khan into Kashmeer, whence he was obliged to fly his country, and Shady Khan was crowned at Serinuggur in his stead. Ally reigned for a period of seven years, and his brother ascended the throne in the year 826.

A.H. 826.
A.D. 1422.

ZEIN-OOL-ABID-DEEN.

The King's character—rivalry of his three sons—civil contentions prevail throughout his reign—his death.

SHADY KHAN ascended the throne under the title of Zein-ool-Abid-Deen, and immediately sent a large force, with Jusrut Gukkur, to conquer the Punjab, and eventually to attack Dehly. Although unable to cope with the King of Dehly, Jusrut completely subdued the Punjab. Zein-ool-Abid-Deen, meanwhile, marched towards Thibet; and having subjected great part of that country to his authority, he associated his brother, Mahomed Khan, in the government, and determined to abolish the odious persecution adopted by Seeva Dew Bhut, the late prime minister. Preliminary to all other measures, he recalled the bramins who had been expelled, and caused a general toleration of all religions to be publicly notified. Temples were again permitted to be built, and each individual worshipped his God agreeably to the faith in which he was educated. The King superintended in person the construction of several canals and aqueducts; and established a code of laws which were engraved on copper-plates, and placed in all the public markets and halls of justice. His lenity was carried to such lengths, that he never put to death any individual of the state for theft or petty crimes; but robbers of all descriptions were fettered, and obliged to gain their livelihood by hard work, in the construction of public edifices. With all these regal virtues, he associated that domestic one so rarely practised, of strict fidelity to his only wife. He encouraged literature and the arts; and the science of music in his days was much improved by the different books written on the subject.* During his reign, the Raja of Thibet sent a pair of birds caught on the lake of Mansurowur. They were excessively beautiful, and were called the royal geese; and possessed the extraordinary faculty of separating particles of milk from water, if they were mixed, after which they used to drink each separately. †

In the beginning of his reign, Zein-ool-Abid-Deen nominated his brother Mahomed Khan to the office of prime minister, and associated him in the government; and after his death, he invested his son, Heidur, with all the dignities of his father. The King also honoured his two foster-brothers, Musaood and Sheeroo, with great confidence and high offices; but having had a dispute, Sheeroo

* The science of music seems to be almost lost in India, though there are books on the subject in the Sanscrit language, the stores of which are as yet scarcely penetrated by our best oriental scholars.

† The royal goose of lake Mansurowur is the swan of Europe; but we have never heard of its possessing the remarkable quality here alluded to.

put his elder brother, Musaood, to death, for which the King caused him to be tried and executed; but afterwards distributed a crore of rupees, equal to four hundred seers* of solid gold among the poor, for the salvation of his soul.

Zein-ool-Abid-Deen had three sons, Adhum, Hajy, and Beiram: the eldest he always disliked; and though the second was his favourite, yet he gave to the third a large tract of country, over which he appointed him governor. After arriving at the age of manhood, the three princes becoming jealous of each other evinced symptoms of direct hostility, and the King thought it better to divide them: he therefore placed the eldest son, Adhum Khan, at the head of an army to invade Thibet, and sent his second son against Lohkote. The former succeeded in overrunning Thibet, and returned, covered with glory, and laden with spoils, to the capital, while the favourite son, Hajy Khan, having subdued Lohkote, marched with his army against his father in Kashmeer. Zein-ool-Abid-Deen collected his troops, and in the mean time sent letters full of kindness and advice to his son, but without effect. He therefore marched with his army, and encamped on the plain of Buleel. Hajy Khan wished to decline attacking his father; but his troops commenced the action without orders, and many brave officers were killed on both sides. Adhum Khan behaved in the most gallant manner during the battle; and Hajy Khan, unable to with-

* Eight hundred pounds weight.

stand the brunt of the royal forces, after a severe engagement, which lasted from sunrise to sunset, was defeated, and fled to Heerpoor, whither he was followed by Adhum Khan, who was restrained by his father from further pursuit. Hajy Khan having collected a small part of his force at that place retreated to the town of Nere. Meanwhile the King, returning to his capital, caused a pillar to be built, round which were suspended the heads of those rebels who had been taken prisoners in the engagement. At this time he deputed Adhum Khan with a force to march and attack the fort of Gujraj; where having seized several of those persons who first promoted the insurrection, he executed them, and seized their property. This measure had the effect of inducing the few Gujraj soldiers who were with Hajy Khan to desert, and go over to Adhum Khan, whom the King at this period declared his representative, and heir to the throne. Adhum Khan ruled for a period of six years, when the inhabitants, suffering severely from his mal-administration, made their complaints to the King at Serinuggur, who sent repeated injunctions to his son. Adhum Khan paid no attention to these communications; but collecting a force at Kootb-ood-Deenpoor, he threatened to attack the capital. The King, however, made terms with him, and pointed out the province of Gujraj as a fit object to gratify his ambition. After his march thither, however, Adhum Khan was reduced to the humiliation of beseeching the assistance of his exiled brother, Hajy Khan. Instead of rendering it, Hajy Khan attacked his brother, but was defeated at the town of Seevapoor, which Adhum Khan laid in ashes. On receipt of this information, the King sent his whole army to attack Adhum Khan, when a severe action took place, in which the latter was defeated, many of his best soldiers killed in the retreat; and, of those who fled to the town of Seevapoor, on the Behut, upwards of three hundred were drowned. The King after this victory joined his army, and marched to Seevapoor, while Adhum Khan was encamped on the opposite bank of the Behut. At this period, Hajy Khan, the King's favourite son, arrived at the town of Baramoola. The King sent his youngest son, Beiram Khan, to congratulate him on his arrival. Adhum Khan now fled with his force by the route of Shahabad to the banks of the Neelab, and the King returned to his capital. At this time he proclaimed his favourite, and now penitent son, Hajy Khan, heir-apparent; who endeavoured to atone for his misconduct by assiduity and attention to his father in his old age. The King was, however, distressed to perceive with what indifference this young man received his advice, with respect to abstaining from the use of wine, and from other licentious habits. Hajy Khan, who conducted all public affairs, was now seized with a bloody flux, and the King's age prevented his transacting business. Seeing matters in this state, the chiefs sent secretly for Adhum Khan, who, appearing at the capital, visited the King, but he refused to forgive him. The Prince Adhum Khan, however, profited by his presence at the capital, and carried on an intrigue against his brother, wishing to be again acknowledged heir; a measure to which he could not induce the chiefs to accede without the King's assent. These chiefs daily urged his Majesty to declare in favour of one or other of his sons, which he obstinately declined; and it is supposed that the dissensions in the palace speedily put an end to the torments of his mind, as he died shortly after, in the sixty-ninth year of his age, A.H. 877, after a reign of nearly fifty-two years.

A. H. 877.
A. D. 1472.

Before the death of the King, the youngest prince, Beiram Khan, gained so much advantage over his eldest brother, Adhum Khan, that the latter, finding himself completely deserted, marched to Kootb-ood-Deenpoor, where he was frequently attacked by the King's forces, commanded by the two younger brothers, Hajy Khan and Beiram Khan; and being at length compelled to fly, he took the route of Badral to Hindoostan, while Hajy Khan's party was strengthened by the arrival of his son Hussun Khan; so that on the death of the King, Hajy Khan ascended the throne without opposition.

HEIDUR.

Hajy Khan ascends the throne, under the title of Heidur—becomes disreputable from his propensity to keep low company, and to indulge in vile pursuits—falls from the terrace of his palace, and is killed.

After the burial of the King, his second son, Hajy Khan, was crowned at Sikundurpoor by his brother Beiram, and assumed the title of Heidur. The new king's first act was to raise his son Hussun Khan to the office of Ameer-ool-Omra, bestowing upon him, at the same time, the district of Gujraj as an estate for life, and proclaiming him heir to the crown. He also conferred the district of Nakam on his younger brother, Beiram Khan, and dismissed with presents the several rajas who had come to Sikundurpoor to celebrate his coronation. His subsequent conduct, however, by no means realised the hopes which the nation had entertained of him. He gave himself up entirely to scandalous excesses, and permitted his ministers to exercise flagrant acts of injustice and oppression on his subjects. As an instance of which, he formed a disreputable connection with one Booby, a barber, who, becoming the medium of communication between the King and the people, took from them large bribes for his pretended or real services. Hussun Kechy,* an officer who

* An inhabitant of the province of Kech, contiguous to Mikran.

had distinguished himself in supporting the claims of Hajy Khan to the throne, suffered death through the intrigues of this miscreant. Affairs were in this state, when Adhum Khan, returning from Hindoostan to Jummoo, induced the raja of that province to support his claim; but in the mean time, an attack being made on Jummoo by a party of Moguls, Adhum Khan was killed by an arrow, which entering the mouth, penetrated his skull. When the King heard of the death of his brother he caused his body to be brought to Kashmeer, and buried in the vault with his father. In consequence of the shameful conduct of the King, the nobles intimated to his younger brother, Beiram Khan, their willingness to aid in deposing Heidur. This plot coming to the ears of Futteh Khan, the son of the late Adhum Khan, he resolved to try his fortune, and therefore marched to the capital, in order, as he stated, to lay at the King's feet the spoils which he had taken from the surrounding countries. Having appeared at court, however, without the royal permission, many of the courtiers whispered stories against him, which induced the King to refuse to see him, or to employ him in any public capacity. Such was the state of parties at the court, when the King, who was one evening carousing on the terrace of his palace, became much intoxicated. On attempting to go below, his foot slipped, and falling from a great height, he was killed, after a short and inglorious reign of fourteen months, A. H. 878.

A.H. 878.
A.D. 1473.

HUSSUN.

Ascends the throne—his title disputed by his uncle, Beiram Khan, who is taken prisoner, and suffers death.—Mullik Taj Bhut minister—gives great offence to the people.—Jehangeer Makry, an officer of rank, is induced to quit the court.—Death of the King.

HEIDUR was succeeded by his son Hussun, through the zealous assistance of one Ahmud Ahoo. Having imprisoned all his opponents, the King established his capital at Nowshehra, appointing Ahmud Ahoo his prime minister, with the title of Mullik Ahmud, and his son, Nowroze, to the office of Ameer-i-Dur.* The King's uncle, Beiram Khan, quitted Kashmeer in disgust, and went to India. Hussun renewed the laws and edicts of his grandfather, Zein-ool-Abid-Deen, which had fallen into disuse during the short reign of his father; but some malecontents, who disliked the new order of things, and expecting to derive advantage from a change in the government, invited Beiram Khan to return, persuading him that he would easily succeed in establishing himself on the throne. Beiram Khan marched from India by the route of Kurmar with this view,

* Ameer-i-Dur, or the Lord of the Entrance, answers to the Kapouchy Bashy of European Turkey.

and penetrating through the hills, arrived without opposition in the province of Gujraj. The King, who had moved towards Depalpoor, now proceeded to Seevapoor, in order to attack his uncle. He was persuaded by some of his officers to invade India; but his minister, Mullik Ahmud, recommended him to suspend all other objects till the force of his uncle was dispersed. A large detachment under Mullik Taj Bhut opposed Beiram Khan, who on his part expected to be joined by many officers of the Kashmeer army. In this hope he was disappointed; and in an action which took place at Looloopoor, Beiram Khan was defeated, and fled to Zeinpoor; and both he and his son being taken prisoners were brought before the King. Hussun ordered his uncle's eyes to be put out, and he only survived the operation three days. This rebellion being subdued, the King deputed his commander-in-chief, Mullik Taj Bhut, at the instigation of the Raja of Jummoo, to march with the united forces of Kashmeer and Jummoo, by the route of Rajoory, against the King of Dehly. Ajeet Dew, the Raja of Jummoo, having joined and taken command of the allied army, was opposed by Tartar Khan, the Dehly governor of the contiguous district, when the Kashmeer troops were defeated, and Tartar Khan, penetrating into Jummoo, sacked the town of Seealkote. At this period, the King had two sons born, the eldest (Mahmood Khan) he delivered over to Mullik Taj Bhut, and the youngest (Hoossein Khan) to Mullik Nowroze, the son of his minister Mullik Ahmud. Unfortunately, about this period, disputes arising between Mullik Ahmud and Mullik Taj Bhut, dissensions spread among the nobles, which eventually caused much bloodshed. These civil feuds went so far, that the combatants, on one occasion, absolutely entered the royal appartments with Mullik Ahmud at their head. Such a mark of disrespect induced the King to imprison the minister, who died in confinement of a broken heart. Syud Nasir, one of the King's favourites, who had been distinguished at the court of Zein-ool-Abid-Deen, was so banished, and he shortly afterwards died. The King, however, made the family of the latter some reparation, by inviting his son, Syud Hussun, from Dehly, and appointing him prime minister. That nobleman entirely disappointed the hopes entertained of him; for as soon as he obtained sufficient influence he exercised it in effecting the destruction of many of the other nobles, and in confining the commander-in-chief, Mullik Taj Bhut. Among other officers who fled from his persecution was Jehangeer Makry, who took protection in the fort of Lohkote. Shortly afterwards, the King being taken dangerously ill, by a relapse of his old complaint, the flux, and seeing that he could not long survive, sent for his minister, and thus addressed him :—"All my "own children are too young to be placed in "charge of the government; it is, therefore, my "wish, that one of my nephews, either Yoosoof "Khan, the son of Beiram Khan, or Futteh "Khan, the son of Adhum Khan, should succeed "me." The minister, pretending submission, promised obedience, and the King shortly afterwards died. But we are not informed of the exact time when this event happened, and, consequently, are unable to fix the precise limit of his reign, which, I am led to believe, must have been about nineteen years.

A.H. 891.
A.D. 1486.

MAHOMED.

Is raised to the throne of his father at the age of seven years.—Civil war ensues between a body of Syuds at the head of the government and the citizens of Serinuggur.—The Syuds defeated and expelled the kingdom.—Futteh Khan, the King's cousin, sets up his claim to the throne, and succeeds in usurping the crown.—Arrival of Shah Kasim Anwar Noorbukhsh.—Establishes a religious persecution.—Hindoo temples destroyed.—The tribe of Chuk become converts.—Futteh Khan divides his kingdom into three parts; giving to Mullik Atchy and Shunkur Zeina two portions.—The King Mahomed makes his escape to Hindoostan, and returning with his army recovers his empire—is expelled again by Futteh Khan.—Mahomed regains his throne.—Futteh Khan dies in India.—His son, Iskundur, sets up his claim to the crown, but is defeated.—Mahomed deposed by his minister, Mullik Atchy.—Ibrahim is raised to the government.—Nazook, the son of Ibrahim, is made an instrument of an intrigue to dethrone his father.—He marches with an army from Dehly for that purpose.—Battle of Sullah.—Nazook on the throne.—Mahomed restored for the fourth time.—Kamran Mirza enters Kashmeer; but is eventually expelled with heavy loss.—The Tartar forces from Kashghar, under Mirza Heidur Doghlat, invade Kashmeer.—The Tartars ravage the country for three months, till at length they are attacked, and a great battle is fought.—Peace concluded, and the Tartars return to Kashghar.—Two comets are seen in Kashmeer.—A severe famine.—Death of the King.

IMMEDIATELY after the burial of the King, his prime minister, Syud Hussun, elevated the Prince Mahomed (the late monarch's eldest son) to the throne of Kashmeer, at the age of seven years. On which occasion the contents of the royal treasury, together with the robes and armoury, being displayed before him, the child put aside the jewels and splendid apparel, and laid hold of a bow; from which circumstance a happy omen was drawn that the young king would be a great warrior. The minister, Syud Hussun, being proclaimed regent, prevented any person from having communication with him; which giving offence to the other nobles, they obtained the support of Pursaram, the Raja of Jummoo, and put Syud Hussun and thirty other Syuds to death; after which, having crossed the Behut and broken the bridge, they encamped on the opposite bank of the river, and collected a force. Syud Mahomed, the son of the regent, and the King's uncle,* mustered the royal guards, and proceeded to the palace for his protection. The inhabitants of the city were desirous of releasing Yoosoof Khan, the son of Beiram Khan, and placing him on the throne, or, indeed, any member of the royal family who had attained manhood, and who was able both to defend his own rights, and protect his subjects from the horrors of another civil war. The Syud party, on obtaining the first intimation of the feeling of the people, rushed into the prison of the unfortunate Yoosoof, headed by Syud Ally Khan, and murdered him. Their hands were yet reeking with his blood, when they encountered Mullik Taj Bhut; who, boldly upbraiding them for their conduct, also fell a victim to their fury on

* The King's mother was the sister of Syud Mahomed.

the spot. Syud Ally Khan, being now at the head of a large body of Syuds, opposed the opposite party, and some severe actions occurred. During these dissensions the town became much infested by thieves. In this state of affairs the Syud dug a ditch round the city. They confiscated the property, and levelled the houses, of those citizens who joined their enemies on the opposite side of the river; while Jehangeer Makry, who had previously sought safety in the fort of Lohkote, joined them, in spite of advantageous offers made to him by the Syuds. Shortly afterwards, Dawood, the son of Jehangeer, crossed the bridge with a small party of the insurgents, and attacked the Syuds; but the most of the assailants falling victims, their heads were elevated on the public minarets, in view of those encamped on the opposite bank of the river. The Syuds, on the following day, made an attack on the lines of the popular party; but they were vigorously opposed by the citizens in their attempt to cross the bridge of boats, on which many of the Syud party were slain; till at length, the bridge giving way, those who were on it at the time were drowned. The Syuds now deputed a messenger to Tartar Khan, governor of the Punjab, for assistance; who, in consequence, sent a considerable force towards the capital of Kashmeer: but on its arrival at Bhimbur it was attacked by Howns, the raja of that place, and completely dispersed. Meanwhile the insurgents kept the Syuds on the alert, and closely besieged them for two months in Serinuggur, till at last they resolved on storming that city; for which purpose they crossed the Behut by three separate boat-bridges. The attacking party was opposed by the Syuds, who were overpowered by numbers, and sought safety behind the ditch within the walls; whither they were so closely pursued by the citizens, that the latter succeeded in entering and setting fire to the town, and slew upwards of two thousand of the Syud party. The Kashmeeries now proceeded in a body to the palace of the young king, and with their own hands placed the crown on his head, in

A.H. 892. A.D. 1486.

the year 892. They then insisted on the banishment of Syud Ally Khan and the rest of the Syuds; and also on the dismissal of Pursaram, Raja of Jummoo, from the King's councils. Having obtained these objects, it remained to be seen what could be done to satisfy their expectations of personal advantage. Each Kashmeery demanded some preferment for his services, which the state being unable to grant, the prospect of another civil war presented itself. At this period Futteh Khan, (the son of Adhum Khan, and grandson of Zein-ool-Abid-Deen,) who had arrived at Rajoory, reached Jalindur, in order to take advantage of circumstances. He was joined by many malecontents, and marched towards Kashmeer. Futteh Khan expected to have been supported by Jehangeer Makry; but after the success of his party, that officer joined the King, and accompanied him with an army to oppose the invader. Futteh Khan, meanwhile, proceeded by the route of Heerpoor as far as the town of Oodown, and encamped, with a marsh covering his front; in which position he was attacked by a body of Kashmeer troops, which were repulsed and put to flight; but the main body of the King's troops behaved with so much intrepidity, particularly the King's personal guard, with Jehangeer Makry at their head, that Futteh Khan was in the end defeated, with the loss of fifty men, and was nearly taken prisoner. Meanwhile a report prevailed through the camp that the King had fallen into the enemy's hands; which induced Jehangeer Makry to give up farther pursuit, and to return to camp, where he found all safe. Futteh Khan's army being dispersed, the King returned to the capital; deputing Mullik Yar Bhut to lay waste the country of the Raja of Rajoory, who had afforded Futteh Khan an asylum in his dominions. Futteh Khan now disappeared for some time; but at length collecting a force in the district of Purmgola, he marched towards Serinuggur. Jehangeer Makry proceeded with the royal army to a place called Gukkur, in the district of Makam; but his attention was again directed towards the capital, on hearing that two state-prisoners, named Suffy and Runga Ray, as well as others confind at Serinuggur, had made their escape. In this conjuncture, Jehangeer Makry resolved to accomplish by stratagem what he thought would be doubtful in fair battle: he therefore held out promises and advantages to the Raja of Rajoory, to induce him to join the King's troops. The intrigue succeeded: Futteh Khan was compelled to retreat to the south, but he attacked and overran the district of Jummoo; and collecting more soldiers, returned to Kashmeer a third time. At this period, the King and Jehangeer Makry recalled

the Syud exiles. After their arrival an action took place between the King's army and that of Futteh Khan, in which both sides displayed great courage, but the pretender was defeated. He was, however, soon again in the field; and having attacked the royalists, gave them a total overthrow. The King, on this occasion, was left without a single attendant; and his general, Jehangeer Makry, being severely wounded, sought safety in flight. Mahomed, thus abandoned even by his servants, was seized by the zemindars of Kashmeer, on his return to the capital, and delivered into the hands of Futteh Khan, after a reign of nearly eleven years. From that period he remained a close prisoner, receiving as mild
A.H. 902. treatment as was consistent with his
A.D. 1496. situation.

On the imprisonment of Mahomed, Futteh Khan, assuming the reins of government, and being formally crowned, was acknowledged King of Kashmeer in the year 902; and appointed Suffy and Runga Ray, the two officers who had lately made their escape, his ministers. About this time, one Meer Shumsood-Deen, a disciple of Shah Kasim Anwur, the son of Syud Mahomed Noorbukhsh, arrived in Kashmeer from Irak. Futteh Khan made over to this holy personage all the confiscated lands which had lately fallen to the crown; and his disciples went forth destroying the temples of the idolaters, in which they met with the support of the government, so that no one dared to oppose them. In a short time many of the Kashmeeries, particularly those of the tribe of Chuk, became converts to the Noorbukhsh tenets. The persuasion of this sect was connected with that of the Sheeas; but many proselytes, who had not stasted of the cup of grace,* after the death of Meer Shums-ood-Deen, reverted to their idols. Religious disputes went to such lengths among the nobles of the state, that they even drew their swords in the King's presence, and slew each other in the hall of audience. During these broils, Mullik Atchy and Shunkur Zeina, two Kashmeer chiefs, having released the late king, Mahomed, carried him to Baramoola, where they intended to raise a force, and replace him on the throne; but as he showed no symptoms of that energy and resolution necessary to carry their project into effect, they determined to deliver him over again into Futteh Khan's hands. Mahomed, discovering their project, made his escape in the night. Futteh Khan now divided his kingdom

* In India, as well as in most Mahomedan countries, the people have their domestic tutelary saints, at whose shrine, after their death, one or more of their disciples reside to receive or to make proselytes; on which occasion the devotee, after receiving *absolution* and hearing a lecture, is sometimes required to repeat from memory a particular creed, and is then initiated among the disciples of the shrine by sipping wine out of a vessel called the miraculous cup, or cup of grace. These saints, in all parts of the East, have great influence over their followers; but no where is that power more extensive than in India, and in no part of India, I believe, is the devotion so complete as throughout the Deccan, from the Nurbudda to Ceylon. The influence of the saints, or fakeers, has frequently been felt in our native army, and may, if not carefully watched, be experienced again, in the most fatal manner.

into three principalities; and having secured one portion for himself, delivered over the other two to Mullik Atchy and Shunkur Zeina. On the former person he bestowed the title of Wuzeer Mootluk, and on the latter, that of Divan-i-Kool. Such was the state of affairs for some years, when at length Ibrahim, the son of Jehangeer Makry, who had been appointed to his father's situation in the army, went to Hindoostan, and returned to Kashmeer, bringing with him the exiled king, Mahomed, to re-establish his claims. An action ensued at Baramoola, which terminated in favour of Mahomed; and Futteh Khan, being compelled to fly, took the route of Heerpoor to Hindoostan.

A.H. 911. A.D. 1505. After the defeat of Futteh Khan, which happened when he had held the reins of government for ten years, Mahomed re-ascended the throne; and nominating Ibrahim Makry to the office of minister, he proclaimed Iskundur Khan, a lineal descendant from Shahab-ood-Deen, heir-apparent. On this occasion he put to death the sons of Mullik Atchy, who were kept at the capital as pledges for their father's behaviour by Futteh Khan. Some time after the second accession of Mahomed, Futteh Khan returned to Kashmeer at the head of a large army; and Mahomed, not having the means or the courage to oppose him, fled, and left the government in the possession of his rival, A. H. 912. A. D. 1506. after a short reign of about ten months, A. H. 912.

Futteh Khan re-assumed his functions as King

of Kashmeer without opposition, and appointed one Jehangeer, of the tribe of Budra, his minister of state, and Shunkur Zeina his minister of finance. After the second expulsion of Mahomed, that monarch sought protection at the court of Sikundur Lody of Dehly, who sent a large force to replace him on his throne; and on the march to Kashmeer he was joined by Jehangeer Budra, who deserted Futteh Khan on account of some slight imposed on him. The army of Mahomed entering Kashmeer by the route of Rajoory, was opposed by the forces of Futteh Khan, commanded by Jehangeer Makry, who with his son were both killed in the action. The Kashmeer troops were defeated, and Futteh Khan again compelled to fly to Hindoostan, where he subsequently died, after his second reign, which lasted for little more than a year.

A.H. 913.
A.D. 1507.

On the third accession of Mahomed, he placed in close confinement Shunkur Zeina, the late minister of finance, retaining Mullik Atchy in his office of minister of state. After being firmly seated on his throne, he put to death many of the nobles of the court of Futteh Khan, among whom were Suffy and Runga Ray; Shunkur Zeina also eventually died in prison.

A. H. 922.
A. D. 1516.

In the year 922, the body of Futteh Khan was brought by his servants from Hindoostan into Kashmeer; and Mahomed went out on foot, attended by a solemn mourning party, to meet it, and followed it to the grave, when it was interred in the family vault of the kings of Kashmeer.

As Mullik Atchy had, during his ministry confined Ibrahim Makry at Serinuggur, his son, Abdal Makry, in the year 931 (being then in India), espoused the cause of Iskundur Khan, the son of the late Futteh Khan, and marched an army for the purpose of placing him on the throne. The King, supported by Mullik Atchy, moved to Alwurpoor, in the district of Fankul, to oppose the invader, who being defeated was compelled to throw himself into the fort of Nakam, wherein he was closely besieged by the Kashmeer army under Mullik Atchy. At this period many of the Kashmeery officers, dissatisfied with Mullik Atchy, who exercised regal power, were on the point of going over to Iskundur Khan, when the minister deputed his son with a force to attack him; and although the minister's son fell in the action, Iskundur was defeated, and evacuating the fort, sought safety in flight: Nakam was accordingly occupied by Kashmeer troops, and the Makry army dispersed. After the return of Mahomed to Kashmeer the third time, the courtiers succeeded in alienating his esteem from his minister; which induced Mullik Atchy to withdraw from court, and settle at Rajoory, where he completely gained the good will of the surrounding rajas. Some time after, Iskundur Khan procuring aid from the Emperor Babur of Dehly, conquered the province of Lohkote. Mullik Yar Chuk, the brother of Mullik Atchy, however, having attacked and made him prisoner, brought him to the King, who caused his eyes to be put out,

A.H. 931.
A.D. 1524.

The conduct of the minister's brother on this occasion restored the confidence of the King to the late minister, whom he sent for, and replaced in his situation. Mullik Atchy conceived that the King had not kept terms with his brother, by putting out the eyes of Iskundur Khan; and in consequence, having, in the first instance, deprived him of most of his personal favourites by imprisoning them, he subsequently deposed the King, and sent him to Lohkote in confinement; after which he raised his son, the Prince Ibrahim, lately arrived from Dehly, to the throne of Kashmeer, in the beginning of the year

A.H. 932.
A.D. 1525.

932, when Mahomed had reigned nineteen years.

The Prince Ibrahim now ascended the throne, and Mullik Atchy retained the office of minister. At this period, Abdal Makry, who had been driven from his country by the intrigues of Mullik Atchy, fled to Hindoostan, where having obtained a situation in the household of Babur Padshah of Dehly, he induced that monarch to attempt the conquest of Kashmeer. Babur accordingly ordered an army, under Sheikh Ally Beg and Mahmood Khan, to be placed at the disposal of Abdal Makry, who was accompanied by Nazook, the son of Ibrahim, King of Kashmeer, then living with his relatives in Dehly, in order that by proclaiming his title to the throne he might have some plea for invading the country, and prevent that resistance which he knew would be made if the Kashmeeries supposed that the throne was to be filled by a stranger. On information of the approach of the Dehly army to place Nazook on the throne, Mullik Atchy Chuk accompanied the King Ibrahim, who proceeded in person to the town of Sullah, in the district of Fankul, where the two armies opposed each other.

A.H. 932.
A.D. 1525.

In this battle the Kashmeer troops lost many men, and were eventually defeated, the King and his minister both flying from the field. Mullik Atchy reached the capital, whence he was subsequently expelled; but we have no account of the fate of Ibrahim on that occasion. His reign lasted for the short space of eight months.

After the battle of Sullah, the Dehly army marched to Serinuggur, and placed on the throne Nazook, the son of Ibrahim, and grandson to Mahomed, who was at that period in confinement; and the people, fearful lest the government should fall into the hands of the King of Dehly, received their new monarch with every demonstration of joy. Having left Serinuggur, he proceeded to Nowshera, his capital, and appointed Abdal Makry his minister. This chief having pursued Mullik Atchy to the town of K'hulnagry, returned and partitioned out the several distircts of Kashmeer among the numerous officers of the army; and after rewarding the services of the officers and soldiers of the King of Dehly, permitted them to return to Hindoostan.

On the occupation of Kashmeer by Abdal Makry, he wrote to Mullik Atchy, condemning him for confining the old king, Mahomed; and having sent for that monarch from Lohkote, reinstated him in the government a fourth time. Seven years

after which, in the year 939, he declared
A.H. 939. A.D. 1532. his grandson, Nazook, heir-apparent. In this year, also, Babur Padshah of Dehly dying, was succeeded by his son Hoomayoon. Mahomed had no sooner ascended the throne again, than Mullik Atchy, who had fled from the battle of Sullah, made his appearance at the head of a body of the Kashmeer highlanders, on the plain of Kohka. Here he was opposed by Abdal Makry, and being defeated, fled to Hindoostan. At this period, Mirza Kamran, brother of Hoomayoon Padshah of Dehly, was governor of the Punjab. This prince being joined by Sheikh Ally Beg and Mahmood, who left the court of Kashmeer in disgust, was prevailed on to send a force, under the orders of Mahram Beg, to conquer that kingdom. The Kashmeer troops could not be brought to oppose the Moguls, but fled to the hills; while the Punjabies, laying waste the fields, and burning the towns, put to death all the inhabitants who fell in their way. Abdal Makry, who at first thought this invation had been undertaken at the instance of Mullik Atchy, being now convinced of the contrary, sent for him and the chiefs of the Chuk and Makry tribes, who mtually exchanged the most solemn oaths to unite in one common cause. The junction of Mullik Atchy, who had great influence over his countrymen, at such a moment, enabled the King to collect a respectable force, with which he completely defeated the Punjabies, and expelled them the country. After the departure of the Punjab army, Mullik Atchy became disgusted with the

duplicity and pride of Abdal Makry, and was on the point of abandoning the King's councils, and proceeding to Hindoostan, when in

A.H. 939.
A.D. 1532.

the year 939 Syud Khan, King of Kashghar, deputed his son, Sikundur Khan, with one Mirza Heidur Doghlat, to march south at the head of an army of twelve thousand men. These troops invaded Kashmeer by the route of Thibet and Lar. The inhabitants fled, panic-struck, to the mountains, while the merciless Tartars laid waste the country, sacked the towns, and levelled, with barbarous malignity, many of the magnificent palaces which the kings of Kashmeer had constructed. The Tartars, meeting with no opposition, loaded themselves with spoil, and put to death such unfortunate wretches as they discovered hid in holes or caves. This devastation continued for upwards of three months, when Abdal Makry, Mullik Atchy Chuk, and other officers, who had taken refuge in the town of Chukdura, finding their retreat insecure, retreated to Baramoola, living occasionally in the hills. They at last resolved to attack the Tartars, which they did with great disparity of numbers. On this occasion the Kashmeeries lost many valuable officers, and the Tartars suffered equally. The former were at one time on the point of giving way, when Abdal Makry and Mullik Atchy Chuk appearing in the ranks, their example induced their countrymen to rally, and they succeeded in repelling the last charge of the Tartars. Night closed the scene, and the morning presented the opposed armies employed in burying their dead, which amounted to many thousands. After this battle a truce was agreed on, and a peace ensued, on which the King of Kashmeer consented to give his daughter in marriage to the young Tartar prince Sikundur, who then returned to Kashghar. In the year 940

A.H. 940.
A.D. 1533.

two comets appeared in Kashmeer; and a severe famine succeeded, which compelled many of the inhabitants to fly their country, during a period of ten months, while the dearth lasted. The old enmity of Abdal Makry and Mullik Atchy Chuk was again renewed; but the former having most influence at the capital, the latter was obliged to quit, and retire to Zeinpoor. The King did not long survive. He was seized with a fever; and after

A.H. 942.
A. D. 1535.

lingering a few months, died, in the year 942, after a checkered and interrupted reign of fifty years.

IBRAHIM.

Is acknowledged King—is expelled the throne—dies.

It appears from the Towareekh Kashmeery that Ibrahim, who had formerly usurped the crown from his father Mahomed, and had escaped during the battle of Sullah, in the year 932, now returned, and was acknowledged king. During his reign we find him alternately the passive pageant of royalty in the hands of his two ministers, Mullik Atchy Chuk and Abdal Makry. Amid the dissensions of these two chiefs, Abdal Makry, collecting an army, marched against the capital; and his rival, accompanied by the King, defeated him in a battle which took place near
A. H. 947. the mountains, and compelled him to
A. D. 1540. fly to Gujraj. At length Ibrahim died
in the year 947.

NAZOOK.

Ascends his father's throne.—The dissensions between the races of Chuk and Makry continue.—Abdal Makry invites Hoomayoon Padshah to invade Kashmeer—accompanies Mirza Heidur Doghlat with a force—subverts the government of the Chuks.—Abdal Makry dies, leaving Mirza Heidur Doghlat at the head of the state.—Atchy Chuk procures the aid of Sheer Shah, King of Dehly.—The Hindoostan troops defeated.—Mirza Heidur removes the seat of government from Serinuggur to Indrakote—invades little Thibet—eventually conquers both great and little Thibet on the north, and the districts of Pugly and Rajoory on the south.—Mirza Heidur is killed in an endeavour to suppress an insurrection.—An oligarchy succeeds, which, for form's sake, acknowledges Nazook as King.—Shortly after which he is deposed.

IBRAHIM was succeeded by his son Nazook. This prince had scarcely ascended the throne three months when he was expelled by the army of Hoomayoon Padshah of Dehly; which invading Kashmeer conquered that province, as we shall proceed to relate.*

A.H. 948.
A.D. 1541.

In the year 948, Hoomayoon Padshah being defeated by Sheer Shah, King of Bengal, fled his country, and retreated

* Ferishta has prefixed, at the head of this section, the name of Mirza Heidur Doghlat, who so long ruled Kashmeer, and to whom we are chiefly indebted for this history; but as Nazook, the lineal heir, subsequently regained his throne, and survived Mirza Heidur, I have considered his rule as a mere usurpation.

to Lahore ; when Abdal Makry, Zungy Chuk, and many other Kashmeery nobles, wrote letters, inviting him to the conquest of their country. These letters were sent by one Mirza Heidur Doghlat, who was accordingly authorised to carry into effect this project. On reaching Mein, Mirza Heidur was joined by Abdal Makry and Zungy Chuk, from whence they proceeded to Rajoory, with a force not exceeding altogether four thousand horse. Mullik Atchy Chuk, then virtually ruler of Kashmeer, advanced with a force of three thousand cavalry and fifty thousand infantry to the Kurmul pass, of which he took possession. Mirza Heidur, on receiving intimation of this movement, countermarched, and took the route of Punnuj. Atchy Chuk, conceiving that pass sufficiently protected by its intricacies to prevent the approach of cavalry, took no precautions to render it more difficult, but he was mistaken ; for the Hindoostan army having penetrated the mountains made their first appearance at the city of Serinuggur, which they sacked. Abdal Makry and Zungy Chuk now assumed the reins of government, and immediately assigned the revenues of some districts solely for the payment of the army. Shortly after which, Abdal Makry, who was now old, having made over his children to the care of Mirza Heidur, died. Atchy Chuk, who found that he could not make head against Mirza Heidur, went in person to Hindoostan, and solicited the assistance of Sheer Shah, who had at that period assumed the title of King of Hindoostan. That monarch deputed Hoossein Khan Sheerwany, with five thousand horse and two war-elephants, to accompany Atchy Chuk. Mirza Heidur and Zungy Chuk, hearing of the approach of the Dehly army, moved out to oppose it. The two forces met between the towns of Dhunuj and Gava, where an action took place, when Mullik Atchy being defeated, fled to Purumgola, and the Dehly army was entirely routed.

In the year 950, Mirza Heidur chang-
A.H. 950. ed his capital from Serinuggur to In-
A.D. 1543. drakote, and at the same period Zungy Chuk, becoming suspicious of his colleague, left the capital and joined Atchy Chuk, when they both collected a force and marched to Serinuggur, for the purpose of subverting the government of Mirza Heidur. Here they were joined by Beiram, the son of Zungy Chuk, who had made his escape from the capital. Mirza Heidur deputed Bundgan Koka and Khwaja Hajy Kashmeery to oppose the confederates, who were completely defeated, and fled to Purumgola.

Mirza Heidur, having left Bundgan Koka as his lieutenant in Kashmeer during his absence, proceeded with an army for the purpose of invading Thibet, where he reduced the district of Looshoo and several others; and on his return being opposed by Zungy Chuk on the fron-
A.H. 952. tier, in the year 952, the latter was
A.D. 1545. killed, and his son, Ghazy Khan, taken prisoner. During the absence of Mirza Heidur, Atchy Chuk, and his son Mahomed Chuk, died of an epidemic disease, so that the most formidable rivals of Mirza Heidur were thus removed;

A.H. 954. A.D. 1547. In the year 954, and ambassador from Kashghar joined Mirza Heidur at Lar.

At this period, Khwaja Beiram, the son of Musaood Chuk, who having asserted his independence had kept possession of Gujraj for the last seven years, was induced to accept of the friendship of Jan Boozoorg Mirza, who took the most solemn oaths to abstain from attacking him; but being one day in his company, he put Beiram Chuk to death, and brought his head to Mirza Heidur at Lar, conceiving by this measure to gain his favour. Abdy Zeina, one of Mirza Heidur's officers, concluding that the act had been preconcerted with Mirza Heidur, quitted the court, and indignantly declared his detestation of the man who could commit murder in violation of his oath. Mirza Heidur, however, denied any connivance or participation in the deed. Shortly afterwards, Mirza Heidur proceeded for the purpose of attacking the country of Kishtwar, and deputed Bundgan Koka with other officers in command of the advance-guard of the army. This detachment made one march from Charloo to Dote, a distance of three days' journey, came up with the Kishtwar army, and encamped on the opposite bank of the river. Neither army could cross, and a sharp discharge of arrows and musketry was kept up, though without much effect. Some stragglers from Mirza Heidur's camp lost their road, and joined the advance at Wary; but upon their arrival there, a violent gale of wind came on, and raised the dust of the whole plain. At this moment a small detachment of the Kishtwar army then in the town, taking advantage of the circumstance, sallied and attacked the invaders. Bundgan Koka and twenty-five officers of note were killed, and the detachment made the best of its way to join Mirza Heidur.

Sortly after, in the year 955, Mirza
A.H. 955. A.D. 1548. Heidur invaded Little Thibet, and not only succeeded in conquering that country, but subsequently added Great Thibet, Rajoory, and Pugly to his dominions.

Moolla Kasim was nominated to the government of Little Thibet, Moolla Hussun to that of Great Thibet, Mahomed Nuzur to that of Rajoory, and Dawood Ally to the province of
A.H. 956. A.D. 1549. Pugly. In the year 956, Mirza Heidur marched against the fortress of Deebul, where he was met by Adum Khan Gukkur, who endeavoured to mediate a reconciliation between Mirza Heidur and Dowlut Chuk, the nephew of the late Atchy Chuk ; but Dowlut Chuk, offended at the reception he met with, left the meeting abruptly, and even carried away the elephant which he had brought to present to Mirza Heidur. Shortly after which, Mirza Heidur returned to Kashmeer. At a subsequent period, Dowlut Chuk, and Ghazy Khan Chuk, the son of Zungy Chuk, who had lately been released from confinement, together with Yehya Chuk, connected themselves with Heibut Khan Neazy, who having fled from Sulim Shah of Dehly, now took refuge at Rajoory. Heibut Khan was pursued by Sulim Shah in person till he reached the confines

of the district of Nowshehra, when the former having deputed Syud Khan Neazy to crave his mercy, Sulim Shah consented to be reconciled, on condition of Heibut Khan sending his mother and son as hostages for his good behaviour into the royal camp; after which he fell back on Bhimbur, in the district of Seealkote. The Kashmeer partisans, who had joined Heibut Khan at Rajoory, prevailed on him to go to Deebul, and endeavoured to persuade him to depose Mirza Heidur. He not only refused his assent, but sent a bramin to inform Mirza Heidur of their intention. Heibut Khan moved to the town of Subzeea, in the district of Jummoo, where the Chuk confederacy, having intimation of his treachery, left him. Ghazy Khan Chuk went direct to the capital, and abandoning his associates joined Mirza Heidur, while the rest, quitting Kashmeer, retired to the court of Sulim Shah, King of Dehly. In the year 957, Mirza Heidur deputed Khwaja Shums-ood-Deen with a large and valuable present of saffron to the King of Dehly, who sent Yaseen Khan Afghan as ambassador, to accompany Khwaja Shums-ood-Deen on his return to Kashmeer, with other presents, consisting of horses and some of the finest Indian muslins, to Mirza Heidur, who having returned to Yaseen Khan Afghan a quantity of saffron with some beautiful shawls, despatched him back to his court.

A.H. 957. A.D. 1550.

In the year 958, Mirza Heidur appointed Kiran Bahadur, a commander of Mogul horse, to the government of

A.H. 958. A.D. 1551.

Bheerbul. This measure gave great offence to the inhabitants, who attacked him, and resisted his authority. Mirza Heidur, in order to support his lieutenant, put himself at the head of the Moguls, and was killed by an arrow in a night-attack made upon his camp, and the Moguls were defeated. Thus fell Mirza Heidur Doghlat,
A.H. 958. A.D. 1551. in the tenth year after his accession to the government of Kashmeer, in the year 958.

After the death of Mirza Heidur, and the defeat of the Moguls, the whole kingdom was thrown into confusion. The leading men, however, having formed a kind of administration, divided the territory into three principalities or districts; that of Dewsur fell to the lot of Dowlut Chuk, that of Dhunuj to Ghazy Khan Chuk, and Gujraj to Yoosoof Chuk and Beiram Chuk, while Abdy Zeina remained at the capital, and was virtually ruler of the whole; though, for form's sake, Nazook, the son of Ibrahim, and grandson of the late Mahomed, was seated on the throne of Kashmeer.

A.H. 959. A.D. 1552. In the beginning of the year 959 the Kashmeer officers, after having each secured a portion of the kingdom, became discontented at the inequality of their shares, and in consequence a civil war arose, in which four parties at first oppose each other, under separate leaders; viz.

1. Abdy Zeina, with the Zeina tribe.
2. Hussun, the son of Abdal, with the Makry tribe.

3. The Kapoories, under Beiram and Yoosoof Chuk, with their tribes.

4. The Kamies, under Ghazy Khan, Atchy, and Dowlut Chuk, with their tribes.

These dissensions continued for some time, till at the end of two months after the accession of Nazook he was deposed a second time, and his brother Ibrahim was raised to the throne in his stead.

IBRAHIM II.

The brother of Nazook, is raised to the throne by Dowlut Chuk.—The party of Ghazy Khan obtains an ascendency, and Ibrahim is deposed.

THE civil dissensions being conducted with the utmost rancour, the party which possessed the person of Nazook deposed him, and placed his son Ibrahim on the throne; on which occasion the Kamies under Dowlut Chuk appear to have gained the advantage, since he assumed the title of minister to the royal pageant at Serinuggur. Meanwhile Mirza Hajy, minister to the late Mirza Heidur Doghlat, made his escape, and fled to Sulim Shah of Dehly. In the year

A.H. 960. A.D. 1552.

960, a disagreement arising between Ghazy Khan and Dowlut Chuk, both of whom were of the Kamy party, another revolution succeeded. On the following year

A.H. 961. A.D. 1553.

Ghazy Khan, having separated himself from Dowlut Chuk, was joined by Hoossein Makry and Shums Zeina, from Hindoostan; while Dowlut Chuk was joined by Yoosoof Chuk and Beiram Chuk. Several trifling skirmishes took place between these parties for a period of two months, when peace was concluded. At this time a body of Thibetians made an inroad into Kashmeer, and drove off some sheep from the district of Gava. The invaders were immediately pursued by a large body of Kashmeeries under Heibut Khan, the son of Ghazy Khan; for men were now ready to follow, at a moment's warning, any leader who offered them an object of plunder. Heibut Khan retaliated by invading Thibet, and sacking every thing in his way; and having spread desolation far and wide, arrived at one of the forts, which he took, and put the governor to death with his own hand. Proceeding far into the interior of the country, he obliged the Thibetians to present him with three hundred horses, five thousand Puttoo cloaks, one hundred sheep, and thirty Kootas cows.* He compelled them also to restore all the good horses they took during their last inroad into Kashghar; which Heibut Khan retained for his father, Ghazy Khan Chuk, to whom he presented them on his return.

A.H. 962.
A.D. 1554.

The year 962 was remarkable for a severe earthquake in Kashmeer; on which occasion the town of Dampoor, with several orchards and gardens, was removed from the eastern to the western bank of the Behut river;† and the town of Jadra, situated under the mountains, was destroyed by the falling of great part of the mountain on the town, in which upwards of six thousand persons perished.

* These are the animals from whose tails are obtained the beautiful fly-flappers used by eastern princes on occasions of state.

† It is not easy to say whether we are to take the text literally, or to suppose that a chasm opening behind the town altered the course of the river, and, consequently, the position of the town.

ISMAEL.

On the ascendency of Ghazy Khan's party, the Prince Ismael, the brother of Ibrahim, is elevated to the throne.—His death.

SCARCELY had five months elapsed from the coronation of Ibrahim, through the agency of Dowlut Chuk, before Ghazy Khan and his party attained such an increase of power, that he deposed and blinded Ibrahim. He also drove Dowlut Chuk from the capital; and in the A.H. 963. A.D. 1555. year 963 he established upon the throne of Kashmeer Ismael, the brother of the late King Ibrahim. At this time Hubeeb, the King's son, wished to unite with Dowlut Chuk, on which Ghazy Khan resolved to seize him; and on hearing that he had gone in a boat on the river to shoot ducks, Ghazy Khan seized the horses of his party. Dowlut Chuk endeavoured to escape to the hills on foot, but was overtaken, and his eyes put out. After this event the Prince Hubeeb became more reconciled to his situation. Ghazy Khan now wished to confer the office of minister on Nanuk Chuk, the nephew of Dowlut Chuk, but he disdained the offer, and fled the country.

HUBEEB.

On the death of Ismael, his son, Hubeeb, is raised to the throne.—Severe struggle for supremacy among the race of Chuk, in which Dowlut Chuk prevails.—Invasion by Shah Abool Maly from Hindoostan—is defeated.—Hubeeb is deposed by Ghazy Khan Chuk.

ISMAEL died two years after his accession, and his son Hubeeb was placed on the throne in his stead. In the latter end of the year 964, the following persons, Noosrut Chuk, Nanuk Chuk, Shunkur Chuk, the brother of Ghazy Khan, Yoosoof Chuk, and Husty Chuk, all bound themselves by oaths to take advantage of Ghazy Khan the first time he became intoxicated to put him to death, and to raise his brother, Hoossein Chuk, then in close confinement, to the throne of Kashmeer. Ghazy Khan, obtaining information of their intentions, contrived to gain over Yoosoof Chuk and Shunkur Chuk, while Noosrut Chuk and Husty Chuk resolved to occupy the country in the neighbourhood with troops. Noosrut Chuk was seized and confined; but Hubeeb Chuk and Nanuk Chuk made their escape, and collecting a few men crossed the river, destroyed the bridges, and formed a junction with Husty Chuk. Ghazy Khan sent troops against them; but in a severe action which took

A.H. 964.
A.D. 1556.

place he was defeated, and compelled to retreat, while Hubeeb Chuk marched with flying colours to Hamoon. Ghazy Khan, upon this, marched on to Domra, where he procured three or four boats, and crossing the river with three elephants, and a force of three hnndred men, attacked Hubeeb Chuk a second time. On his arrival at Khalidgur, the forces were again opposed to each other. Hubeeb Chuk was defeated, and being seized in crossing the Muchbul, his head was cut off, and suspended in the town of Kulanamut, where he usually resided.

About this period, Beiram Chuk arriving from Hindoostan received from Ghazy Khan the district of Kohtahamoon in jageer; and having taken his departure from Serinuggur, he repaired to Mulunchah, in the district of Rutungur, his native town, whither Shunkur Chuk and his other associates joined him, when they began to collect troops at Soopapoor. Ghazy Khan sent his sons and relations to attack them, but the rebels fled into the hills. Ghazy Khan now proceeded to the district of Kohtahamoon, where he remained for several days; when at length Ahmud Hoorein, a son of his brother Heidur Chuk, pledged himself to seize Beiram Chuk, and bring him to Serinuggur.

Ahmud Hoorein went to Sumurkote, a place occupied by a people called Russies,* a description of Sofy. He seized some of these people, and enquired of them where Beiram Chuk had gone.

* The circumstance of a convent of Russian missionaries being in Thibet (for the philosophical and horticultural Russies can be no others) is certainly a very extraordinary fact.

They replied, that they had conveyed him in a boat to Nadily, and delivered him safe over to Ameer Zeina. These Russies are an agricultural people, employing themselves either in sowing gain or planting fruit trees. They live in a society by themselves, and do not marry. Ahmud Hoorein now proceeded to the house of Ameer Zeina, and after much search he seized Beiram Chuk, whom he brought to Serinuggur, where he was strangled.

At this time Shah Abool Maly, who had been expelled from Lahore, fell into the hands of some Gukkurs. In this condition, notwithstanding his fetters, he made his escape on the back of Yoosoof Chuk, and procuring the aid of Humal Gukkur and Heidur Chuk, he resolved to attack Kashmeer. On reaching Rajoory he was joined by several persons of that place, as well as by Dowlut Chuk (the blind), Futteh Chuk, and other Chuks, as also by Gowhur Makry; and in the year 965 Shah Abool Maly invaded Kashmeer. On approaching Baramoola, Heidur Chuk and Futteh Chuk, whose duty it was to guard the passes, went to Madooky, while Shah Abool Maly preserved such strict discipline among his troops, that no soldier dared molest the inhabitants on any pretence. On reaching Baramoola, which is not far from Madooky, the invaders occupied a height. Ghazy Khan was encamped at a place called Gahwar, and detached his brother Hoossein Khan to a short distance in advance. This movement gave an opportunity to the confederate Chuks who had joined Shah Abool Maly to attack Hoossein Khan,

A. H. 965.
A. D. 1557.

and oblige him to fall back. Ghazy Khan allowed the Chuks to penetrate into his lines before he became the assailant, when his troops attacked them vigorously, and nearly annihilated the whole force of the enemy. This event compelled Shah Abool Maly to retreat out of the country without risking another engagement. Ghazy Khan returned to Mein, where he put to death all the Mogul prisoners which had fallen into his hands in the late engagement, excepting only one, Hafiz Mirza Hoosseiny, who was a favourite singer of Hoomayoon Padshah.

A. H. 966. A. D. 1558. In the year 966, Ghazy Khan, instead of continuing that benevolent prince which he had before proved himself to his subjects, became so inflated with pride and the importance of his situation, that he disgusted his old friends and adherents, who withdrew from about his person in consequence of his giving a loose to his passions, and committing many flagrant acts of injustice and cruelty. At this period, a report reached the ear of Ghazy Khan that his son, Heidur Chuk, was plotting his destruction, in order to hasten his own elevation to the throne. Ghazy Khan directed his minister, Mahomed Jooneid, to reprove him severely; but the young man, irritated at the liberty of speech which the minister thought proper to use on the occasion, drew his dagger, and stabbed him to the heart. On which Ghazy Khan, without seeing his son, ordered him to be carried to Zeingur, and executed.

A. H. 967. A. D. 1559. In the year 967, Kiran Bahadur arriving at Jowlapoor from Hindoostan with seven war elephants and a large army, remained there three months, where he was joined by Noosrut Chuk, Futteh Chuk, and others, as well as by some Gukkur officers of distinction. There he delayed some time longer, expecting to be joined by more of the malecontents. Those who had already united with him, now becoming disgusted with his apparent indifference, quitted him, and went over to Ghazy Khan. Kiran Bahadur's army being, in consequence, much weekened, Ghazy Khan sent a strong detachment of infantry from Nowrozekote to attack it. Kiran Bahadur was defeated, and fled to the fort of Duria, leaving his elephants in the hands of his enemies.

GHAZY SHAH CHUK.

After his accession a dreadful disease breaks out on the King.—Civil war throughout Kashmeer.—The sons of Ghazy Khan wage war against Thibet.—Ghazy Khan abdicates the throne in favour of his brother Hoossein Khan.

FIVE years had elapsed since the elevation of Hubeeb, when Ghazy Chuk, imprisoning him, declared himself king, and caused public prayers to be read, and coin to be struck, in his name; but shortly after his accession, the leprosy,* which had formerly made its appearance on him, broke out so violently that he nearly lost all his fingers.

A. H. 968.
A. D. 1560.

In the year 968, Futteh Chuk, Gowhur Chuk, and Rung Ray, fled from the capital, and collected a force in the hills. They were pursued by Hoossein Chuk, the brother of Ghazy Shah, with two thousand men; and a heavy fall of snow coming on, most of the insurgents, being without camp-equipage, fell victims to its effects. The few persons, however, who did escape, fled to Gohore, and in the following year threw themselves on the mercy of Hoossein Chuk, who interceded with his brother in their behalf.

A.H. 970.
A.D. 1562.

In the year 970, Ghazy Shah marched at the head of his army to Lar, from whence he sent his son, Ahmud Khan, accompanied by Futteh Khan and Nasir Kutaby,

* The particular shape which the disease assumed in Ghazy Chuk was that usually denominated elephantiasis.

to invade the territory of Thibet. When they arrived within ten miles of the border, Futteh Khan proceeded to the capital without receiving Ahmud Khan's orders; and as the Thibetians were neither capable nor willing to oppose the Kashmeer troops, they agreed to pay a large sum of money as a ransom for their country. The Prince Ahmud Khan, who was entrusted with the expedition into Thibet, was so much vexed that he had had no share in the invasion conducted by Futteh Khan that he resolved to enter Thibet in spite of the conditions made by the Thibetians. On this occasion, however, Futteh Khan lost his life, and the Prince Ahmud sustained so severe a defeat, that he was constrained to return with disgrace. Ghazy Shah, being altogether disappointed at the conduct of his son, recalled him.

A. H. 971. A. D. 1563. In the year 971, Ghazy Shah, advancing in person to the confines of Thibet, encamped at a place called Mokudkar; but the leprosy having now deprived him of his eyesight he grew irritable and peevish, and committed so many unpopular and cruel acts that the nation anxiously desired his death, while his brother, Hoossein, and his son, Ahmud, each endeavoured to gain popularity, in order to establish his claim to the crown. The moment Ghazy Shah ascertained that these two parties existed he returned to Serinuggur, and secured the succession to his brother, Hoossein Khan, by abdicating the throne in his favour, after a short reign of four years.

HOOSSEIN SHAH CHUK.

Ascends the throne of his brother.—Remarkable mode of distributing his property adopted by the late king.—Hoossein Khan causes his nephew, Ahmud, to be blinded.—Death of the ex-king.—Hoossein Shah receives an embassy from Akbur, and sends his daughter to Agra to marry that emperor.—The Kashmeer princess is sent back to her father.—This insult tends to break the King's heart.—His abdication and death.

AFTER the secession of Ghazy Shah he divided his personal effects into two lots, giving one to his children, and sending the other half to the shops, requiring the shop-keepers to pay him a certain sum of money. The demand being treble the value of the property, the merchants came to Hoossein Khan, and entreated him to advise his brother to give up so strange an intention as that of a monarch selling his personal effects. Ghazy Shah, who was reduced by age as well as disease to a state of second childhood, insisted on the shop-keepers purchasing his goods; and he became so enraged against Hoossein Shah that he regretted having abdicated in his favour, and now wished to establish his son, Ahmud Khan, on the throne; for which purpose he collected a force in the suburbs, with the intention of dethroning his brother Hoossein. The new King, however, was enabled, without coming to action, to dismember the old King's army, and to reduce his brother to the necessity of retreating to Zeinpoor, where he remained three months, and then returned to Serinuggur. Meanwhile Hoossein Shah, being firmly seated on the throne, made new regulations for the financial departments. In the year 972 he sent his brother, Shunkur Chuk, to assume charge of the government of Nowshehra and Rajoory; but the latter shortly afterwards appeared at the head of a force in open rebellion. Hoossein Shah deputed an army under the command of Mahomed Khan Makry to attack his brother, whom having defeated, the general returned to the capital, where he was greeted by Hoossein Shah, who went out to meet and congratulate him. Shortly after the arrival of the army, some of the officers concerted a scheme to put the King to death; but he discovered the plot, and seizing the ringleaders, caused their eyes to be put out.

A.H. 972.
A.D. 1564.

In the following year, 973, his prime minister, Khan-ooz-Zuman, was induced to attack the palace during his absence, with the intention, after seizing the treasures, of proclaiming himself king; but his scheme was defeated by the exertions of Musaood Paik, the officer of the King's body-guard, who seizing the minister's son, and having cut off his head, exposed it to his party, which fled. The minister was shortly after secured, and the King ordered his execution; while Musaood Paik was elevated to the situation of minister, with the title of Moobariz Khan, and the estate of the district of Fankul was made over to him.

A. H. 973.
A. D. 1565

In the following year, Hoossein Shah, perceiving that attempts were so frequently made to dethrone him, conceived it necessary, for his personal safety, to incapacitate his nephew and rival, Ahmud Khan, from reigning, by causing him to be blinded. The news of this event had such an effect on the old king, Ghazy Khan, who was still living, that he died of a broken heart.

A. H. 975.
A. D. 1567.

In the year 975, the King growing jealous of the rising power of his minister, Moobariz Khan, seized and confined him, and appointed one Booly Govind to his situation; but the latter being detected in embezzling forty thousand bales of shawls, he was also imprisoned, and Ally Koka was raised to the office of minister.

A. H. 976.
A. D. 1568.

In the year 976, Kazy Hubeeb, a person of the Hunefy persuasion, after leaving the great mosque on Friday, went to pay his devotions at the tombs of some holy persons at the foot of the Maran hills. On this occasion one Yoosoof, a person of the Sheea persuasion, being present, drew his sword, and wounded the Kazy on the head. He levelled also another blow at the Kazy, who, in endeavouring to save his head with his hand, had his fingers cut off. This attack arose out of no other cause than the animosity which existed between the two sects. On this occasion, Mowlana Kumal, the Kazy of Seealkote, was present. Yoosoof, after wounding Kazy Hubeeb, made his escape. The King, although himself of the Sheea persuasion, sent persons to seize Yoosoof; and he required several holy and learned men, such as Moolla Yoosoof, Moolla Feroze, and others, to investigate the matter, and to award punishment according to the law. It is related that these worthies said that it was lawful to put, Yoosoof to death. The Kazy who was wounded declared, that as he had not died of his wounds the law did not admit of the culprit being executed. He was; however, notwithstanding, stoned to death. About this time a number of persons of the Sheea sect arrived with Mirza Mookeem and Meer Yakoob, who came as ambassadors to Serinuggur from Akbur, Emperor of Dehly. Hoossein Shah caused his own tents to be pitched for them at Heerapoor; and when they arrived there, he went forth to meet and escort them. After which, embarking in boats with the son of Hoossein Shah, they proceeded in state to the city of Serinuggur. Hoossein Shah did not go in the boat, but rode on horseback, and prepared the house of Hoossein Makry for the reception of the ambassadors. After some days, Mirza Mookeem, being of the same persuasion as the assassin Yoosoof required of Hoossein Shah that he should send those learned men who had pronounced the sentence of death on that culprit to him; with which Hoossein Shah complied. Kazy Zein, himself a Sheea, insisted that the sentence pronounced by the persons by whom Yoosoof had been tried was erroneous. The judges said that they had not positively sentenced Yoosoof to death, but declared that it was lawful to execute a person convicted of the crime of which he was found guilty. Mirza

Mookeem now ordered the judges into confinement, and made them over to Futteh Khan. Hoossein Shah left the city, and went in a boat to Kamraj; and Futteh Khan, at the instance of Mirza Mookeem, the Dehly ambassador, caused the holy men to be put to death; after which, ropes were tied to their feet, and they were dragged through the streets and markets of the town. Hoossein Shah, on his return, after presenting the Indian ambassadors with some valuable articles for their master, sent his daughter to be married to Akbur Padshah, and acknowledged his supremacy. In the year 977 (A.D. 1569) news arrived in Kashmeer that the Emperor Akbur, on hearing of the conduct of his ambassadors at Kashmeer, ordered them to be publicly executed at Agra; and as a token of his indignation and horror at the conduct of Hoossein Shah, who had sanctioned such a proceeding in his kingdom, he refused to receive his daughter, and sent her back to Kashmeer.* This circumstance had such an effect on the mind of Hoossein Shah, that he

* When I consider that Hoossein Shah Chuk was himself a Sheea of rigid principles, it is fair to conclude that the trial of Yoosoof by a conclave of divines, and his subsequent execution, arose solely out of the necessity of yielding to the voice of the people. The unwillingness which Hoossein Shah felt in giving up Yoosoof to public feeling seems plainly indicated by his subsequently permitting Akbur's ambassadors to assume the power, in his capital, of punishing the bench of judges who condemned the criminal. The conduct of Akbur (himself a Sheea), in making an example of those ambassadors on their return, and in refusing to espouse the daughter of a king who had acted with such baseness and duplicity as Hoossein Shah Chuk, are equally honourable to his character as a prince and as a man.

was seized with a violent illness, and was soon rendered totally unfit to transact public business. Most of the chiefs now quitting the court, waited on his brother, Ally Khan, at Shewpoor; whence they induced him to march to the capital. On his arrival within fourteen or fifteen miles of Serinuggur, the whole of the court-party deserted Hoossein Shah; and that monarch was compelled to abdicate his throne in favour of his brother. He accordingly sent to him the Koottas canopy, and the other insignia of royalty. Ally Khan was formally acknowledged King; while Hoossein Shah, leaving Serinuggur, went to Zeinpoor, where he died, three months afterwards, of dysentery, in the same year, viz. A. H. 977.

A.H. 977.
A. D. 1569.

ALLY SHAH CHUK.

Succeeds his brother on the throne.—An imposter, called Shah Arif, enters Kashmeer.—The King gives him his daughter in marriage.—The imposter exposed and expelled from the country.—An embassy from Dehly.—Death of Ally Chuk.

On the death of Hoossein, his brother Ally was formally crowned at Serinuggur; and Dookna, the late minister to Hoossein Shah, received from the new monarch the seals of office. At this time, Shah Arif, a dervish of the Sheea persuasion, and who claimed relationship to Shah Tahmasp of Persia, arrived in Kashmeer from Lahore; where he had for some time lived under the protection of Hoossein Kooly Khan, governor of the Punjab. Ally, who was himself a Sheea, was so pleased with this stranger, that he gave him his daughter in marriage; while Ally Chuk, the son of Nowroze Chuk, and Ibrahim, the son of Ghazy Khan, absolutely worshipped this holy personage, and declared him to be the Imam Mehdy, who is to appear again in the last days. This infatuation carried them so far, that they resolved to dethrone Ally, and to raise Shah Arif to the government. The moment the King heard this, he took measures to persecute the dervish. The holy man gave out that he would, by means of his sanctity, convey himself to Lahore in one day; and on the following morning having disappeared, his disciples concluded that he had been transported by means of his art to some other country; but he was discovered to have paid a large sum to the ferryman to carry him across the river, and was taken at Baramoola, whither he had travelled. He again escaped, and was taken at the hill of Mehtur Sooliman; after which the King fined him in the sum of one thousand ashrufies, and taking away his daughter from him, compelled him to quit the kingdom. In the year 979, Ally, the son of Nowroze Chuk, represented that the minister, Dookna, had plundered the country, and that when spoken to on the subject he had conducted himself with great insolence. The King accordingly caused Dookna to be seized and sent to Gujraj, whence he effected his escape to the court of Hoossein Kooly Khan, governor of the Punjab; but that chief not receiving him with the cordiality he expected, he returned to Nowshehra, in Kashmeer, where he was apprehended, and sent to Serinuggur. In the year 980 Ally Shah marched at the head of his army to Gunwar, commonly called Kishtwar, and having espoused the daughter of the prince of that country, returned to his capital, where he received an embassy, consisting of Moolla Eshky and Kazy Sudr-ood-Deen, from the court of Dehly; the result of which was, that Akbur was proclaimed Emperor of Kashmeer in the public prayers. Ally Shah Chuk

A. H. 979.
A. D. 1571.

A. H. 980.
A. D. 1572.

at the request of. Akbur, now sent his niece* to be married to the Prince Sulim.† In
A. H. 984. A. D. 1575. the year 984 a severe famine was experienced in Kashmeer, in which many thousands of the inhabitants died. In
A. H. 986. A. D. 1578. the year 986 Ally Shah was killed by a fall from his horse, after a reign of nine years.

* This Princess was probably the daughter of Hoossein Shah, whom Akbur thought it politic, three years before, to send back to her father; but relenting in his severity towards her, he seems to have sent an embassy to escort her to Dehly.

† This prince afterwards ascended the throne of Dehly, under the title of Jehangeer.

YOOSOOF SHAH CHUK.

Succeeds his father on the throne—attacks and slays his uncle, Abdal Khan—is eventually driven from his country by Gowhur Chuk—proceeds to India—obtains the aid of Akbur Padshah—returns to Kashmeer—defeats Gowhur Chuk, and deprives him of sight.—A new insurrection created, which is suppressed.—Ambassadors arrive from Akbur.—The King's two sons return with them to the Dehly court.—Akbur arrives at Lahore, and proposes to visit Kashmeer.—Yoosoof Shah wishes to meet and escort him, but is prevented by his chiefs.—Akbur causes Kashmeer to be invaded.—Peace concluded.—A second invasion.—The Kashmeer prince makes considerable resistance.—Final conquest of Kashmeer by Akbur.

ON the death of Ally he was succeeded by his son Yoosoof, while the late King's brother, Abdal Khan, apprehensive of his nephew's designs on his person, withdrew from the capital. Yoosoof wrote to his uncle, entreating him to lay aside all suspicion, and even requested him to come to court, promising faithfully to abide by his advice, and even offering to make over to him the government, if he were disposed to assume the charge of public affairs. This communication, which was sent by Syud Moobarik Khan, was not delivered to Abdal Khan, as was intended; and the messenger returned to Serinuggur, assuring the King that his uncle not only refused to come to the capital, but was raising a force secretly to oppose his coronation. On this Yoosoof Shah marched against him, and Abdal Khan, collecting his retainers, resolved to die like a soldier; so that on the occasion of meeting with the government troops both himself and his son were killed. After this event, Yoosoof Shah, returning to the capital, buried his father agreeably to the custom of the Sheeas, and he was proclaimed King in his stead. In the course of two or three months Syud Moobarik Khan, Ally Chuk, and others, crossing the Behut, raised the standard of revolt. Yoosoof Shah, with Mahomed Khan his minister, marched to oppose them; and in an action which ensued Mahomed Khan, with sixty of the King's personal guard, were slain, and himself being defeated, fled to Heerpoor, whither he was pursued by Syud Moobarik Khan. Thence the King was compelled to retreat into the woods, to a place called Hurunpal Nursak, and eventually to the hills, while Syud Moobarik Khan, returning in triumph to Serinuggur assumed the reins of government. The first act of his administration was to confine his colleague, Ally Chuk; a measure which so enraged those persons who had supported him, that on quitting the court to proceed to their jageers, they resolved to raise Yoosoof again to the throne; but before that could be effected, the Chuks had again disagreed, and having separate interests, they endeavoured to establish Gowhur Chuk on the throne. Syud Moobarik Khan, perplexed with the intrigues by which he was surrounded, wished Yoosoof Shah to resume charge of the government: but the latter having fled from Kashmeer during the late commotion, went direct to the court of Dehly, and laid his petition at the feet of Akbur Padshah. Akbur ordered Raja Man Sing and Syud Yoosoof Khan with a force to re-establish him: for which purpose they marched from Futtehpoor in the year 987.

A.H. 987.
A.D. 1579.

At this period, Gowhur Chuk being at the head of the government of Kashmeer, Yoosoof Shah thought it advisable to send his son, Yakoob, in advance, in order to gain over some of his former adherents; and, at any rate, by his appearance in the country to create a sensation in his favour among the inhabitants.

When Yoosoof Shah arrived at Seealkote his affairs looked so prosperous that he marched on direct to Rajoory, which district he subdued, and then proceeded to Lassa, where he was met by one Yoosoof Khan, a Kashmeery sent to oppose him, but who joined him with his whole army, and enabled the King to enter his country by the route of Jeehbul. This is the most difficult approach to the valley; notwithstanding which he proceeded direct to the fort of Shewpur, where he found Gowhur Chuk ready to oppose him, on the opposite bank of the Behut. A severe engagement took place shortly after, when the Kashmeeries were defeated, and Yoosoof Shah entered the city of Serinuggur, where Gowhur Chuk was seized and imprisoned.

Yoosoof Shah, again seated on the throne, resorted the several districts of Kashmeer, as before, to his own officers, and concluded the revolution by putting out the eyes of his rival Gowhur Chuk.

A.H. 988. A.D. 1580. In the year 988, Shums Chuk, Ally Chuk, and Mahomed Khan, being suspected to treason, were seized, while Hubeeb Khan, afraid of sharing the same fate, fled to a place called Gaheer; and Yoosoof, the son of Ally Chuk, having escaped from prison with his four brothers, joined Hubeeb Khan at the same place, whence they all proceeded to the court of Thibet. having procured reinforcements, they directed their arms against their own country; but by the time they arrived on the frontier, such dissensions arose among them that their troops left them, they were themselves seized, brought to the capital, and their noses and ears were cut off.

A. H. 989. A. D. 1581. In the year 989, when Akbur Padshah returned from Lahore to Agra, that monarch deputed Mirza Tahir and Mahomed Saleh as envoys to Kashmeer. On their arrival at Baramoola, they were met by Yoosoof Shah in person, who, kissing the letter from Akbur Padshah, placed it on his head. After a short time the ambassadors returned to Dehly, accompanied by the Princes Heidur and Yakoob, the King's sons, to the court of Akbur, were having staid some time they returned to Kashmeer.

A. H. 990. A. D. 1582. In the year 990, Yoosoof marched in the direction of Lar; during which journey, Shums Chuk, escaping from prison, joined Heidur Chuk, who had fled to Kishtwar; but as they were pursued by the Kashmeer army, they fled further, and Yoosoof returned to Serinuggur.

A. H. 991.
A. D. 1584.
In the year 991, Heidur Chuk having returned to Kishtwar collected a force and marched to invade Kashmeer, but was defeated on the frontier by the King in person.

A.H. 992.
A.D. 1585.
In the year 992, the Prince Yakoob, having left Kashmeer, had the honour of again paying his respects to Akbur Padshah; and when that monarch reached Lahore, Yakoob wrote to his father, that Akbur intended to visit Kashmeer; and in the mean time Hukeem Ally Geelany arrived at Lassa, as envoy from his court. Yoosoof Shah met the envoy, put on the honorary robe sent to him, and intended to proceed to court to pay his respects; but Baba Khuleel, Baba Mehdy, and others of the Kashmeer nobles, told Yoosoof Shah that he must not quite the kingdom; and if he insisted upon it, they declared they would proclaim his son Yakoob, lately arrived in Kashmeer, King. The King was thus compelled to forego his intention, and dismissed the ambassador, who reported the whole of the proceedings to his court. Akbur, who had all along intended to conquer Kashmeer, made the conduct of the nobles on this occasion a plea for doing so; and he in consequence deputed Mirza Shahrokh, Shah Ally, and Raja Bhugwundas, with a large force, for that purpose. When the Indian army arrived at the Hoolias pass they found it occupied by Kashmeer troops; and the Indian generals were glad to make terms, requiring only that the King of Kashmeer should pay an annual tribute to Akbur Padshah. On the return of the Dehly

troops, Yoosoof Shah accompanied them to the court of Akbur; but the Emperor, by no means satisfied with the terms, refused to ratify the treaty; and in the year 995 he appointed Mahomed Kasim Khan, who held the rank of Ameer-ool-Behr (Admiral), to march and subdue Kashmeer.

A. H. 995.
A. D. 1586.

Yakoob, who had now succeeded to the throne, in consequence of his father's detention at the court of Dehly, collected an army and occupied the passes; but the treacherous Kashmeeries, as usual, forsook their sovereign, and joined the foreign invaders. Some of the nobles, who were at Serinuggur, also threw off their allegiance, and rebelled. Yakoob, conceiving it advisable to check the insurrection in his own kingdom, before opposing the foreign enemy, returned from the frontier to the capital; and the forces of Akbur entering Kashmeer, proceeded, without, opposition, to Serinuggur. Officers being now appointed to subdue the several districts, the conquest in a short time was rendered complete. On the successful approach of the Indian army, Yakoob fled to the hills; but collecting a force, he attacked Mahomed Kasim Khan, and in one action which took place many Indian chiefs were killed, though the Prince Yakoob was eventually defeated. Not disheartened by this reverse, he again assembled troops, and marched to the gates of Serinuggur, where he was opposed by Mahomed Kasim Khan, whom he defeated, and compelled to seek protection in the citadel of that town, whence Mahomed Kasim wrote to his court for assistance. Akbur

Padshah having recalled Mahomed Kasim, nominated Syud Yoosoof Khan Mushedy to the government of Kashmeer; and on his approach the Prince Yakoob withdrew his forces from the citadel, and fled to the hills, whither he was pursued for two years; he was at last seized and sent to Dehly, where Akbur enrolled both Yoosoof Shah Chuk and his son Yakoob among the nobles of his government. They each received estates in the fertile province of Behar, and from that period the kingdom of Kashmeer has been a province of Dehly; before which, for upwards of one thousand years that principality had been independent, and was never subdued by any of the monarchs of Hindoostan.

CHAPTER XI.

SOME ACCOUNT OF THE MAHOMEDANS IN MALABAR.

All the materials of the history of the Mahomedans of the Malabar coast that I have been able to collect are derived from the Tohfut-ool-Mujahi-deen; from which we learn that the province of Malabar is situated on the southern part of the peninsula of India, and that the Hindoo princes of that country previously to the reign of Ramraj* paid tribute, and acknowledged fealty, to the rays of Beejanuggur and the Carnatic.

Anterior to the propagation of the Mahomedan faith, the Christans and Jews had established themselves as merchants in that country; till at length, during the reign of a prince called Samiry,† some vessels from Arabia having Mahomedans on board, going on a pilgrimage to the footsteps of Adam, on the island of Selandeep (Ceylon), which is also called Lunka, were driven into the port of Cranganore, where the Samiry raja resided. This prince received the strangers with hospitality, and was so pleased with the

* For the history of Ramraj, see vol. iii. p. 80, &c.

† *Zamorin* of the Portuguese historians.

society of some holy men who were among the pilgrims, that having enquired respecting the Mahomedan faith, he became a convert; and leaving his kingdom, went to Mecca, and died in one of the ports of the Red Sea. Before his death, he wrote to his representative in Malabar to receive the Mahomedans in future with hospitality, and permit them to settle and build musjids. This communication was written in the language of Malabar, whose ruler henceforward assumed the title of Samiry.

In consequence of this letter the Mahomedans were treated with kindness by the reigning prince, who wrote to the governors of his districts in these words:—"Whereas Mullik, the son of Hu-"beeb, and certain other Mahomedans, have come "to visit this our country, and intend residing "among us, it is our royal order, agreeably to "the imperial command of the late Samiry, that "wherever the said Mullik or any of his tribe "wish to reside, ground shall be allotted to them, "in order to build either habitations or places "of worship." Mullik first settled at Cranganore, where he built a musjid, and cultivated some garden land; afterwards, having gone farther into the country, he established a colony of Mahomedans in the town of Quilon. Thence he went to Hurryputtun, Daraputtun, Mundra, Jay-Faknoor, Mangalore, and Kalinjurkote;* in each of which towns he built musjids, and established Moollas to preach the true faith; and as the

* Many of these places are either erroneously written in my MS., or they have changed their names.

Mahomedans in Malabar are mostly of the Shafay* persuasion, I conclude that Mullik, the son of Hubeeb, was also of the same faith. From this period, the Mahomedans extended their religion and their influence in Malabar; and many of the princes and inhabitants becoming converts to the true faith, gave over the management of some of the sea-ports to the strangers, whom they called Nowayits (literally, the New Race). The rajas of the ports of Goa, Dabul, and Choul, were the first who gave them this appellation, and encouraged emigration from Arabia; and though their elevation to public offices gave umbrage to the Christians and Jews,† who became their determined enemies; yet, as the countries of Deccan and Guzerat were gradually brought under Mahomedan subjection, their enemies were unable to do these Arabian settlers any material injury, until the tenth century of the Hijra, when

* Mahomedans adopting the doctrines of Aboo Abdoolla, surnamed Shafay, who lived in the eighth century of the Christian era. He was the first and most able of the Mahomedan doctors who wrote on the civil and canonical law. His tenets and opinions are in conformity with those of Aboo Huneefa, who died in the year 782. Aboo Abdoolla Shafay was born in the same year at Gaza, in Palestine, and died in Egypt at the age of fifty-four, A.D. 836. The followers of these divines are entitled Soonies or orthodox, in contradistinction to other Mahomedan schismatics, whom they call Rafzy, or Heretics.

† The Jews and Christians here alluded to are those which came from western Asia; and it seems not improbable that their emigration to the East occurred during the period of the early Christian schisms of Nestorians, Manicheans, &c. which emigration continued, perhaps, even down to the time of Mahomed.

in the decline of the Mahomedan empire of Dehly the Portuguese invaded India.

A. H. 904.
A. D. 1498.

In the year 904, four vessels belonging to the King of Portugal arrived at the ports of Calicut* and Koilad; when, having made observations on the nature of the country and its inhabitants, they returned to Portugal. On the following year six vessels arrived; and the Portuguese endeavoured to persuade the Raja of Calicut to shut his ports against the traders from Arabia, telling him that by such a measure the Indians would gain more advantage than by carrying on a small traffic annually by the Red Sea; but Samiry not consenting to this proposal, the Portuguese declared war against the Arabs, and attacked their vessels; which so incensed the Raja, that he ordered several of the Portuguese then on shore to be attacked, and seventy were killed. The rest made their escape to their ships, and took refuge with the Raja of Cochin, an enemy of Samiry. The Cochin chief permitted the Portuguese to build a fortified factory at that place; they also destroyed a mosque, and built a chapel in its stead, which was the first building erected by Europeans in India. From Cochin they sailed to Cananore, where they also made friends with the Raja; and having built a fort, established a factory there; and while they transported pepper and ginger to Europe, they prevented any other vessels from doing so also.

A. H. 905.
A. D. 1499.

Samiry, hearing of these proceedings, attacked

* Faria-e-Souza says, Vasco de Gama reached Calicut on the 20th May, 1498. Vol. i. part i. chap. iv.

the Raja of Cochin; and having killed three petty rajas in action, and taken their country, he returned to his capital: but, the heirs of those slain, collecting a large force, retook their countries, and the rajas of Cochin and Cananore continued to support and befriend the Portuguese. Samiry, a thousand times more incensed than ever, distributed largesses to his troops, and marched to Cochin; but finding the Portuguese had sailed and left the place, he returned to his capital, and immediately despatched ambassadors to Judda, in the Red Sea, to the Deccan, and to Guzerat; informing the respective sovereigns of those countries, that the Portuguese had behaved in the most cruel manner to his Mahomedan subjects, and that he was unable to withstand their forces. He states:—"I am not apprehensive for my own "country, but for my Mahomedan subjects; for, "although myself a Hindoo, I conceive it my "duty to protect them as if they were also of the "same persuasion. But the King of Portugal is "wealthier than I; and as I find that by destroy- "ing these invaders they increase their numbers "on the following year, I am reduced to solicit "the assistance of the Mahomedan kings; so that "I entreat you, by the value you place on your "religion, to send your ships filled with victori- "ous troops into these seas, to attack the Euro- "peans, and entitle yourselves to have your "names enrolled in the list of holy warriors, who "in supporting the cause of religion have become "inhabitants of paradise."*

* This *orthodox* letter, if actually written, was probably penned in Arabic by some worthy Moslem scribe; and it is

Munsoor Ghoory, the Caliph of Egypt, accordingly deputed his admiral, Ameer Hoossein, with thirteen ships of war, to proceed to the Indian coasts. Mahmood Shah of Guzerat, and Mahmood Shah Bahmuny of the Deccan, also sent ships from Diù, Surat, Gogo, Dabul, and Choul, which all met at the island of Diù; from whence the combined fleets proceeded, under the command of Mullik Eiaz Sooltany, the Guzerat admiral, and Ameer Hoossein, the admiral from Egypt, to the south. This armament fell in with the Portuguese off the port of Choul, where an engagement took place, in which some Arab vessels fell into the hands of the Portuguese, and the Mahomedan fleet was dispersed, after which the Portuguese returned to their own ports. At this period an army from Constantinople arriving in Egypt, the Ghoory dynasty became subservient to the Turkish government of Europe. Samiry, hearing this news, was much dejected, despairing of subduing the Portuguese, who every day became more and more powerful. During the absence of Samiry, in the year 915, from Calicut, the Portuguese landed and plundered the town, and burned the principal mosque; but on the following day, the inhabitants rising on the invaders, five hundred Portuguese were killed, and many drowned in endeavouring to reach their boats. Notwithstanding this circumstance, they obtained a grant of land from a neighbouring zemindar, on which

A. H. 915.
A. D. 1509.

likely its contents were never clearly explained to the Hindoo prince.

they built a fort within three miles of Calicut. It has been before related in the Deccan history, that during the same year they attacked and took by storm the fort of Goa, which was, however, shortly after retaken by stratagem ; but they subsequently became possessed of it again by bribing the governor with large presents ; since which period Goa has been considered the principal Portuguese settlement in India, and a governor-general is appointed from Europe.

Samiry, finding all his efforts against the Portuguese of no avail, was reduced to such a state of despair, that being taken seriously ill, he died of a broken heart in the year 921,

A. H. 921.
A. D. 1515.

when he was succeeded by his brother, who shortly after his accession made peace with the Portuguese. In this treaty the latter were authorised to build a factory at Calicut, and to trade without molestation, on condition of permitting four ships laden with pepper and ginger to sail annually to the Arabian coast. The Portuguese immediately built a fortified factory ; and after establishing themselves, not only refused to allow the transport of the pepper and ginger to take place agreeably to compact, but persecuted the Mahomedans, on all occasions, with great cruelty. The Jews, also, who resided at Cranganore, taking advantage of the weakness of the Samiry government, following the example of the Portuguese, put to death many of the Mahomedans in that town and its vicinity. Samiry, repenting of having come to any terms with these Europeans, and seeing that their example had induced the Jews to commit these outrages, marched with a force to Cranganore, and succeeded in expelling all the Jews from every part of his country; after which, calling upon the Mahomedans in Malabar to join his standard, he proceeded to attack the Portuguese factory at Calicut, which he stormed, and took by assault; and he was enabled to despatch the four Arab vessels laden with pepper and ginger.

The Portuguese, however, resolved to have a factory near the town of Calicut, for two reasons: in the first place, on account of its great trade; and, secondly, because their factory being contiguous to that port, they could blockade it, and entirely monopolise the export of pepper and ginger. Inspite of remonstrance, therefore, in the year 938 they built a fort at the port
A.H. 938. A.D. 1531. of Jaliat, seven miles distance from Calicut, and also the fort of Reevadunda, near Choul.

In the year 941 they took possession
A.H. 941. A.D. 1534. of the port of Swally and Daman, and of the island of Diù, in Guzerat, from Bahadur Shah, as has been already related in the history of that monarch; and in
A.H. 943. A.D. 1536. the year 943 they attack the town of Cranganore, and built a fort, notwithstanding the efforts of Samiry to prevent it. At this time, Sooliman, the Grand Signior of Constantinople, resolved, if possible, to deprive the Portuguese of the trade to India, and to attack their factories, after which he proposed to conquer the empire of Hindoostan. For this purpose he appointed his vizier, Sooliman Aga, to the

command of an armament, consisting of upwards of one hundred vessels, which sailed from the Red Sea in the year 944. Sooliman Aga
A. H. 944. first attacked and took the port of
A. D. 1537. Adun, which lies at the mouth of the Red Sea, whence he sailed towards the island of Diù, in Guzerat; but fiinding, on his arrival, that his treasury was low, and his provisions nealry exhausted, he was compelled, after a few days, to return, without accomplishing his purpose.

Before the year 963 we find that
A. H. 963. other nations of Europe had sent vessels
A. D. 1555. to India, and settled in the several ports and island of the East. They built factories at Pûlicat, Mylapoor, Negapatam, Madras, Bracelore, Mangalore, and in Bengal. They also settled on the islands of Sumatra, Malacca, Timoor, and Ceylon, and even established factories on the coast of China; but Sooltan Ally Akhy attacked the Europeans on the island of Sumatra, and drove them from their factory, as did also the King of Ceylon. Samiry, the King of Calicut, being much oppressed by the Portuguese, sent ambassadors to the Mahomedan kings of Beejapoor and the Deccan, requesting their assistance.

In the year 979, the Deccan and
A.H. 979. Beejapoor monarchs marched against
A.D. 1571. Reevadunda and Goa, while Samiry attacked and captured the fort of Jaliat; but the Mahomedan kings were compelled to raise the sieges both of Reevadunda and Goa, and return to their respective capitals. The Portuguese now became more and more exasperated against the

Mahomedans; and having the entire command of the seas, they plundered several ships (belonging to Akbur Padshah of Dehly) returning from Judda in the Read Sea, whither they had conveyed pilgrims to the holy shrine at Mecca. They also landed and burned the towns of Adilabad and Carapatam, on the shore of the Beejapoor empire, and went to Dabul for the same purpose; but the governor, Khwaja Ally Shirazy, having heard of their intentions, permitted them to land, and put to death upwards of a hundred and fifty Portuguese. From the time the vessels belonging to Akbur Padshah were taken, that monarch laid an embargo on all his ships sailing either to the Red Sea or to the Gulf of Persia, as heretofore, conceiving that to obtain passes from the Europeans would be derogatory to his dignity; and the ships being plundered incurred both disgrace to the King and loss to his subjects. Some of the governors on the sea-coast, however, such as Abdool Raheem of Surat, and others, obtaing passes for their vessels, still continued to trade. In the year 1020,

A.H. 1020.
A.D. 1611.

the Emperor of Dehly, Jehangeer, the son of Akbur Padshah, granted a spot for the English to build a factory in the city of Surat, in the province of Guzerat, which is the first settlement that people made on the shores of Hindoostan. The persuasion of this nation is different from that of other Europeans, particularly the Portuguese, with whom they are in a state of constant warfare. They assert that Jesus was a mortal, and the Prophet of God; that there is only one God; and that he is without equal, and has no wife, nor son, according to the belief of the Portuguese. The English have a separate king, independent of the King of Portugal, to whom they owe no allegiance; but on the contrary, these two nations put each other to death wheresoever they meet. At present, in consequence of the interference of Jehangeer Padshah, they are at peace with each orther, though God only knows how long they will consent both to have factories in the same town, and to live on terms of amity and friendship.

CONCLUSION.

It is stated in the history of Babur, that the territory of Hind (India) is confined to the first, second, and third climates, but that no part is in the fourth climate. This country is quite peculiar, and the manners of its inhabitants are very remarkable. Its towns bear little resemblance to those of other countries ; but the customs of the people have some affinity with those of Yemun in Arabia, with the Bedouins, and especially with the inhabitants of Madagascar. Hind is bounded on the north by Kashmeer, whence issue the great rivers which flow to the south-west. These all unite, near Mooltan, with the river Indus, and flow in one stream to Tutta, where they disembogue into the Indian ocean. These rivers are the Sutlooj, the Beea, the Ravy, the Chunab, the Behut, and, lastly, the Sind, or Indus. The Behut used to be called the Jheelum, as at present the Sind is in some places denominated the Neelab. Besides these rivers are several other large streams issuing from those mountains, such as the Joon (Jumna), the Great Gung (or Ganges), the Kaly Nye, the Gunduk, the Surjoo, and many others, all of which streams, rising in the east, and passing through the province of Bengal, unite with the Ganges and flow into the Eastern sea. Independently of these there are other numerous rivers in Hindoostan, which do not take their rise in the mountains that form the Indian barrier. Among them we may reckon the Chumbul, the Bunas, and the Soane, all of which unite with the Ganges, and fall into the ocean. In the Deccan are also several rivers; such as the Nurbudda, the Tapty, the Poorna, the little Gunga (Godavery), the Krishna, the Bheema, and the Toongbudra. The three former rivers flow to the west, and the three latter-eastward. So superficially do many of the rivers of the Deccan pass through the open country, that their waters might be rendered applicable to its irrigation; and although in some villages it is usual to dig channels and convey the water into their fields, it is not sufficiently practised; for the inhabitants do no appear to enjoy the sight of running streams, or to feel refreshed by breezes blowing over water. It sometimes happens, indeed, that men of rank, in travelling, prefer pitching their tents on the banks of streams, but they usually have the female apartments in the vicinity of the water.*

* In order to understand this sentence it is necessary to observe, that the mode of encampment adopted by travellers of distinction in India is quite systematic and uniform. In front is the chief's guard of honour and his flag; behind is his state tent for holding levees and receiving visitors; next in order come his private tents, surrounded by screens embracing a square area of several yards, and in the rear of all are the female apartments, which for convenience and privacy are placed close to the edge of the water, or stream, if there should be one. On both

The houses of India are built like prisons, and the towns and cities are filthy and uncleanly. I must, however, except the Hydrabad of Golconda, which has lately been constructed by Mahomed Ally Kootb Shah, and which not only bears a fair comparison with the cities in other parts of the world, in appearance as well as in cleanliness, but is superior to many. The cause of this excellence arises out of the fine stream of water that flows throughout the streets and bazars, which are beautiful and wide. The shops and private houses in Hydrabad are throughout constructed of stone and mortar, and on each side of the stream is a row of trees affording abundance of shade. India abounds with forests and extensive wildernesses, full of all sorts of trees; so much so, that these wastes seem to offer inducements, both to rajas and subjects, to revolt from the government. The agricultural population, and the abundance of cattle, in this country, exceed that of all others; but its depopulation and desolation are sudden and rapid beyond conception. This is owing principally to the inhabitants building their houses of thatch, and having their domestic utensils of earthen-ware, both of which they relinquish without remorse; so that by taking their cattle with

flanks of the chief's establishment are his retainers and the cattle and carriages: an arrangement which effectually deprives him and his guests of enjoying the sight of running streams, or being refreshed by the breezes blowing over the water. Ferishta's countrymen (the Persians) are absolute enthusiasts on the subject of running waters and green fields.

them, and departing to some other spot, they easily construct houses like those they have deserted, and, after obtaining a few earthen vessels, they again apply themselves to husbandry.

The autumnal crops are produced in the months when the sun is in Cancer, Leo, Virgo, and Libra, and are brought forward by the rain of the monsoon; while the spring crops, which grow during the months when the sun is in Scorpio, Sagittarius, Capricornus, and Aquarius, require no rain, nor the aid of streams or wells, but are brought to great perfection by the dews and the cool nights at that season of the year, a fact which has always surprised me. The air of the Deccan, owing to its proximity to the sea, and the abundance of the rain which falls, is extremely moist.

The Indians divide the year into three seasons, each having four months. These they call the hot season, the wet season, and the cool season. They calculate their months according to the revolutions of the moon; but their three seasons are rendered subservient to both the solar and lunar year. This they contrive in the following manner:—Whenever the beginning of the lunar month falls on a Tuesday, for instance, and the sun enters Leo on the fifteenth or twentieth of that month, supposing it to be the month of Srawun (August), they commence the month of Bhadown (September) from the day on which the sun enters the new sign of the zodiac. This makes a difference of ten days, and some hours, in every solar year. Thus in every third year they have an extra month, which they include in that division they call the rainy season; and in that year they have five lunar months for the wet season. On the occasion of the extra month again recurring they include it in the cold season, and on the third occasion, in the hot season. The seasons, according to the Indian phraseology, are as follow:—

Srawun (August) Bhadown (September) Asween (October) Kartik (November)	The season of rain,

answering to Cancer, Leo, Virgo, and Libra. They reckon only twenty-six days, and something over, for Libra; and this difference they carry to the account of the lunar year, to make it correspond with the solar calculations.

Margsirsh (December) Poos (January) Mag'h (February) P'halgoon (March)	The cold season,

which lasts from the end of Libra to the beginning of Aquarius, including part of both.

Cheitr (April) Veishak (May) Jesht (June) Ashar (July)	The hot season.

The rains are usually the heaviest in the two months of Srawun and Bhadown (August and September); whereas the cold is in the extreme in the months of

Poos and Mag'h (January and February); and the hottest months are Cheitr and Ashar (April and July). According to this account the Hindoos subdivide the year into six portions, each of which has its particular name; for instance,

Srawun and Bhadown (August and September) are called Burk Root, or Veersha;

Asween and Kartik (October and November) Surrid Root;

Margsirsh and Poos (December and January) Heemunt Root;

Mag'h and P'halgoon (February and March) Seeshir Root;

Cheitr and Veishak (April and May) Busunt Root;

Jeisht and Ashar (June and July) Greeshm Root.

The Hindoos divide the day and night into twelve hours each; and they subdivide their twelve hours into minutes in the same way as in other countries. They also separate the day and night into eight pe'hrs, or watches. A pe'hr is the same as the pas of the Persians, from which is derived the word pasban, a watchman. The Hindoos also subdivide their twelve hours into thirty gurries; so that there are seven gurries and a half in each pe'hr, or watch. The variations in the length of the day and the night are minutely observed, and recorded by their astronomers and learned men.

Let it not remain concealed from those persons who peruse history in general, that the central portion of Hind has been subjected to the arms of the kings of Islam, (may God perpetuate their good works!) while the territories of the confines are still in possession of several great Hindoo princes; who having submitted to pay tribute are permitted to retain their countries, which they thus preserve from foreign invasion. Of these princes, there are five principal rajas on the north, and five others on the south, each of whom has numerous tributary rajas dependent on him. There are several great rajas, too, in the Deccan who possess extensive regions, and who have also tributary chiefs subordinate to them. Of the five former great rajas are.

The Raja of Kooch,
The Raja of Jummoo,
The Raja of Nagrakote,
The Raja of Kumaoon, and
The Raja of Bhimbur.

The rajas of Kooch are lineally descended, from father to son, from Shunkul, who was once a great ruler of that territory. In modern times there have been four dynasties of kings; and he who is now on the throne is of the race of hill-bramins, which are not held in much estimation by the inhabitants of Hindoostan. The territory of Kooch is bounded on one side by Chittagong, on another by China, and on another by Bengal. The Raja of Jummoo in ancient times was held to be very powerful, because he possessed seventy forts. He is of the tribe of Moolbas, or Boolbas: this tribe is connected with the Nowair Purwary. Raja Rig is the first person of this hill-race who is mentioned as famous in history. In the time of Gooshtasp of Persia, Kedaraj, the nephew of Mahraj, King of Kunowj, constructed the fort of Jummoo, and made it over, with the neighbouring country, to Raja Rig. He, accompanied by four hundred blood relations, raised an army, and fixing himself in that mountainous region, established a kingdom for his descendants. The Raja who is now on the throne is the sixty-first lineal decendant of Raja Rig; but he does not possess all the power which his ancestors once did.

The Raja of Nagrakote is of a family which traces its pedigree through a long ancestry of one thousand three hundred years; anterior to which, the race of Beis, or Byce, held sovereign sway in that territory for nearly one thousand years, when the present family ascended the throne; but I have been unable to trace its origin. The Raja of Nagrakote obtains consideration from the Hindoos for two reasons: first, because he holds in his possession so strong a fortress as that of Nagrakote; secondly, because the celebrated temple dedicated to Doorga is within his dominions. From this source he derives a considerable revenue, on account of the pious Hindoos who come annually to make offerings there.

The Raja of Kumaoon also possesses an extensive dominion, and a considerable quantity of gold is procured by washing the earth mounds in his country, which also cotains copper mines. His territory stretches to the north as far as Thibet, and on the south reaches to Sumbhul, which is included in India. He retians in pay an army of eighty thousand men, both cavalry and infantry, and commands great respect from the emperors of Dehly. His treasures, too, are vast. It is a rule among the kings of Kumaoon not to encroach on the hoards of their ancestors; for it is a saying among them, that whoever applies his father's treasures to his own use will become mean and beggarly in spirit; so that at the present day fifty-six distinct treasures exist, which have been left by the rajas of Kumaoon, each of which has the owner's seal on it. The sources of the Jumna and Ganges are both to be found within the Kumaoon territory.

The Raja of Bhimbur is also a prince of great power, and has an extensive dominion. These five rajas have numerous petty princes dependent on them, whose countries are situated in their vicinity. Such are the great Hindoo princes of the Sewalik mountains, which lie on the north of Hindoostan. These mountains extend from Swad and Bijour in a continuous chain as far as Bengal; and they embrace Hindoostan on the north, so that both ends are lost in flat and sandy deserts on the south. From the boundaries of Ketch and Mikram, as far as the mountains, is a desert tract. In these regions are the territories of the Raja of Kutch, the Raja of Amurkote, the Raja of Bhikaneer, the Raja of Jeselmere, and the Jam Raja. The Raja of Kutch, whose territory lies proximate to Sind, is dependent on the King of Guzerat. Water is so scarce in this country that some of the wells are two hundred yards deep, and the element is drawn up by camels. In consequence of this deficiency, agriculture is very limited, and provisions are scarce.

The Raja of Amurkote is one of the rajas of Sind. Like Kutch, it is deficient in water and cultivation. The Emperor Akbur was born at Amurkote.

The Raja of Bhikaneer claims the priviledge of receiving daughters from the several other rajas of India. He is of the race of Bhurteea.

The Raja of Jeselmere is also a great prince: his country lies between Guzerat and Sind. This tract abounds in fearful deserts and forests, and is very deficient in water. Its resources are chiefly derived from breeding horses and camels; for, like the countries of Kutch and Sind, it suffers for want of water, and the cultivation, therefore, is very limited.

The country of the Jam Raja is situated near to Guzerat. When the King of Guzerat is powerful, the Jam Raja pays tribute, otherwise he refuses to do so. His country is ill supplied with water, and his subjects are not only in want of clothing, but frequently suffer from the absence of food. They subsist, for the most part, on the milk of camels and buffaloes. Fine horses are procured in abundance in that country, and the Arabians* which are brought to India are imported through Kutch, and pay a considerable revenue to the government.

* The finest horses produced in India are bred in Kattywer; and it is to the circumstance of crossing them with Arabian blood to which alone we can refer the great superiority of these animals over the other horses of the country.

Within the territories of these five rajes little other grain but bajry and jowar is cultivated. The revenue is for the most part derived from horses and camels.

Among the great rajas of the Deccan is the Raja of the Carnatic. Of this line the most illustrious was Beejy Sing, who, nine hundred years ago, founded the city of Beejanuggur, so called after him; and his decendants considered it incumbent on them to add to its extent and beauty, so that it became seven coss* in circumference. The first person who displayed the banners of revolt in India, and pretended to establish his independence from the kings of Kunowj, was the ancestor of the rajas of the Carnatic, as has been before related;† and in the reign of Mahraj he expelled his lieutenant, Shew Ray, from the Deccan. His descendants, however, from father to son, succeeded to the kingdom, when at length Ramraj, in the year 972 (A. D. 1564), opposed the kings of the Deccan, and was slain; after which period no such raja has sat on the throne.

As ample details regarding the other rajas of the Deccan are to be found by referring to the histories of that part of India which have been before given in this work, I have not thought proper to lengthen it out by again dwelling on those subjects.

* Fourteen miles. † Introductory chapter, vol. i. p. xxix.

COMPARATIVE CHRONOLOGY

OF

THE MINOR KINGDOMS WHICH EVENTUALLY FELL INTO THE POWER OF THE GREAT MOGUL.

A. D.	GENERAL CHRONOLOGY OF INDIA.	GUZERAT.	MALWA.	KANDEISH.
1370	FEROZE TOGHLUK, King of Dehly	....	....	The district of Talnere conferred on Mullik Raja.
1387	....	....	Dilawur Khan Ghoory made governor	
1389	MAHMOOD TOGHLUK, King of Dehly			
1391	....	Moozuffur Khan, governor		
1397	....	——————assumes the title of King		
1399	Teimoor invades India............	....	....	Death of Mullik Raja.—MULLIK NUSEER, King.
1400	———sacks Dehly, and expels the King	Mahmood Toghluk of Dehly solicits an asylum	——————affords a refuge to the exiled King of Dehly	
1401	....	The districts of Idur and Diù taken from the Hindoos	The King of Dehly quits Malwa to reoccupy his throne.—DILAWUR KHAN assumes the title of King	
1406	The kingdom of Dehly limited to within a few miles of the city	....	Dilawur Khan dies.—SOOLTAN HOOSHUNG, King	
1407	....	Moozuffur Shah wage war with the King of Malwa	Sooltan Hooshung is defeated, and made prisoner	
1408	....	....	——————is restored to his throne	
1410	....	——————dies.—AHMUD SHAH I. King		
1411	....	Ahmud Shah has to contend with his cousins for the throne	——————invades Guzerat in aid of the pretenders	Mullik Nuseer occupies Aseer by treachery.
1415	SYUD KHIZR KHAN, King—he recovers part of the Doab			
1417	....	——————levies tribute from the Raja of Buglana	....	——————receives the regalia from the King of Guzerat, and the title of Khan.

A.D.	GENERAL CHRONOLOGY OF INDIA.	GUZERAT.	MALWA.	KANDEISH.
1418	......	Formidable confederacy of the Hindoos against Ahmud Shah	Sooltan Hooshung invades Guzerat to aid the Hindoos	
—	......	Ahmud Shah exacts tribute from the Raja of Champanere, and invades Malwa.—Peace concluded	——is defeated at the battle of Kaliada.—Peace with Guzerat	
1421	Syud Khizr Khan dies, and is succeeded by SYUD MOOBARIK	War renewed with Malwa......	——proceeds to Jajnuggur to obtain elephants, and returns to Mando.—Battle of Sarungpoor.—Levies tribute from the Raja of Kehrla	
—	......	Ahmud Shah retreats.—end of the war		
1426	......	——builds the fort of Ahmudnuggur, near Idur		
1427	War with the King of Joonpoor			
1428	War with the Gukkurs in the Punjab	......	The Raja of Kehrla attacked by the Bahmuny King of the Deccan	
1429	......	——invades the Deccan.—Battle of Manukpoonj	The King of Malwa proceeds to the Deccan, but is defeated	
1430	......	Bombay and Tanna taken by the Deccan troops, but recovered by the Guzeratties		
1432	Lahore temporarily occupied by the Moguls	......	Death of Sooltan Hooshung.—SOOLTAN MAHOMED GHOORY, King	
1435	Death of Syud Moobarik.—SYUD MAHOMED, King	......	Mahomed is murdered by his relative Mahmood Khiljy	
1436	......	Ahmud opposes the pretensions of Mahmood Khilji to the throne of Malwa	Severe contests for the crown, which finally terminate in the firm establishment of SOOLTAN MAHMOOD KHILJY	
1437	......	......	......	Mullik Nuseer becomes involved in war with the King of the Deccan
1440	Dehly besieged by the king of Malwa	......	Sooltan Mahmood proceeds to Dehly by invitation, but meets with little encouragement, and in consequence return	Battle of Lulling.—Death of Nuseer Khan
1441	......	......	——invades Rajpoothana—besieges Koombulmere and Chittoor	MEERAN ADIL KHAN.—MEERAN MOOBARIK KHAN
1443	......	Death of Ahmud Shah I.—MAHOMED SHAH, King		

A. D.	GENERAL CHRONOLOGY OF INDIA.	GUZERAT.	MALWA.	KANDEISH.
1444	....	....	Sooltan Mahmood wages war with the King of Joonpoor	
1446	SYUD ALLA-OOD-DEEN, King of Dehly	....	——levies tribute from the Rana of Mundulgur	
1447	Thirteen independent Mahomedan kings in India			
1450	....	Mahomed Shah proceeds to impose tribute on Champanere	—— ——marches to assist the Raja of Champanere	
1451	....	——retires hastily to Ahmudabad, and dies.—KOOTB SHAH, King	——invades Guzerat	
1453	BHEILOLE LODY, King..........	War with Malwa.—Battle of Surkech, wherein the King of Malwa captures the crown jewels of Guzerat		
1455	——recovers a part of the Dehly empire	Kootb Shah invades the territory of the Rana	——takes Kerowly, Ajmere, and Runtunbhore	
1457	....	——takes Aboogur by strom —dies.—DAWOOD SHAH, King	——invades the territory of the Rana, and exacts tribute	Meeran Moobarik Khan dies.—ADIL KHAN, King
——	....	MAHMOOD BEGURRA, King		
1461	....	....	——invades the Deccan—gains the battle of Bidur	
1462	....	——marches to the relief of the King of the Deccan	——is compelled to retreat with heavy loss	
1464	....	....	Kehrla taken by the army of the Deccan	
1465	....	——levies tribute on the rajas along the coast south of Surat	——gains the battle of Elichpoor.— Kehrla restored. —Peace with the King of the Deccan	
1467	....	....	The Raja of Kehrla retakes that fortress, but it is again wrested out of his hands	
——	....	....	An Ambassador arrives from Aboo Syeed, King of Bokhara	
1469	....	——invades western Guzerat, and takes Girnal or Girnar	——dies. —GHBIAS-OOD-DEEN, King—confides the whole management of his government to his son	
1470	....	——invades Kutch and Sind—builds Moostufabad, in western Guzerat		

A. D.	GENERAL CHRONOLOGY OF INDIA.	GUZERAT.	MALWA.	KANDEISH.
1474	Bheilole Lody conquers the kingdom of Joonpoor			
1482	....	Mahmood Begurra commences the seige of Champanere		
1484	....	———— ————Champanere taken, after a siege of more than two years		
1490	Death of Bheilole Lody.—SIKUNDUR, King			
1494	....	Bombay attacked by Bahadur Geelany, a Deccan chief.—Reparation made by the King of the Deccan		
1495	....	....	Commencement of the civil war	
1498	The Portuguese reach India by the route of the Cape of Good Hope	————————compels Adil Khan of Kandeish to pay tribute—invades the Deccan	Death of Gheias-ood-Deen.—NASIR-OOD-DEEN, King	
1500	A Portuguese fleet of thirteen sail of ships arrives.—The Portuguese make war with the Mahomedan fleets.—The latter well supplied with cannon, and make use of fire-ships			
1503	Severe naval action of Cochin......	....	....	Adil Khan dies.—DAWOOD KHAN, King
1507	Two Portuguese fleets, consisting of thirty-five vessels, reach India			
1508	A fleet of twelve vessels reaches India.—Naval action of Choul.—The Portuguese first employ the Indians against their enemies	————————sends his admiral to join the Turkish admiral from the Red Sea to engage the Portuguese fleet		
1510	Goa taken by the Portuguese—recaptured by the King of Beejapoor	———— ————places his grandson, ADIL KHAN II. on the throne of Kandeish—receives an embassy from the King of Dehly—also from the King of Persia	....	Dawood Khan dies.—ADIL KHAN. II.
1511	Goa retaken by the Portuguese, on which occasion five thousand native troops are employed	————————dies.—MOOZUFFUR II. King		
1512	....	....	Death of Nasir-ood-Deen.—MAHMOOD II. King	

A. D.	GENERAL CHRONOLOGY OF INDIA.	GUZERAT.	MALWA.	KANDEISH
1512	....	....	Contests for the throne among his brothers—his Hindoo chiefs prove their attachment to him—he becomes jealous of them	
1517	Sikundur Lody dies.—IBRAHIM, King of Dehly	Moozuffur Shah marches into Malwa	He flies to Guzerat........	Adil Khan II. accompanies the King of Guzerat into Malwa
1518	....	....	Mando captured from the Hindoos after a dreadful slaughter, and Mahmood II. reinstated on his throne	
1519	....	....	Rana Sanka invades Malwa.—defeats Sooltan Mahmood II. and makes him prisoner.—Mahmood restored to his throne by Rana Sanka	
1520	The Portuguese fail in a attempt to take Diù	Rana Sanka invades Guzerat......	....	———dies.—MEERAN MAHOMED, King
1521	A second attempt also fails.........	Moozuffur Shah invades the dominions of the Rana		
1524	....	The Prince Bahadur quits his father's court in disgust, and proceeds to Dehly		
1526	Babur ascends the throne of Dehly	Death of Moozuffur Shah II.—SIKUNDUR, King—his death.—MAHMOOD II. King.—BAHADUR SHAH, King		
1527	....	Contests for the throne..............	Sooltan Mahmood affords an asylum to the Guzerat princes	Meeran Mahomed engages in war with the King of the Deccan, and is defeated—solicits the aid of his uncle Bahadur Shah of Guzerat
1529	———dies.—HOOMAYOON, King of Dehly	Bahadur Shah invades the Deccan, and causes himself to be acknowledged King in Berar and Ahmudnuggur		
1531	The Portuguese armada of four hundreds ships and twenty-two thousand men sails from Bombay against Diù	———invades Malwa and subdues it.—The Portuguese fleet and expedition repulsed off Diù	Mando taken by escalade.—Death Mahmood II.	———attends his uncle, Bahadur Shah in the campaign in Malwa
1533	Battle of Agra gained by Hoomayoon, who invades Malwa	———affords an asylum to the malcontent Mogul chiefs		
———	....	———defies the power of Hoomayoon—besieges and takes Chittoor		

A. D.	GENERAL CHRONOLOGY OF INDIA.	GUZERAT.	MALWA.	KANDEISH.
1534	War with Bahadur Shah.—Defeat at Mundsoor.—Mando and Champanere taken.—Guzerat occupied by the Moguls	Bahadur Shah defeated, and pursued by Hoomayoon through Malwa to Cambay.—Guzerat held by the Moguls		
—	Insurrection of the Afghans in Bengal	————recovers his kingdom		
1535	…	————is killed in an affray with the Portuguese at Diù.—MEERAN MAHOMED SHAH, King		
1536	…	His death MAHMOOD III. King	…	Meeran Mahomed called to the throne of Guzerat.—MEERAN MOOBARIK KHAN, King
1539	Hoomayoon expelled from India by Sheer Shah Soor			
1541	…	…	Malwa conquered by Sheer Shah Soor	
1543	Conquers Malwa—takes Runtunbhore — besieges Kalunjur—is killed by the explosion of a shell. —SULIM SHAH, King			
1552	Sulim Shah dies. — MAHOMED SHAH SOOR ADILY, King			
1553	…	Mahmood III. dies.—AHMUD II. King		
1554	Hoomayoon crosses the Indus from Persia, and regains his crown			
1556	————his death.—AKBUR, King			
1558	Final re-establishment of the Mogul empire			
1561	…	Death of Ahmud II.—MOOZUFFUR III. King	BAZ BAHADUR, King—is attacked by the Moguls	Meeran Moobarik Khan aids Baz Bahadur
—	…	Dissensions in the state…	The Mogul general killed, and Baz Bahadur restored	
1566	…	…	…	————dies.—MEERAN MAHOMED KHAN
1567	Akbur invited into Guzerat…	Invasion by Akbur		
1572	————enters Guzerat to expel the Mirzas.—GUZERAT CONQUERED	Occupation by Akbur, and abdication of Moozuffur III.		
1575	————invades and occupies Behar. —BEHAR CONQUERED			
1576	…	…	…	Meeran Mahomed Khan dies.—RAJA ALLY KHAN

A. D.	GENERAL CHRONOLOGY OF INDIA.	GUZERAT.	MALWA.	KANDEISH.
1578	MALWA CONQUERED................	....	Baz Bahadur abdicates his throne in favour of Akbur	
1583	....	Death of Moozuffur III. the last of his race		
1584	Death of Bahadur Shah, the last of the kings of Luknowty			
——	BENGAL CONQUERED			
1586	KASHMEER CONQUERED			
1590	SIND CONQUERED.—Berar ceded to Akbur			
1592	MOOLTAN CONQUERED..............	....	....	Boorhanpoor is sacked by a body of mutineers from Ahmudnuggur
1595	Battle of Soopa in the Deccan......	....	....	Raja Ally Khan killed.—BAHADUR KHAN
1599	AHMUDNUGGUR CONQUERED. — KANDEISH CONQUERED	....	....	Aseer besieged and taken—Bahadur Khan deposed

APPENDIX.

No. I.

AN ALPHABETICAL LIST

OF

THE PROPER NAMES, TITLES, AND ORIENTAL WORDS.

WHICH OCCUR IN THIS WORK,

WITH EXPLANATIONS ATTACHED.

Akil	عاقل	*A.* The wise
Abbas	عبّاس	*A.* The fierce
Abdool		
Abdoolla	عبدالله	*A.* The servant of God
Abdy Zeina	عبدي زيبا	*A.* Contraction for Abdoolla Zein
Abia	ابيا	*A.* Abia
Abool Asakir	ابو العساكر	*A.* The father of the host
Abool Fuzl	ابوالفضل	*A.* The father of excellence
Abool Kasim	ابوالقاسم	*A.* Father of Kasim (a divider)
Adeena	آدينه	*A.* Swarthy

Note.—The capital letters denote the language from which each word is derived :—viz. *A.* Arabic. *Af.* Words of Afghan origin. *C.* Canarese. *H.* Hindvy. *Ka.* Kashmeerian, *M.* Marratta. *P.* Persian. *S.* Sanscrit. *T.* Toorky.

Adhum	ادهم	*A.* Swarthy
Adil	عادل	*A.* The just
Adil Shahy	عادل شاهي	*A.P.* Of or belonging to the dynasty of Beejapoor so called
Adum	آدم	*A.* Adam
Afghan	افغان	*Af.* People so called
Afra	افرا	*A.* The nimble
Afrasiab	افراسیاب	*P.* (An ancient king of Persia)
Afreedoon	افریدون	Ditto
Afshar	افشار	*P.* Tribe
Afzul	افضل	*A.* The excellent
Agha	آقا	*T.* Lord
Agny	اگني	*S.* Fire. A lamb
Ahdy	احدي	*A.* (The fierce). The one
Ahmud	احمد	*A.* The praiseworthy
Ahrar	احرار	*A.* The free born (title of a poet)
Ajda	اژده	*P.* The dragon
Ajdur	اژدر	*P.* The dragon
Ajeet Dew	اجيت ديو	*S.* The invincible prince
Akbur	اکبر	*A.* The great
Akheel	اخيل	*A.* Freckled
Ak Koovinloo	اق قونيلو	*T.* Tribe of the white ram
Akta	اکتا	*T.* Foster mother's relative

Alankoo	الانکو	*T.* Tribe
Alberg	البري	*T.* Tribe
Alingez	النگز	*T.* Tribe
Alkadur Billa	القادر بالله	*A.* The powerful in God
Alla-ood-Deen	علا الدين	*A.* Glory of the faith
Alla-ool-Moolk	علا الملک	*A.* Glory of the state
Allay	علا ي	*A.* Of or belonging to Alla-ood-Deen
Ally	علي	*A.* Glorious
Ally Shukur	علي شکر	*A.* Of high praises
Allytugeen	عليتگين	*P.* The glorious hero
Almas	الماس	*P.* Diamond
Altoon	التون	*T.* Gold
Altoonea	التونيه	*T.* Golden
Altumish	التمش	*T.* Sixty (so called from being purchased for sixty tomans)
Aluf	الف	*A.* Upright
Alugh	الغ	*T.* The great
Alum	عالم	*A.* Intelligent
Aluptugeen	الپتگين	*T.* The impetuous tiger
Alwund	الوند	*P.* The name of a mountain
Amarry	اماري	*H.* The seat on an elephant having a canopy
Ambur	عمبر	*A.* Ambergris

Ameen	امين	*A.* Faithful, *m.*
Ameena	امينه	*A.* Faithful, *f.*
Ameen-ool-Moolk	امين الملک	*A.* Faithful of the state
Ameer	امير	*A.* A Prince
Ameer-ood-Deen	امير الدين	*A.* Prince of the faith
Ameer-ool-Momineen	امير المومنين	*A.* Prince of the faithful
Ameer-ool-Omra	امير الامرا	*A.* Prince of princes
Ameerzada	امير زاده	*P.* Son of a prince
Amroo	عمرو	*A.* Proper name
Amurgoey	امرگوي	*P.* Title of inspector of agriculture
Amur Sing	امر سنگ	*S.* The lion chief
Anchul	انچل	*H.* Proper name
Andeel	انديل	*Af.* Proper name
Andly	اندلي	*H.* Blindfold
Anjoo	انجو	*T.* The Precious
Anka	انكا	*T.* A wet nurse
Ankoos	انكوس	*S.* An elephant goad
Ansar	انصار	*A.* Auxiliaries
Anund	انند	*S.* Joyous
Anundpal	انندپال	*S.* The joyous prince
Anwur	انور	*A.* The resplendent
Anwury	انوري	*A.P.* The resplendent
Arab Khan	عرب خان	*A.* The Arab chief
Ardsheer Babegan	اردشير بابگان	*P.* Babegan, the lion of the host
Arghoon	ارغون	*T.* Red or fair
Arif	عارف	*A.* Intelligent

Arizy	عارضي	*H.* The officer who forwards petitions to the throne
Arjoon	ارجُن	*S.* Name of a hero god
Armian	ارمیان	*Af.* Projector (Jeremiah)
Arsapa	ارسپا	*C.* Proper name
Arslan	ارسلان	*T.* The lion
Arustoo	ارسطو	*A.* Aristotle
Asa	اسا	*H.* Proper name
Asghur	اصغر	*A.* The little
A'shab	اصحاب	*A.* Companions
Ashruf	اشرف	*A.* Most noble
Ashruffy	اشرفي	*P.* Most noble
Ashwat'hama	اشوتهمه	*S.* The restrainer of horses (the name of a Hindoo demigod)
Askurry	عسکري	*A.* Chieftain
Assamy	اسامي	*P.* The inhabitants of Assam
Assud	اسد	*A.* Lion
Assudy	اسدي	*A.* A tribe of Arabs occupying Arabia Petra
Assumud	الصمد	*A.* The eternal
Asuf	اصف	*A.* Azof
Asy Row	اسي راو	*M.* Proper name
Atabuky	اتابکي	*T.* The tutor of the prince

Atba	عتبه	*A.* The excellent
Atchy	اچي	*S.* Virtuous
Atka	اتکا	*T.* Relative of a wet-nurse
Atmeer	اتمير	*Af.* Proper name
Attar	عطّار	*A.* The perfumer
Atushpara	آتشپاره	*P.* Spark of Fire
Aurungzeeb	اورنگزيب	*P.* The ornament of the throne
Azad	آزاد	*P.* Free
Azeez-ool-Moomalik	عزيز الممالک	*A.* Beloved of the universe
Azeez-ool-Moolk	عزيز الملک	*A.* Dear to the state
Azum	عظم	*A.* The magnificent
Azmut	عظمت	*A.* Magnificence
Azoory	اذري	*P.* The fire-worshipper
Baba	بابا	*T.* Father
Babajee	باباجي	*T.* Paternal
Baboo	بابو	*S.* Master
Babur	بابر	*T.* The lion-hearted
Bahadur	بهادر	*T.* The valiant
Baha-ood-Deen	بها الدين	*A.* The splendour of the faith
Baha-ool-Moolk	بها الملک	*A.* The splendour of the state
Bahmun	بهمن	*P.* An ancient king of Persia
Bahmuny	بهمني	*P.* Sagacious, appertaining to a Brahmin

Baikra	بايقره	*T.* Proper name
Bain	باين	*A.* The distinguished
Baisanghar	بايسنغر	*T.* Proper name
Bakur	باقر	*T.* Brown or copper-coloured
Baky	باقي	*A.* The resolute
Baky Khuteer	باقي خطير	*A.* The illustriously resolute
Bala Row	بالا راو	*S.* The illustrious prince
Balyrow	باليراو	*S.* Ditto
Banoo Begum	بانو بگم	*T.* Lady queen
Bany	باني	*A.* Builder or architect
Barbik	باربک	*T.* Chief of the council
Bargeer	بارگير	*H.P.* A cavalry soldier (literally, one carrying heavy arms)
Barha	بارها	*Af.* Tribe
Basheer	بشير	*A.* Comely
Bastugeen	باستگين	*T.* Of great valour
Bayezeed	بايزيد	*T.* The illustrious prince
Baz	باز	*P.* A hawk
Bedar	بيدار	*P.* Vigilant
Beeby	بيبي	*H.* Lady
Beeby, By	بيبى بي	*H.* Lady queen
Beeby Rajy	بيبى راجي	*H.* Lady queen
Beerbul	بيربل	*H.* Powerful
Beg	بگ	*T.* Prince

Begum	بگم	*T.* Princess
Begurra	بیگره	*S.* Surname of Mahmood of Guzerat
Behroze	نهروز	*P.* Probably a corruption of Feroze, victorious
Behzad-ool-Moolk	بهزاد الملک	*A.* The most noble of the state
Beiooka	بیوقا	*T.* Proper name
Beiram	بیرام	*T.* A feast
Beiramgoor	بیرامگور	*T.* The name of an ancient king of Persia
Bereed	برید	*T.* Royal, illustrious
Bereed Shahy	برید شاهي	*T.* Of or belonging to the dynasty so called which reigned at Bidur
Bergy	برگي	*M.* Light-armed cavalry
Bhagmutty	بهاگمتي	*S.* The name of a favourite mistress of the king of Golconda
Bhardevy	نهاردیوي	*M.* The Princess Bhar
Bharjy	بهارجي	*M.* Proper name
Bharloo	بهارلو	*T.* Name of a tribe
Bharmul	بهارمل	*S.* Proper name
Bhaybulundur	بهایبلندر	*S.* Of exalted dignity
Bheel	بهل	*S.* Name of a tribe of hill people

Bheem	بهيم	*S.* Awful
Bheer Khan	بهير بهان	*S.* Lord of the war-car
Bheilole	بهيلول	*Af.* Proper name
Bheiry	بهيري	*H.* A falcon
Bhew Ray	بهيو راي	*S.* The awful king
Bhikun	بهكن	*H.* Proper name
Bhoje	بهوج	*S.* Dominion
Bhoje Mul Naig	بهوج مل نايگ	*S.* The chief holding dominion
Bhojut	بهجت	*P.* Joyful
Bholy	بهولي	*Af.* Vulgar
Bhoola	بهوله	*Af.* Ditto
Bhoory	بهوري	*Af.* Red haired
Bhowany Das	بهواني داس	*S.* The slave of the goddess
Bhowput	بهوپت	*S.* The lord of the earth
Bhugwandass	بهگواندا س	*S.* The servant of God
Bhungera	بهنگيره	*Af.* Tribe
Bhurt	بهرت	*S.* Proper name
Bhyleem	بهيليم	*Af.* Proper name
Bhyrew	بهيرو	*S* Awful
Bijly	بيجلي	*H.* Lightning
Bilal Dew	بلال ديو	*S.* The great prince
Birkana	برکانه	*C.* Proper name
Birlas	برلاس	*T.* Tribe
Boghtudy	بغتدي	*T.* Proper name
Bokraz	بقراز	*T.* Proper name
Booboojee	بوبوجي	*T.* Lady
Boochuna	بوچنه	*C.* Proper name

Boodagh	بداغ	*T.* Proper name
Boodhun	بودهن	*S.* The wise
Boodoo	بودو	*H.* Corruption of the above
Boolbas	بلباس	*T.* Tribe
Boorhan-ood-Deen	برهان الدين	*A.* Chief of the faithful
Boostamy	بستامي	*P.* An inhabitant of Boostam
Boot-Shikun	بت شكن	*P.* Destroyer of idols
Boozoorg	بزرگ	*P.* Great
Boozunjur	بوزنجر	*T* Destroyer
Borish	بورش	*T.* Hardy, flinty
Bramha	برمه	*S.* Brahma
Brahmin	برهمن	*S.* A Brahmin
Bubun	ببن	*Af.* Proper name
Buddoo	بدو	*Af.* Ditto
Budee-ooz-Zuman	بديع الزمان	*A.* The wonder of the age
Budmeen	بدمين	*A.* Proper name
Budr	بدر	*A.* Full moon, resplendent
Budra	بدره	*Ka.* Tribe in Cashmeer
Budukhshy	بدخشي	*P.* Inhabitant of Budukshan
Bukshshy	بخشي	*P.* Fortunate
Buktyar	بختيار	*P.* Fortunate tribe in Persia
Bulbhudar	بلبهدر	*H.* Powerful

Bulbun	بلبن	*P.* *Portulaca*
Buleel	بليل	*A.* Humid, soft
Buloch	بلوچ	*P.* Tribe
Bulochy	بلوچي	*P.* One of the tribe
Bundgan	بندگان	*P.* Servile
Bungush	بنگش	*Af.* Tribe
Bungy	بنگي	*H.* Scavenger
Burkhoordar	برخوردار	*P.* Fortunate
Burny	برني	*H.* An inhabitant of Birun
Buswunt Row	بسونت راو	*S.* Resembling the bull
Chahar minar	چهار منار	*P.* Palace of four pillars
Chand	چاند	*H.* Resplendent
Cheen	چين	*P.* Chinese
Chehlgany	چهلگاني	*T.* Tribe
Chinia	چينيه	*C.* Diminutive
Chishty	چشتي	*T.* An inhabitant of Chisht
Chitnevees	چتنويس	*P.* Secretary
Chitty	چتي	*S.* Letter
Choban	چوبان	*P.* The shepherd
Choghtay	چغتاي	*T.* Name of a tribe
Choldy Khan	چلدي خان	*T.* A lance
Chougan	چوگان	*T.* A game played with bat and ball
Chowbeea	چوبيه	*T.* Tribe
Chowhan	چوهان	*H.* Ditto
Chuk	چک	*Ka.* Ditto

Chunchul	چنچل	*S.* Unsteady
Chund Ray	چند راي	*S.* King Chand, or the resplendent
Chundur Sein	چندر سين	*S.* Moonlike chief
Chungiz	چنگيز	*T.* Proper name
Chushawimdy	چشاوندي	*T.* An inhabitant of Cheshawand
Chutr	چتر	*S.* A canopy or umbrella used by kings
Coss	کوس	*S.* A measure of length, varying from one and a half to three miles in different parts of India
Dabishleem	دابشليم	*S.* Proper name
Daby	دابي	*H.* Tribe in Sowrashtra
Dad	داد	*P.* Justice
Dahir	داهر	*H.* Proper name
Daniel	دانيال	*A.* Daniel
Danieltugeen	دانيالتگين	*A T.* Daniel the chief
Danishmund	دانشمند	*P.* The wise
Dara	دارا	*P.* Darius
Darab	داراب	*P.* Corruption of Dara
Dawood	داود	*A.* David
Dawoodzye	داود زاي	*Af.* Tribe of David
Deena	دينا	*A.* Faithful
Denar	دينار	*P.* Deenar
Deilimy	ديلمي	*P.* Inhabitants of Deilim

Deotee	ديوتي	*H.* Lamplighter
Depul Hurry	ديوپال هري	*S.* The supreme lord
Dervish	درويش	*P.* Dervise
Dewul Devy	ديول ديوي	*S.* The lady queen
Devy Das	ديوي داس	*S.* The lord and master
Dew	ديو	*S.* Prince
Dew Naig	ديونايگ	*S.* The regal chief
Dewraj	ديورا ج	*S.* The regal prince
Dhurma	دهرمه	*S.* The just
D'hurmarow	دهرمه راو	*S.* The just king
Dhurmchund	دهرمچند	*S.* The just prince
Dilaram	دل ارام	*P.* The comforter
Dilawur	دل اور	*P.* The brave
Diljoo	دلجو	*P.* The conciliator
Dilshad	دلشاد	*P.* The gladdener
Diwan Khana	ديوان خانه	*P.* The public hall of audience
Doaspa	دواسپه	*P.* Double horsed
Doghlat	دغلات	*T.* Tribe
Dongur See	دنگرسي	*S.* The hill chief
Dongur Sein	دنگرسين	*S.* Ditto
Dookna	دكنه	*M.* Family name
Dooldy	دولدي	*T.* Tribe
Doorga	درگه	*S.* Goddess of destruction
Dooryodhun	دوريودهن	*S.* One of the princes of the Mahabharut
Dost	دوست	*P.* Friendly
Doung	دوانگ	*M.* Having two weapons in war

Dowla	دوله	*P.* Prosperous
Dowlut	دولت	*P.* Ditto, the state
Droupdy	دروپدي	*S.* A heroine of the Mahabharut
Dubeer	دبير	*P.* Secretary
Dukeeky	دقيقي	*P.* Name of a poet
Duffady	دفعدار	*A.* A subordinate military officer
Dundany	دنداني	*P.* having projecting teeth
Durbar	دربار	*P.* The court
Darea	دريه	*P.* Ocean
Dustoor	دستور	*P.* The pillar
Dustoor-ool-Moolk	دستور الملک	*A.P.* The pillar of the state
Dutrashtur	دتراشتر	*S.* The lord of the country
Duvaly	دوالي	*H.* Tribe
Eedgah	عيدگاه	*P.* Place of holding a festival
Eesa	عيسي	*A.* Jesus
Eiaz	اياز	*A* Refulgent
Eibuk	ايبک	*T.* Crested
Ein-ool-Moolk	عين الملک	*A.* The glory of the state
Eisha	عايشه	*A.* Voluptuous
Eiz-ood-Deen	عزالدين	*A.* The glory of the faith
Elderim	يلدرم	*T.* Lightning

Elias	الياس	*A.* Elias
Elik	الک	*T.* Fireball
Enoch	انوخ	*A.* Enoch
Eritch	ایر	*T.* Proper name
Etibar	عتبار	*A.* Faithful
Etimad	اعتماد	*A* Right arm
Faik	فایق	*A.* Superior
Farooky	فرخي	*P.* Propitious
Fatima	فاتمه	*A.* Name of the daughter of the prophet
Fazie	فاضل	*A.* Most excellent
Ferishta	فرشته	*P.* An angel, a messenger
Feroze	فیروز	*P.* Propitious
Fetteh	فتح	*A.* Victorious
Fidwy	فدوي	*P.* Obedient
Firdowsy	فردوسي	*P.* Name of the poet
Firman	فرمان	*P.* A royal mandate
Firmully	فرملّي	*Af.* Tribe
Folad	فولاد	*P.* Steel
Folady	فولادي	*P.* Of steel
Fowjy	فوجی	*P.* Soldier
Fukhr-ood-Deen	فخر الدین	*A.* Pride of the faithful
Fukhr-ool-Moolk	فخر الملک	*A.* Pride of the state
Furash	فرّاش	*P.* A person who pitches tents
Furash Khana	فراش خانه	*P.* Camp-equipage establishment

Fureed	فريد	*A.* Precious
Fureedon	فريدون	*P.* King of Persia
Furhad	فرهاد	*P.* A celebrated statuary
Furhut-ool-Moolk	فرحت الملک	*A.* The joy of the state
Furokh	فرخ	*P.* Propitious
Furokhy	فرخي	*P.* Ditto
Furokhzeed	فرخزاد	*P.* Nobly born
Futtehy	فتحي	*A.* Victorious
Fuzeel	فضيل	*A.* Learned
Fuzeelut	فضيلت	*A.* Excellence
Fuzl	فضل	*A.* Superior
Fuzl-oolla	فضل الله	*A.* Possessing excellence from God
Fyz-oolla	فيض الله	*A.* Possessing liberality from God
Gand'hary	گندهاري	*S.* Name of a heroine of the Mahabharut
Gawan	گاوان	*P.* Proper name
Geelany	گيلاني	*P.* Native of Geelan
Geesoo-duraz	گيسو دراز	*P.* Longhaired
Ghalib	غالب	*A.* Powerful
Ghazy	غازي	*A.* Hero of the faith
Ghazy-mehaly	غازي محلي	*A.* Name of a slave
Gheias-ood-Deen	غياث الدين	*A.* The aid of religion
Ghiza-Toorkman	غزا ترکمان	*T.* Tribe

Ghizny	غزني	*P.* Proper name
Gholam-i-Ally	غلام علي	*P.* The servant of Ally
Gholam-i-K'has	غلام خاص	*P.* Royal slaves. The household troops
Ghows	غوث	*A.* The beseecher
Ghuffary	غفاري	*A.* The pardoner
Ghuneem	غنيم	*A.* The fortunate
Ghuzunfur	غضنفر	*P.* Hero or Lion
Gimgadas	گنگا داس	*S.* Lord of the Ganges
Gungoo	گنگو	*S.* Of or belonging to the Ganges
Giran	گران	*P.* Dear, precious
Giras	گراس	*S.* Mouthful
Girassia	گراسيه	*S.* Hindoo tribe
Gokultash	گوکلتاش	*T.* Tribe
Gond	گوند	*H.* Tribe
Goodurz	گودرز	*P.* Ancient king of Persia
Goojur	گوجر	*S.* Hindoo tribe
Gool	گل	*P.* Flower, roseate
Goolbuden	گلبدن	*P.* Delicate as a rose
Goolrokh	گلرخ	*P.* Rosy cheek
Goolrung	گلرنگ	*P.* Roseate, rose coloured
Goolzar	گلزار	*P.* Rose garden
Goony	گوني	*S.* One possessing high qualities
Goorgandaz	گرگ‌انداز	*P.* Wolf-slyer

Gooshtasp	گشتاسپ	*P.* Ancient king of Persia
Gopal	گوپال	*S.* Cowherd, appellation of Krishna
Gopraj	گوپراج	*S.* A synonime of Krishna
Govind	گوبند	*S.* Appellation of Krishna
Gowhur	گوهر	*P.* Jewel
Gudda	گدا	*P.* Begger
Guja	گجا	*S.* Possessing elephants
Gujputty	گجاپتي	*S.* The lord of the elephants
Gukkur	گکر	*H.* A tribe in Punjab
Gunesh	گنيش	*S.* Ganesa
Gunga	گنگا	*S.* The Ganges
Gunghadhur	گنگادهر	*S.* The restrainer of the Ganges
Gunj-Shukr	گنج شکر	*P.* Repository of sweetness
Hafiz	حافظ	*A.* Protector
Hajib	حاجب	*P.* Groom of the bedchamber
Hajy	حاجي	*A.* Pilgrim
Hamid	حامد	*A.* Praiseworthy
Haroon	هارون	*A.* Impatient
Hatim	حاتم	*A.* A Judge
Hawaldar	هوالدار	*P.* A subordinate military officer

Heiat	حيات	*A.* Life
Heibut	هيبت	*A.* Awe
Heidur	حيدر	*A.* Lion
Heidur-ool-Moolk	حيدر الملک	*A.* Lion of the state
Hemajee	هماجي	*S.* Golden
Hemoo	هيمو	*S.* Ditto
Hemraj	هيمراج	*S.* Golden prince
Hijaz	حجاز	*A.* Mecca
Hijubr-ood-Deen	حجبر الدين	*A.* Lion of the faith
Hindal	هندال	*T.* Black
Hindoo	هندو	*T.* Ditto
Himmut	همّت	*P.* Resolution
Hirawul	هراول	*T.* The advanced guard of an army
Hirvy	هروي	*P.* An inhabitant of Hirat
Hissam-ood-Deen	حصام الدين	*A.* The sowrd of the faith
Hoolakoo	هولاكو	*T.* Proper name
Hoomayoon	همايون	*P.* Propitious
Hoon	هون	*C.* A golden coin, pagoda
Hoorein	هورين	*A.* Proper name
Hoormooz	هرمز	*P.* The Deity
Hooshung	هشنگ	*P.* An ancient king of Persia
Hooshiar	هوشيار	*P.* Vigilant
Hoossein	حسين	*A.* Virtuous

Howda	هوده	*H.* An uncovered seat on an elephant
Hubeeb	حبيب	*A.* Affectionate
Hubush	حبش	*A.* Abyssinian
Hudeea-Sooltana	هديه شلطانه	*P.* Proper name of a princess
Hukeem	حكيم	*A.* Philosopher
Humadany	همداني	*P.* An inhabitant of Hamadan
Humad-ood-Deen	هماد الدين	*A.* The most praiseworthy of the faithful
Humbur Dew	همبر ديو	*S.* A corruption of Amra Deva, the immortal prince
Humeed	حميد	*A.* Praised
Hunzvy	حمزوي	*A.* Tribe
Handeatum	هندياتم	*C.* Proper name
Humeef	حنيف	*A.* Faithful
Hunefy	حنفي	*A.* Name of a sect
Hurdevy	هرديوي	*S.* Lady queen
Hurdut	هردت	*S.* Adopted lord
Hurry	هري	*S.* Lord
Hurrychundur	هريچندر	*S.* Refulgent lord
Hurry Sa	هري سا	*S.* Lord and king
Hursook	هرسوک	*S.* The comfort of his prince
Hurum or Haram	حرم	*A.* Seraglio (sanctuary)
Hussun	حسن	*A.* Virtue

Hutpal	هتپال	*S.* Lord of the elephant
Huzara	هزارا	*Af.* Name of a tribe
Hye	حي	*A.* Living
Ibrahim	ابراهيم	*A.* Abraham
Idrees	ادريس	*A.* Esdras
Iftikhkar-ool-Moolk	افتخار الملک	*A.* Ornament of the state
Imad-ood-Deen	عماد الدين	*A.* Pillar of religion
Imad-ool-Moolk	عماد الملک	*A.* Pillar of the state
Imad Shahy	عماد شاهي	*A.* Of or belonging to the kings of Berar so called
Imam	امام	*A.* The high priest
Imam-ool-Moolk	امام الملک	*A.* High priest of the state
Inayut	عنايت	*A.* Liberality
Intishar	انتشار	*A.* Famous
Issac	اسحاق	*A.* Isaac
Isfahany	اسفهاني	*P.* Inhabitant of Isfahan
Isferahy	اسفراهي	*P.* A native of Isfirah
Isfundyar	اسفنديار	*P.* An ancient king of Persia
Iskunder	اسکندر	*P.* Alexander
Islam	اسلام	*A.* Salvation
Ismael	اسماعيل	*A.* Ismaeel
Jafur Beg	جعفر بگ	*P.* Name of a prince
Jageerdar	جاگردار	*P.* Feudal chief

Jahirba	جاهربا	*H.* Proper name
Jahir Dew	جاهر ديو	*H.* Ditto
Jakur	جاقر	*T.* Ditto
Jakurtugeen	جاقرتگين	*T.* Ditto
Jam	جام	*S.* Appellation for a prince in Sind
Japheth	يافث	*A.* Japheth
Jazim	جازم	*A.* Resolute
Jeevundas	جيوندا س	*S.* A corruption of Jeiwunt-dasa, the servant of the victorious
Jewum Ray	جيونراي	*S.* The victorious prince
Jehangeer	جهانگير	*P.* Conqueror of the world
Jehan Shah	جهانشاه	*P.* King of the world
Jehansooz	جهانسوز	*P.* Incendiary of the world
Jeichund	جيچند	*S.* The victor king
Jeipal	جيپال	*S.* The victor lord
Jelabur	جلابر	*T.* Name of a tribe
Jemedar	جمعدار	*P.* A military chief (captain)
Joodry	جودري	*P.* The plague
Joojhar	جوجهار	*H.* Proper name
Joojy	جوجي	*T.* Ditto
Jookan	حوقان	*T.* Ditto
Joomla	جمله	*P.* Collector

Joomun	جمن	*H.* Proper name
Joona	جونه	*H.* Old, ancient
Jooneid	جنيد	*T.* Proper name
Joorjeea	جورجيه	*T.* Ditto
Joorjy	جورجي	*P.* Inhabitant of Joorjan
Joshun	جوشن	*P.* Coat of mail
Jotumraj	جوتمراج	*S.* Proper name
Jowhur	جوهر	*P.* Precious (jewel)
Jubbar	جبّار	A. Superior, overbearing
Judeed	جديد	*A.* New, novel
Jug Dew	جگديو	*S.* Lord of the earth
Jugdew Row	جگديو راو	*S.* Lord and king of the earth
Juggut Row	جگت راو	*S.* King of the world
Jugmal	جگمل	*S.* Ditto
Jugnat	جگنات	*S.* Lord of the universe
Jugut	جگت	*S.* The world
Julal	جلال	*A.* Glorious, *m.*
Julala	جلاله	*A.* Glorious, *f.*
Julal-ood-Deen	جلا الدين	*A.* Glory of religion
Julaly	جلالي	*P.* Name of a tribe
Julwany	جلواني	*P.* A. native of Julwan
Jumad-ool-Awul	جماد الاوّل	*A.* Name of the third Mahomedan month
Jumad-oos-Sany	جماد الثاني	*A.* Name of the fourth Mahomedan month

Jumal	جمال	*A.* Beauty, *m.*
Jumaly	جمالي	*A.* Beauty, *f.*
Jumsheed	جمشيد	*P.* Ancient king of Persia
Jumvy	جموي	*H.* An inhabitant of Jumoo
Jusrut	جسرت	*H.* Proper name
Jut or Getæ	جت	*H.* Name of a tribe
Kadur	قادر	*A.* Powerful
Kafila	قافله	*A.* Caravan
Kafoor	كافور	*A.* Camphire
Kajar	قاجار	*T.* Name of a tribe
Kajooly	كاجولي	*T.* Proper name
Kaky	كاكي	*P.* A bun, small loaf
Kala Phar	كالاپهار	*H.* The black rock
Kaloo	كالو	*H.* Black
Kaly	كالي	*H.* Ditto
Kamil	كامل	*A.* Perfect
Kanajee	كاناجي	*H.* Proper name
Kanha	كانها	*H.* Ditto
Karooba	كاروبه	*P.* Ambur
Kashany	كاشاني	*P.* A native of Kashan
Kasim	قاسم	*A.* A divider
Kasy Row	كاسي راو	*M.* Proper name
Katty	كاتي	*S.* A native of Kattywar
Kawur Sein	كاور سين	*S.* Proper name
Kazy	قاضي	*A.* Cadi, judge

Kazy-ool-Koozat	قاضي القضات	*A.* The chief judge
Kedar	كيدار	*S.* Proper name
Keert Varma	كيرة ورما	*S.* Ditto, mentioned in the Mohabharut
Kehtry	كهتري	*S.* Royal race
Kei Kaoos	كيكاوس	*P.* An ancient king of Persia
Kei Kobad	كيقباد	*P.* Ditto
Keiomoors	كيومرس	*P.* Ditto
Keis	قيس	*A.* Proper name
Keisur	قيصر	*P.* Cæsar
Ketoo	كيتو	*S.* Castor
Kezilbash	قزلباش	*T.* Red caps (the Persians are so called)
Khakshal	خاكشال	*T.* Name of a tribe
Khan	خان	*T.* Lord
Khan Khanan	خان خانان	*T.* Lord of lords
Khanum	خانم	*T.* Lady
Khas	خاص	*P.* Private and personal
Khasa Kheil	خاص خيل	*P.* Personal guards
Khanzada Begum	خانزاده بگم	*T.* The noble lady
Kheir	خير	*A.* Excellent
Khilat	خلعت	*P.* Honorary robes
Khiljy	خلجي	*Af.* Name of a tribe
Khing Sowar	خنگ سوار	Horseman (name assumed by a saint)
Khizr	خذر	Evergreen, eternal

Khizr Khyle	خذرخیل	*Af.* Name of a tribe
Khodeija	خدیجه	*A.* Proper name, *f.*
Kholasut-ool-Moolk	خلاصة الملک	*A.* The elect of the state
Khondemeer	خندامیر	*A.* Name of a celebrated historian
Khonza	خَنزه	*A.* Proper name, *f.*
Khoodabunda	خدابنده	*P.* Servant of God
Khoodawund	خداوند	*P.* Lord
Khoorsheed	خُرشید	*P.* Resplendent
Khoorum	خُرّم	*A.* Joyful
Khoosh	خوش	*P.* Ditto
Khooshal	خوشحال	*P.* Ditto
Khoosh Geldy	خوش گلدي	*T.* Welcome
Khoosh Kuddum	خوشقدم	*P.* Graceful
Khoosrow	خُسرو	P. Fairfaced
Khootba	خُطبه	*A.* Prayers for the king
Khowas	خواص	*A.* Personal
Khuleel	خلیل	*A.* Friend (Abraham)
Khuleelzye	خلیلزاي	*Af.* Name of a tribe
Khulf	خلف	*A.* Progeny
Khumar Tash	خمار طاس	*T.* Proper name
Khutab	خطاب	*A.* Renowned
Khuteer	خطیر	*A.* Great
Khwaja Jehan	خواجه جهان	*P.* Lord of the universe
Kiran Bahadur	قران بهادر	*T.* Proper name

Kirany	كراني	*Af.* Tribe
Kishtum	كشتم	*H.* Corruption from Krishna
Kishwar	كشور	*P.* Country
Kitabdar	كتابدار	*P.* Librarian
Kocheen	قوچين	*T.* Tribe
Koka	كوكه	*T.* Foster-brother
Koly	كولي	*H.* Predatory race in Guzerat
Koly Row	كولي راو	*M.* The Koly chief
Koochy	كوچي	*P.* An inhabitant of Kooch
Koofy	كوفي	*A.* Inhabitant of Koofa
Koohpara	كوهپاره	*P.* Burster of mountains
Koolkurny	كولكرني	*M.* Village registrar
Koolly	قلي	*T.* Slave
Koombho	كومبهو	*H.* Proper name
Koonty	كونتي	*H.* Name of the mother of the Pandoos
Koorban	قربان	*A.* Sacrifice
Koord	كورد	*P.* A native of Carduckia
Koorshasip	كرشاسپ	*P.* An ancient king of Persia
Kootb	قطب	*A.* The pole star
Kootb Nooma Alum	قطب نما عالم	*A.* The compass of the universe

Kootb-ood-Deen	قطب الدين	*A.* The pole star of the faith
Kootb-ool-Moolk	قطب الملک	*A.* The pole star of the state
Kootb Shahy	قطب شاهي	*A.P.* Family name of the kings of Golconda
Kootloogh	قتلغ	*T.* A proper name
Kootloogh Nigar Khanum	قتلغ نگار خانم	*T.* A proper name, *f.*
Koowur	کور	*S.* Heir-apparent
Koran	قران	*A.* The Koran
Koreish	خوریش	*A.* Tribe of the prophet Mahomed
Korkan	کورکان	*T.* Turkish tribe
Kotwal	کوتوال	*P.* Mayor
Kowam-ool-Moolk	قوام الملک	*A.* Supporter of the state
Kowla Devy	کوله دیوي	*S.* The water-lily queen
Kowlanundy	کولانندي	*S.* The joyous lily
Kowry	کَوڑي	*H.* The small white shell called the Negro's tooth
Kripa Acharia	کرپا اچاریه	*S.* One of the heroes of the Mahabharut
Krishn	کرشن	*S.* The black god
Kubacha	قباچه	*T.* A family name
Kubool	قبول	*A.* Consent
Kubeer	کبیر	*A.* Great

Kuchun	کچن	*T.* A family name
Kuddum	قدم	*A.* Advanced
Kuddur	قدر	*A.* Power
Kudroo	قدرو	*H.* Powerful
Kufshdar	کفشدار	*P.* One who has charge of the royal slippers
Kujuk	کجک	*H.* An elephant goad
Kulaby	کلابي	*P.* A family name
Kulan	کلان	*P.* Great
Kulany	کلاني	*P.* Ditto
Kuleem	کليم	*A.* Eloquent
Kullian	کليان	*S.* Propitious
Kullich	قلچ	*Af.* Tribe
Kumal	کمال	*A.* Complete
Kumboh	کنبوه	*Af.* Tribe
Kumbur	قنبر	*H.* Full moon, corruption of Kumra
Kumbur-i-Dewana	قنبر ديوانه	*H.* Silly, one who is lunatic at the full moon
Kundoo	کندو	*H.* Proper name
Kundy	کندي	*H.* Ditto, a defile
Kuns	کنس	*H.* Proper name
Kupoory	کپوري	*H.* Camphorated
Kureem	کريم	*A.* Clement
Kurghoo	کرگهو	*H.* Rhinoceros-like
Kurra	قره	*T.* Black
Kurragooz	قره‌گوز	*T.* Black-eyed
Kurra Koovinloo	قره قوينلو	*T.* Tribe of the black ram

Kurun	کرن	*S.* Sunbeam
Kushka	قشقه	*T.* The mark worn on the forehead by Hindoos
Kussab	قساب	*P.* The butcher
Kustoory	کستوري	*S.* Fair, resembling camphor
Kutaby	کتابي	*P.* The book-worm
Kutry	کهتري	*S.* A caste so called
Kuzil-Arslan	قزل أرسلان	*T.* The tawny lion
Kuzil Hukum	قزل حکم	*T.* The red chief
Lacheen	لاچين	*T.* Tribe
Ladoo	لادو	*H.* Beloved
Laghiry	لاغري	*A.P.* Slender
Lalcheen	لالچين	*T.* Family name
Larun	لارن	*H.* Favourite
Lary	لاري	*P.* Of or pertaining to the province of Lar, in Persia
Leith	ليث	*A.* Proper name
Lody	لودي	*Af.* Tribe
Lohany	لُهاني	*Af.* A tribe of Afghans
Lokmun	لقمان	*A.* Æsop
Looly	لولي	*P.* An actress
Loor	لُر	*P.* An ancient Persian tribe
Lootf	لُطف	*A.* Kindness

Luchmun	لچمن	*H.* Proper name
Luddur Dew	لدّر ديو	*H.* Proper name of a Hindoo Raja
Luky	لكي	*P.* One of the most ancient tribes of Parsia
Lunga	لنگه	*Af.* Tribe
Lushkur	لشكر	*P.* Camp
Lushkury	لشكري	*P.* A soldier
Lutchuna	لتچنه	*H.* Proper name
Luteef	لطيف	*A.* Exquisite
Maazim	معزظم	*A.* The noble
Maaly	معلي	*A.* The exalted
Maasoom	معسوم	*A.* The orphan
Madhoo	مادهو	*H.* Proper name
Mahabharut	ماهابهارت	*S.* The great war
Mahkaly	ماهكالي	*S.* Time the goddess of destruction
Mahmood	محمود	*A.* Praiseworthy
Mahomed	محمد	*A.* Praised
Mahraj	ماهراج	*S.* The great king
Mahrum	مهرم	*T.* Family name
Mahtab	ماهتاب	*P.* Moonlight
Mahy	ماهي	*P.* The standard of the fish
Makry	ماكري	*Ka.* Family name
Maldeu	مالديو	*H.* Proper name
Mamish	مامش	*T.* Tribe
Maratib	مراتب	*A.* Dignity

Marratta	مرهته	*H.* A nation so called
Mandlik	ماندلک	*H.* A petty prince, chief of a host
Meamun Oolla	میامن الله	*A.* Reposing in God
Meean	میان	*H.* Sir, Mr.
Meeana	میانه	*Af.* Tribe
Meekur	میکر	*C.* Canarese appellation
Mere	میر	*S.* Highlander
Meer Akhoor	میر اخور	*P.* Groom
Meeran	میران	*P.* Affix to a proper name
Meer Joomla	میر جمله	*A.* Prime minister
Meer Nobut	میر نوبت	*A.* Captain of the guards
Meeruk	میرک	*P.* Affix to a proper name
Mehd Eerak	محد ایراق	*P.* The Eerakian mother
Mehdvy	مهدوي	*P.* A sect
Mehdy	مهدي	*P.* The twelfth imam, so called
Mehrum	محرم	*A.* Honoured
Munsubdar	منصبدار	*P.* A military chieftain
Mifta	مفته	*A.* Proper name
Mirza	میرزا	*P.* Secretary
Misry	مصري	*P.* Native of Egypt
Mittun	متّن	*S.* Tasty

Mlecha	ملچه	*S.* Impure
Moatimid	معتمد	*A.* Faithful
Modood	مودود	*A.* Endeared
Moghyss	مغيث	*A.* Intercessor
Mohabut	مهابت	*A.* Awful
Mohafiz	محافظ	*A.* Preserver
Mohib	محب	*A.* Attached
Mohsun	محسن	*A.* Beauteous
Mohulla	محله	*A.* A ward or parish
Mohurrum	محرّم	*A.* Honoured
Moiz-ood-Deen	معز الدين	*A.* Dear to religion
Moiz-ool-Moolk	معز الملک	*A.* The darling of the state
Mokbil	مقبل	*A.* Leader
Mokeem	مقيم	*A.* Steadfast
Mokhlis	مخلص	*A.* Faithful
Momin	مؤمن	*A.* Ditto
Moobarik	مبارک	*A.* Propitious
Moobariz	مبارز	*A.* Champion
Moobushir	مبشر	*A.* Comely
Moodna	مودنه	*C.* Proper name
Moozuffury	مظفري	*A.* Victorious
Moogh	مغ	*P.* The magian
Mookudur	مقدر	*A.* Powerful
Mookul	موکل	*H.* Proper name
Mookummil	مکمل	*A.* Accomplished
Mookund	مکند	*S.* Great
Mookurrib	مقرب	*A.* Approximate
Moolk	ملک	*A.* Country, the empire

Moolla	ملا	*A.* A priest
Moottea	متعه	*A.* A temporary marriage
Moonshy	منشي	*P.* A secretary
Moonyim	منعم	*A.* Favoured
Moorad	مراد	*A.* Object of desire
Moorhary Row	مرهاري راو	*H.* Proper name
Moortuza	مرتضي	*A.* Approved
Moosahib	مصاحب	*A.* Associated
Moostowly	مستولي	*A.* Overcome
Moostufa	مصطفي	*A.* Intercessor
Moosvy	موسوي	*A.* Of or pertaining to Moses
Moozuffur	مظفر	*A.* Victorious
Moty	موتي	*H.* Pearl
Movyud Dewana	مويد ديوانه	*P.* Movyud the silly
Movyud-ood-Deen	مويد الدين	*A.* Support of the faith
Mowas	مواس	*H.* A predatory tribe in Guzerat
Mowjy	موجي	*Af.* Tribe
Mowlana	مولانا	*A.* High priest
Mowlanazada	مولانا زاده	*A.P.* Descended from a high priest
Mowullid	مولّد	*A.* A native born of foreign parents
Moyin	معين	*A.* Select
Mudkurn	مدكرن	*S.* The honied ray
Mudun	مدن	*S.* The god of love
Mujlis	مجلس	*A.* Assembly

Mujnoon	مجنون	*P.* Insane
Mujahid	مجاهد	*A.* Persevering
Mujdood	مجدود	*A.* Novel
Mukbool	مقبول	*A.* Approved, handsome
Mukdooma Jehan	مقدومه جهان	*A.* The queen of the universe
Mukhsoos	مخصوص	*A.* Select
Mullik	ملک	*A.* King
Mullika Jehan	ملکه جهان	*P.* Queen of the world
Mullik-ool-Mushaikh	ملک المشایخ	*A.* Chief of the priests
Mullik-ool Toojir	ملک التجار	*A.* Chief of the merchants
Mulloo	ملو	*H.* Proper name
Mumby Devy	منبي ديوي	*S.* The goddess Mumby
Mumlikut	مملکت	*A.* Kingdom
Mundul	مندل	*S.* Host
Munery	منيري	*H.* A native of Munere
Munewar	منيوار	*H.* Teloogoo millitia
Munga	منگه	*H.* Proper name
Mungoo	منگو	*T.* Proper name
Mungul	منگل	*S.* The planet Mars
Munjoo	منجو	*H.* Proper name
Munjun	منجن	*H.* Ditto
Munoochehr	منوچهر	*P.* Celebrated Persian minister

Munoopraj	منوپراج	*S.* Proper name
Muntuky	منتقي	*A.* Logician
Munsoor	منصور	*A.* Victorious
Murdan	مردان	*P.* Manly
Murghoob-ool-Koolloob	مرغوب القلوب	*A.* Title of a book. The desire of hearts
Muryum	مريم	Mary
Musheer	مشير	*A.* Arrangement
Musheer-ool-Moolk	مشير الملک	*A.* The regulator of the state
Musjid	مسجد	*A.* Mosque
Muskaty	مسقتي	*A.* native of Muscat
Musnud	مسند	*A.* A throne
Musseety	مصيتي	*A.* Proper name
Mutroo	مترو	*H.* A native of Mutra
Mymindy	ميمندي	*P.* A native of Mymund
Nadir	نادر	P. The pole star
Nadiry	نادري	*P.* Relating to the pole
Nahir	ناهر	*S.* Lion
Naib	نايب	*A.* Deputy
Naig	نايگ	*S.* Chief
Naigwaries	نايگوار	*H.* Teloogoo militia
Naik	نايک	*S.* Leader
Nasir	ناصر	*A.* Victorious
Nat	نات	*S.* Chief
Nawab	نواب	*P.* Nabob

Nazook	نازک	*P.* Delicate
Neamut	نعمت	*A.* Luxury
Neeaz	نیاز	*P.* Humility
Neeazy	نیازي	*P.* Name of a tribe
Nehal	نهال	*P.* A young tree
Nehr Dew	نهر دیو	*S.* The lion king
Nehung	نهنگ	*P.* A crocodile
Nevayets	نوایت	*P.* The new race
Niamut	نعمت	*A.* Delicacy
Nigaristan	نگارستان	*P.* The gallery of pictures
Nisar	نثار	*A.* An offering
Nizam	نظام	*A.* Arrangement
Nizam-ool-Moolk	نظام الملک	*A.* The regulator of the state
Nizam Shahy	نظام شاهي	*A.* Title of the kings of Ahmudnuggur
Noah	نوح	*A.* Noah
Nobut	نوبت	*P.* Watch, guard
Nooh	نوح	*A.* Noah
Noor	نور	*P.* Light
Noorbukhsh	نوربخش	*P.* Imparting light
Noor-ood-Deen	نور الدین	*P.A.* Light of the faith
Noosrut	نصرت	*A.* Victory
Nooyan	نویان	*T.* Name of a tribe
Noshtugeen	نشتگین	*T.* Proper name
Mowlapa	نولیه	C. Ditto
Nowroze	نوروز	*P.* Festival held on the 21st of March

Nowshaba	نوشابه	*P.* Alexander's queen (so called)
Nowsherwan	نوشیروان	*P.* An ancient king of Persia
Nudeem	ندیم	*A.* Companion
Nujm	نجم	*A.* A star
Nujm-oos-Sany	نجم الثاني	*A.* The second star
Nujuf	نجف	*A.* Holy
Nukara	نقاره	*A.* Kettle-drum
Nukeeb	نقیب	*T.* An usher
Nukhwut	نخوت	*A.* Affectation
Nul	نل	*H.* Proper name
Nunda	ننده	*S.* Joyful
Nundraj	نندراج	*S.* The joyful king
Nunny	نني	*H.* Little
Nurd	نرد	*P.* Backgammon-men
Nureeman	نریمان	*P.* An ancient hero of Persia
Nursa	نرسه	*H.* Proper name
Nursing	نرسنگ	*S.* The lion of men
Nursing Row	نرسنگ راو	*S.* The lion king
Nurswundy	نرسوندي	*H.* Proper name
Nuseeb	نصیب	*A.* Fortunate
Nuseer	نصیر	*A.* Victorious
Nutty	نتي	*H.* Proper name
Nuzeery	نظیري	*Af.* Name of a tribe
Nuzr	نظر	*A.* Sight
Nyshapoory	نیشاپوري	*P.* A native of Nyshapoor

Oghloo	اغلو	*T.* A son
Oghz	عغز	*T.* An ox
Oghzloo	عغزلو	*T.* Name of a tribe
Oktay	آقتاي	*T.* Proper name
Olcha	اولچه	*T.* A measure
Oobeid	عُبيد	*A.* Obedient
Oody Sing	اودي سنگ	*S.* The exalted chief
Oogur Sein	اوگر سين	*S.* The lord of an awful army
Ooloos Beg	آلوس بگ	*T.* Chief of the tribe
Oomdut-ool-Moolk	عمدت الملک	*A.* Pillar of the state
Oomr	عمر	*A.* Life, existence
Oomra	آمرا	*A. pl.* of Ameer, ae prince
Oomr Sheikh	عمر شيخ	*A.* Proper name, th-father of the em peror Babur
Oonsury	عنصري	*A.* Fundamental
Oorea	اوريا	*H.* Family name
Oostajloo	استاجلو	*T.* The brave
Ootarid	عطارد	*A.* The planet Mercury
Oothman	عثمان	*A.* The caliph
Ooveis or Veis	اويس	*T.* Proper name
Oozbuk	عزبک	*T.* Proper name
Oozery Rozey	عزيري رازي	*P.* Proper name
Oozun	اوزن	*T.* Lengthy
Owlia	اوليا	*A.* Saint

Padshah	پادشاه	*A.* A king
Palky	پالکي	*H.* A letter, plankeen
Pan	پان	*H.* The aromatic leaf which is eaten by the Indians
Pandoo	پندو	*S.* The fair, yellow
Papia	پاپیه	*C.* Proper name
Patan	پتهان	*Af.* The tribe of Afghan. Deck of a vessel
Pavia	پاویه	*C.* Proper name
Peala	پیاله	*P.* The cup
Peer	پیر	*P.* Venerable
Peeranweisa	پیرانویسه	*P.* Minister of Ky Kaoos
Peroo	پیرو	*H.* Holy
Peihlwan	پهلوان	*P.* A champion
Perguna	پرگنه	*H.* A division of a province
Perychehra	پریچهره	*P.* Fairy face
Peshdadian	پیشادیان	*P.* An ancient race of kings of Persia
Pesh Nimaz	پیش نماز	*P.* Champlain
Peshwa	پیشوا	*P.* A leader
Pirmal	پرمال	*H.* Proper name
Poonja	پونجه	*H.* Proper name
Poorby	پُربي	*S.* Eastern
Poorunmal	پورنمل	*H.* Lord of the towns and forests

Pota	پوته	*H.* Proper name, treasure
Powar	پوار	*H.* Tribe so called
Prem	پریم	*H.* Proper name
Pritvy Raja	پرتوي راج	*S.* Lord of the earth
Pundit	پندت	*S.* Learned, doctor
Pundoo	پندو	*S.* Yellow
Purdan	پردان	*S.* Minister
Purizada	پریزاده	*P.* Fairy born
Pursaram	پرسارام	*S.* Hindoo demigod
Purtab	پرتاب	*S.* Good fortune
Purtab Sa	پرتاب سا	*S.* Prosperous king
Purveez	پرویز	*P.* An ancient king of Persia
Purwanchy	پروانچي	*T.* The officer issuing royal mandates
Puttuck	پتک	*S.* Division
Raab	رعب	*A.* Awe
Raees	رأیس	*A.* Chief
Rafezy	رافضي	*A.* Heretical
Raheem	رحیم	*A.* Merciful
Raheem Dad	رحیم داد	*A.P.* Merciful and just
Raj or Raja	راج or راجه	*S.* King
Rajoo	راجو	*S.* Regal
Rajpoot	راجپوت	*S.* Tribe so called, of royal descent
Rajy	راجي	*H.* Regal
Ramchund	رامچند	*S.* Hindoo demigod
Ramchundur	رامچندر	*S.* Hindoo demigod

Ram Raj	رام راج	*S.* King Rama
Ram Sa	رام سا	*S.* King Rama
Ramzan	رمضان	*A.* The ninth Mahomedan month, the month of fasting
Rana	رانا	*S.* Title of the kings of Oodipoor
Ranoo	رانو	*H.* Proper name
Rany	راني	*S.* Title of the queens of Oodipoor
Rawoot Row	راوت راو	*H.* Proper name. The cavalier
Rawul	راول	*S.* Prince
Rawul Dew	راول ديو	*S.* Royal prince
Ray	راي	*S.* King
Raymul	رايمل	*S.* The chief of lords
Ray Rayan	راي رايان	*S.* Chief of princes
Ray Row	راي راو	*S.* Chief of chiefs
Razy	راضي	*A.* Contented
Reddywar	رديوار	*H.* Landholders of Telingana
Rusheed	رشيد	*A.* Valiant
Reihan	ريحان	*P.* Sweet marjoram
Risaladar	رسالهدار	*P.* Commandant of a rissala, or regiment of horse
Roohany	روحاني	*A.* Name of a tribe
Roohpurwur	روح پرور	*A.P.* Soul's delight
Rookn-ood-Deen	ركن الدين	*A.* Pillar of religion

Roomy	رومي	*P.* A native of Asia Minor
Roosoomdar	روسم‌دار	*P.* Collector of customs
Roostoom	رستم	*P.* The Persian hero (so called)
Roshuye	روشنائي	*P.* Illuminati (a sect)
Row	راو	*H.* Chief
Roze Afzoon	روز افزون	*P.* Daily increasing
Rubbee-ool-Akhur	ربيع الاخر	*A.* The fourth month of the Arabians
Rubbee-ool-Awul	ربيع الاوّل	*A.* The third month of the Arabians
Rubeea	ربيع	*A.* The spring
Ruffeea-ood-Deen	رفيعه الدين	*A.* Exalted of the faith
Ruffut	رفعة	*A.* Exalted
Ruffut-ool-Moolk	رفعة الملک	*A.* Exalted in the state
Ruheem	رحيم	*A.* The merciful
Ruhman	رحمان	*A.* The benevolent
Rujub	رجب	*A.* The seventh month of the Arabians
Rumul-i-Moosudus-i-Mujnoon	رمل مسدس مجنون	*A.* Metre in poetry
Runga	رنگه	*S.* Variegated
Rungia	رنگيه	*H.* High coloured
Runmul	رنمل	*S.* The lord of the fight

Ruttun See	رتن سي	*S.* The precious prince
Ruzak	رضاق	*A.* Provider
Ruzeea Begum	رضيه بگم	*T.* The approved princess
Sa	سا	*S.* King
Saadut	سعادت	*A.* Propitiousness
Sabajy	ساباجي	*H.* Proper name
Sabat	سابات	*A.* Trenches
Sadhoo	سادهو	*S.* The simple
Sadik	صادق	*A.* The upright and just
Sadiky	صادقي	*A.* The righteous
Sady	سعدي	*A.* Propitious
Sahadew	سهاديو	*H.* Proper name
Sahib	صاحب	*A.* Lord
Sahibzada	صاحبزاده	*A.P.* Noble
Salar	سالار	*P.* Chief
Salivahan	ساليواهن	*S.* Proper name of a prince
Sam	سام	*P.* An ancient Persian hero
Samiry	سامري	*H.* The zamorin of Malabar
Samywar	ساميوار	*H.* Holy chief
Sanka or Sanga	سانکه	*H.* Prince of Oodipoor
Sar	سار	*T.* King

Sarung	سارنگ	*H.* Tuneful. An instrument of six strings
Sawunt	سارنت	*H.* Chief
Seeta Bund	سيتا بند	*H.* The bridge of Seeta
Seetaputty	سيتاپتي	*H.* Appellation for Rama the husband of Seeta
Setul Dew	سيتل ديو	*H.* Proper name
Seeva	سيوه	*S.* The god of destruction
Sehra	سهره	*H.* Proper name
Seif	سيف	*A.* The sword
Sena	سنه	*A.* Sinai
Serpa Devy, or Sooroop Devy	سرپه ديوي	*S.* The fair faced queen
Setty	ستي	*H.* Chief of a mercantile
Sew, Shew, or Seeva (*vide supra*)	شيو	*S.* Seeva, the god of destruction
Sewund	سيوند	*S.* Resembling Seeva
Shaban	شابان	*P.* The eighth Mahomedan month
Shadman	شادمان	*P.* Joyful
Shady	شادي	*P.* Joy
Shafye	شفيع	*A.* Intercessor
Shah	شاه	*P.* A king

Shahab-ood-Deen	شهاب الدين	*A.* The strength of the faith
Shaheen	شاهين	*P.* The falcon
Shahida	شاهده	*P.* A mistress
Shahoo	شاهو	*Af.* Proper name
Shahrokh	شاه‌رخ	*P.* Having a royal countenance
Shahrokhy	شاه‌رخي	*P.* The name of a coin bearing the king's head
Shah Toorkan	شاه ترکان	*P.* Prince of the Toorks
Shahzada	شاهزاده	*P.* Prince of the blood
Shaista	شايسته	*P.* Worthy
Sheea	شيع	*A.* Name of a sect
Sheebany	شيباني	*T.* Proper name
Sheebuk	شيبک	*T.* Proper name
Sheer	شير	*P.* The lion
Sheerchung	شيرچنگ	*P.* Having a lion's grasp
Sheeroo	شيرو	Hindvy corruptions of Sheer, a lion
Sheerum	شيرم	
Sheery	شيري	
Sheida	شيدا	*P.* Insane
Sheikh	شيخ	*A.* A chief
Sheikha	شيخا	Hindvy corruptions of the above
Sheikhjee	شيخ‌جي	Hindvy corruptions of the above

Sheikh-ool-Islam	شیخ الاسلام	*A.* Chief priest of islamism
Sherooya	شیرویه	*P.* An ancient king of Persia
Shew-Dew-Bhutt	شیو دیو بهٹ	*S.* Seeva Dew, the beggar
Shimran	شمران	*Af.* Proper name
Shimur	شمر	*Af.* Proper name
Shirazy	شیرازي	*P.* A native of Shiraz
Shist	شست	*P.* The mark
Shooja-ool-Moolk	شجع الملک	*A.* The most valiant of the state
Shoojat	شجاعت	*A.* Valour
Shubkoor	شبکور	*P.* Blind at night
Shudad	شداد	*A.* Proper name
Shukdar	شقدار	*P.* Governor of a district or division of land
Shukhfy	شخفي	*A.* Proper name
Shukoor	شکور	*A.* Grateful
Shukur Khatoon	شکر خاطون	*T.* The sweet lady
Shumsheer	شمشیر	*P.* Scymitar
Shumsheer-ool-Moolk	شمشیر الملک	*P.* The sword of the state
Shums	شمس	*A.* The sun
Shunkul	شنکل	*H.* Proper name
Shunkur	شنکر	*H.* Proper name
Shunkur Zeina	شنکر زینا	*Ka.* Proper name
Shureef	شریف	*A.* Highness

Shurf-ood-Deen	شرف الدين	*A.* Upholder of the faith
Shurky	شرقي	*A.* Eastern
Shuval	شوال	*A.* The tenth Mahomedan month
Siamook	سيامک	*P.* An ancient prince of Persia
Siddy	سدّي	*A.* Chieftain
Siddy Mowla	سدّي مولا	*A.* The holy chief
Sideek	صديق	*A.* The just
Sidpal	سدپال	*S.* Proper name
Sidraj	سدراج	*S.* Proper name
Sikundur	سکندر	*P.* Alexander
Silehdar	سلحدار	*P.* Heavy-armed horseman
Silhuddy	سلهدي	*S.* Proper name
Simeon	سمعون	*A.* Simeon
Sing	سنگ	*S.* Lion, chieftain
Singhasun	سنگهاسن	*S.* Royal litter
Sipah Salar	سپه سالار	*T.* Commander-in-chief
Sipustageen	سپستگين	*T.* Proper name
Siraj	سراج	*A.* The lamp
Sirka	سرکه	*H.* The name of a Marratta family
Sirvodhun	سرودهن	*H.* Proper name
Sisodia	سيسوديه	*H.* The name of a race of Rajpoots

Soheil	سهيل	*P.* An ancient hero of Persia, a planet
Sohrab	سهراب	*P.* An ancient hero of Persia
Sooba	صوبه	*A.* Contraction of Soobahdar, governor
Soobhan	سبحان	*A.* Praise
Sookpal	سُکپال	*S.* Proper name
Sooliman	سليمان	*A.* Solomon
Sooltan	سلطان	*A.* A king
Soombul	سنبل	*P.* Hyacinth
Soomur	سومر	*H.* Proper name
Soonut	سُنّت	*A.* Orthodox
Soony	سُنّي	*A.* Religious sect
Soor	سور	*Af.* Name of a tribe
Soorijmul	سورجمل	*H.* The sunlike lord
Soorjim	سورجن	*H.* Sun-born
Sooria	سوريا	*S.* The sun
Sooria Row	سوريا راو	*S.* The sunlike chief
Soorkha	سرخا	*H.* The red
Soorsing	سورسنگ	*S.* Lion of the sun
Soorut Rany, or Sooroop Rany	سورت راني	*S.* The Surat queen, or the beauteous queen
Sree	سري	*S.* Prosperous
Sreeputty	سريپتي	*S.* The master of prosperity
Subah-ool-Kheir	صباح الخير	*A.* The glory of the morning

Subooktugeen	سبکتگین	*T.* Proper name
Sudanund	سدانند	*S.* Proper name
Sudashew	سداشیو	*S.* Proper name
Sudda	سده	*S.* Proper name
Suddoh	سدوه	*S.* Proper name
Suddur Khan	صدر خان	*A.* The principal chief
Sudr-i-Jehan	صدر جهان	*A.* The select of the universe
Sudrnisheen	صدر نشین	*P.* The chief seat of justice
Sudr-oos-Su door	صدر الصدور	*A.* The lord chief justice
Sufdur	صفدر	*A.* Arranger
Sufeedasp	سفیداسپ	*P.* An ancient king of Persia
Sufeer	سفیر	*A.* An envoy
Suffur	سفر	*A.* Travelled
Suffy	صفي	*A.* Virtuous
Suf Shikun	صف شکن	*P.* Breaker through the line
Sufvy	صفوي	*A.* Sofy
Sugga	سگه	*H.* Proper name
Sulabut	صلابت	*A.* Proper name
Sulim	سلیم	*A.* Safety
Suljook	سلجوق	*T.* Toorkman tribe
Sultanut	سلطنت	*A.* Dominion
Sumbajee	سمباجي	*S.* The lion chief
Sumud	سمد	*A.* The virtuous
Sundul	سندل	*P.* Sandal
Sungut	سنگت	*S.* Proper name

Sunjur	سنجر	*T.* Proper name
Sunjye	سنجي	*S.* Proper name
Surabuny	سرابني	*Af.* A family name
Suraf or Shroff	سراف	*A.* Banker, money-changer
Surmust	سرمست	*P.* Haughty
Survur-ool-Moolk	سرور الملک	*A.* Noble of the state
Surwaraj	سرواراج	*S.* Lord of all
Syud	سيد	*A.* Descendant of Mahomed
Syud-oos-Sadate	سيد السعادت	*A.* The chief of the Syuds
Tahir	طاهر	*A.* The just, the good
Tahmasp	طهماسپ	*P.* An ancient king of Persia
Tahmorasp	طهمراسپ	*P.* An ancient king of Persia
Taj	تاج	*P.* The diadem
Tajik	تاجک	*T.* A Tartar race of merchants
Taj-ool-Moolk	تاج الملک	*A.* The diadem of the state
Talib	طالب	*A.* The petitioner
Talish	تالش	*T.* Name of a tribe
Tardy	تردي	*T.* Proper name
Tash	تاش	*T.* Hardy, flinty as stone

Tatar	تاتار	*T.* Tartar
Teimoor	تیمور	*T.* Teimour
Teiub	طیب	*A.* Good
Teloogoo	تلوگو	*H.* Of or pertaining to Telingana.
Tilla	طلا	*A.* Gold
Tilok Chund	تلوکچند	*S.* Shining forehead
Tima	تیمه	*C.* Proper name
Timapa	تماپه	*C.* Proper name
Tim Raj	تم راج	*C.* Proper name
Timuna	تمنه	*C.* Proper name
Tiriak	تریاک	*T.* Inebriating, a drug
Tirmul	ترمل	*C.* Proper name
Tirmuny	ترمنی	*T.* Proper name
Todur Mul	تودر مل	*S.* Proper name
Togha	طغا	*T.* Proper name
Toghan	طغان	*T.* Proper name
Toghantugeen	طغانتگین	*T.* Proper name
Toghay	طغاي	*T.* Proper name
Toghluk	طغلق	*T.* Proper name
Toghrul	طغرل	*T.* Proper name
Tohfa	تحفه	*P.* The rare
Toofal	توفال	*Af.* Proper name
Tooly	تولی	*T.* Proper name
Toomnayee	تومنائي	*T.* Proper name
Toorab	تراب	*A.* Earthy
Tooraghay	تراغاي	*T.* Proper name
Toork	ترک	*T.* Turk
Toorkman	ترکمان	*T.* Name of a tribe

Toorky	ترکي	*T.* Of or belonging to a Turk
Toormish	ترمش	*T.* Proper name
Toormooshreen	ترمشرين	*T.* Proper name
Toormoozy	ترمذي	*T.* A native of Toormooz or Turmed
Toosin	توسن	*T.* Proper name
Toozuky	تزوکي	*T.* A framer of institutes
Toozun	توزن	*T.* Proper name
Tora Beg	تورابگ	*T.* Proper name
Tubatibba	تباتبه	*A.* An Arabian tribe
Tubligha	تبلغه	*T.* Proper name
Tucky	تقي	*A.* Supported
Tugeen	تگين	*T.* The brave
Tumajy	تماجي	*H.* Proper name
Tumbole	تنبول	*T.* Proper name
Tunka	تنکه	*H.* A coin
Turkhan	ترخان	*T.* Tribe
Tursoon	ترسون	*T.* Proper name
Turufdar	طرفدار	*P.* Provincial governor
Tusheea	تشيه	*A.* Professing the Sheea doctrine
Ul-Messeeh-ool-Khoreish-ool-Kadirry	المسيح الخوريش القادري	*A.* Messiah of the most potent family of the Khoreish
Vakeel-i-Dur	وکيل در	*P.* The deputy of the threshold, lord in waiting

Vakeel-ool-Mootluk	وکیل المتلق	*P.* The supreme deputy, regent
Vakeel-oos-Sultanut	وکیل السلطنت	*P.* The viceroy
Vasdew	واسدیو	*S.* The lord of treasures
Veechitrveeria	ویچترویرہ	*S.* Of manifold strength
Veija Nat Dew	ویجا نات دیو	*S.* Lord of victory
Veis	ویس	*T.* Proper name
Veis Laghiry	ویس لاغری	*T.* Proper name
Velapa	ولاپا	*C.* The fair
Velluparaj	واپراج	*C.* The fair prince
Venkaputty	ونکپتی	*C.* Proper name
Venkutadry	ونکتادری	*C.* Proper name
Venkutraj	ونکتراج	*C.* Proper name
Venkut Row	ونکت راو	*H.* Proper name
Venkutty	ونکتی	*C.* Proper name
Vias	ویاس	*S.* The commentator
Vidiadry	ودیادری	*C.* The learned
Vikramajeet	وکرماجیت	*S.* Sun of victory
Vinaik Dass	ونایکداس	*S.* Servant of the king
Vinaik Dew	ونایکدیو	*S.* Lordly prince
Viswas Row	ویسواس راو	*S.* The chief possessing confidence
Vizier	وزیر	*P.* Minister or deputy
Vizier-i-Kool	وزیر کل	*P.* The sole minister

Vizier-ool-Moomalik	وزير المممالک	*A.* The minister of the state
Vusnad Dew	وسناد ديو	*H.* A corruption of Veija Nat Dew
Wahab	واهاب	*A.* Bountiful
Wasil	واصل	*A.* Uniter
Woorea or Oorea	ووريه	*H.* Of or belonging to Orissa
Wostad	اوستاد	*P.* Preceptor
Wufa	وفا	*A.* Grateful
Wujee-ool-Moolk	وجيع الملک	*A.* Support of the state
Wuleed	وليد	*A.* Proper name
Wully	ولي	*P.* Saint, sanctified
Wurmish	ورمش	*T.* Proper name
Wurmunish	ورمنش	*T.* Proper name
Yadgar	يادگار	*P.* Memorial
Yado	يادو	*S.* The race of Krishna
Yaghy	ياغي	*T.* Rebellion
Yakoob	يعقوب	*A.* Jacob
Yakoob Beg	يعقوب بگ	*A.* The chief Jacob
Yakoot	ياقوت	*P.* Ruby
Yar	يار	*P.* The friend
Yehya	يحيا	*A.* Jehu
Yekbal	يقبال	*P.* Prosperity
Yekbalmund	يقبالمند	*P.* Prosperous
Yakhlass	يخلاص	*P.* Friendly
Yekhtyar	يختيار	*P.* Free, uncontrolled

Yekung	یکنگ	*H.* Single stick, or singly armed
Yeldooz	یلدوز	*T.* A star
Yelloo	یلو	*H.* Proper name
Yeltum Raj	یلتم راج	*C.* Proper name
Yesavul	یساول	*T.* Aid-de-camp
Yesoo	یسو	*S.* Prosperous
Yeswunt Row	یسونت راو	*S.* Prosperous lord
Yevun	یون	*S.* An Ionian, applied by the Hindoos to all races from the west
Yezdijerd	یزدجرد	*P.* The last of the Kaianian kings of Persia
Yezdy	یزدي	*P.* An inhabitant of Yezd
Yezeed	یزید	*P.* Godlike
Yezeedyar	یزیدیار	*P.* Friend of God
Yoodeeshteer	یودشتیر	*S.* Form in battle
Yooghrish	یوغرش	*T.* Proper name
Yoonoos	یونس	*A.* Jonas
Yoorish	یورش	*T.* Assaulting
Yoosof	یوسف	*A.* Joseph
Yooyoocha	یویوچه	*S.* Desiring war
Yumny	یمني	*A.* A native of Yemen or Arabia Felix
Zacharia	زکریا	*A.* Zacharia
Zal	زال	*P.* A famous hero of Persian fable

Zalim	ظالم	*A.* The cruel
Zeead	زیاد	*P.* Increasing
Zeehuj	زالحج	*A.* The month of pilgrimage, the twelfth Mahomedan month
Zeekad	زالقعده	*A.* The eleventh Mahomedan month
Zeenut	زینت	*A.* Beauteous
Zein	زین	*A.* Ornamental
Zein-ood-Deen	زین الدین	*A.* Ornament of religion
Zein-ool-Abideen	زین العابدین	*A.* Ornament of the servants of God
Zeitoon	زیتون	*P.* An olive
Zungy	زنگي	*P.* Persian family name
Zemindar	زمیندار	*P.* One who belongs to the land
Zohak Marry	ضحاک ماري	*P.* An ancient king of Persia
Zoobdut-ool-Moolk	زبدة الملک	*A.* The choice of the state
Zoolkudur	ذوالقدر	*A.* Powerful
Zoolnoon	زوآلنّون	*A.* Proper name
Zoora	زراع	*A.* Agricultural
Zowzun Hussun	زوزن حسین	*T.* Red, Hussein
Zuffur	ظفر	*A.* Victory
Zuheer	ظهیر	*A.* Enlightened
Zuhoory	ظهوري	*A.* Famous, celebrated

Zuman	زمان	*P*. An age
Zund	زند	*P*. An ancient Persian tribe
Zundah Kafur	زنده كافر	*P*. A race of people in Kashghar
Zunjany	زنجاني	*P*. A native of Zungan
Zureef-ool-Moolk	ظريف الملك	*A*. The most active in the state

No. II.

AN ALPHABETICAL LIST

OF

NAMES OF COUNTRIES, MOUNTAINS, RIVERS, AND TOWNS,

WHICH OCCUR

THROUGHOUT THE WORK.

		E.Long. °	′	N.Lat. °	′
Abhur	ابهر	46	10	36	42
Aboogur	ابوکهر	74	11	30	9
Acburpoor ...	اکبرپور	78	42	28	25
		79	51	26	23
		82	26	26	27
Adilabad	عدلاباد	76	8	21	6
Adony or Adwany	ادونی	77	30	16	0
Aden	عدن	52	20	15	12
Agra	اگرا	78	2	27	11
Aheerwara ...	اهیروارا	76	29	21	25
Ahmadabad ...	احمداباد	72	0	23	0
Ahmudnuggur ...	احمدنگر	74	50	19	8
		73	0	23	35
Ahroony	اهرونی	—		—	
Ahsunabad ...	احسناباد	76	54	17	23
Ahwan	اهوان	—		—	
Ahwas	اهواس	76	34	22	31
Ajdur	اجدر	67	29	35	2
Ajoodhun	اجودهن	72	25	30	40

			E.Long. °	′	N.Lat. °	′
Ajmere ...	...	اجمیر	74	52	26	28
Ajum ...	...	عجم	*The country of Persia*			
Ajunta, Pass	...	اجنته	75	50	20	37
Allapoor ...	...	علاپور	75	19	18	31
Alund ...	...	النذ	76	32	17	34
Alwur ...	...	الور	76	41	27	35
Alwurpoor	...	الورپور	*Kashmeer*			
Ambala ...	...	انباله	76	44	30	23
Ambur ...	...	انبر	75	53	19	40
Amerkote	...	امرکوت	70	3	25	36
Amol ...	...	امول	77	57	25	30
Amroha ...	...	امروهه	78	25	28	56
Anagoondy	...	اناگنذدي	76	34	15	23
Andkhoo ...	...	اندخو	65	12	36	40
Anterbede...	...	انتربید	*A province lying between the Jumna and Ganges, called the Dooab*			
Antoor ...	...	انتور	75	20	20	32
Anumbole...	...	انمبول	—		—	
Anundpoor	...	انندپور	77	45	12	11
Anuntgeer...	...	اننتگیر	79	18	14	12
Ardinga ...	...	اردنگه	80	4	15	40
Ardustan ...	...	اردستان	51	5	36	0
Arele ...	...	اریل	79	40	28	7
Armenia ...	...	ارمنیه	*The Province*			

Name		E.Long. °	′	N.Lat. °	′
Armun	ارمن	—		—	
Asawul	اساول	72	0	23	0
Asheera	اشیره	—		—	
Ashta	اشته	76	15	19	24
		76	49	18	32
		76	51	23	0
Ashty	اشتي	75	41	18	25
Ashnuggur, Kashmere	اشنگر	75	29	17	50
Asny	اسني	87	19	24	21
Asseer	اسیر	76	24	21	30
Astrabad	استراباد	54	50	35	50
Atehur	اتیهر	78	35	26	40
Atraoly	اتراولي	78	21	28	3
Attock	اٹک	72	22	33	55
Azoorbaijan ...	اذربایجان	*A province of Persia*			
Badghees	بادغیس	—		—	
Badowly	بادولي	82	53	27	10
Badrul	بادرل	76	34	28	20
Badulgur	بادلگر	81	57	24	54
Badwerd	بادورد	52	15	39	50
Bagdad	بغداد	42	20	33	30
Bagrakote ...	باگراکوت	75	48	16	14
Bahmunhully ...	بهمنهلي	77	51	17	7
Bahmunypoora ...	بهمنیپوره	70	36	17	36
Balapoor	بالاپور	77	31	13	20
		76	50	20	43
Bamyan	بامیان	67	50	34	30

		E.Long. °	′	N.Lat. °	′
Bandagur	باندا گهر	74	50	23	2
Banswala	بانسواله	74	34	23	32
Bawy	باري	75	38	18	32
Baramoola ...	بارامولا	74	20	34	40
Barcelore	بارسيلور	—		—	
Barely	بريلى	79	25	28	23
Baroche	بهروچ	73	8	21	47
Baroda	برودہ	76	49	25	31
Basouda	بسودہ	78	17	23	17
Bawur	باور	74	6	22	3
Beea	بيه	*The River*			
Beejagur	بيجا گڈہ	75	30	21	37
Beejanuggur ...	بيجانگر	76	33	15	19
Beejapoor... ...	بيجاپور	75	48	16	50
Beejwara	بيجوارا	80	40	16	35
Beema	بهيمه	*The River*			
Beer	بير	75	49	19	2
		75	0	26	24
		73	20	34	19
Beerbhoom ...	بيربهوم	86	21	23	4
Beesuinuggur ..	بيسلنگر	72	20	23	45
Behar	بهار	85	32	25	11
Behut	بهت	*The River*			
Bejour	بجور	78	46	25	29
Belgam	بيلگام	79	50	19	23
Belumconda ...	بلمكنده	80	5	16	31
Benares	بنارس	82	40	25	20
Bengal	بنگال	*The Province*			
Bensrode	بنسرود	75	35	25	

Name		E.Long. °	′	N.Lat. °	′
Berah … …	بهره	73	10	32	7
		73	15	33	20
Berar … …	برار	*The Province*			
Bete … …	بیت	68	20	22	27
Betwa … …	بیتوه	*The River*			
Bhagnuggur …	بهاکنکر	78	32	17	22
Bhandere … …	بهاندیر	79	57	25	48
Bhattia … …	بهتیه	76	30	24	18
Bheelwara …	بهیلوارا	77	39	22	32
Bheema … …	بهیمه	*The River.*			
Bheerbul … …	بهیربل	*Kashmeer.*			
Bhikanere… …	بهکانیر	72	20	27	56
Bhilsa … …	بهلسا	77	54	23	37
Bhimbur … …	بهمبر	74	18	33	4
Bhimkul … …	بهمکل	—		—	
Bhimra … …	بهمرا	73	7	19	19
Bhind … …	بهند	78	41	26	32
Bhorup … …	بهورپ	73	35	18	25
Bhowungeer …	بهونکیر	70	10	21	30
Bhugwanpoor …	بهکوانپور	83	0	24	57
Bhukkur … …	بهکر	71	12	31	38
		69	35	27	13
Bhuraich … …	بهرایچ	81	30	27	33
Bhurtpoor… …	بهرتپور	77	32	27	15
Bhurtwara …	بهرتوارا	75	0	22	4
Bidur … …	بیدر	77	34	17	55
Bilála … …	بلاله	70	40	20	56
Bingar … …	بنکار	74	50	19	8
Birha … …	بره	84	28	22	31

		E.Long. °	′	N.Lat. °	′
Birhala	برهاله	80	18	23	56
Birun	برن	87	13	24	45
Bisowly	بسولي	{ 74	48	21	51
		78	56	28	19
Bituhnda	بتهنده	{ 72	50	27	20
		74	50	30	8
Bokhara	بخارا	62	48	39	30
Bongeer	بنكير	79	50	17	31
Boodwul	بودول	74	28	21	38
Boondy	بوندي	75	40	25	26
Boorhanpoor ...	بورهانپور	73	40	23	0
Boost	بست	65	0	32	0
Brahmunabad ...	براهمن آباد	68	18	24	43
Budukhshan ...	بدخشن	70	0	36	25
Budry, (*Ford*) ...	بدري	77	30	24	33
Buglana	بكلانه	*The Province*			
Bukhshypoor ...	بخشيپور	80	54	25	21
Bulamia	بلاميه	70	35	33	17
Bulkh	بلخ	66	20	36	31
Bulnat	بلنات	*Mountains in the Punjab, so called.*			
Buleel	بليل	*Kashmeer.*			
Bulochistan ...	بلوچستان	*The Province.*			
Bulsar	بلسار	73	2	20	40
Bunas	بناس	*The River*			
Bundelcund ...	بهندلكند	*The Province*			
Bundwa	بندوه	84	21	23	49
Bung	بنك	*Prov. Bengal.*			

		E.Long. °	′	N.Lat. °	′
Bunkapoor ...	بنکاپور	75	19	14	44
Burkistwar ...	برکستوار	—		—	
Burungaum ...	برنگام	76	22	23	48
Bussora	بسره	47	50	30	18
Bustar	بستر	87	5	21	45
		82	26	19	33
Butnere	بتنیر	73	55	29	34
Butwa	بتوه	87	23	22	52
Byana	بیانه	77	15	26	57
Cacherlacota ...	کاچرلاکوته	79	25	15	50
Cairo	قایره	23	30	30	5
Calicut	کالیکوت	75	52	11	15
Calistry	کالستري	79	48	13	45
Cambay	کنبیت	72	51	22	5
Cananore	کنانور	75	26	11	54
Canara	کنر	*The Province*			
Carnatic	کرناتک	*The Province*			
Caroor	کرور	78	9	10	50
Ceylon	سلندیب	*The Island*			
Chakun	چاکن	74	1	18	44
Chaliskole ...	چالیسکول	—		—	
Champanere ...	چانپانیر	77	57	23	8
		75	1	25	57
		73	39	22	30
Changdevy ...	چانکدیوي	73	59	17	0
Chawund	چاوند	74	6	19	11
Chicacole	چکاکول	84	0	18	13

		E.Long. ° ′	N.Lat. ° ′
Chickly	چکلي	77 29 76 13 76 10	19 29 20 22 18 14
Chilka, Ahungeran	چلکه اهنکران	*A Pass in Transoxania*	
Chilkoor	چلکور	86 58	24 58
Chinoor	چنور	79 48	18 50
Chunab, ...	چناب	*The River*	
Chitcole	چتکول	84 0 74 47	18 13 24 55
Chittoor	چتور	79 11	13 14
Choly	چراي	80 0	23 7
Choul	چول	73 0	18 33
Chukdura	چکدره	*A Pass in Kashmeer.*	
Chumbul, ...	چنبل	*A River.*	
Chunar	چنارکده	82 49	25 6
Chundery	چنديري	78 16	24 38
Chundergiry ...	چندراکري	75 5 79 24	12 28 13 36
Chundergooty ...	چنراکوتي	75 3	14 27
Chupurgutta ...	چپرکته	87 3	26 7
Churwul	چرول	75 53	11 54
Cochin	کوچين	76 17	9 59
Compila	کمپله	76 30	15 24
Concan	کونکن	*The Low Country lying between Surat and Goa*	
Condapilly ...	کنداپلي	80 36	16 40
Condbeer	کندبير	80 20	16 21

Name		E.Long. °	′	N.Lat. °	′
Canjeveram ...	کنچن	79	57	12	51
Cosimcota ...	کسمیکوته	80	12	17	40
Cranganore ...	کرانکانور	76	16	10	13
Cuddapa	کرپا	78	55	14	30
Culloor	کلور	76	53	13	12
Cumamett ...	کمامت	80	11	17	15
Cummum	کمم	79	11	15	34
Dabul	دابل	73	14	17	47
Daigloor	دایکلور	77	57	18	34
Damodry	دامودري	*A pass*			
Dampoor (*on the Behut*)	دامپور	78	17	28	11
		78	30	29	19
Damrá	دامره	78	0	16	55
Damra		*Kashmeer*			
Danwur	دانور	79	32	19	50
Daraputun ...	داراپتن	77	36	10	45
Darasun	داراسن	76	5	18	10
Dâria	داریا	71	30	31	34
Darwar	داروار	75	5	15	29
Deboon	دیبون	—		—	
Deccan	دکهن	*The Province*			
Deebul	دیبل	68	8	24	45
Deebul		*Kashmeer*			
Deebur	دیبر	74	41	21	51
Deenpuna	دینپنه	71	15	30	30
Dehly	دهلي	77	16	28	40
Depalpoor ...	دیپالپور	73	48	30	58
Depalpoor ...		*Kashmeer*			

		E.Long. °	′	N.Lat. °	′
Dervishpoor ...	درويشپور	—		—	
Devy	ديري	81	0	15	55
Dewgur or Devagiry	ديوكده ديواكري	75	29	19	53
		76	11	24	11
Dewly	ديولي	82	52	20	8
Dewnary	ديوناري	72	48	26	2
Dewpooral ...	ديوپورال	*Kashmeer*			
Dewsur	ديوسر	76	8	28	45
Dewurconda ...	ديوركنده	77	51	16	37
Dhamony	دهاموني	83	11	24	10
Dhâmungaum ...	دهامنگاون	76	7	20	22
Dhar	دهار	75	22	22	37
Dharanuggury ...	دهرانگري	78	9	29	19
D'harore	دهارور	76	9	18	52
Dholpoor	دهولپور	77	52	26	40
Dhoor	دهور	78	44	14	41
Dhowleswur ...	دهوليسور	75	10	16	19
Dhunkote, Kashmeer	دهنكوت	86	28	28	12
Dhunna Sodra ...	دهنه سودره	*Pass*			
Dhuntoor	دهنتور	73	38	34	27
Dhunuj	دهنج	*Kashmeer*			
Dhuny	دهني	84	39	24	30
Dilgoosha... ...	دلكوشه	*Garden*			
Diu	ديو	71	15	20	45
Doab	دواب	*A name given to any tract lying between two rivers*			

		E.Long. °	′	N.Lat. °	′
Dohud	دهد	74	20	22	55
Dole	دول	75	22	25	55
Dongurpoor ...	دنگرپور	73	50	25	48
Doorgy	دورکي	75	50	25	40
Dopamow... ...	دوپامو	—		—	
Dowlka	دوالکه	84	56	23	8
Dowlutabad ...	دولتاباد	75	29	19	53
Dulmow	دلمو	81	10	27	35
Duman	دمان	72	54	20	26
Dunda	دنده	73	47	18	18
Dundana	دندانه	76	31	29	6
Dundanakon, or Dundan Shikun (a pass)	دندانکن	67	50	35	0
Dundooka ...	دندوکه	72	10	22	24
Dura	دره	79	27	28	51
Dura Ismael Khan	دره اسمعيل خان	71	10	31	50
Durseela	درسيله	—		—	
Dwarka	دوارکا	69	8	22	16
Dwar Sumoodra ...	دوار سمودره	76	55	14	30
Dydla	ديدله	74	49	21	57
Eelak	ايلاق	*Summer residencies.*			
Erak, or Irak ...	عراق	*A term applied both to Persia and Mesopotamia*			
Eerich	ايرچ	79	3	25	48
Elgundel	الکندل	79	6	18	24

			E.Long.		N.Lat.	
			°	′	°	′
Elichpoor ...	...	الچپور	77	34	21	14
Elloora ...	...	ایلوره	75	16	20	7
Ellore ...	...	ایلور	81	9	16	41
Etawa ...	...	اتاوه	78	59	26	45
Etgeer ...	...	ایتکیر	77	11	16	48
Faukul ...	...	فانکل	*District of Kashmere*			
Fars }		فارس	*A Province of Persia.*			
Farsistan }	...	فارسستان				
Ferozabad	...	فیروزاباد	{ 78	27	27	10
			{ 76	52	17	7
Furas ...	...	فراس	*A Province in Transoxania*			
Furghana ...	...	فرغانه				
Furghunian	...	فرغنیان	68	20	42	30
Futtehpoor	...	فتحپور	{ 72	15	29	40
			{ 73	11	30	51
			{ 86	45	24	35
Gáhgrone ...	...	گاکرون	76	15	24	38
Gaheer ...	...	گهیر	*Kashmeer.*			
Galna ...	...	گالنه	74	37	20	50
Ganjam ...	...	گنجعام	85	10	19	50
Gava ...	...	گاوه	*Kashmeer.*			
Gavul ...	...	گاول	89	56	24	49
Gavulgur ...	...	گاولکر	77	24	21	22
Geelan ...	...	گیلان	*A Province in Persia.*			
Ghazipoor	...	غازیپور	{ 80	44	25	51
			{ 83	33	25	35

		E.Long. °	′	N.Lat. °	′
Ghizny	غزني	68	53	33	10
Ghoor	غور	78	28	27	4
Ghoorbund ...	غوربند	68	31	34	41
Girnal or Girnar ...	گرنال	77	6	14	53
Girnary	گرناري	75	58	25	15
Goa	گوه	73	59	15	30
Godavery	گوداوري	*A River*			
Godra	گودرا	{ 78	22	21	35
		73	41	22	48
Gogo	گوکو	72	28	21	42
Gogy	گوکي	76	45	16	35
Gohery	گوهري	79	7	24	31
Gokudkur... ...	گهکدکر	*Kashmeer*			
Gohore	گهور	*Kashmeer*			
Golconda	گلکنده	82	31	17	39
Gombroon ...	گنبرون	57	30	26	40
Gondel	گندل	71	42	21	51
Gondwâna ...	گوندوانه	*The Province.*			
Goolâmât	غلامات	*Kashmeer.*			
Goonta Cummum	گونتا کمم	*River.*			
Goorum	گورم	82	16	18	0
Gopalpilly ...	گوپالپلي	83	23	18	4
Gorowly	گوررلی	—		—	
Gorukpoor ...	گورکپور	{ 83	18	26	44
		79	22	22	40
Gowr	گور	83	58	26	31
Gualiar	گواليار	78	4	26	17
Gujraj	گجراج	75	20	23	53
Do.					

		E.Long. °	′	N.Lat. °	′
Gujweel, Kashmeer	گجویل	77	24	12	32
Gukkur	گکر	*Kashmeer*			
Gundicota ...	گندیکوته	78	22	14	49
Gungrar	گنگرار	75	42	23	56
Gunjowty... ...	گنجوتي	—		—	
Gunpoor	گنپور	78	9	16	34
Gunwar or Kishtwar	گنوار	*A province of Thibet*			
Gurhy	گرهي	78	12	23	29
		77	18	29	38
		71	5	20	10
Gurmseer	گرمسیر	*A Province*			
Gurra	گرّه	91	20	22	52
		77	25	23	50
		79	57	23	3
Gurra Kota ...	گرّه‌کوته	79	17	23	43
Guzerat	گجرات	*The Province*			
Gya	گیه	77	58	33	31
Hajypoor	حاجیپور	70	42	28	41
		75	0	25	7
		85	17	25	41
Hamadan	همدان	48	0	24	20
Hamoon, Kashmeer	هامون	—		—	
Hansy	هانسي	75	57	29	6
Hatmutty	هاتمتي	*A River.*			
Heerpoor	هیرپور	*Kashmeer.*			
Hindoo Cooh ...	هندوکوه	*Mountains of Pishawur.*			

		E. Long. °	′	N. Lat. °	′
Hindown	هنداون	77	0	26	44
Hírat	هرات	62	18	34	48
Holkar	هولكار	76	33	13	25
Hookery	هوكري	75	2	15	4
Hoolias	هولياس كهات	Pass			
Hooshungâbâd ...	حشنكآباد	75	50	22	45
Hoot	هوت	—		—	
Houz-i-Burma(*Lake*)	حوض برمه	87	43	24	50
Houz-i-Kumt'hana	حوض كمتهانه	*Lake*			
Houz-i-Kootloo ...	حوض قوتلو	*Lake*			
Houz-i-Rany ...	حوض راني	*Lake*			
Hulkant	هلكانت	78	30	26	44
Hundia	هنديه	82	10	25	20
Hunwutgur ...	هنوتكر	74	54	19	52
Hurdwar	هردوار	78	9	29	58
Hurryputtun ...	هريپتن	—		—	
Hurunpal, Nursak	هرنپال نرساک	*Kashmeer*			
Hussunabdal ...	حسنابدال	75	46	20	9
Hustnapoor ...	هستناپور	78	52	14	11
Hydrabad... ...	حيدراباد	{ 68	40	25	21
		{ 80	18	28	3
Ibrahimputtun ...	ابراهيم پتن	78	41	17	11
Idur	ايدر	73	1	25	50
Ilahy, Mahal ...	الهي محل	*A palace*			
Inaconda	اندكنده	79	48	16	3
Indapoor	انداپور	75	6	18	7
Inderkote	اندركوت	—		—	
Indgy	اندجي	78	12	16	5
Indoor	اندور	—		—	

		E.Long. ° ′	N.Lat. ° ′
Indraconda ...	اندراکونده	75 50 78 8	22 42 18 40
Indrakote	اندراکوت	*Kashmeer*	
Indijan	اندجان	68 40	41 40
Isfahân	اصفهان	52 30	31 10
Islâmâbâd	اسلاماباد	91 54 76 20	22 21 34 29
Islâmuggur ...	اسلامنگر	85 56 77 30 78 11	24 57 23 24 28 18
Islâmpoor	اسلامپور	90 28 75 40 85 13 74 28 71 30	23 59 28 6 25 8 17 0 28 27
Jadra, Kashmeer ...	جادرا	—	—
Jajnuggur... ...	جاجنگر	85 1	20 30
Jalesur	جليسر	78 20	27 30
Jaliat	جليات	75 54	11 5
Jâlna	جالنه	75 58	19 54
Jalundur	جالندر	—	24 0
Do. Kashmeer ...			
Jâm (Pass) ...	جام	77 6	20 27
Jay Faknoor ...	جاي فاكنور	—	—
Jeebul	جهيبل	*Kashmeer*	
Jeelput	جهيلپت	—	—
Jeeoor	جيرر	75 30	22 45
Jehrund	جهرند	73 27	22 29

		E.Long. °	′	N.Lat. °	′
Jeipoor, (or Jypoor)	جيپور	75	50	26	55
Jeipoor Kotly, (or Jypoor)... ...	جيپور گوتلي	76	23	20	42
Jesselmere... ...	جسلمير	71	13	26	52
Jhayin	جهاين	75	18	28	5
Jhalode	جهالود	74	13	23	7
Jharkund	جهاركند	*A Province.*			
Jheelum	جهيلم	*River.*			
Jhirka	جهيركه	—		—	
Jirconda	جركنده	—		—	
Jood	جود	*Mountains*			
Joodhun, or Ajoodhun	جودهن	72	35	30	40
Joodry	جودري	79	31	26	56
Joonagur	جوناگر	70	40	21	30
Joonere	جنير	74	7	19	14
Joonpoor	جونپور	82	40	25	44
Joorjan	جورجان	*Provinces S. E. of the Caspian Sea*			
Joorjistan	جورجستان				
Joorjoora	جرجره	75	22	28	4
Jowlapoor ...	جولاپور	*Kashmeer*			
Judda	جدّه	39	30	20	45
Juggut, or Jyrgat	جگت	69	8	22	15
Juhjur	جهجر	80	28	16	45
Jujur	ججر	*River*			

		E.Long. °	′	N.Lat. °	′
Julalabad	جلال آباد	79	33	27	46
		70	45	34	9
		77	24	29	33
		83	23	25	51
Julaly	جالي	78	18	27	53
Julmoor	جلمور	84	10	18	25
Julwan	جلوان	*Province in Persia.*			
Jumkindy	جمکندي	75	21	16	30
Jummoo	جمّو	74	55	32	53
Jumna	جمنه	*River*			
Jumulmooroo ...	جملمورو	78	28	14	52
Kabul	کابل	69	12	34	7
Kadurabad ...	قادرآباد	74	50	19	8
Kakny	کاکني	76	16	11	53
Kakreea	کاکریه	76	8	23	35
Kala Chubootra ...	کالاچبوترا	*An encamping ground so called*			
Kaliada	کالیاده	76	16	23	16
Kalinjur	قالنجر	80	27	25	4
Kalinjurkote ...	کالنجرکوت	*A town west of Attock*			
Kalpy	کالپي	79	44	26	8
Kamraj	کامراج	*Kashmeer*			
Kandahar... ...	قندهار	77	16	18	53
Kandeish	کهاندیش	*The Province*			
Kandy	قندي	80	47	7	10

		E.Long. ° ′	N.Lat. ° ′
Kaplan	قاپلان	*A town in Transoxania.*	
Karapatam ...	كراپتن	73 26	16 26
Kasan	كاسان	68 28	42 11
Kashan	كاشان	51 30	35 0
Kashgar, a Province of Tartary ...	كاشغار	74 0	37 50
Kashmeer	كشمير	*The Province.*	
Katáén	كتاين	84 10	26 29
Katgur	كاتكر	88 52	24 45
Kattack	كتك	85 52	20 26
Kava	كاوه	*District of Kashmeer*	
Kaziroon	كاذرون	52 0	32 0
Keechiwara ...	كيچيوارا	*District in Malwa.*	
Kech	كيچ	*Prov. of Sind.*	
Keid	قيد	*Desert.*	
Kehlna, (Vishalgur)	كهلنه	73 50	17 30
Kehrla	كهيرله	72 32	28 48
Kelookery, (*Suburb of Dehli*) ...	كيلوكهري	76 16	28 40
Kerowly	كرولي	{ 79 0 77 53	27 22 27 8
Khalidgur ...	خالدگر	*Kashmeer.*	
Khanbaligh ...	خان‌بالغ	*City in Tartary*	
Khânpoor... ...	كانپور	{ 73 17 73 8	30 0 33 32

		E.Long. °	′	N.Lat. °	′
Khaspoor	خاسپور	74	4	32	38
Khoojund	خوجند	66	52	41	8
Khooshab	خوشاب	72	38	32	2
Khoozar	خوزار	66	46	27	54
Khorasan	خراسان	*A Province of Persia.*			
Khowaspoor ...	خواصپور	74	4	32	38
Khozarbund ...	خزارابند	*Kabul.*			
Khuleefâbâd ...	خليفاباد	—		—	
Khulijpoor ...	خلجپور	76	50	24	6
Khullij	خلج	70	30	34	40
Khuteebpoor ...	خطيبپور	—		—	
Khutta, (also a Province of Tartary)	ختّه	82	40	25	57
Khutuk	ختّک	85	52	20	26
Khwaja, Deedar ...	خواجه دیدار	*District in Kabul.*			
Khwaruzm ...	خوارزم	*The Province of Chorasmmia.*			
Kirman	کرمان	70	21	33	29
Kish	قش	65	12	39	23
Kishlakat-i-Huzara	قشلاکات حزاره	*A Province of Kabul.*			
Kishtwâr	کشتوار	*Province of Thibet.*			
Kittoor	کتّور	74	50	15	38
Koheer	کوهیر	82	39	23	45
Kohrâm	کهرام	—		—	
Koilad	کویلاد	—		—	

		E.Long. °	′	N.Lat. °	′
Kohka, Plain of	میدان کوکه	*Kashmeer.*			
Kolapoor	کولاپور	77	34	20	53
		74	20	16	45
Kolarus	کلارس	77	41	25	16
Kole	کول	78	0	27	52
Kole, (Julaly) ...	کول جلالي	73	25	33	12
Kolhar	کلهار	75	48	16	25
Kondana or Singur	کندانه	73	54	18	22
Kooary	کواري	71	37	24	3
Kooch	کوچ	*A Province in Bengal.*			
Koofa	کوفه	44	0	32	10
Kooh-toor ...	کوه‌تور	*Mount Sinai*			
Koolburga ...	کلبرکه	76	54	17	23
Koolgam ...	کلکام	—		—	
Koombulmere ...	کومبهلمیر	73	31	25	9
Kooncby	کونچی	75	50	16	15
Koondly	کوندلي	71	34	21	21
Koondooz... ...	قندز	82	9	16	46
Koorkan	کورکان	74	53	31	10
Koorshy	قرشي	80	59	27	0
		80	41	27	10
Koowurket ...	کورکهیت	*A field of Battle near Tahneswur.*			
Korla	کورله	73	54	16	36
Kota	کوته	78	54	26	18
		72	51	34	13
Kotgeer	کوتکیر	77	28	31	20

		E.Long. °	′	N.Lat. °	′
Kotgirour... ...	كوتكرور	*Kashmeer.*			
Kothamoon ...	كوت نامون	*Kashmeer.*			
Kotla	كوتله	78	28	27	17
Kowilconda ...	كويلكنده	77	51	16	56
Kowlâs	كولاس	76	54	22	32
Kowrial	كوريال	—		—	
Krishna	كرشنه	*The River*			
Kuchwaha ...	كچواها	80	25	26	6
Kuggur, *River* ..	ككهر	75	55	26	35
Kuhndwa... ...	كهندوه	76	25	21	52
Kujdewan ...	كجديوان	73	50	26	50
Kulgoor	كلكور	—		—	
Kulnugry	كلنگري	*Kashmeer.*			
Kullanore... ...	كلانور	75	20	31	51
Kulanumut ...	كلانمت	*Kashmeer.*			
Kulliany	كلياني	83	34	24	24
Kullum	كلّم	76	15	18	38
		74	7	19	5
Kumaoon	كماون	*Province in Nepaul*			
Kumtana, (or Cumtànà)	كمتانه	77	29	17	52
Kundoo-Deva Pully	كندوديواپلي	—		—	
Kunikdizin ...	كنكدز	*Transoxania*			
Kunoory	كنوري	72	19	23	36
Kunowj, or Canowj	قنوج	79	49	27	4
Kurbela	كربلا	44	0	32	20
Kurgone	كرگون	71	30	22	3
Kurmar	كرمار	*Kashmeer.*			

Name		E.Long. °	′	N.Lat. °	′
Kurmulla	کرملا	75	17	18	27
Kurnool	کرنول	78	7	15	50
Kurnal	کرنال	76	58	29	30
Kuronde	کروند	73	28	21	18
Kurpa	کرپه	78	55	14	30
Kurra	کرّه	75	11	18	51
Kurrakole... ...	قراکول	*Tartary*			
Kurry	کري	75	54	22	19
		73	34	19	32
		72	28	23	18
Kutch	کچ	*The territory so called.*			
Kutcha Ghât ...	کچه کهات	*Ford.*			
Kutehr	کتهر	78	59	24	49
Kutra	کتره	78	59	24	49
Kuzveen, (or Casven)	قزوين	53	0	36	0
Kythul	کيتهل	76	20	29	48
Lahore	لاهور	74	12	31	35
Lâr	لار	*Province of Persia.*			
Lâr	لار	*Kashmeer.*			
Larky	لارکی	*Pass*			
Lassa	لاسه	91	8	29	32
Lodhana	لدهانه	75	27	24	0
Lohgur	لهکره	73	35	18	40
		69	20	33	49
Lohkote	لهکوت	*Kashmeer.*			
Looloopoor, Kashmeer	لولوپور	81	35	25	18

		E.Long. ° ′	N.Lat. ° ′
Looshoo	لوشو	*Dist. of Thibet.*	
Lowluk	لولک	*Kashmeer.*	
Luchmynuggur ...	لچمینکر	76 53	27 24
Luknow	لکنو	80 50	26 53
Luknowty ...	لکنوتي	88 11	24 55
Lulling	للنک	75 50	20 40
Lumghân	لمغان	*Province near Peshawur.*	
Lungur	لنکر	87 30	21 53
Madras	مدراس	80 22	13 4
Madoky	مادوکي	*Kashmeer.*	
Madurgy	مدرکي	76 56	16 20
Machiwara ...	ماچیوار	76 14	30 54
Mâhânudda ...	ماهاندہ	*River.*	
Mahoba	ماهوبه	79 51	25 20
Mâhim (Bombay Island)	ماهم	72 49	19 40
Maholy	مهولي	80 24	27 40
Mahmoodabad ..	محموداباد	{ 83 43 83 27	25 37 26 2
Mahomedabad ...	محمّداباد	79 21	27 80
Mahomednuggur...	محمّدنکر	82 31	17 29
Mahomedpoor ...	محمّدپور	{ 70 40 76 27	29 3 30 8
Mâhoor	ماهور	77 58	19 49
Mahrasa (or Mow-rasa)	مهراسه	77 6	34 45

		E.Long. °	'	N.Lat. °	'
Malabar	مليبار	*Province on the Western Coast of India.*			
Malacca, an Island	ملكه	102	0	2	30
Mallygur	ماليكهره	78	11	22	71
Malwa	مالوه	*The Province.*			
Malycota	ماليكوته	81	59	28	23
Man, River ...	مان	91	14	18	11
Mandese	مان ديس	*A district of Beejapoor.*			
Mando	ماندو	75	29	22	22
Mangalore ...	منگلور	74	53	12	52
Mankote, Kashmeer	مانكوت	48	20	24	25
Manoory	مانوري	78	55	11	50
Manserovûr ...	مانسروار	*Lake.*			
Manukpoonj ...	مانكپونج	79	30	24	23
Manukpoor ...	مانكپور	73	28	26	50
Maran-Hills ...	ماران	*Kashmeer.*			
Marwar	ماروار	*Province of Upper India.*			
Masulipatam ...	مچليپتن	81	11	16	9
Mavur-ool-nehr ..	ماورالنهر	*Transoxania.*			
Mâzinderân ...	مازندران	*A Province of Persia.*			
Mecca	مكّه	50	30	20	40
Medina	مدينه	48	5	22	10
Mednypoor, Kashmeer	ميدنيپور	83	23	25	33
		87	20	22	26

			E.Long. °	′	N.Lat. °	′
Meduk ...	...	مدک	—		—	
Mehkur ...	...	مهکر	78	23	27	35
Mehndry ...	...	مهندري	*River*			
Mehrowly ...	...	مهرولي	82	40	24	9
Mehyswur ...	...	مهيسور	75	41	22	11
Mein ...	...	مين	*Kashmeer.*			
Merkol ...	...	مرکول	82	56	19	45
Merut ...	...	ميرت	77	42	28	59
Mewar ...	...	ميوار	*Province of Upper India.*			
Mewât ...	...	موات	*Province do.*			
Mikran ...	...	مکران	*Province of Southern Persia.*			
Mirch ...	...	مرچ	74	43	16	55
Moghat ...	...	مغات	*A Bridge in Transoxania.*			
Mogulistan	...	مغلستان	*Province of Tartary.*			
Mohâbilla ...	...	مهابله	70	50	21	25
Mohatila ...	...	مهاتله	69	18	23	10
Mhowkehr	...	مهرکيهر	74	24	20	0
Moodkul ...	...	مودکل	76	32	16	1
Mokudkar ...	...	موکدکار	*Kashmeer.*			
Mooltân ...	..	مولتان	75	18	23	6
Moorghab ...	...	مرغاب	67	15	31	29
Moostufâbad	...	مصطفاباد	70	20	21	0
Moosulmooroo	...	مسلمورو	78	38	15	58
Moosy ...	...	موسي	73	43	18	26

		E.Long. °	′	N.Lat. °	′
Mootapilly ...	متاپلي	78	6	11	3
Muchbul, River ...	مچبول	*Kashmeer*			
Muchlyputtun, (or Masulipatam) ...	مچليپتن	88	11	16	9
Mudun, (hill at Runtunbhore) ...	مدن	86	51	24	24
		86	10	25	58
Mudwara	مدوارا	78	23	16	38
		80	57	16	17
Mukna	مكنه	83	18	18	26
		73	48	22	14
Mulungoor ...	ملنكور	79	24	18	19
Mulwut	ملوت	84	9	25	7
Mundra	مندره	70	0	22	48
Mundla	منداه	80	29	22	40
Mundlere	مندلير	77	13	26	20
Mundsoor	مندسور	75	7	24	3
Mundul	مندل	72	4	23	14
Mundulgur ...	مندلكره	75	9	25	20
Mundry (hills) ...	مندري	78	30	28	41
Munsoorpoor ...	منصورپور	76	20	30	25
Murhera	مرهره	78	38	27	4
Murhutt	مرهة	*Province of Mahrashtra.*			
Muriala	مرياله	70	43	22	4
Murv	مرو	61	15	37	30
Mushed	مشهد	56	0	38	0
Mylapoor	ميلاپور	86	16	25	0
Myne	مين	85	30	25	38
Mysoor	ميسور	76	44	12	18

		E.Long. °	′	N.Lat. °	′
Nadly	نادلي	*Kashmeer*			
Nâdool	نادول	76	39	26	2
Nâdote	نادوت	73	40	21	51
Nagdurry	ناكدري	80	17	6	56
Nagoonda... ...	ناكنده	80	33	24	36
Nâgoor	ناكور	76	5	16	2
Nâgry	ناكري	79	40	13	20
Nakam	ناكام	*Kashmeer.*			
Nakavy	ناكوي	*Kashmeer.*			
Nâlchâ	نالچه	75	30	22	26
Namumpilly, (Lake)	ناممپلي	84	45	19	47
Nandere	نانديڑ	75	10	21	42
Narain	نارايں	75	20	26	45
Narainkehra ...	نارايںكهره	76	21	15	12
Narainpatam ...	نارايپتم	83	10	18	31
Nardeim	ماردين	84	36	24	7
Nargy	ناركی	78	27	27	18
Narnol	نارنول	76	11	28	4
Natolia	ناتوليه	*Province in Asia Minor.*			
Neelab	نيلاب	72	20	33	56
Neerdole	نيردول	76	37	19	23
		81	50	16	53
Negapatam ...	ناكپتن	79	53	10	36
Nehawund ...	نهاوند	49	0	35	0
Nehrwâla	نهرواله	72	8	23	50
Nere	نير	86	7	26	12
Nere	نير	*Kashmeer.*			
Nikâla	نكاله	*Kashmeer.*			

		E.Long. °	′	N.Lat. °	′
Nindoona	نندونه	76	29	29	0
Nizampatam ...	نيزاپتن	80	44	15	56
Nowlaye	نولاي	75	27	23	2
Nowlgoond ...	نولكوند	75	29	15	30
Nowrus	نورس	75	52	16	51
Nowrozkote ...	نوروزكوت	*Kashmeer.*			
Nowsary	نوساري	73	1	21	0
Nowshehra, Kashmeer	نوشهره	74	51	31	19
		72	2	34	6
		69	10	25	51
Nowulgoond ...	نولكند	75	32	15	43
Nubat Ghat ...	نبات كهات	*A Palace at Hydrabad.*			
Nuddy Mahal ...	ندّي محل	*Palace.*			
Nuggur	نكر	87	22	23	28
		74	10	32	43
		71	37	25	21
Nuggurkote ...	نكركوت	*Kashmeer.*			
Nuldoorg	نلدّرگ	76	20	17	52
Nunda	نندە	82	28	18	15
		77	16	19	33
Nundial	نندیال	78	33	15	30
Nundoorbar ...	نندربار	74	25	21	26
Nurbuda	نربده	*River.*			
Nurnalla	نرناله	77	2	21	15
Nurwur	نرور	78	3	23	24
Nuseerpoor ...	نصيرپور	73	16	33	48
Nyshapoor ...	نشاپور	88	35	25	6

		E.Long. °	′	N.Lat. °	′
Ocha	ارچه	49	20	22	25
Oodgeer	اودكير	77	10	18	27
Okshy	اخشي	78	5	33	41
Ongole	اونكول	80	7	15	31
Oodown	اودون	{ 68	35	28	12
		69	24	24	15
Oodown	اودون	*Kashmeer.*			
Oojein	اجين	75	52	23	11
Ookey	اكي	*Kashmeer*			
Ooman	امان	*Arabia.*			
Oomruzpoor ...	اُمرزپور	75	36	17	14
Oorconda	اُركنده	77	20	14	57
Oosh	اوش	69	15	41	30
Ootgy	اوتكي	77	50	16	59
Oozkund	اُزكند	69	40	41	53
Oran	اران	*Kashmeer.*			
Orcha (where Abool Fuzl was killed)	اورچه (جايكه ابو الفضل كشته شد)	78	39	25	23
Orissa	اوريسه	69	6	30	22
Ormuz	هرمزد	57	30	26	40
Owsa	اوسه	76	30	18	20
Pagtoor	پاكتور	78	3	15	55
Pail	پايل	73	22	19	2
Pâl...	پال	74	15	17	34
Palum	پالم	76	59	19	7
Palunchinoor ...	پالنچينور	81	30	17	0
Pangul	پانكل	78	13	16	15
Pâniput	پانيپت	76	45	29	25

		E.Long. °	′	N.Lat. °	′
Par	پار	73	47	17	51
Patna	پتنه	87	27	21	42
		85	9	25	35
		83	40	26	18
Patry	پاتري	72	0	23	8
Paunch, *Kashmeer*	پارنچ	75	2	34	10
Peitun	پيتن	82	44	27	57
Penkonda... ...	پنکونده	77	40	14	8
Pentapoondi ...	پنتاپرندي	82	10	16	58
Pentapoor ...	پنتاپور	82	40	17	15
Pernala	پرناله	74	16	16	48
Pery Kehra ...	پري كهره	69	38	28	59
Peshâwur	پشاور	71	41	34	5
Pettapoor... ...	پتاپور	75	16	22	25
P'harpully ...	پهارپلي	78	4	14	34
Pholo	پهولو	75	14	30	20
Pitlâud	پتلاود	72	58	20	30
Poona	پونه	74	0	18	31
Poorundhur ...	پورندهر	74	10	18	0
Potnoor	پوتنور	—		—	
Pudmawutty ...	پدماوتي	*Words in Bengal.*			
Pugly, Kashmeer...	پكلي	74	36	33	24
Pulicat	پليكت	80	23	13	24
Punala	پنهالا	74	16	16	48
Punjab	پنجاب	*Province.*			
Punjur River ...	پنجر	*Kashmeer.*			
Punna	پنّه	80	9	24	44

		E.Long. °	′	N.Lat. °	′
Punnuj, Kashmeer	پنّج	89	33	27	23
Purenda	پرنده	76	52	18	45
Purmgolla ...	پرمكوله	*Kashmeer.*			
Pursuroor	پرسراور	80	19	15	56
Putialy	پتيالي	76	18	30	10
Puttun	پتين	{ 76	5	27	51
		{ 72	9	23	49
Rabery, or Rewary	رابيري	76	40	28	10
Rachore	راچور	77	24	10	12
Radunpoor ...	رادنپور	71	40	23	40
Rairee	رايري	73	43	15	46
Raiseen	رايسين	{ 75	0	18	28
		{ 78	2	23	25
Rajmurda... ...	راجمرده	74	18	18	24
Rajanuggur ...	راجانگر	{ 90	25	23	20
		{ 82	36	19	27
Rajapoor	راجاپور	39	89	23	15
Rajconda	راجكنده	78	50	17	11
Rajoory	راجوري	74	40	17	58
Rajmundry ...	راجمندري	81	50	17	1
Rajpoondy ...	راجپوندي	74	50	17	19
Rajpoor	راجپور	{ 77	33	30	13
		{ 74	30	22	20
Rameswur ...	راميسور	80	50	29	33
Ramgir	رامگر	79	37	18	35
Rampinjun ...	رامپينجن	79	29	24	11
Râmpoora ...	رامپوره	79	12	19	71
Ranoory	رانوري	74	40	19	4

		E.Long. °	′	N.Lat. °	′
Ravy	راوي	*The River.*			
Ray-Afzây	راي افزاي	*A Palace, so called.*			
Raybagh	راي باغ	74	51	16	34
Reeva	ريوه	81	19	24	33
Rewary	ريواري	76	40	28	10
Rewdunda	ريودنده	73	31	16	43
Roh	روه	85	42	24	54
Rohtas	رهتاس	73	43	33	1
Rohtuk	رهتک	76	36	28	54
Rohunkehra	رهنکهره	*Pass to the N. W. of Ahmud-nuggur*			
Rohut	روهت	83	6	24	48
Room	روم	*Asia Minor.*			
Rubat Ameer	ربات امير	*Transoxania.*			
Rungpoor	رنكپور	89	22	26	43
		71	41	30	30
Runtunbhore	رنتنبهور	76	23	26	1
Rusoolâbâd	رسولاباد	—		—	
Rutungur	رتنگر	*Kashmeer.*			
Rye, or Tehran	ري	*Capital of Persia.*			
Saadabad	سعدآباد	83	10	25	31
Saburmutty	سابرمتي	*The River.*			
Sâgur	ساكر	77	13	24	21
		75	8	14	10
Saharun	سهارن	80	10	23	28

		E.Long. °	′	N.Lat. °	′
Sahsaram	سهسرام	83	59	24	59
Samarkand ...	سمرقند	64	50	39	41
Sarangur	سارنكر	82	54	21	29
Sarungpoor ...	سارنكپور	76	35	23	38
Sasny	ساسني	78	11	27	42
Satara	ستاره	74	11	17	42
Sâvâ	ساوه	52	0	31	50
Seekry	سيكري	70	35	23	11
Seepry	رود سيپري	*River.*			
Seestan	سيستا	*Province in South-Eastern Persia.*			
Seetulpoor ...	سيتلپور	87	17	25	7
Seevapoor... ...	سيواپور	*Kashmeer.*			
Seewas	سيواس	{ 78	27	23	42
		76	14	24	20
Sehaṣnuk	سهسنك	78	11	27	42
Sehwan	سهوان	68	50	26	15
Selandeep	سلنديپ	*Island Ceylon.*			
Selim	رود سليم	*The River.*			
Sena	رود سنه	*The River.*			
Sendooz	سندوز	—		—	
Seray Lado ...	سراي لادو	*Caravansera on the Indus.*			
Serhind (or Surhind)	سرهند	76	22	30	38
Serinuggur, *Capital of Kashmeer* ...	سرينكر	79	50	34	40
Setpoor	سيتپور	71	8	29	7
Ṣevana	سوانه	73	4	21	26

Name		Persian	E.Long. °	′	N.Lat. °	′
Sewalik ...	...	سیوالک	*Mountains.*			
Sewee ...	...	سیوي	75	20	19	21
Sewgaum ...	...	سیوکاؤن	76	41	25	47
Sewly ...	...	سیولي	{ 76	4	20	24
			85	51	23	23
Sewust'han	...	سیوستهان	*Province West of the Indus*			
Shadiabad	...	شدیاباد	83	23	25	41
Shadman ...	...	شادمان	*Transoxania.*			
Shahabad...	...	شاه‌آباد	87	29	25	16
Shahabpoor	...	شاهبپور	*Kashmeer.*			
Shahdroog	...	شاهدرک	77	35	14	11
Shahnowaz	...	شاهنواز	*Transoxania.*			
Shapoor ...	...	شاپور	75	23	34	18
Sharokhia	...	شرخیه	*Transoxania.*			
Sheergur ...	...	شیرکیر	70	37	21	18
Sheerwan ...	...	شیروان	*Province in Persia.*			
Sheevur ...	...	شیور	*District N.W. of Moultan.*			
Shewala ...	...	شواله	*A name for Ceylon.*			
Shewpoor...	...	شیوپور	76	54	25	45
Shiraz ...	...	شیرزا	55	0	32	0
Sholapoor	...	شولاپور	75	5	17	35
Shoojalpoor	...	شوجلاپور	76	50	23	26
Shooturgurdana (the Camel's pass)		شترکردنه	*Transoxania.*			
Shujawund	...	شجاوند	*Transoxania.*			

		E.Long. °	′	N.Lat. °	′
Shumsabad ...	شمساباد	78	10	27	2
		72	32	33	57
Sicacolum ...	سکاکولم	80	55	16	15
Sidpoor	سدپور	72	21	23	57
Sikundurpoor ...	سکندرپور	*Kashmeer.*			
Sind	سند	*Province.*			
Sind	رود سند	*River Indus.*			
Singram	سنگرام	82	21	25	54
Sinoor	سنور	73	31	21	55
Sirala	سراله	74	15	17	0
Siry	سري	82	32	5	13
Soane	سون	*River*			
Somâpoor... ...	سوماپور	89	27	26	20
Somnat	سمنات	70	20	21	45
Songeer	سنگیر	74	58	21	8
Songhur	سنگهر	73	48	21	12
Sonkehra	سنگهره	77	10	24	52
Sonput	سنپت	76	20	19	3
Sooltanpoor ...	سلطانپور	77	7	31	59
Soonam	سنام	75	53	30	8
Soonargam ...	سنارگاون	89	27	23	17
Soonere	سنیر	76	27	23	32
Soopa (near the Godavery River	سپه	74	38	15	16
Soorkhab	سرخاب	*Tnansoxania.*			
Soorsutty	سورستي	90	49	24	33
Soorsutty	رود سورستي	*The River.*			
Sorut	سورت	*Prov. Western Guzerat.*			

		E.Long. °	′	N.Lat. °	′
Sialkote	سیالکوت	74	32	32	35
Sreenuggur ...	سرینگر	75	50	34	40
Subooly	سبولي	87	9	24	9
		90	35	23	49
Subzeea	سبزیه	*Kashmeer.*			
Subzwar	سبزوار	67	15	39	20
Suisapoor	سویساپور	—		—	
Sukeet	سکیت	78	38	27	4
Sulah	صلح	*Kashmeer.*			
Sumatra	سمتره	*The Island.*			
Sumbhul	سنبهل	78	38	28	37
Sumnan	سمنان	—		—	
Sumthur	سمتهر	79	3	25	40
Sumurkote ...	سمرکوت	*Kashmeer.*			
Sunja	سنجه	*Kashmeer.*			
Sunkeswur ...	سنکسور	71	54	23	23
Suntravul	سنتراول	73	27	22	40
Surgooja	سرگوجه	83	10	23	8
Surgdewary, or Hurdwar ...	سرگدیواري	78	9	29	58
Surhind or Serhind	سرهند	76	22	30	38
Surjoo (or Suroo)	سرجو	*River.*			
Surkech	سرکیچ	72	40	23	0
Surmore	سرمور	*Hills.*			
Surohy	سروهي	72	49	24	52
Surtuk	سرتک	76	19	29	54
Suruksh	سرخش	*Transoxania.*			
Sutgam (Chitagong)	ستگاون	91	48	24	15
Sutlooj	ستلج	*River.*			

		E.Long. ° ′	N.Lat. ° ′
Sutnoor	ستنور	76 27	21 48
Sutwas	ستواس	76 45	22 30
Swad	سواد	71 50	34 30
Sydpoor	سیدپور	87 13	24 52
Tabreez (Tauris)...	طبریز	47 30	38 0
Taee	طاي	*Messopotamia.*	
Tahneswur ...	تهانسیر	76 50	29 58
Talikhan	تالیخن	68 50	36 40
Talikota	تلیکوته	76 22	16 29
Tâlnere	تهالنیر	75 7	21 21
Tanda	تانده	67 20	24 55
Tandla	تاندله	74 39	22 3
Tanna	تهانه	{77 18 / 73 4	26 26 / 19 12
Tapty	تپتي	*River.*	
Târâpoor	تاراپور	88 3	23 50
Tarpully	تارپلي	79 46	16 38
Tatpak	تاتپک	*Transoxania.*	
Tedzen	تدزن	*Transoxania.*	
Teergiram ...	ترکیران	*Transoxania.*	
Thibet	تیبت	*Province.*	
Tikona	تکونه	73 30	18 20
Timoor	تیمور	*Island East of India.*	
Tiprah	تپراه	83 29	26 43
Tirhoot	تیرهت	*Province.*	
Tirma	تیرمه	*Kashmeer (famous for its shawls.)*	

		E.Long. °	′	N.Lat. °	′
Tirowry	تروري	81	8	24	44
Toglukabad, *suburb of Delhi*	تغلقاباد	77	19	28	32
Tokharistan ...	تخارستان	*Transoxania.*			
Toohana	طوهانه	75	54	29	41
Toolumba ...	طولمبه	72	20	30	34
Toong	تونك	75	13	13	18
Toongbudra ...	تونكبدره	*River.*			
Tooran	توران	*E. Persia and Transoxania.*			
Toorkistan ...	تركستان	*Prov. of Tartary, country of the Turks*			
Toorkul	توركل	77	40	18	11
Toormooz... ...	ترمذ	—		37	17
Toos	طوس	57	0	39	0
Trebizond... ...	تريبزند	40	0	30	30
Tuckul	تكل	78	8	16	1
Tukeeabad ...	تكياباد	66	2	33	40
Tul-Ghât	تل‌كهات	*Below the passes.*			
Tulingana ...	تلينكنه	*The Province.*			
Tulwara	تلواره	72	18	25	21
Tumbola	تمبوله	74	14	31	50
Tallygaum ...	تاليگام	{ 74 75	59 48	20 18	28 43
Tutta	تته	68	8	24	45

		E.Long. °	′	N.Lat. °	′
Udgerrydoorg ...	اُدکویدرک	79	22	14	52
Ulmulla	الموله	73	3	23	12
Veeragootun ..	ویراکوتم	83	40	18	32
Velumpultun (perhaps Belumconda)	ولمپتن	80	5	16	31
Verool or Ellora ...	ویرول	75	16	20	7
Vishâlgur	وشالکر	73	50	17	30
Waee	واي	74	3	18	0
Wâgur	واکر	72	3	22	24
Wâlwâ	والوا	74	35	17	4
Wâr	وار	74	47	20	50
Warapully ...	وارابلي	79	43	16	45
Wooreea	اوریه	79	9	9	50
Woshagur... ...	اوشاکر	75	45	20	33
Wully	ولي	74	16	19	4
Wurungole ...	اورنکول	79	41	17	57
Wyrâgur	اویراکر	80	2	20	26
Yehar	یهار	79	2	24	43
Yekdulla	یکدله	81	0	25	38
Yelgundel... ...	یلکندل	78	10	17	58
Yesâvul	یساول	72	40	23	0
Yezd	یزد	57	0	36	0

			E.Long. ° ′	N.Lat. ° ′
Zeinabad ...	...	زیناباد	73 41	23 0
Zeingur ...	...	زینگر	*Kashmeer.*	
Zeinpoor ...	...	زینپور	*Kashmeer.*	
Zemeen Dawir	...	زمین داور	*District of Khorassan.*	

Note.—Circumstances have prevented this table from being so complete as it might have been made, chiefly owing to the want of good maps of Kashmeer and Transoxania.

THE END.